Beginning Hibernate 6

Java Persistence from Beginner to Pro

Fifth Edition

Joseph B. Ottinger
Jeff Linwood
Dave Minter

Apress®

Beginning Hibernate 6: Java Persistence from Beginner to Pro

Joseph B. Ottinger
Youngsville, NC, USA

Jeff Linwood
Austin, TX, USA

Dave Minter
London, UK

ISBN-13 (pbk): 978-1-4842-7336-4
ISBN-13 (electronic): 978-1-4842-7337-1
https://doi.org/10.1007/978-1-4842-7337-1

Managing Director, Apress Media LLC: Welmoed Spahr
Acquisitions Editor: Steve Anglin
Development Editor: Matthew Moodie
Coordinating Editor: Mark Powers

Cover designed by eStudioCalamar

Cover image by Greg Rosenke on Unsplash (www.unsplash.com)

Distributed to the book trade worldwide by Apress Media, LLC, 1 New York Plaza, New York, NY 10004, U.S.A. Phone 1-800-SPRINGER, fax (201) 348-4505, e-mail orders-ny@springer-sbm.com, or visit www.springeronline.com. Apress Media, LLC is a California LLC and the sole member (owner) is Springer Science + Business Media Finance Inc (SSBM Finance Inc). SSBM Finance Inc is a **Delaware** corporation.

For information on translations, please e-mail booktranslations@springernature.com; for reprint, paperback, or audio rights, please e-mail bookpermissions@springernature.com.

Apress titles may be purchased in bulk for academic, corporate, or promotional use. eBook versions and licenses are also available for most titles. For more information, reference our Print and eBook Bulk Sales web page at http://www.apress.com/bulk-sales.

Any source code or other supplementary material referenced by the author in this book is available to readers on GitHub via the book's product page, located at www.apress.com/9781484273364. For more detailed information, please visit http://www.apress.com/source-code.

Printed on acid-free paper

Table of Contents

About the Authors

Joseph B. Ottinger is a systems architect, consultant, and Senior Engineer for Delos Living. He's been messing around with computers since the 1980s, thinking about systems and architecture through war games and music. He's worked as a developer, architect, consultant, and writer since then, including editing stints at *Java Developer Journal* and TheServerSide.com.

A musician, programmer, artist, writer, father, and husband, his interests tend to range far and wide, through philosophy, history, science, art, basketball, education, and – apparently – hamsters.

Jeff Linwood has been involved in software programming since he had a 286 in high school. He got caught up with the Internet when he got access to a UNIX shell account, and it has been downhill ever since.

When he's not playing on the computer, his hobby is running ultramarathons. Jeff is based in Austin, Texas, and helps large companies solve tough problems with content management, search engines, and web application development. Jeff also co-authored *Professional Struts Applications* (Apress), *Building Portals with the Java Portlet API* (Apress), and *Pro Hibernate 3* (Apress).

Dave Minter has adored computers since he was small enough to play in the boxes they came in. He built his first PC from discarded, faulty, and obsolete components; and he considers that to be the foundation of his career as an integration consultant. Dave is based in London, where he helps large and small companies build systems that "just work." He wrote *Beginning Spring 2: From Novice to Professional* (Apress) and co-authored *Building Portals with the Java Portlet API* (Apress) and *Pro Hibernate 3* (Apress).

About the Technical Reviewer

Manuel Jordan Elera is an autodidactic developer and researcher who enjoys learning new technologies for his own experiments and creating new integrations. Manuel won the Springy Award – Community Champion and Spring Champion 2013. In his little free time, he reads the Bible and composes music on his guitar. Manuel is known as dr_pompeii. He has tech-reviewed numerous books for Apress, including *Pro Spring MVC with WebFlux* (2020), *Pro Spring Boot 2* (2019), *Rapid Java Persistence and Microservices* (2019), *Java Language Features* (2018), *Spring Boot 2 Recipes* (2018), and *Java APIs, Extensions and Librarie*s (2018). Read his 13 detailed tutorials about many Spring technologies, contact him through his blog at `www.manueljordanelera.blogspot.com`, and follow him on his Twitter account, `@dr_pompeii`.

Acknowledgments

Joseph would like to thank various people for encouraging and enabling him to write this book, and so he will: first, his wife and children for allowing him the time and energy to put into the project; various project leads for Hibernate like Steve Ebersole and Chris Cranford; Jonas Konrad, who provided some advice and much-needed pointers in a few critical spots; friends like Tracy Snell, Andrew Lombardi, Eugene Ciurana, Michael Rasmussen, and Justin Lee for serving as sounding boards and source material; his editors, for putting up with his quirks;[1] bands like Rush, Pink Floyd, Tool, Yes, and Porcupine Tree for providing the soundtrack to the book;[2] the letter Ξ, for having one of the most fun letters' names to pronounce;[3] his Gibson guitars, because they care; and lastly, Stan Lee, for giving Joseph a worthwhile impetus to learn to read when he was very young.

[1] Quirks like his endless footnotes; when asked, they allowed Joseph to have one footnote for every three pages, to which the response was, "Thanks! Three footnotes maximum for every page, got it!" ... and then he promptly exceeded his allotted count anyway.

[2] A soundtrack you won't hear, nor is it likely to be easily detected unless you listen very well. Listen more than that - no, more than that, too. Keep going. Let him know which song you hear, okay?

[3] Ξ is pronounced like "see." He learned this from his youngest son.

Acknowledgments

Introduction

Hibernate is an amazing piece of software. With a little experience and the power of annotations, you can build a complex, database-backed system with disturbing ease. Once you have built a system using Hibernate, you will never want to go back to the traditional approaches.

While Hibernate is incredibly powerful, it presents a steep learning curve when you first encounter it - steep learning curves are actually a good thing because they impart profound insight once you have scaled them. Yet gaining that insight takes some perseverance and assistance.

Our aim in this book is to help you scale that learning curve by presenting you with the minimal requirements of a discrete Hibernate application, explaining the basis of those requirements, and walking you through an example application that is built using them. We then provide additional material to be digested once the fundamentals are firmly understood. Throughout, we provide examples rather than relying on pure discourse. We hope that you will continue to find this book useful as a reference text long after you have become an expert on the subject.

Who This Book Is For

This book assumes a good understanding of Java fundamentals and some slight familiarity with database programming using the Java Database Connectivity (JDBC) API. We don't expect you to know anything about Hibernate - but if you buy this book, it will probably be because you have had some exposure to the painful process of building a large database-based system.

All of our examples use open source software - primarily the Hibernate API itself - so you will not need to purchase any software to get started with Hibernate development. This book is not an academic text. Our focus is, instead, on providing extensive examples and taking a pragmatic approach to the technology that it covers.

To true newcomers to the Hibernate API, we recommend that you read at least the first three chapters in order before diving into the juicy subjects of later chapters. Very experienced developers or those having experience with libraries similar to Hibernate will want to skim the latter half of the book for interesting chapters.

This book uses Java 11, which was the "current release" when it was drafted, and ignores Java's module system. By print time, Java 17 had become the current long-term supported release, and this book *still* ignores the module system; while modules are useful (and, arguably, important) their use is tangential at best for the subject matter. For the record, Hibernate works well with Java modules, but this book doesn't cover them at all, because they don't necessarily help one master Hibernate; modules' focus is on engineering and creation of better executables, neither subject being a core focus *here.*

How This Book Is Structured

This book is informally divided into three parts. Chapters 1 through 8 describe the fundamentals of Hibernate, including configuration, the creation of mapping files, and the basic APIs. Chapters 9 through 11 describe the use of queries, criteria, and filters to access the persistent information in more sophisticated ways. Chapter 12 addresses the use of Hibernate to talk to nonrelational data stores, providing an easy "on ramp" to NoSQL.

The following list describes more fully the contents of each chapter:

Chapter 1 outlines the purpose of persistence tools and presents excerpts from a simple example application to show how Hibernate can be applied. It also introduces core terminology and concepts.

Chapter 2 discusses the fundamentals of configuring a Hibernate application. It presents the basic architecture of Hibernate and discusses how a Hibernate application is integrated into an application.

Chapter 3 presents an example application, walking you through the complete process of creating and running the application. It then looks at a slightly more complex example and introduces the notion of generating the database schema directly from Hibernate annotations.

Chapter 4 covers the Hibernate lifecycle in depth. It discusses the lifecycle in the context of the methods available on the core interfaces. It also introduces key terminology and discusses the need for cascading and lazy loading.

Chapter 5 explains why mapping information must be retained by Hibernate and demonstrates the various types of associations that can be represented by a relational database. It briefly discusses the other information that can be maintained within a Hibernate mapping.

Chapter 6 explains how Hibernate lets you use the annotations to represent mapping information. It provides detailed examples for the most important annotations and discusses the distinctions between the standard JPA 2 annotations and the proprietary Hibernate ones.

Chapter 7 explains some of the uses of the Java Persistence API (as opposed to the Hibernate-native API), as well as the lifecycle and validation of persisted objects.

Chapter 8 revisits the Hibernate `Session` object in detail, explaining the various methods that it provides. The chapter also discusses the use of transactions, locking, and caching, as well as how to use Hibernate in a multithreaded environment.

Chapter 9 discusses how Hibernate can be used to make sophisticated queries against the underlying relational database using the built-in Hibernate Query Language (HQL).

Chapter 10 introduces Hibernate's filtering capabilities, allowing easy and convenient selection of subsets of data.

Chapter 11 demonstrates some core concepts in integrating Hibernate into a full-stack architecture, leveraging the Undertow servlet engine as a container.

Chapter 12 demonstrates the integration of Hibernate into application frameworks like Spring, Spring Boot, ActiveJ, and Quarkus.

Chapter 13 covers Hibernate Envers, which is a library that provides versioned data for entities stored through Hibernate.

Downloading the Code

The source code for this book is available to readers via the **Download Source Code** link located at `www.apress.com/9781484273364`. Please feel free to visit the Apress website and download all the code from there.

Contacting the Authors

We welcome feedback from our readers. If you have any queries or suggestions about this book, or technical questions about Hibernate, or if you just want to share a really good joke, you can email Joseph Ottinger at `joeo@enigmastation.com`, Dave Minter at `dave@paperstack.com`, and Jeff Linwood at `jlinwood@gmail.com`.

CHAPTER 1

An Introduction to Hibernate 6

Most significant development projects involve a relational database.[1] The mainstay of most commercial applications is the large-scale storage of ordered information, such as catalogs, customer lists, contract details, published text, and architectural designs.

With the advent of the World Wide Web, the demand for databases has increased. Though they may not know it, the customers of online bookshops and newspapers are using databases. Somewhere in the guts of the application, a database is being queried and a response is offered.

Hibernate is a library (actually, a set of libraries) that simplifies the use of relational databases in Java applications by presenting relational data as simple Java objects, accessed through a session manager, therefore earning the description of being an "Object/Relational Mapper," or ORM. It provides two kinds of programmatic interfaces: a "native Hibernate" interface and the Jakarta EE[2] standard Java Persistence API.

---

[1] A relational database is a collection of data, each of which is formally described and organized into "rows" - data related to a given thing, like a person, a product, a message - and columns, like a person's first name, a person's last name, a product number, a product description, and so on and so forth. Rules can also be put into place such that rows are described as relating to one another, so an order might be described as "owning" line items, and a line item's product number has to exist. There are other database types, but relational databases are probably the most common database types out there.

[2] Jakarta EE is a set of specifications that allows the Java community to use "enterprise-level" specifications to accomplish common tasks. This includes things like building applications for the World Wide Web, talking to databases (including direct SQL or via the Java Persistence API, or "JPA"), or using message queues, among many other possibilities. It used to be called "Java EE" (and before that, "J2EE"), but in 2019 Oracle handed ownership to the community, and it was renamed for legal reasons.

J. B. Ottinger et al., *Beginning Hibernate 6*, https://doi.org/10.1007/978-1-4842-7337-1_1

This edition focuses on Hibernate 6. As this sentence is being written, it's still at Alpha8, so it's not formally released, but chances are that the actual release is going to be very similar to the code used here.

There are solutions for which an ORM - like Hibernate - is appropriate and some for which the traditional approach of direct access via the Java Database Connectivity (JDBC) API is appropriate. We think that Hibernate represents a good first choice, as it does not preclude the simultaneous use of alternative approaches, even though some care must be taken if data is modified from two different APIs.

To illustrate some of Hibernate's strengths, in this chapter we take a look at a brief example using Hibernate and contrast this with the traditional JDBC approach.

Plain Old Java Objects (POJOs)

Java, being an object-oriented language, deals with objects. Usually, objects that represent program states are fairly simple, containing properties (or attributes) and methods that alter or retrieve those attributes (mutators and accessors, known as "setters" and "getters," colloquially). In general, these objects might encapsulate some behavior regarding the attributes, but usually their sole purpose is containing a program state. These are known typically as "plain old Java objects," or POJOs.

In an ideal world, it would be trivial to take any Java object - plain or not - and persist it to a database. No special coding would be required to achieve this, no performance penalty would ensue, and the result would be totally portable. In this ideal world, we would perhaps perform such an operation in a manner like this.

Listing 1-1. A Rose-Tinted View of Object Persistence

```
POJO pojo=new POJO();
ORMSolution magic=ORMSolution.getInstance();
magic.save(pojo);
```

There would be no nasty surprises, no additional work to correlate the class with what the table schema might be, and no performance problems.

Hibernate actually comes remarkably close to this idea, at least when compared with many of its alternatives,[3] but there are configuration files to create and subtle performance and synchronization issues to consider. Hibernate does, however, achieve its fundamental aim: it allows you to trivially store POJOs in the database. Figure 1-1 shows how Hibernate fits into your application between the client code and the database.

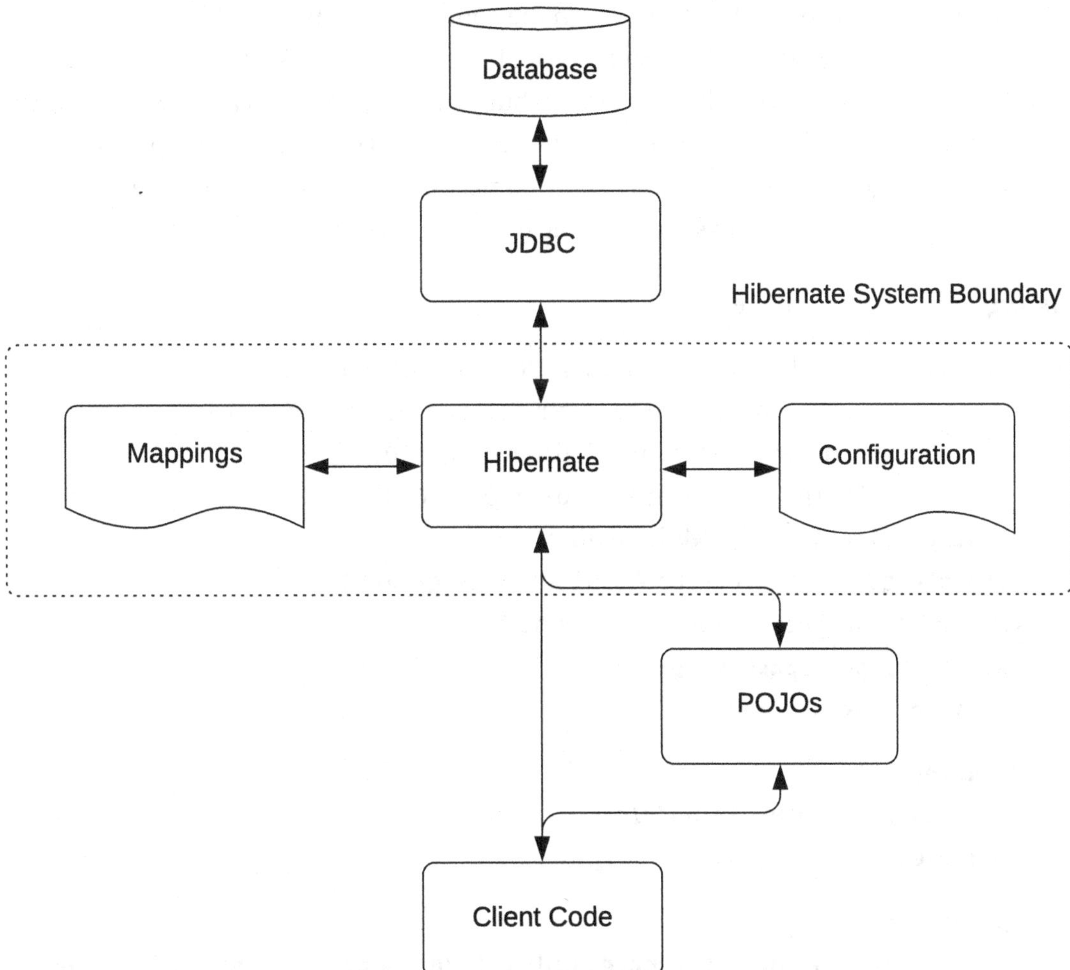

Figure 1-1. *The role of Hibernate in a Java application*

[3] Note also that there are *many* alternatives that have sprouted up after Hibernate was released, many of which address areas where Hibernate appears suboptimal. They're mostly different paradigms, and generally what you'll find is that Hibernate does an *excellent* job of being a go-between for a relational database and Java's object model, where the alternatives tend to want you to think of your Java objects in terms of the data model, instead.

Building a Project

We're going to use Maven (`https://maven.apache.org`) to build a project for this book. It'll be organized as a top-level project with a subproject (or "module") for every chapter, and we'll also have a few extra modules to provide common functionality. You can do the same thing with Gradle (`https://gradle.org`), and there's no real reason for this book to prefer one over the other, but Maven won the coin toss,[4] so Maven it is.

Create a directory on your filesystem; it can be anything you like. (On my system, it's `/Users/joeo/work/publishing/bh6/src`, but you can name it anything appropriate for your tastes and preference and, obviously, filesystem.) This will be our top-level directory; we're going to put chapters in it by name, like `chapter01` and the like. We're using two digits because it looks nicer and also collates properly.[5]

Listing 1-2. The Top-Level `pom.xml`

```
<project xmlns:xsi="http://www.w3.org/2001/XMLSchema-instance"
         xsi:schemaLocation="http://maven.apache.org/POM/4.0.0
          http://maven.apache.org/xsd/maven-4.0.0.xsd"
         xmlns="http://maven.apache.org/POM/4.0.0">
    <modelVersion>4.0.0</modelVersion>
    <groupId>com.autumncode.books.hibernate</groupId>
    <artifactId>hibernate-6-parent</artifactId>
    <packaging>pom</packaging>
    <version>5.0</version>

    <modules>
        <module>chapter01</module>
    </modules>

    <properties>
        <project.build.sourceEncoding>UTF-8</project.build.sourceEncoding>
        <maven.compiler.source>11</maven.compiler.source>
```

[4] Maven called "heads," and out of 11 coin flips, Maven won 6 of them.

[5] If you download the source, you'll see some really funny comments in the XML. These are `asciidoctor` tags, and they're used here to hide information that isn't relevant; the idea is that if you actually typed in this code, it'd be what you actually needed, as opposed to presenting information that's not relevant yet.

```
    <maven.compiler.target>11</maven.compiler.target>
    <testng.version>7.4.0</testng.version>
    <hibernate.core.version>6.0.0.Alpha8</hibernate.core.version>
    <h2.version>1.4.200</h2.version>
    <logback.version>1.2.3</logback.version>
    <lombok.version>1.18.18</lombok.version>
    <hibernate.validator.version>
        6.2.0.Final
    </hibernate.validator.version>
    <javax.el-api.version>3.0.0</javax.el-api.version>
    <ignite.version>2.10.0</ignite.version>
    <jackson.version>2.12.3</jackson.version>
</properties>

<dependencyManagement>
    <dependencies>
        <dependency>
            <groupId>org.hibernate.orm</groupId>
            <artifactId>hibernate-core</artifactId>
            <version>${hibernate.core.version}</version>
        </dependency>
        <dependency>
            <groupId>org.testng</groupId>
            <artifactId>testng</artifactId>
            <version>${testng.version}</version>
        </dependency>
        <dependency>
            <groupId>com.h2database</groupId>
            <artifactId>h2</artifactId>
            <version>${h2.version}</version>
        </dependency>
        <dependency>
            <groupId>ch.qos.logback</groupId>
            <artifactId>logback-classic</artifactId>
            <version>${logback.version}</version>
        </dependency>
```

```
            <dependency>
                <groupId>org.projectlombok</groupId>
                <artifactId>lombok</artifactId>
                <version>${lombok.version}</version>
            </dependency>
            <dependency>
                <groupId>org.apache.ignite</groupId>
                <artifactId>ignite-core</artifactId>
                <version>${ignite.version}</version>
            </dependency>
            <dependency>
                <groupId>org.hibernate.orm</groupId>
                <artifactId>hibernate-jcache</artifactId>
                <version>${hibernate.core.version}</version>
            </dependency>
            <dependency>
                <groupId>org.hibernate</groupId>
                <artifactId>hibernate-envers</artifactId>
                <version>${hibernate.core.version}</version>
            </dependency>
            <dependency>
                <groupId>com.fasterxml.jackson.core</groupId>
                <artifactId>jackson-databind</artifactId>
                <version>${jackson.version}</version>
            </dependency>
            <dependency>
                <groupId>com.fasterxml.jackson.datatype</groupId>
                <artifactId>jackson-datatype-jsr310</artifactId>
                <version>${jackson.version}</version>
            </dependency>
        </dependencies>
    </dependencyManagement>

    <dependencies>
        <dependency>
            <groupId>org.hibernate.orm</groupId>
```

```
            <artifactId>hibernate-core</artifactId>
        </dependency>
        <dependency>
            <groupId>ch.qos.logback</groupId>
            <artifactId>logback-classic</artifactId>
        </dependency>
        <dependency>
            <groupId>com.h2database</groupId>
            <artifactId>h2</artifactId>
            <scope>test</scope>
        </dependency>
        <dependency>
            <groupId>org.testng</groupId>
            <artifactId>testng</artifactId>
            <scope>test</scope>
        </dependency>
    </dependencies>

    <build>
        <plugins>
            <plugin>
                <groupId>org.apache.maven.plugins</groupId>
                <artifactId>maven-compiler-plugin</artifactId>
                <version>3.8.1</version>
                <configuration>
                    <release>11</release>
                </configuration>
            </plugin>
        </plugins>
    </build>
</project>
```

So what is this pom.xml actually doing? It turns out, quite a bit – although almost all of it's related to common configuration for the rest of the book, so the module pom.xml files are much simpler than they otherwise would be.

The first few lines describe the "parent project," described as having a `groupId` of `com.autumncode.books.hibernate` and an artifact id of `hibernate-6-parent`. It's also set to a *version* of `1.0-SNAPSHOT` – none of this is particularly relevant.

We then have a `<modules>` block, with a single module in it. As we progress through the book, we'll add modules here for each chapter, and if you look at the source code that accompanies this book, you'll see a full complement of modules in this section.

Up next is the `<properties>` block, which we use to set the default compiler version and target (Java 11, which is the current "production" version of Java[6]), followed by a lot of specific dependency versions, like `<h2.version>1.4.200</h2.version>`.[7]

Next, we have a `<dependencyManagement>` block. This doesn't actually set up any dependencies, as such: it simply allows us to centralize references for dependencies. Note that modules will inherit the dependencies of the parent project, so we can declare all of our specific dependencies **here** and the modules can simply use the names, instead of having to include the versions as well. If a new version of Hibernate were to come out, for example, we'd only have to change the version used in `<dependencyManagement>`, and the change would propagate throughout the whole project.

After `<dependencyManagement>`, we have dependencies we expect to be common for the entire project. This *is* a Hibernate book, so it makes sense to have Hibernate itself here, as well as a relatively standard logging framework (Logback (`https://logback.qos.ch/`), which itself includes Slf4j (`www.slf4j.org/`) as a transitive dependency), and we also import TestNG (`https://testng.org`) and H2 (`www.h2database.com/`), a popular embedded database written in pure Java, as test dependencies.

Lastly, we have a `<build>` section, which forces Maven to use a recent version of the `maven-compiler-plugin`, required to set the language version correctly, because while Maven is horribly useful, it's also designed to support legacy JVMs very well, to the point where you have to tell it specifically to use more recent JVMs.

We haven't even gotten to this chapter's build yet! We declared the module, but we haven't described it yet. Thankfully, with so much work being done in the parent `pom.xml`, the chapter's project model is really rather simple.

---

[6] It's actually the current LTS version of Java – with LTS meaning that it's got long-term support. The *actual* "current" version of Java as this is being written is Java 16, with Java 17 – the next LTS version of the JVM – right around the corner, but 16 isn't an LTS version, and 17 hasn't been released at draft time.

[7] If you are using the downloaded source code, note that the current version of H2 **might** be more recent than this reference. Of course, that's exactly why the property is being set in the first place, to make tracking current versions easier.

Listing 1-3. chapter01/pom.xml

```
<?xml version="1.0" encoding="UTF-8"?>
<project xmlns="http://maven.apache.org/POM/4.0.0"
         xmlns:xsi="http://www.w3.org/2001/XMLSchema-instance"
         xsi:schemaLocation="http://maven.apache.org/POM/4.0.0
          http://maven.apache.org/xsd/maven-4.0.0.xsd">
    <parent>
        <groupId>com.autumncode.books.hibernate</groupId>
        <artifactId>hibernate-6-parent</artifactId>
        <version>5.0</version>
    </parent>
    <modelVersion>4.0.0</modelVersion>

    <artifactId>chapter01</artifactId>
</project>
```

Here, all we do is declare what **this** module is (`chapter01`) and include a reference to the parent module. Everything is inherited.

Now that we have all the icky project stuff out of the way, let's circle back around to what Hibernate is designed to do for us.

Hibernate is, as already pointed out, an "Object/Relational Mapper," meaning that it maps Java objects to a relational schema, and vice versa. Programmers actually have a *lot* of control over what the actual mapping looks like, but in general it's easiest to follow a few simple idioms to create easily mapped objects. Let's start with a simple object, representing a message that we'll store in a database for absolutely no good reason at all, other than to serve as the basis for a simple example.

Listing 1-4. chapter01/src/main/java/chapter01/pojo/Message.java

```
package chapter01.pojo;

import java.util.Objects;

public class Message {
  String text;
```

```
  public Message(String text) {
    setText(text);
  }

  public String getText() {
    return text;
  }

  public void setText(String text) {
    this.text = text;
  }

  @Override
  public boolean equals(Object o) {
    if (this == o) return true;
    if (!(o instanceof Message)) return false;
    Message message = (Message) o;
    return Objects.equals(getText(), message.getText());
  }

  @Override
  public int hashCode() {
    return Objects.hash(getText());
  }

  @Override
  public String toString() {
    return String.format("Message{text='%s'}", getText());
  }
}
```

You can't get much simpler than that object; it's doable, of course, because you could create an object that had no state (therefore, no `text` field and no accessor or mutator to reference to it), and we could ignore the `equals()` and `hashCode()` and `toString()` as well. Such objects would be useful as *actors*, objects that act on other objects. But Listing 1-4 is a good example of what *most* POJOs will look like, in that most Java classes that represent program state *will* have attributes, accessors, mutators, `equals`, `hashCode`, and `toString` as well.

Hibernate could map Listing 1-4 fairly easily, but it does *not* follow the idioms you'll find in most Hibernate entities. Getting there is really simple, though.

Let's create a `MessageEntity` class, which still doesn't fit the Hibernate idiom perfectly, but is ready for persistence – and along the way, it'll serve as the basis for an *actual* Hibernate entity, which we'll see right after we see what Hibernate actually does for us behind the scenes.

Listing 1-5. chapter01/src/main/java/chapter01/pojo/MessageEntity.java

```
package chapter01.pojo;

import java.util.Objects;

public class MessageEntity {
  Long id;
  String text;

  public MessageEntity() {
  }

  public MessageEntity(Long id, String text) {
    this();
    setId(id);
    setText(text);
  }

  public Long getId() {
    return id;
  }

  public void setId(Long id) {
    this.id = id;
  }

  public String getText() {
    return text;
  }
```

```
  public void setText(String text) {
    this.text = text;
  }

  @Override
  public boolean equals(Object o) {
    if (this == o) return true;
    if (!(o instanceof MessageEntity)) return false;
    MessageEntity message = (MessageEntity) o;
    return Objects.equals(getId(), message.getId())
        && Objects.equals(getText(), message.getText());
  }

  @Override
  public int hashCode() {
    return Objects.hash(getId(), getText());
  }

  @Override
  public String toString() {
    return String.format("MessageEntity{id=%d,text='%s'}",
        getId(),
        getText());
  }
}
```

There are a few changes here. We've added an id field (a Long), along with an accessor and a mutator for the id, and we've added the id to the standard utility methods (equals(), hashCode(), and toString())... and we've added a no-argument constructor. The id field is pretty common for relational mapping, because such fields are much easier to search and refer to when working with the database, but the no-argument constructor is *primarily* a concession to convenience, because it allows us to create a sort of "blank canvas" object that we can fill in later, through the mutators or by direct field access, if we allow that.

In strict OOP terms, this can be a bad thing, because it means we can legitimately construct an object that lacks legitimate state; consider our poor old MessageEntity. If we define a "valid MessageEntity" as having a valid id field (any number will do, as long as it's not `null`) and a populated `text` field (anything but `null`), then calling our no-argument constructor creates a `MessageEntity` that is *not* valid. In fact, if we call the *other* constructor, we have similar problems, because we aren't checking the values of the attributes as we set them.

This is actually a characteristic of the Java Persistence API, or JPA specification, which says that the class *must* have a `public` or `protected` no-argument constructor with no arguments. Hibernate extends the JPA specification, and while it is looser in some requirements than the JPA specification is, it generally follows the constructor requirement (although the constructor can also have `package` visibility).

We also should not have the class be marked `final`. There are actually ways around this, but Hibernate by default creates an extension of the class to enable some potentially very useful features (like lazy-loading data in attributes).

You should also provide standard accessors and mutators (like `getId()` and `setId()`).

So how would we *use* this class in an actual persistence story? Here's a test class that actually initializes a database, saves a `MessageEntity` into it, and then tests that the message can properly be retrieved.

Listing 1-6. `chapter01/src/test/java/chapter01/jdbc/PersistenceTest.java`

```
package chapter01.jdbc;

import chapter01.pojo.MessageEntity;
import org.testng.annotations.BeforeClass;
import org.testng.annotations.Test;

import java.sql.*;
import java.util.ArrayList;
import java.util.List;

import static org.testng.Assert.assertEquals;

public class PersistenceTest {
  Connection getConnection() throws SQLException {
    return DriverManager.getConnection("jdbc:h2:./db1", "sa", "");
  }
```

```
@BeforeClass
public void setup() {
  final String DROP = "DROP TABLE messages IF EXISTS";
  final String CREATE = "CREATE TABLE messages ("
      + "id BIGINT GENERATED BY DEFAULT AS IDENTITY "
      + "PRIMARY KEY, "
      + "text VARCHAR(256) NOT NULL)";
  try (Connection connection = getConnection()) {
    // clear out the old data, if any, so we know the state of the DB
    try (PreparedStatement ps =
            connection.prepareStatement(DROP)) {
      ps.execute();
    }
    // create the table...
    try (PreparedStatement ps =
            connection.prepareStatement(CREATE)) {
      ps.execute();
    }
  } catch (SQLException e) {
    e.printStackTrace();
    throw new RuntimeException(e);
  }
}

public MessageEntity saveMessage(String text) {
  final String INSERT = "INSERT INTO messages(text) VALUES (?)";
  MessageEntity message = null;
  try (Connection connection = getConnection()) {
    try (PreparedStatement ps =
            connection.prepareStatement(INSERT,
                Statement.RETURN_GENERATED_KEYS)) {

      ps.setString(1, text);
      ps.execute();
      try (ResultSet keys = ps.getGeneratedKeys()) {
        if (!keys.next()) {
```

```
                throw new SQLException("No generated keys");
            }
            message = new MessageEntity(keys.getLong(1), text);
        }
    }
  } catch (SQLException e) {
    e.printStackTrace();
    throw new RuntimeException(e);
  }
  return message;
}

@Test
public void readMessage() {
  final String text = "Hello, World!";

  MessageEntity message = saveMessage(text);

  final String SELECT = "SELECT id, text FROM messages";
  List<MessageEntity> list = new ArrayList<>();
  try (Connection connection = getConnection()) {
    try (PreparedStatement ps =
             connection.prepareStatement(SELECT)) {
      try (ResultSet rs = ps.executeQuery()) {
        while (rs.next()) {
          MessageEntity newMessage = new MessageEntity();
          newMessage.setId(rs.getLong(1));
          newMessage.setText(rs.getString(2));
          list.add(message);
        }

      }
    }
  } catch (SQLException e) {
    e.printStackTrace();
    throw new RuntimeException(e);
  }
```

```
    assertEquals(list.size(), 1);
    for (MessageEntity m : list) {
      System.out.println(m);
    }
    assertEquals(list.get(0), message);
  }
}
```

So what's going on here? First, we have a simple utility method that returns a `Connection`; this mostly saves the length of the statement and reduces repetition.

We also have a `setup()` method, marked with `@BeforeClass`. This annotation means this method will be invoked before any of the tests in the class are executed. (We could also have used `@BeforeTest` or `@BeforeSuite`, but in this case, `@BeforeClass` is probably the right granularity, assuming we have more functionality to test than we actually do.)

The annotations indicate when the annotated method runs, in context of the test class. `@BeforeTest` runs before every method annotated with `@Test` runs. `@BeforeClass` runs before *any* test method in the class runs; `@BeforeSuite` runs before any test in *any* test class runs. There are also `@AfterClass`, `@AfterTest`, and `@AfterSuite` methods that run at the end of their corresponding phases.

Next, we have another utility method, `saveMessage()`, which takes message text to save. This will insert a new record in the database table. It requests the generated key from the database so that it can populate a `MessageEntity` and return it, mirroring convenient behavior (we can now query for *that message* and test for equivalency, as we see done in the `readMessage()` test). It's functional; it's not very good, honestly, but it's not worth improving. Hibernate does this sort of thing far better than we are here, and in less code; we could mirror much of what Hibernate does, but it's just more effort than it's worth.

Lastly, we have our actual test: `readMessage()`. This calls `saveMessage()` and then reads through all of the "saved messages" - which, given that we've taken pains to create a deterministic database state, will be a list of *one* message. As it reads the messages, it creates `MessageEntity` objects for each one and stores them in a `List`, and then we validate the `List` - it should have one element only, and that element should match the `MessageEntity` we saved at the beginning of the method.

Whew! That's a lot of work; there's some boilerplate, in the acquisition of resources (done with automatic resource management, to handle clean deallocation in the case of exceptions), and the JDBC code itself is pretty low level. It's also rather underpowered and very manual. We're still managing the specific resources like `Connection` and `PreparedStatement`, and the code's very brittle; if we added a field, we'd have to look for and modify every statement that would be affected by that field, since we're manually mapping the data from JDBC into our object.[8]

We also run into the issue of *types* with this code. This is a very simple object, after all; it stores a simple numeric identifier with a simple string. However, if we wanted to store a geolocation, we'd have to break the geolocation into its component properties (latitude and longitude, for example) and store each separately, which means your object model no longer cleanly matches your database.

All of this makes using the database directly look more and more flawed, and that's before factoring in other issues around object persistence and retrieval.

Want to *run* these tests? It's really simple: run the Maven lifecycle with `mvn build`, which will download all of the dependencies for our project (if necessary), compile our "production" classes (the ones in `src/main/java`), then compile our test classes (the ones in `src/test/java`), and then execute the tests, dumping any console output (to the console, naturally) and halting on failures. It then builds a jar of our production resources. We can also limit the lifecycle to only doing enough to run the tests with `mvn test`.

Hibernate As a Persistence Solution

Hibernate fixes almost everything we don't like about the JDBC solution. We don't use complex types in this example, so we won't see how that's done until later in this book, but it's easier to do in nearly every metric.[9]

[8] This actually affected the draft of this chapter; the reviewer actually caught an error where your author had done the mapping incorrectly, because it was done manually.

[9] The only metric by which the Hibernate code is "worse than" the JDBC code is in the metric of "doesn't require any Hibernate knowledge." You have to have some understanding of Hibernate to use Hibernate, which is a given; if you don't have any Hibernate knowledge, but you *do* have JDBC knowledge, the Hibernate version necessarily seems rather foreign by comparison.

First, we need to fix our `MessageEntity` to be an actual Hibernate entity. We do this by adding some annotations to the class, making it conform to the JPA requirements. We're also going to change the constructors slightly to fit the *domain* of a `Message` in a better fashion; a `Message`'s core attribute is its `text`, and the `id` is incidental. We can map that *better* with Hibernate than in our `MessageEntity`.[10] There are four annotations we want to add for JPA, and they actually cover the annotations Hibernate users will use most often:[11]

1. `@javax.persistence.Entity`: Which marks the class as an entity class to be managed by Hibernate
2. `@javax.persistence.Id`: Which makes the field to which it applies as a primary key for the database
3. `@javax.persistence.GeneratedValue`: Which provides information to Hibernate about how the value should be populated
4. `@javax.persistence.Column`: Which allows us to control aspects of the field in the database

Here's the `Message` entity itself.

Listing 1-7. `chapter01/src/main/java/chapter01/hibernate/Message.java`

```
package chapter01.hibernate;

import javax.persistence.*;
import java.util.Objects;

@Entity
public class Message {
  Long id;
  String text;

  public Message() {
```

[10] To be fair, we could have done that with `MessageEntity` as well, but it's a throwaway class, and it needed the `id` for the population phase in the JDBC test.

[11] Two annotations, `@Entity` and `@Id`, are necessary if you're using annotations to configure your mappings. If you're not using annotations, you'll need to use equivalents to them, at the very least - equivalents that aren't going to be covered in depth in this book.

```
}

public Message(String text) {
  this();
  setText(text);
}

@Id
@GeneratedValue(strategy = GenerationType.IDENTITY)
public Long getId() {
  return id;
}

public void setId(Long id) {
  this.id = id;
}

@Column(nullable = false)
public String getText() {
  return text;
}

public void setText(String text) {
  this.text = text;
}

@Override
public boolean equals(Object o) {
  if (this == o) return true;
  if (!(o instanceof Message)) return false;
  Message message = (Message) o;
  return Objects.equals(getId(), message.getId())
      && Objects.equals(getText(), message.getText());
}
```

```
    @Override
    public int hashCode() {
      return Objects.hash(getId(), getText());
    }

    @Override
    public String toString() {
      return String.format("Message{id=%d,text='%s'}",
          getId(),
          getText());
    }
}
```

The @GeneratedValue here has a strategy of GenerationType.IDENTITY, which specifies that Hibernate will mirror the behavior of our manually created JDBC schema: the keys for each Message will be automatically generated by the database.

The @Column(nullable = false) likewise indicates that the text field can't store a null in the database. The column name will be derived from the field name, mangled slightly if it matches a reserved word; in this case, our database is fine with a column called text so no mangling occurs, and we *can* provide an explicit column name if we so desire.

Apart from the annotations and the constructors, the Message and the MessageEntity are very similar.

Next, we need to look at how we tell Hibernate to connect to a database and how it should behave. We do this with a configuration file, conventionally named hibernate.cfg.xml and located in the execution classpath; in general, the files will all look the same with the exception of the JDBC URLs and the mapping references. Because this is written for a test, we'll put it in our src/test/resources directory.

Listing 1-8. chapter01/src/test/resources/hibernate.cfg.xml

```
<?xml version="1.0"?>
<!DOCTYPE hibernate-configuration PUBLIC
        "-//Hibernate/Hibernate Configuration DTD 3.0//EN"
        "http://www.hibernate.org/dtd/hibernate-configuration-3.0.dtd">
<hibernate-configuration>
    <session-factory>
```

```
        <!-- Database connection settings -->
        <property name="connection.driver_class">org.h2.Driver</property>
        <property name="connection.url">jdbc:h2:./db1</property>
        <property name="connection.username">sa</property>
        <property name="connection.password"/>
        <property name="dialect">org.hibernate.dialect.H2Dialect</property>
        <!-- Echo all executed SQL to stdout -->
        <property name="show_sql">true</property>
        <!-- Drop and re-create the database schema on startup -->
        <property name="hbm2ddl.auto">create-drop</property>
        <mapping class="chapter01.hibernate.Message"/>
    </session-factory>
</hibernate-configuration>
```

Most of our configurations will look pretty similar to this, honestly. But what is it telling us?

`connection`[1]`.driver.class`	This is the fully qualified name of the JDBC driver class for the session factory.
`connection.url`	This is the JDBC URL used to connect to the database.
`connection.username`	The connection's username, surprisingly enough.
`connection.password`	Another surprise – the connection's password. In an uninitialized H2 database, "sa" and an empty password are sufficient.
`dialect`	This property tells Hibernate how to write SQL for the specific database.
`show_sql`	This property sets Hibernate to echo its generated SQL statements to a specified logger.
`hbm2ddl.auto`	This property tells Hibernate whether it should manage the database schema; in this case, we're telling it to create on initialization and drop the database when it's done.

`hbm2ddl.auto` is *dangerous* in production environments. For temporary, or testing, environments, it's no big deal, but when you're talking about real data that needs to be preserved, this property can be destructive, a word one rarely wants to hear when talking about valuable data.

The last line tells Hibernate that it has one entity type to manage, the `chapter01.hibernate.Message` class.

There's one more configuration file to consider, although it's optional. (It's included in the source for the book.) The parent project specifies `logback-classic` as a dependency, which means that every chapter receives Logback and its transitive dependencies as classpath elements. Logback has a default configuration, but it tends to be extraordinarily noisy for our purposes. Here's a `logback.xml` configuration file that trims out some of the noise.

Listing 1-9. `chapter01/src/main/resources/logback.xml`

```
<configuration>
  <appender
      name="STDOUT"
      class="ch.qos.logback.core.ConsoleAppender">
    <encoder
        class="ch.qos.logback.classic.encoder.PatternLayoutEncoder">
      <Pattern>
        %d{yyyy-MM-dd HH:mm:ss} %-5level %logger{36} - %msg%n
      </Pattern>
    </encoder>
  </appender>
  <logger name="org.hibernate.SQL"
          level="debug"
          additivity="false">
    <appender-ref ref="STDOUT"/>
  </logger>
  <logger name="org.hibernate.type.descriptor.sql"
          level="trace"
          additivity="false">
    <appender-ref ref="STDOUT"/>
  </logger>
  <root level="info">
    <appender-ref ref="STDOUT"/>
  </root>
</configuration>
```

Note that the default logger level is set to `info`. This tends to create a lot of information on the logger's output stream (the console); it's interesting to look at and can be very helpful for diagnostic purposes, but if you want, you can set the logger level to `error` and reduce the chattiness of Hibernate quite dramatically.

Now we have all the plumbing and secondary configuration files out of the way: it's finally time to look at what some actual Hibernate code looks like. Our test actually mirrors what the JDBC test does, almost exactly. It's far more succinct code than the JDBC code was.

Listing 1-10. `chapter01/src/test/java/chapter01/hibernate/PersistenceTest.java`

```
package chapter01.hibernate;

import org.hibernate.Session;
import org.hibernate.SessionFactory;
import org.hibernate.Transaction;
import org.hibernate.boot.MetadataSources;
import org.hibernate.boot.registry.StandardServiceRegistry;
import org.hibernate.boot.registry.StandardServiceRegistryBuilder;
import org.testng.annotations.BeforeClass;
import org.testng.annotations.Test;

import java.util.List;

import static org.testng.Assert.assertEquals;

public class PersistenceTest {
  private SessionFactory factory = null;

  @BeforeClass
  public void setup() {
    StandardServiceRegistry registry =
        new StandardServiceRegistryBuilder()
            .configure()
            .build();
    factory = new MetadataSources(registry)
```

```
        .buildMetadata()
        .buildSessionFactory();
  }

  public Message saveMessage(String text) {
    Message message = new Message(text);
    try (Session session = factory.openSession()) {
      Transaction tx = session.beginTransaction();
      session.persist(message);
      tx.commit();
    }
    return message;
  }

  @Test
  public void readMessage() {
    Message savedMessage = saveMessage("Hello, World");
    List<Message> list;
    try (Session session = factory.openSession()) {
      list = session
          .createQuery("from Message", Message.class)
          .list();
    }
    assertEquals(list.size(), 1);
    for (Message m : list) {
      System.out.println(m);
    }
    assertEquals(list.get(0), savedMessage);
  }
}
```

The first thing to notice is the way we're accessing resources. In the JDBC version, we had a simple `getConnection()` that we called whenever we happened to need a `Connection`; here, we're creating a reference to a `SessionFactory` and initializing it before the class' tests run. The way we build it is ... not complex, but it's verbose for something we're likely to do over and over again.[12]

Once we **have** the `SessionFactory`, though, the idioms are very straightforward. We create a block for which a `Session` is in scope - again, with automatic resource management - and then we begin a transaction. (In the JDBC example, we did the same thing, just implicitly.) Then we `save()` the object, or query for one, as we need.

Once we've done something with the database, we commit the transaction.

We're going to discuss a lot more about the actual configuration and mapping in future chapters; it's okay if you're wondering what settings are available, and what operations there are, and why one would want a transaction for a read operation. We're going to cover all of that.

If you run this code (again, with `mvn test` or `mvn build`), you might see a *ton* of logging output, largely because of the `show_sql` property being set to `true` in the Hibernate configuration file.

Summary

In this chapter, we have considered the problems and requirements that have driven the development of Hibernate. We have looked at some of the details of a trivial example application written with and without the aid of Hibernate. We have glossed over some of the implementation details, but we will discuss these in depth in Chapter 2.

[12] We're actually going to create a utility module in Chapter 3 and use that to hide the process of building a `SessionFactory`. If we use an application framework like Jakarta EE or Spring, they'll have their own ways of initializing a `SessionFactory` such that such repetitive, verbose code is hidden away like it should be.

CHAPTER 2

Integrating and Configuring Hibernate

Integrating Hibernate into a Java application is easy. The designers of Hibernate avoided some of the more common pitfalls and problems with the existing Java persistence solutions and created a clean but powerful architecture. In practice, this means that you do not have to run Hibernate inside any particular Java EE container or framework. As of Hibernate 6, Java 8 or later is required, thanks to the integration of the date and time API and other such useful features.[1]

Just because you *can* use Java 8 doesn't mean you *should be* using Java 8. As noted in Chapter 1, the current release of Java when this was written is Java 16, with Java 17 peeking around the corner of the calendar; the "long-term" current version of Java is 11, with 17 designated to be the next long-term support release. Java 8 should only be used when you literally have no choice, such as an unavoidable dependency on a library that is supported on 8 and on nothing later.

At first, adding Hibernate to your Java project looks intimidating: the distribution includes a large set of dependencies. To get your first Hibernate application to work, you have to set up the database references and the Hibernate configuration, which might include mapping your objects to the database. You also have to create your POJOs, including any annotation-based mapping. After you have done all of that, you need to write the logic in your application that uses Hibernate to actually accomplish something! But once you learn how to integrate Hibernate with your application, the basics apply for any project that uses Hibernate.

[1] That means that if you're on an older version of the JVM, you'll have to stick to older versions of Hibernate. That shouldn't be too much of a bother; Java 7 has been end-of-lifed since April of 2015. It's time to move up if you haven't already, thanks to security concerns and, of course, the fact that Java 8 is nice.

J. B. Ottinger et al., *Beginning Hibernate 6*, https://doi.org/10.1007/978-1-4842-7337-1_2

One of the key features of Hibernate's design is the principle of least intrusiveness: the Hibernate developers did not want Hibernate to intrude into your application more than was necessary. This led to several of the architectural decisions made for Hibernate. In Chapter 1, you saw how Hibernate can be applied to solve persistence problems using conventional Java objects. In this chapter, we explain some of the configuration details needed to support this behavior.

The Steps Needed to Integrate and Configure Hibernate

This chapter explains configuration and integration in detail, but for a quick overview, refer to the following list to determine what you need to do to get your first Hibernate application up and running. Then Chapter 3 will lead you through the building of a pair of small example applications that use Hibernate. The first of these examples is as simple as we could make it, so it is an excellent introduction to the following necessary steps:

1. Identify the POJOs that have a database representation.
2. Identify which properties of those POJOs need to be persisted.
3. Annotate each of the POJOs to map your Java object's properties to columns in a database table (covered in more detail in Chapter 6).
4. Create the database schema using the schema export tool, use an existing database, or create your own database schema.
5. Add the Hibernate Java dependencies to your application's classpath (covered in this chapter).
6. Create a Hibernate XML configuration file that points to your database and your mapped classes (covered in this chapter).
7. In your Java application, create a Hibernate Configuration object that references your XML configuration file (covered in this chapter).
8. Also in your Java application, build a Hibernate SessionFactory object from the Configuration object (covered in this chapter).

9. Retrieve the Hibernate Session objects from the SessionFactory, and write your data access logic for your application (create, retrieve/read, update, and delete).

Don't worry if you don't understand every term or concept mentioned in this list. It's actually more straightforward than you might think, looking at the list! After reading this chapter, and then following the example in the next chapter, you will know what these terms mean and how they fit together.

Understanding Where Hibernate Fits into Your Java Application

You can call Hibernate from your Java application directly, or you can access Hibernate through another framework, like Spring Data (`https://spring.io/projects/spring-data`). You can call Hibernate from a Swing application, a servlet, a portlet, a JSP page, or any other Java application that has access to a database.[2] Typically, you would use Hibernate to either create a data access layer for an application or replace an existing data access layer.

Hibernate supports the Java Management Extensions (JMX), J2EE Connector Architecture (JCA), and Java Naming and Directory Interface (JNDI) Java language standards. Using JMX, you can configure Hibernate while it is running. Hibernate may be deployed as a JCA connector, and you can use JNDI to obtain a Hibernate session factory in your application. In addition, Hibernate uses standard Java Database Connectivity (JDBC) database drivers to access the relational database. Hibernate does not replace JDBC as a database connectivity layer; Hibernate sits on a level above JDBC.

In addition to the standard Java APIs, many Java web and application frameworks now integrate with Hibernate. Hibernate's simple, clean API makes it easy for these frameworks to support Hibernate in one way or another. The Spring Framework provides excellent Hibernate integration, including generic support for persistence objects, a generic set of persistence exceptions, and transaction management. Chapter 12 explains how Hibernate can be configured within a Spring application.

[2] Note that it's typically not very wise to call Hibernate or *any* storage mechanism directly from a servlet, et al. We'll see some better strategies for this explained in Chapters 11 and 12, but for the sake of brevity will do things inefficiently.

Regardless of the environment into which you are integrating Hibernate, certain requirements remain constant. You will need to define the configuration details that apply; these are then represented by a ServiceRegistry object. From the ServiceRegistry object, a SessionFactory object is created; and from this, Session objects are instantiated, through which your application accesses Hibernate's representation of the database.

Deploying Hibernate

There are two sets of components necessary for the integration of Hibernate into your application: a database driver and the Hibernate dependencies themselves.

The example code for this book uses H2 as a small, embeddable database;[3] this can be found at `http://h2database.com/`. This is not to indicate that other databases are of less value than H2, but it is simply an expedient choice; H2's sort of sibling project HSQLDB is also workable, as is Derby; if you have a MySQL or PostgreSQL data server handy, those work as well, but an embedded database means that you don't have to have an external process running, nor do you have to configure a special database or user account.[4] H2 also provides a *very* convenient web-based console with which you can interact with a database (or any database, if you provide the driver to the classpath), if you need that sort of thing.

If you're using the Hibernate binary download (from a "release bundle," via `https://hibernate.org/orm/releases/`), all of the jars contained in the `lib/required` directory are mandatory in order to use Hibernate.

---

[3] The third edition of this book actually used HSQLDB, and we switched to H2 for the fourth edition. There was not a concrete reason for the switch, but research among the community showed a preference for H2 over HSQLDB, for various reasons (mostly centering on the fact that H2 is written by HSQL's original author). Your authors listen to the people.

[4] It's also worth noting that there are plug-ins for Maven that can embed external databases like MariaDB (a variant of MySQL); see MariaDB4J at `https://github.com/vorburger/MariaDB4j` if you're interested. But H2 is smaller and faster for our purposes, and since Hibernate is database independent, the actual database you use should largely be irrelevant.

Perhaps[5] an easier way to integrate Hibernate is through the use of a build tool, like Gradle (`www.gradle.org/`, used by the Hibernate project itself), SBT (`www.scala-sbt.org/`), or Maven (`http://maven.apache.org/`), the latter which is arguably the most popular of the build tools, if not the best.[6]

All of these build tools are able to bundle dependencies into a deliverable artifact. They're also able to include dependencies transitively, which means that projects that depend on a given subproject also inherit that subproject's dependencies.

We'll target Maven as a build environment for the rest of the book; users of other build tools are generally able to migrate from Maven fairly easily.[7]

Installing Maven

There are many ways to install Maven. This is a cursory overview; different operating systems (and different system configurations) can affect the installation procedure, so when you are in doubt, you can refer to `http://maven.apache.org/download.cgi#Installation` for the actual documentation.

To save you some time, however, you can download Maven from `http://maven.apache.org/download.cgi/`; you should get the most recent version. UNIX users (including Linux and MacOS users) should download the file ending in tar.gz; Windows users should download the zip file.

In UNIX, untar the file into a directory of your choice; an example of the command that might be run is this:

```
mkdir ~/tools || cd ~/tools; tar xf apache-maven-3.8.1-bin.tar.gz
```

[5] "Perhaps" is being used here rather ironically. Use a build tool like Maven or Gradle. Other options are doable, much like it's perfectly okay to build a rope bridge to cross a chasm, when a suspension bridge has already been built for you.

[6] Arguments about "which build tool is best" are a lot like arguments about relative merits of IDEA, Emacs, NetBeans, Eclipse, and others. Everyone has an opinion, and that opinion is perfectly valid for the one who holds it, as long as the understanding is that SBT is the worst; however, Maven is generally agreed upon not to be the "best build tool," much like Eclipse is not the "best editor." They're popular. They're common. That's about it.

[7] If you don't use a build tool, please see your IDE's instructions for adding libraries to projects. However, it's worth noting that using a build tool is wise; it means that your builds are easily duplicated. For example, if you want to show your code to someone else, without a build tool you will have to make sure their environment matches yours; but with a build tool, all you have to do is make sure they have the tool installed. You can see this in this book; I describe the build with Maven, and readers can use any editor or IDE they like without affecting the content whatsoever.

This will create `~/tools/apache-maven-3.8.1/`, and the mvn executable will be in `~/tools/apache-maven-3.8.1/bin`; add this to your command path.

For Windows, open the archive and extract it into a known location (e.g., `C:\tools\`). Add the location of `mvn.bat` (in this example, `C:\tools\apache-maven-3.8.1\bin`) to your path via the System Properties dialog, and you should be able to run Maven with "mvn" in the command prompt.

Maven uses a project object model, typically written in XML, called "pom.xml". This file describes the project's name and versions and builds configurations (if any), as well as any subprojects and any project dependencies. When Maven is run, it will automatically download any resources it needs in order to complete the build as specified, and then it will compile the project source code; if the project includes tests, it will run the tests and complete the build if (and only if) no test failures occur.

This book uses a parent project that contains global dependencies for the book and subprojects corresponding to the chapters; much of the operating code is written as a set of tests in the subprojects. Chapter 1, for example, used two methods to write data to and read data from a database; those tests were written as TestNG[8] test classes: `chapter01.hibernate.PersistenceTest` and `chapter01.jdbc.PersistenceTest`.

The parent project's configuration file, after Chapter 1 was written, looked like Listing 2-1.

Listing 2-1. The Top-Level `pom.xml`

```
<project xmlns:xsi="http://www.w3.org/2001/XMLSchema-instance"
        xsi:schemaLocation="http://maven.apache.org/POM/4.0.0
         http://maven.apache.org/xsd/maven-4.0.0.xsd"
        xmlns="http://maven.apache.org/POM/4.0.0">
    <modelVersion>4.0.0</modelVersion>
    <groupId>com.autumncode.books.hibernate</groupId>
    <artifactId>hibernate-6-parent</artifactId>
    <packaging>pom</packaging>
    <version>5.0</version>

    <modules>
```

[8] TestNG (`https://testng.org/`) is a unit testing framework. It's a popular alternative to JUnit (`https://junit.org/junit5`). It's probably perfectly acceptable to also like JUnit 5, which has many features inspired by TestNG and some nice features of its own.

```
    <module>chapter01</module>
</modules>

<properties>
    <project.build.sourceEncoding>UTF-8</project.build.sourceEncoding>
    <maven.compiler.source>11</maven.compiler.source>
    <maven.compiler.target>11</maven.compiler.target>
    <testng.version>7.4.0</testng.version>
    <hibernate.core.version>6.0.0.Alpha8</hibernate.core.version>
    <h2.version>1.4.200</h2.version>
    <logback.version>1.2.3</logback.version>
    <lombok.version>1.18.18</lombok.version>
    <hibernate.validator.version>
        6.2.0.Final
    </hibernate.validator.version>
    <javax.el-api.version>3.0.0</javax.el-api.version>
    <ignite.version>2.10.0</ignite.version>
    <jackson.version>2.12.3</jackson.version>
</properties>

<dependencyManagement>
    <dependencies>
        <dependency>
            <groupId>org.hibernate.orm</groupId>
            <artifactId>hibernate-core</artifactId>
            <version>${hibernate.core.version}</version>
        </dependency>
        <dependency>
            <groupId>org.testng</groupId>
            <artifactId>testng</artifactId>
            <version>${testng.version}</version>
        </dependency>
        <dependency>
            <groupId>com.h2database</groupId>
            <artifactId>h2</artifactId>
            <version>${h2.version}</version>
```

```
</dependency>
<dependency>
    <groupId>ch.qos.logback</groupId>
    <artifactId>logback-classic</artifactId>
    <version>${logback.version}</version>
</dependency>
<dependency>
    <groupId>org.projectlombok</groupId>
    <artifactId>lombok</artifactId>
    <version>${lombok.version}</version>
</dependency>
<dependency>
    <groupId>org.apache.ignite</groupId>
    <artifactId>ignite-core</artifactId>
    <version>${ignite.version}</version>
</dependency>
<dependency>
    <groupId>org.hibernate.orm</groupId>
    <artifactId>hibernate-jcache</artifactId>
    <version>${hibernate.core.version}</version>
</dependency>
<dependency>
    <groupId>org.hibernate</groupId>
    <artifactId>hibernate-envers</artifactId>
    <version>${hibernate.core.version}</version>
</dependency>
<dependency>
    <groupId>com.fasterxml.jackson.core</groupId>
    <artifactId>jackson-databind</artifactId>
    <version>${jackson.version}</version>
</dependency>
<dependency>
    <groupId>com.fasterxml.jackson.datatype</groupId>
    <artifactId>jackson-datatype-jsr310</artifactId>
    <version>${jackson.version}</version>
</dependency>
```

```
        </dependencies>
    </dependencyManagement>

    <dependencies>
        <dependency>
            <groupId>org.hibernate.orm</groupId>
            <artifactId>hibernate-core</artifactId>
        </dependency>
        <dependency>
            <groupId>ch.qos.logback</groupId>
            <artifactId>logback-classic</artifactId>
        </dependency>
        <dependency>
            <groupId>com.h2database</groupId>
            <artifactId>h2</artifactId>
            <scope>test</scope>
        </dependency>
        <dependency>
            <groupId>org.testng</groupId>
            <artifactId>testng</artifactId>
            <scope>test</scope>
        </dependency>
    </dependencies>

    <build>
        <plugins>
            <plugin>
                <groupId>org.apache.maven.plugins</groupId>
                <artifactId>maven-compiler-plugin</artifactId>
                <version>3.8.1</version>
                <configuration>
                    <release>11</release>
                </configuration>
            </plugin>
        </plugins>
    </build>
</project>
```

This specifies a number of things about the project (such as the Java version, which is the current maintained version of Java[9]), and includes four dependencies: Hibernate itself; the H2 database; a logging framework, named "logback"; and TestNG, the last which is limited to the testing phase (as the "scope" node instructs).

The child projects - in this listing, this is only chapter01 - will receive this configuration and its set of dependencies automatically, which means we don't have to repeat ourselves very often.

To build and run this project after installing Maven, you simply have to go to the directory that contains pom.xml and execute `mvn package` - that will, as stated, download all the required dependencies, build them, test the projects in order, and build deployable artifacts for each project, whether as jar files or any other type of deployable unit.

Maven projects have a specific folder layout, although it's configurable; by default, the Java compiler compiles all code found in `src/main/java`, and Maven bundles the compiled classes with whatever is in `src/main/resources` into the deliverable artifact, the library or package being built. The `src/test/java` directory contains test classes in Java, which are then compiled and run, with the classpath being built from the tests, the resources in `src/test/resources`, and whatever is in `src/main` in the classpath as well.

Wow, that's a lot of non-Hibernate discussion - and all of it can be found (and subverted) on the websites for each given build environment. In general, you can (and should) use what you like; this book uses Maven because of how common it is, not because it's the One True Build Tool.

Let's look at the actual code we've been running so far and explain it all. That will give you a basis for future discussion, even if you're not going to use it much beyond this chapter.

We've already mentioned the top-level `pom.xml` file; we're going to start in the `chapter02` directory (which is almost a clone of the `chapter01` directory, except with `chapter02` instead of `chapter01` - and a change we'll see soon). Our project description file (our `pom.xml`) is very simple, specifying only the parent project and the current project's name (see Listing 2-2).

[9] The current "supported" version of Java, in terms of long-term support, as of this writing is Java 11, as has been said *at least* three times now. You can, however, still use Java 8 with Hibernate.

Listing 2-2. Chapter 2's Project Object Model

```
<project xmlns:xsi="http://www.w3.org/2001/XMLSchema-instance"
         xmlns="http://maven.apache.org/POM/4.0.0"
         xsi:schemaLocation="http://maven.apache.org/POM/4.0.0
         http://maven.apache.org/xsd/maven-4.0.0.xsd">
    <parent>
        <groupId>com.autumncode.books.hibernate</groupId>
        <artifactId>hibernate-6-parent</artifactId>
        <version>5.0</version>
    </parent>
    <modelVersion>4.0.0</modelVersion>

    <artifactId>chapter02</artifactId>
</project>
```

Our Message.java is held in src/main/java/chapter02/hibernate/Message.java. This is basically the same POJO as in Listing 1-7, renamed and placed in a different package. Since everything else is the same, we won't list it here.

Our actual running code is in the src/test directory and consists of two relevant files:[10] src/test/java/chapter02/hibernate/PersistenceTest.java and src/test/resources/hibernate.cfg.xml.

We've already seen PersistenceTest.java from Chapter 1, but let's take a look at it again, with a little more detail.

Listing 2-3. chapter02/src/test/chapter02/hibernate/PersistenceTest.java

```
package chapter02.hibernate;

import org.hibernate.Session;
import org.hibernate.SessionFactory;
import org.hibernate.Transaction;
import org.hibernate.boot.MetadataSources;
import org.hibernate.boot.registry.StandardServiceRegistry;
import org.hibernate.boot.registry.StandardServiceRegistryBuilder;
```

[10] There are other classes in the tree, but we no longer care about JDBC in this chapter; they're here because you were promised that chapter02's tree was the same as chapter01's. All of the JDBC stuff is going to be ignored.

```
import org.testng.annotations.BeforeClass;
import org.testng.annotations.Test;

import java.util.List;

import static org.testng.Assert.assertEquals;

public class PersistenceTest {
  private SessionFactory factory = null;

  @BeforeClass
  public void setup() {
    StandardServiceRegistry registry =
        new StandardServiceRegistryBuilder()
            .configure()
            .build();
    factory = new MetadataSources(registry)
        .buildMetadata()
        .buildSessionFactory();
  }

  public Message saveMessage(String text) {
    Message message = new Message(text);
    try (Session session = factory.openSession()) {
      Transaction tx = session.beginTransaction();
      session.persist(message);
      tx.commit();
    }
    return message;
  }

  @Test
  public void readMessage() {
    Message savedMessage = saveMessage("Hello, World");
    List<Message> list;
    try (Session session = factory.openSession()) {
      list = session
          .createQuery("from Message", Message.class)
          .list();
    }
```

```
    assertEquals(list.size(), 1);
    for (Message m : list) {
      System.out.println(m);
    }
    assertEquals(list.get(0), savedMessage);
  }
}
```

The setup() method is where Hibernate is initialized. Hibernate gets Session objects – which do the actual database interaction – from the SessionFactory type, here named factory; it gets the SessionFactory from a service registry. In our test, we're building the service registry explicitly; if you were using something like Spring or Jakarta EE, the SessionFactory would probably be initialized as part of the application startup for you, and you'd simply request a value for it.

We do not, however, store Session references for very long. They're much like database connections; if you need one, you acquire one and discard it as soon as you are done with it. This has real impact on how you write your application, in some cases.[11]

You can provide a resource name to StandardServiceRegistryBuilder().configure(), if you like; the default is hibernate.cfg.xml, but if you want to use a different configuration explicitly – for example, for testing purposes – this is where you would provide the configuration name:

```
StandardServiceRegistry registry =
  new StandardServiceRegistryBuilder()
      .configure("my-special-hibernate.cfg.xml")
      .build();
```

Looking at the methods that use Session, we can use automatic resource management on a Session itself; try-with-resources requires a close() method to be present on a type. There's a way we can fake it out so that we could automatically try to commit transactions, and that might work in simple code like this (where the conditions under which a transaction would fail would be very limited and, for that matter, catastrophic for the test), but normally your code will want to make explicit decisions about whether to commit a transaction or not. We cover transactions a good bit more thoroughly in Chapter 8.

[11] It's also wise to use a database connection pool. Hibernate has one built-in, but it's not meant for production use; we'll see the use of more capable database connection pools in the next section, and Hibernate makes their usage trivial.

The last piece of the puzzle is the actual configuration file itself, which is in src/test/resource/hibernate.cfg.xml. See Listing 2-4.

Listing 2-4. chapter02/src/test/resources/hibernate.cfg.xml

```
<?xml version="1.0"?>
<!DOCTYPE hibernate-configuration PUBLIC
        "-//Hibernate/Hibernate Configuration DTD 3.0//EN"
        "http://www.hibernate.org/dtd/hibernate-configuration-3.0.dtd">
<hibernate-configuration>
    <session-factory>
        <!--  Database connection settings  -->
        <property name="connection.driver_class">org.h2.Driver</property>
        <property name="connection.url">jdbc:h2:./db2</property>
        <property name="connection.username">sa</property>
        <property name="connection.password"/>
        <property name="dialect">org.hibernate.dialect.H2Dialect</property>
        <!--  Echo all executed SQL to stdout  -->
        <property name="show_sql">true</property>
        <!--  Drop and re-create the database schema on startup  -->
        <property name="hbm2ddl.auto">create-drop</property>
        <mapping class="chapter02.hibernate.Message"/>
    </session-factory>
</hibernate-configuration>
```

This file might serve as a boilerplate for every Hibernate configuration. In it, we specify the JDBC driver class; the JDBC URL, username, and password used to access the database; a dialect (which allows Hibernate to correctly produce SQL for each given database); some configuration, such as whether to dump the generated SQL to the console; and what to do for the schema. Lastly, it specifies the classes that should be managed - in this case, only our Message class.

There are a lot of things we can control from this file; we can even use it to specify the mapping of our objects to the database (i.e., ignoring the annotations we've been using so far). You'll see a little more of how to do this in later chapters of this book; it helps quite a bit in mapping existing database schemata[12] to object models.

[12] "Schemata" is the plural of "schema." See www.merriam-webster.com/dictionary/schema.

Most coders will (and should) prefer the annotation-based mappings.

Connection Pooling

As you've seen, Hibernate uses JDBC connections in order to interact with a database. Creating these connections is expensive - probably the most expensive single operation Hibernate will execute in a typical use case.

Since JDBC connection management is so expensive, you can pool the connections, which can open connections ahead of time and reuse them (and close them only when needed, as opposed to "when they're no longer used").

Thankfully, Hibernate is designed to use a connection pool by default, an internal implementation. However, Hibernate's built-in connection pooling isn't designed for production use. In production, you would use an external connection pool by using either a database connection provided by JNDI (the Java Naming and Directory Interface) or an external connection pool configured via parameters and classpath.

Hibernate is designed to be able to use any of a *huge* number (well, as long as seven is a huge number) of available database pools. It will attempt to use a given connection pool if it can; that's as simple as putting a connection pool implementation in the classpath, really. If there is more than one connection pool in the classpath, it follows a fairly simple algorithm to determine which one to use - if you attempt to configure a specific connection pool, it'll use that connection pool or use a "sane default" otherwise.

The right way to put a connection pool in the classpath for Hibernate is, well, to simply include it as a dependency. For HikariCP, for example, it's a simple `<dependency>` block in Maven, which itself belongs in the `<dependencies>` block.

Listing 2-5. Changes for the Object Model to Include HikariCP

```
<dependencies>
    <dependency>
        <groupId>org.hibernate.orm</groupId>
        <artifactId>hibernate-hikaricp</artifactId>
        <version>${hibernate.core.version}</version>
    </dependency>
</dependencies>
```

It actually supports five different connection pools, aside from its internal connection pool and the pooling provided by JNDI: HikariCP (as described!), c3p0, Proxool, Vibur DBCP, and Agroal. There are analogs to the `hibernate-hikaricp` artifact that support every one of these; you can choose which one you wish to use explicitly if you include multiple implementations in the classpath through the use of configuration elements.[13]

Of these, which is best? That's really not a trivial question to answer; most of the connection pools have their own characteristics, and which one is best suited for a specific application really depends on *exactly* what requirements need to be met. In general, all of them work well and for their intended purpose. For the purposes of this book, even Hibernate's connection pool is sufficient; at no point is severe enough connection stress introduced to actually worry about resource starvation. However, if you *pressed* me to make a recommendation, it'd be for HikariCP, which has an excellent balance of size and performance, if JNDI connections are not available.

Using JNDI

If you're using Hibernate in a Java EE context - in a web application, for example - then you'll want to configure Hibernate to use JNDI. JNDI connection pools are managed by the container (and thus controlled by the deployer), which is generally the "right way" to manage resources in a distributed environment.

For example, WildFly (`http://wildfly.org/`) comes preinstalled with an example data source, named (helpfully) "java:jboss/datasources/ExampleDS." It's an H2 database, so the dialect is already correct; the new configuration would look something like what is shown in Listing 2-6.

Listing 2-6. Hibernate Configured to Use JNDI for the Data Source

```
<?xml version="1.0"?>
<!DOCTYPE hibernate-configuration PUBLIC
    "-//Hibernate/Hibernate Configuration DTD 3.0//EN"
```

[13] See `https://docs.jboss.org/hibernate/orm/6.0/userguide/html_single/Hibernate_User_Guide.html#database` for details.

```
"http://www.hibernate.org/dtd/hibernate-configuration-3.0.dtd">
<hibernate-configuration>
    <session-factory>
        <!-- Database connection settings -->
        <property name="jndi.url">java:jboss/datasources/ExampleDS</property>
        <property name="dialect">org.hibernate.dialect.H2Dialect</property>
        <!-- Echo all executed SQL to stdout -->
        <property name="show_sql">true</property>
        <!-- Drop and re-create the database schema on startup -->
        <property name="hbm2ddl.auto">create-drop</property>
        <mapping class="chapter02.hibernate.Message"/>
    </session-factory>
</hibernate-configuration>
```

Ideally, the java:jboss tree wouldn't be used; you'd use a name scoped to the application component, in the java:comp/env tree.[14]

Summary

In this chapter, we've presented a brief overview of how to use Maven to build and test your projects, as well as how to specify dependencies. We've also shown the usage of TestNG as a simple harness to run code. Lastly, we've explained how to configure Hibernate, starting from acquiring the SessionFactory and concluding with the SessionFactory's configuration, covering the simple JDBC connection management included with Hibernate, the use of a connection pool, and employment of JNDI to acquire database connections.

You should now have enough of a harness in place such that you can focus on using Hibernate to help you manage a persistent object model. We will add more detail on this as needed in the example code.

In the next chapter, we're going to build some slightly more complex (and useful) object models to illustrate more of Hibernate's core concepts.

[14] See `www.ibm.com/developerworks/library/j-jndi/?ca=dnt-62` for an article that discusses this concept in some detail, although the implementation specifics are slightly dated.

CHAPTER 3

Building a Simple Application

In this chapter, we're going to create the shell of an application, which will allow us to demonstrate a number of concepts common for systems that use Hibernate. We'll be covering the following:

- Object model design, including relationships between objects
- Operations that view and modify persisted data (inserts, reads, updates, and deletes)

Ordinarily, we'd use a service layer to encapsulate some operations, and in fact we will be adding a service layer as we proceed, but at this point we want to see more of how to interact with Hibernate itself. The goal here is not to waste time with a sample application that is "one to throw away." We're definitely not going to be able to have a full and ideal codebase, but it will be a model for how one might actually use Hibernate in the real world.

Of course, such a statement has a caveat: different applications and architects have different approaches. This is but one way to create an application of this sort; others will take different approaches that are just as valid as this one.

Plus, our model will be progressive, meaning that its quality at its genesis will not be very high. We're going to be introducing various new concepts as we proceed; and we'll have plenty of opportunities to go back to previously written code and improve it.

A Simple Application

What we're trying to create is an application that allows peer ranking in various skill areas.

J. B. Ottinger et al., *Beginning Hibernate 6*, https://doi.org/10.1007/978-1-4842-7337-1_3

The concept is something like this: John thinks that Tracy is pretty good at Java, so on a scale of 1 to 10, he'd give Tracy a 7. Sam thinks Tracy is decent, but not great; he'd give Tracy a 5. With these two rankings, one might be able to surmise that Tracy was a 6 in Java. Realistically, with such a small sample set, you wouldn't be able to gauge whether this ranking was accurate or not, but after 20 such rankings, you would have a chance at a truly legitimate peer evaluation.

So what we want is a way for an observer to offer a ranking for a given skill for a specific person. We'd also like a way to determine the actual ranking for each person, as well as a way to find out who was ranked "the best" for a given skill.

If you're looking at these paragraphs with an eye toward application design, you'll see that we have four different types of entities - objects to manage in a database - and a few services.

Our entities are these: People (which are observers and subjects; thus we can use a single type that can refer to both an observer and a subject), Skills, and Rankings.

Our relationships look something like this:

A subject - a Person - has zero, one, or many skills. A person's Skills each have zero, one, or many Rankings.

A Ranking has a score ("on a scale of 1 to 10") and an observer (a Person who submits a particular ranking).

Relationships and Cardinality

Before we start diving into object models, it's worth revisiting the idea of how relationships are specified in database terminology.

Consider a person and a federal identification number. A person might not have a federal identification, so it makes sense that you might have two database tables to consider (a `Person` table and a `FIN` table, for "federal identification number"). We can express this as having a relationship of "one to zero or one," meaning that one `Person` record can have zero or one `FIN` record. We can also express the relationship from the perspective of the `FIN` table, such that a `FIN` has a "one-to-one" relationship with `Person`, meaning that every `FIN` record is related to one and exactly one `Person` record.

The relationship types you see typically fit into the following groups:

1. **One to one**, or 1:1. In this case, you have exactly one record or entity on both sides of the relationship. In Hibernate, this is a relationship that is marked as *not* being optional.

2. **One to zero or one**. With this relationship, the "destination" record - the "zero or one" - is optional, but otherwise it matches the 1:1 relationship.
3. **One to many**, or 1:M. This might be shown as a relationship between a `Person` and their `BankAccount` records, for example, since a person might have a savings account, a checking account, and a revolving loan.
4. **Many to many**, or M:M. With this structure, you have high cardinality on both sides of the relationship; you could imagine here a structure consisting of `SchoolCourse` and `Student`, because each student can be enrolled in many different courses and each course can have many students. Typically, this isn't a particularly efficient structure, in practice - you're more likely to have a school course that has many `Schedule` records, representing each student enrolled at a particular time, and each `Student` would have multiple `Schedule` records as well, meaning that `Course` to `Schedule` is a 1:M relationship, as is the relationship between `Student` and `Schedule`.
5. **Many to one**, or M:1, is the inverse expression of 1:M and is used to indicate dependency on another entity type.

We will cover using these relationship types as we go through this and other chapters.

A First Attempt

Our project will allow us to write, read, and update Rankings for different subjects, as well as tell us who has the highest average score for a given Skill.

It won't do these things very efficiently at first, but along the way, we'll fulfill our desire for (somewhat) agile development practices, and we'll learn quite a bit about how to read and write data with Hibernate.

As usual, we'll be using test-driven development. Let's write some tests and then try to get them to pass. Our first bits of code will be very primitive, testing only our data model, but eventually we'll be testing services.

Our data model is shown in the following. As you can see, it has three object types and three relationships: a Person is related to a Ranking in two ways (as subject and observer), and each Ranking has an associated Skill.

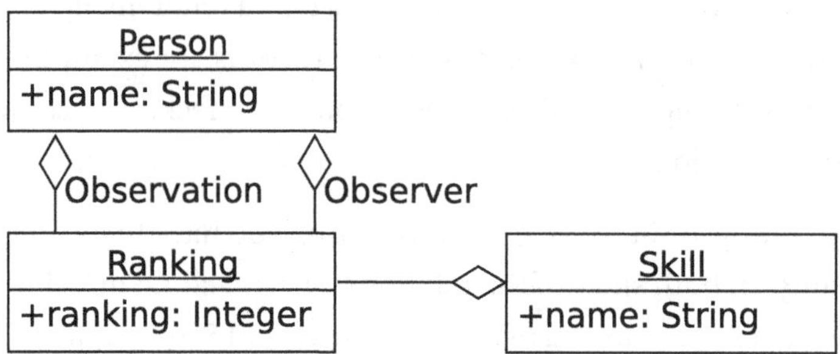

Figure 3-1. *A simple entity relationship diagram*

It's probably worth pointing out that this data model is not ideal. For now, that's all right – we're trying to build something that gives us a starting point, and we'll factor in our full requirements as we proceed.

We're also admittedly underspecifying our entities. For example, a Person can be more than just a name. (A Person can also be a number, correct? ... Oh, wait, that's not as funny as it could be because we're eventually going to add a numeric identifier to every Person as an artificial key.) Perhaps we'll fix this and other issues as we develop our model.

So let's start by designing our objects.

Since our problem description centers on the concept of a Person (as subject and observer), let's start with that. The simplest JavaBean that can represent a Person might look like Listing 3-1.

Listing 3-1. A POJO Representing Our Person Object

```
package chapter03.simple;
public class Person {
  String name;
  public Person() {}
  public void setName(String name) { this.name=name; }
  public String getName() { return name; }
}
```

Note that the "simple" versions of these classes don't exist in the source code for this book, as they don't actually contribute value and they're not used by what we're going to write. Your humble author tried to figure out a way to efficiently represent different stages of a codebase as it was being written, but failed; `git tag` can help, but it's a nightmare to represent in a book.

For the sake of brevity, from here on we're going to ignore simple mutators and accessors (the `setName()` and `getName()`, respectively, in the `Person` class) unless and until we need to include them. We're also going to ignore implementations of `toString()`, `equals()`, and `hashCode()` here, although the sample code for the chapter has examples of it.

This `Person` implementation only includes the concept of a `Person` and ignores the other object types. Let's see what they look like, so we can revisit `Person` and flesh it out, so to speak.

The `Skill` class looks almost exactly like the `Person` class, as it should; they could inherit from a common base class, but for now let's leave them completely separate, as shown in Listing 3-2.

Listing 3-2. A POJO Representing Our Skill Object

```
package chapter03.simple;
public class Skill {
  private String name;
  public Skill() {}
}
```

The `Ranking` class is a little more complicated, but not by much. Really, all it does is encode one side of the associations shown in the UML. It's worth noting that we don't have to consider database associations at all when we're designing our objects; a `Ranking` has an attribute matching a subject, so that's what it uses. We only need to consider the relationships between objects at this point, as Hibernate can help us map the relationships in the database when we get that far. Take a look at Listing 3-3.

Listing 3-3. A POJO Representing Our Ranking Object

```
package chapter03.simple;
public class Ranking {
  private Person subject;
  private Person observer;
```

```
  private Skill skill;
  private Integer ranking;
  public Ranking() { }
  // accessors and mutators omitted for brevity
}
```

Writing Data

At this point, we have a fully working data model in Java. We can use this data model (with some slight changes to include the mutators and accessors the listings don't include) to create entities representing the Person types, the Skill types, and Rankings; and we can use the associations to pull data enough to fit our requirements. Creating our data model might look like that shown in Listing 3-4.

Listing 3-4. A Test That Populates a Simple Model

```
package chapter03.simple;
import org.testng.annotations.Test;
public class ModelTest {
  @Test
  public void testModelCreation() {
    Person subject=new Person();
    subject.setName("J. C. Smell");
    Person observer=new Person();
    observer.setName("Drew Lombardo");
    Skill skill=new Skill();
    skill.setName("Java");
    Ranking ranking=new Ranking();
    ranking.setSubject(subject);
    ranking.setObserver(observer);
    ranking.setSkill(skill);
    ranking.setRanking(8);
    // just to give us visual verification
     System.out.println(ranking);
  }
}
```

However, being able to use the data model isn't the same as being able to persist or query the data model. This is a good start to see how the data model might work, but isn't much as far as actually using it.

In order to allow Hibernate to work with our model, we're going to first convert the `Person` object to an entity by marking it with the `@Entity` annotation.[1] Next, we mark the name as a column (with `@Column`) for our data model, and then we're going to add an artificial key - a unique identifier - to allow us to use something other than a name for a primary key.

We'll describe more about the `@Id` and `@GeneratedValue` annotations later; for now, this marks the attribute as a unique primary key, autogenerated by the database. The form of the key generation will depend on the database itself. (In this case, the key generation will use a database sequence. This may not be what you want; it's also something you can control.)

The Person object now looks something like what's shown in Listing 3-5.

Listing 3-5. `src/main/java/chapter03/hibernate/Person.java`

```
package chapter03.hibernate;

import javax.persistence.*;
import java.util.Objects;

@Entity
public class Person {
  @Column(unique = true)
  private String name;
  @Id
  @GeneratedValue(strategy = GenerationType.AUTO)
  private Long id;

  public Person() {
  }
}
```

[1] Marking an entity with `@Entity` feels almost logical.

Note that we're not showing the full source for Person here; the source code also includes mutators, accessors, toString(), equals(), and hashCode().

Now we can create a test that writes an instance into the database. Here's a snippet of code for that purpose. Again, we're going to be refactoring this code quite a bit in future iterations; see Listing 3-6.

Listing 3-6. src/test/java/chapter03/hibernate/PersonTest.java

```
package chapter03.hibernate;

import org.hibernate.Session;
import org.hibernate.SessionFactory;
import org.hibernate.Transaction;
import org.hibernate.boot.MetadataSources;
import org.hibernate.boot.registry.StandardServiceRegistry;
import org.hibernate.boot.registry.StandardServiceRegistryBuilder;
import org.testng.annotations.BeforeClass;
import org.testng.annotations.Test;

public class PersonTest {
  SessionFactory factory;

  @BeforeClass
  public void setup() {
    StandardServiceRegistry registry =
        new StandardServiceRegistryBuilder()
            .configure()
            .build();
    factory = new MetadataSources(registry)
        .buildMetadata()
        .buildSessionFactory();
  }

  @Test
  public void testSavePerson() {
    try (Session session = factory.openSession()) {
      Transaction tx = session.beginTransaction();
      Person person = new Person();
```

```
            person.setName("J. C. Smell");

            session.save(person);

            tx.commit();
        }
    }
}
```

This is a near mirror image of our Message example from Chapters 1 and 2, with some changes to reflect that we're saving a Person and not a Message, as one might expect.

The actual test is very simple. It creates a Person, and it does nothing but persist it. We're not even trying to validate that it persists - we're just running the persistence mechanism. Assuming that's the case (and it is), we can also assume the same code works for the Skill object; but the Ranking object - with its associations - needs a little more work.

One of the things we need to think about before writing a Ranking object is how to find one of our entities. For one thing, that sort of ability would help us in the simple persistence test: to validate that not only did the save() method execute but that it also actually persisted our data. For another, in the testSavePerson() code, we're creating a Person when we know that Person doesn't exist; with Ranking, however, we fully expect to reuse Person instances as well as Skill instances.

So we need to create a mechanism by which we can query our database. We'll create a method to return a Person reference from the session, using a query; and we'll revisit the query mechanism in the future to optimize it quite a bit.

Rounding Out the Data Model

For sanity's sake, here are the other entities for this chapter: Ranking and Skill. We'll be referring back to these as we go along.

Listing 3-7. src/main/java/chapter03/hibernate/Ranking.java

```
package chapter03.hibernate;

import javax.persistence.*;

@Entity
public class Ranking {
```

```
  @Id
  @GeneratedValue(strategy = GenerationType.AUTO)
  private Long id;
  @ManyToOne
  private Person subject;
  @ManyToOne
  private Person observer;
  @ManyToOne
  private Skill skill;
  @Column
  private Integer ranking;

  public Ranking() {
  }

  public Long getId() {
    return id;
  }

  public void setId(Long id) {
    this.id = id;
  }

  public Person getSubject() {
    return subject;
  }

  public void setSubject(Person subject) {
    this.subject = subject;
  }

  public Person getObserver() {
    return observer;
  }

  public void setObserver(Person observer) {
    this.observer = observer;
  }
```

```
  public Skill getSkill() {
    return skill;
  }

  public void setSkill(Skill skill) {
    this.skill = skill;
  }

  public Integer getRanking() {
    return ranking;
  }

  public void setRanking(Integer ranking) {
    this.ranking = ranking;
  }

  @Override
  public String toString() {
    return "Ranking{" +
        "id=" + id +
        ", subject=" + subject +
        ", observer=" + observer +
        ", skill=" + skill +
        ", ranking=" + ranking +
        '}';
  }
}
```

Listing 3-8. src/main/java/chapter03/hibernate/Skill.java

```
package chapter03.hibernate;

import javax.persistence.*;

@Entity
public class Skill {
  @Column
  private String name;
```

```
  @Id
  @GeneratedValue(strategy = GenerationType.AUTO)
  private Long id;

  public Skill() {
  }

  public Long getId() {
    return id;
  }

  public void setId(Long id) {
    this.id = id;
  }

  public String getName() {
    return name;
  }

  public void setName(String name) {
    this.name = name;
  }

  @Override
  public String toString() {
    return "Skill{" +
        "id=" + id +
        ", name='" + name + '\'' +
        '}';
  }
}
```

There's still room for improvement and completion in both classes - they're not including `equals()` and `hashCode()`, and the `toString()` isn't even done very well yet - but this will do for this stage of the book.

Reading Data

Listing 3-9 is the code to look for a Person, given a name. This snippet uses the Hibernate Query Language (HQL), which is loosely related to SQL; we'll see more about HQL in later chapters.

Listing 3-9. A Method to Find a Specific Person

```
private Person findPerson(Session session, String name) {
  Query<Person> query = session.createQuery(
      "from Person p where p.name=:name",
      Person.class
  );
  query.setParameter("name", name);
  Person person = query.uniqueResult();
  return person;
}
```

This code declares a reference to `org.hibernate.query.Query` (`https://docs.jboss.org/hibernate/orm/6.0/javadocs/org/hibernate/query/Query.html`), and it builds a rough analog to an SQL select statement. This form of the query selects data from the table created from the `Person` entity (which may or may not have a table name of "person"), aliased to "p," and limited to objects whose "name" attribute is equal to a named parameter (helpfully called "name"). It also specifies the reference type of the query (with `Person.class`) to cut down on typecasting and potential errors of incorrect return types.[2]

We then set the parameter value of "name" to the name for which we're searching.

As we're interested in only one possible match at this point (a limitation of our implementation for now), we return a unique result: a single object. If we have five records with that name in our database, an exception will be thrown; we could fix this by using `query.setMaxResults(1)` and returning the first (and only) entry in `query.list()`, but the right way to fix it is to figure out how to be very specific in returning the right `Person`.

[2] The ability to return a type in a query was added in Hibernate 5, and it was *much* appreciated.

If no result is found, a signal value - `null` - will be returned.[3]

Astute readers (thus, all of them) will notice that we pass a `Session` to this method and that the method is declared `private`. This is so that we manage resources more cleanly; we're building tiny blocks of functionality, and we don't want each tiny bit of functionality to go through a process of acquiring resources. We have an expectation that callers will manage the `Session` and, by implication, the transaction that would affect this method. If we need a version of this method exposed that does not burden the caller with session management, we can overload the method name - and we will. (This method is actually designed to be used specifically by other methods in our service - those methods are the ones that are expected to acquire the `Session` and manage transactions.)

We can now write a `findPerson()` method that returns an existing `Person` if one exists by that name, creating a new `Person` object if none is found; see Listing 3-10.

Listing 3-10. A Method to Create or Return a Specific `Person`

```
private Person savePerson(Session session, String name) {
  Person person = findPerson(session, name);
  if (person == null) {
    person = new Person();
    person.setName(name);
    session.save(person);
  }
  return person;
}
```

Our first cut at code to build a `Ranking` (in `RankingTest`) might then look something like what's shown in Listing 3-11.

This method assumes a working `saveSkill()` method, which hasn't been shown yet; we're going to show the *entire class*, with every method included, soon.

Listing 3-11. A Method to Test Creating a `Ranking`

```
@Test
public void testSaveRanking() {
  try (Session session = factory.openSession()) {
```

[3] Returning a signal value like `null` is a stylistic choice for *this code*. There are ways to throw exceptions on such queries. We're just using a signal value *here*.

```
    Transaction tx = session.beginTransaction();

    Person subject = savePerson(session, "J. C. Smell");
    Person observer = savePerson(session, "Drew Lombardo");
    Skill skill = saveSkill(session, "Java");

    Ranking ranking = new Ranking();
    ranking.setSubject(subject);
    ranking.setObserver(observer);
    ranking.setSkill(skill);
    ranking.setRanking(8);
    session.save(ranking);

    tx.commit();
  }
}
```

The chapter code has this method encoded as it is, but this method also gives us the beginnings of another method,[4] one that abstracts all of the repeated code such that we can offer the four important pieces of information and generate data very rapidly.

With that in mind, let's look at queries again. We have shown that queries can return single results; let's look at queries that return multiple results, in order, with the understanding that we're still very far away from being efficient - or even correct, in many ways.

One of our requirements is to be able to determine the Ranking of a given `Person` for a given `Skill`. Let's write another test as a proof of concept.

First, we'll write a method that adds a few more rankings for J. C. Smell; we've already shown him as having an 8 in Java; let's add a 6 and a 7, which would give him an average skill of 7, obviously. With that, our test method might look like what is shown in Listing 3-12.

Listing 3-12. A Method to Test Ranking Operations

```
@Test
public void testRankings() {
  populateRankingData();
  try (Session session = factory.openSession()) {
```

[4] We'll see the `createData` method later in this chapter.

```
    Transaction tx = session.beginTransaction();

    Query<Ranking> query = session.createQuery(
        "from Ranking r "
            + "where r.subject.name=:name "
            + "and r.skill.name=:skill", Ranking.class);
    query.setParameter("name", "J. C. Smell");

    query.setParameter("skill", "Java");

    IntSummaryStatistics stats = query.list()
        .stream()
        .collect(
            Collectors.summarizingInt(Ranking::getRanking)
        );

    long count = stats.getCount();
    int average = (int) stats.getAverage();

    tx.commit();
    session.close();
    assertEquals(count, 3);
    assertEquals(average, 7);
  }
}

private void populateRankingData() {
  try (Session session = factory.openSession()) {
    Transaction tx = session.beginTransaction();
    createData(session, "J. C. Smell", "Gene Showrama", "Java", 6);
    createData(session, "J. C. Smell", "Scottball Most", "Java", 7);
    createData(session, "J. C. Smell", "Drew Lombardo", "Java", 8);
    tx.commit();
  }
}

private void createData(Session session,
                        String subjectName,
```

```
                        String observerName,
                          String skillName,
                          int rank) {
  Person subject = savePerson(session, subjectName);
  Person observer = savePerson(session, observerName);
  Skill skill = saveSkill(session, skillName);

  Ranking ranking = new Ranking();
  ranking.setSubject(subject);
  ranking.setObserver(observer);
  ranking.setSkill(skill);
  ranking.setRanking(rank);
  session.save(ranking);
}
```

The `testRanking()` method uses a slightly more advanced query: the query walks the attribute tree from the `Ranking` object to match the subject's name and skill's name. With the entity references in our object model, it's very easy to do an `SQL JOIN` without having to know specific database syntax or capabilities; Hibernate takes care of writing all of the SQL for us, and we can use the objects "naturally."

By the way, this isn't a particularly good use of the query facility; we'll be revisiting it quite a bit as we progress, especially in the last section of this chapter, where we use Hibernate's query capability to do all of the work of calculating the average for us.[5]

Updating Data

What if we want to change data? Suppose that Gene Showrama, who in our example code ranked J. C. Smell as a 6 in Java, realizes that he has changed his opinion. Let's see what we have to do to update data.

First, let's take our Ranking average calculation routine and refactor it into a reusable method. Next, we'll write our test to update the data and then recalculate the average, testing it to make sure our data is persisted correctly. See Listing 3-13.

[5] We can let the database generate the average of a set of numbers, instead of letting the Java stream calculate it for us, which is also pretty easy. However, doing it in the database avoids the transfer of data from the database to our code, which can save a lot of time and, potentially, network traffic. Generally, doing it with the database is better, and as we'll see, it's easy as well.

Listing 3-13. A Method to Test Ranking Operations

```
private int getAverage(String subject, String skill) {
  try (Session session = factory.openSession()) {
    Transaction tx = session.beginTransaction();

    Query<Ranking> query = session.createQuery(
        "from Ranking r "
            + "where r.subject.name=:name "
            + "and r.skill.name=:skill", Ranking.class);
    query.setParameter("name", subject);
    query.setParameter("skill", skill);

    IntSummaryStatistics stats = query.list()
        .stream()
        .collect(
            Collectors.summarizingInt(Ranking::getRanking)
        );

    int average = (int) stats.getAverage();
    tx.commit();
    return average;
  }
}

@Test
public void changeRanking() {
  populateRankingData();
  try (Session session = factory.openSession()) {
    Transaction tx = session.beginTransaction();
    Query<Ranking> query = session.createQuery(
        "from Ranking r "
            + "where r.subject.name=:subject and "
            + "r.observer.name=:observer and "
            + "r.skill.name=:skill", Ranking.class);
    query.setParameter("subject", "J. C. Smell");
    query.setParameter("observer", "Gene Showrama");
    query.setParameter("skill", "Java");
```

```
    Ranking ranking = query.uniqueResult();
    assertNotNull(ranking, "Could not find matching ranking");
    ranking.setRanking(9);
    tx.commit();
  }
  assertEquals(getAverage("J. C. Smell", "Java"), 8);
}
```

What are we doing here? After we populate the data with known values, we're building a query to locate the specific `Ranking` we want to change (a `Ranking` on Java for "J. C. Smell," written by "Gene Showrama"). We check to make sure we have a valid `Ranking` - which we should, as that data was created by our `populateRankingData()` method - and then we do something very curious.

We set a new ranking score, with `ranking.setRanking(9);` ... and that's it. We commit the current transaction and let the session close because we're done with it.

Hibernate watches the data model, and when something is changed, it automatically updates the database to reflect the changes.[6] The transaction commits the update to the database so that other sessions - as contained in the `findRanking()` method that we'll see shortly - can see it.

There are a few caveats for this (with workarounds, naturally). When Hibernate loads an object for you, it is a "managed object" - that is, it's managed by that session. Mutations (changes) and accesses go through a special process to write data to the database, or pull data from the database if the session hasn't already loaded it, as some data might not be retrieved automatically. (For example, an object might have a large binary object that we don't want loaded every time we retrieve the entity. The proxy here would load it when it was specifically accessed, as opposed to when the entity was first retrieved.) We refer to this object as being in "persisted state," which leads us to a concept that will become important for us as we use persistence in Java.[7]

[6] It generally does this by using a proxied object. When you change the data values in the object, the proxy records the change so that the transaction knows to write the data to the database on transaction commit. If this sounds like magic, it's not - but it's also not trivial to do. Appreciate Hibernate's authors.

[7] We'll be revisiting the topic of managed objects in more detail in our next chapter.

Persistence Contexts

There are four states for an object with relation to a session: persistent, transient, detached, or removed.

When we create a new object, it's *transient* – that is, no identifier has been assigned to it by Hibernate, and the database has no knowledge of the object. That doesn't mean the database might not have the data. Imagine if we'd created a `Ranking` manually for J. C. Smell, from Gene Showrama, on Java. The new Ranking would have an analog in the database, but Hibernate wouldn't know that the object in memory was an equivalent to the object representation in the database.

When we call `save()` on a new object, we're marking it as "persistent," and when we query the session for an object, it's also in persistent state. Changes are reflected in the current transaction, to be written when the transaction is committed. This is what's going on in `changeRanking()` – we are altering an object that's in *persistent state*, and when the transaction is committed, any changes to objects in persistent state have their changes written to the database. We can convert a transient object to a persistent object by using `Session.merge()`, which we haven't seen yet (but we will).

A detached object is a persistent object whose session has been closed or has otherwise been evicted from a `Session`. In our example of changing a `Ranking`, when the session is closed, the `Ranking` object we changed is in detached state for the `findRanking()` call even though we loaded it from the database and it used to be in persistent state.

A removed object is one that's been marked for deletion in the current transaction. An object is changed to removed state when `Session.delete()` is called for that object reference. Note that an object in removed state is removed in the database but not in memory, just as an object can exist in the database without an in-memory representation.

Removing Data

The last thing we want to see is how to delete data or, rather, how to move it into removed state with respect to the persistence context – which almost amounts to the same thing. (It's not actually "removed" until the transaction is committed, and even then the in-memory representation is available until it goes out of scope, as we described in the paragraph on "removed state.")

Let's say, for the sake of an example, that Gene Showrama has realized that he really doesn't have enough information to offer a valid Ranking for J. C. Smell on Java, so he wishes to delete it. The code for this is very similar to our update: we're going to find the Ranking and then call Session.delete().

We can refactor our mechanism for finding a Ranking (from the changeRanking() test), which will give us a Ranking in persistent state. Then we remove it via the session and commit the change; we can then ask for the new average to see if our changes are reflected in the database.

Our code is shown in Listing 3-14.

Listing 3-14. Removing a Ranking

```
private Ranking findRanking(Session session,
                            String subject, String observer, String skill)
                            {
  Query<Ranking> query = session.createQuery(
      "from Ranking r "
          + "where r.subject.name=:subject and "
          + "r.observer.name=:observer and "
          + " r.skill.name=:skill", Ranking.class);
  query.setParameter("subject", subject);
  query.setParameter("observer", observer);
  query.setParameter("skill", skill);
  Ranking ranking = query.uniqueResult();
  return ranking;
}

@Test
public void removeRanking() {
  populateRankingData();
  try (Session session = factory.openSession()) {
    Transaction tx = session.beginTransaction();
    Ranking ranking = findRanking(session, "J. C. Smell",
        "Gene Showrama", "Java");
    assertNotNull(ranking, "Ranking not found");
    session.delete(ranking);
```

```
    tx.commit();
  }
  assertEquals(getAverage("J. C. Smell", "Java"), 7);
}
```

It's like magic, except that it's not: it's just Hibernate managing the database to reflect the changes we're showing it.

A Note on Transactions

We've mentioned "transactions" quite a bit, too, using them with every session reference. So what are they?

A transaction is a "bundled unit of work" for a database.[8]

When you start a transaction, you're saying that you want to see the database as it exists at a certain point in time ("now"), and any modifications affect only the database as it exists from that starting point.

Changes are committed as a whole, so that no other transaction can see them until the transaction completes. This means that transactions allow the application to define discrete units of work, with the user only having to decide the boundaries of when a transaction begins or ends. If the transaction is abandoned - that is, `commit()` is not called explicitly - then the transaction's changes are abandoned, and the database is left unmodified.

Transactions can be aborted ("rolled back," with the `Transaction.rollback()` method) such that any changes that have taken place as part of that transaction are discarded. This allows you to guarantee consistency in your data model.

For example, imagine you're creating an order entry system, with an order consisting of an `Order` object, `LineItem` objects, and a `Customer` object. If you were writing an order with seven line items and the sixth line item failed because of invalid data,[9] you wouldn't want an incomplete order to be lingering in the database. You'd want to roll back the changes and offer the user a chance to try again, with correct data.

Naturally, there are exceptions to the definitions of transactions, and Hibernate provides multiple types of transactions (e.g., you might have a transaction that allows

[8] We're going to be revisiting transactions quite a bit in the next chapter.

[9] Note that Hibernate has validation facilities that make validation of data very easy to do; the way the text describes manual validation is rather unglamorous.

reads of uncommitted data, a "dirty read"). Also, different databases might define transactional boundaries in their own ways. Thankfully, this is a pretty important concern for databases, so each one tends to document how transactions are defined.[10]

The Full Test for Rankings

We've seen a lot of pieces of our test, but let's put it all together. Hold on, it's not a short listing, but this is the *full* class, tags for printing included and all.

Listing 3-15. `src/test/java/chapter03/hibernate/RankingTest.java`

```
package chapter03.hibernate;

import org.hibernate.Session;
import org.hibernate.SessionFactory;
import org.hibernate.Transaction;
import org.hibernate.boot.MetadataSources;
import org.hibernate.boot.registry.StandardServiceRegistry;
import org.hibernate.boot.registry.StandardServiceRegistryBuilder;
import org.hibernate.query.Query;
import org.testng.annotations.AfterMethod;
import org.testng.annotations.BeforeMethod;
import org.testng.annotations.Test;

import java.util.IntSummaryStatistics;
import java.util.stream.Collectors;

import static org.testng.Assert.assertEquals;
import static org.testng.Assert.assertNotNull;

public class RankingTest {
  private SessionFactory factory;

  @BeforeMethod
  public void setup() {
```

[10] See `www.h2database.com/html/advanced.html#transaction_isolation` for H2's documentation of transactions, for example. Other databases have similar documentation.

```
    StandardServiceRegistry registry =
        new StandardServiceRegistryBuilder()
            .configure()
            .build();
    factory = new MetadataSources(registry)
        .buildMetadata()
        .buildSessionFactory();
  }

  @AfterMethod
  public void shutdown() {
    factory.close();
  }

  //tag::testSaveRanking[]
  @Test
  public void testSaveRanking() {
    try (Session session = factory.openSession()) {
      Transaction tx = session.beginTransaction();

      Person subject = savePerson(session, "J. C. Smell");
      Person observer = savePerson(session, "Drew Lombardo");
      Skill skill = saveSkill(session, "Java");

      Ranking ranking = new Ranking();
      ranking.setSubject(subject);
      ranking.setObserver(observer);
      ranking.setSkill(skill);
      ranking.setRanking(8);
      session.save(ranking);

      tx.commit();
    }
  }
  //end::testSaveRanking[]

  //tag::testRankings[]
  @Test
```

```
public void testRankings() {
  populateRankingData();
  try (Session session = factory.openSession()) {
    Transaction tx = session.beginTransaction();

    Query<Ranking> query = session.createQuery(
        "from Ranking r "
            + "where r.subject.name=:name "
            + "and r.skill.name=:skill", Ranking.class);
    query.setParameter("name", "J. C. Smell");

    query.setParameter("skill", "Java");


    IntSummaryStatistics stats = query.list()
        .stream()
        .collect(
            Collectors.summarizingInt(Ranking::getRanking)
        );

    long count = stats.getCount();
    int average = (int) stats.getAverage();

    tx.commit();
    session.close();
    assertEquals(count, 3);
    assertEquals(average, 7);
  }
}
//end::testRankings[]

//tag::changeRanking[]
@Test
public void changeRanking() {
  populateRankingData();
  try (Session session = factory.openSession()) {
    Transaction tx = session.beginTransaction();
    Query<Ranking> query = session.createQuery(
        "from Ranking r "
```

```
          + "where r.subject.name=:subject and "
          + "r.observer.name=:observer and "
          + "r.skill.name=:skill", Ranking.class);
    query.setParameter("subject", "J. C. Smell");
    query.setParameter("observer", "Gene Showrama");
    query.setParameter("skill", "Java");
    Ranking ranking = query.uniqueResult();
    assertNotNull(ranking, "Could not find matching ranking");
    ranking.setRanking(9);
    tx.commit();
  }
  assertEquals(getAverage("J. C. Smell", "Java"), 8);
}
//end::changeRanking[]

//tag::removeRanking[]
@Test
public void removeRanking() {
  populateRankingData();
  try (Session session = factory.openSession()) {
    Transaction tx = session.beginTransaction();
    Ranking ranking = findRanking(session, "J. C. Smell",
        "Gene Showrama", "Java");
    assertNotNull(ranking, "Ranking not found");
    session.delete(ranking);
    tx.commit();
  }
  assertEquals(getAverage("J. C. Smell", "Java"), 7);
}
//end::removeRanking[]

//tag::getAverage[]
private int getAverage(String subject, String skill) {
  try (Session session = factory.openSession()) {
    Transaction tx = session.beginTransaction();

    Query<Ranking> query = session.createQuery(
```

```
        "from Ranking r "
            + "where r.subject.name=:name "
            + "and r.skill.name=:skill", Ranking.class);
    query.setParameter("name", subject);
    query.setParameter("skill", skill);

    IntSummaryStatistics stats = query.list()
        .stream()
        .collect(
            Collectors.summarizingInt(Ranking::getRanking)
        );

    int average = (int) stats.getAverage();
    tx.commit();
    return average;
  }
}
//end::getAverage[]

//tag::populateRankingData[]
private void populateRankingData() {
  try (Session session = factory.openSession()) {
    Transaction tx = session.beginTransaction();
    createData(session, "J. C. Smell", "Gene Showrama", "Java", 6);
    createData(session, "J. C. Smell", "Scottball Most", "Java", 7);
    createData(session, "J. C. Smell", "Drew Lombardo", "Java", 8);
    tx.commit();
  }
}

private void createData(Session session,
                        String subjectName,
                        String observerName,
                        String skillName,
                        int rank) {
  Person subject = savePerson(session, subjectName);
  Person observer = savePerson(session, observerName);
```

```
    Skill skill = saveSkill(session, skillName);

    Ranking ranking = new Ranking();
    ranking.setSubject(subject);
    ranking.setObserver(observer);
    ranking.setSkill(skill);
    ranking.setRanking(rank);
    session.save(ranking);
  }
  //end::populateRankingData[]

  //tag::findPerson[]
  private Person findPerson(Session session, String name) {
    Query<Person> query = session.createQuery(
        "from Person p where p.name=:name",
        Person.class
    );
    query.setParameter("name", name);
    Person person = query.uniqueResult();
    return person;
  }
  //end::findPerson[]

  private Skill findSkill(Session session, String name) {
    Query<Skill> query = session.createQuery(
        "from Skill s where s.name=:name",
        Skill.class
    );
    query.setParameter("name", name);
    Skill skill = query.uniqueResult();
    return skill;
  }

  private Skill saveSkill(Session session, String skillName) {
    Skill skill = findSkill(session, skillName);
    if (skill == null) {
      skill = new Skill();
```

```
      skill.setName(skillName);
      session.save(skill);
    }
    return skill;
  }

  //tag::savePerson[]
  private Person savePerson(Session session, String name) {
    Person person = findPerson(session, name);
    if (person == null) {
      person = new Person();
      person.setName(name);
      session.save(person);
    }
    return person;
  }
  //end::savePerson[]

  //tag::findRanking[]
  private Ranking findRanking(Session session,
                              String subject, String observer, String skill) {
    Query<Ranking> query = session.createQuery(
        "from Ranking r "
            + "where r.subject.name=:subject and "
            + "r.observer.name=:observer and "
            + " r.skill.name=:skill", Ranking.class);
    query.setParameter("subject", subject);
    query.setParameter("observer", observer);
    query.setParameter("skill", skill);
    Ranking ranking = query.uniqueResult();
    return ranking;
  }
  //end::findRanking[]
}
```

Writing Our Sample Application

What have we seen so far? We've seen the following:

1. The creation of an object model

2. The mapping of that object model to a data model, albeit incomplete and rather simply done

3. The writing of data from an object model into a database

4. The reading of data from the database into an object model

5. The updating of data in the database via our object model

6. The removal of data from the database via our object model

With all of this, we're ready to start designing our actual application, armed with the knowledge that our object model works (although efficiency hasn't been considered yet) and with example code to perform most of our tasks as our requirements specify.

We're going to design our application much as we've written our example code; that is, we're going to define an application layer (services) and call that application from tests. In the real world, we'd then write a user interface layer that used the services, just as the tests do.

Just to be clear, our user interactions are

1. Add a Ranking for a subject by an observer.

2. Update a Ranking for a subject by an observer.

3. Remove a Ranking for a subject by an observer.

4. Find the average Ranking for a particular skill for a subject.

5. Find all the Rankings for a subject.

6. Find the highest-ranked subject for a particular skill.

It sounds like a lot, but we've already written much of this code; we just need to refactor it into a service layer for ease of use.

We're going to put these methods into an interface, starting at Listing 3-16, but before we do that, we want to abstract out some basic services – primarily, the acquisition of a Session. To do this, we're going to add a new module to our parent project – the "util" module – with a single class for now, the `SessionUtil`.

In an application server (such as WildFly, GlassFish, or Geronimo), the persistence API is accessed through resource injection; the application deployer configures a context for the Java Persistence API, and the application automatically acquires an `EntityManager` (the JPA equivalent to the `Session`). It's entirely possible (and possibly preferable) to configure Hibernate as the JPA provider; you can then use the Hibernate APIs with a conversion to `Session`.

You can also get this same kind of resource injection via libraries such as Spring or Guice. With Spring, for example, you'd configure a persistence provider, just as you would in a Java EE application server, and Spring would automatically provide a resource through which you could acquire `Session` objects.

However, while each of these platforms (Spring, Jakarta EE, and others) is extremely useful and practical (and probably necessary, in Jakarta EE's case), we're going to avoid them for the most part because we want to limit the scope of what we're doing to Hibernate and not get into a discussion of various competing architecture choices.

In the source code, there's a "util" module, apart from the chapter modules. The `com.autumncode.hibernate.util.SessionUtil` class is a singleton that provides access to a `SessionFactory` – something we've been putting in our test initialization code so far. It looks like what you see in Listing 3-16.

Listing 3-16. `../util/src/main/java/com/autumncode/hibernate/util/SessionUtil.java`

```
package com.autumncode.hibernate.util;

import org.hibernate.Session;
import org.hibernate.SessionFactory;
import org.hibernate.Transaction;
import org.hibernate.boot.MetadataSources;
import org.hibernate.boot.registry.StandardServiceRegistry;
import org.hibernate.boot.registry.StandardServiceRegistryBuilder;
import org.slf4j.Logger;
import org.slf4j.LoggerFactory;

import java.util.function.Consumer;
import java.util.function.Function;

public class SessionUtil {
  private static final SessionUtil instance = new SessionUtil();
```

```
  private static final String CONFIG_NAME = "/configuration.properties";
  private SessionFactory factory;
  private Logger logger = LoggerFactory.getLogger(this.getClass());

  private SessionUtil() {
    initialize();
  }

  public static Session getSession() {
    return getInstance().factory.openSession();
  }

  public static void forceReload() {
    getInstance().initialize();
  }

  private static SessionUtil getInstance() {
    return instance;
  }

  private void initialize() {
    logger.info("reloading factory");
    StandardServiceRegistry registry =
      new StandardServiceRegistryBuilder()
        .configure()
        .build();
    factory = new MetadataSources(registry)
      .buildMetadata()
      .buildSessionFactory();
  }
}
```

This class has a "forceReload()" method (used in initialization) that gives us an easy way to reload a new database context. If we were to need to reset the database to a known state, we can call this method and force Hibernate to reinitialize itself. We'll see this late in the book (in Chapter 13, specifically), where we have the database set to drop itself when we're done with it; reinitialization means the database will be dropped and recreated in pristine state.[11]

The actual source code for the SessionUtil has some extra methods. They're why there are so many classes imported that aren't being used, like Consumer. We will cover them later in the book.

We actually have a really, really simple test that asserts that this returns a Session, shown in Listing 3-17.

Listing 3-17. ../util/src/test/java/com/autumncode/hibernate/util/SessionBuilderTest.java

```
package com.autumncode.hibernate.util;

import com.autumncode.util.model.Thing;
import org.hibernate.Session;
import org.hibernate.query.Query;
import org.testng.annotations.Test;

import static org.testng.Assert.assertEquals;
import static org.testng.Assert.assertNotNull;

public class SessionBuilderTest {
  @Test
  public void testSessionFactory() {
    try (Session session = SessionUtil.getSession()) {
      assertNotNull(session);
    }
  }

}
```

As with SessionUtil, there are extra methods in the actual chapter source code not included here; we'll cover them soon.

[11] It's inadvisable to use create-drop for anything other than tests like the ones we see in this book. The functionality exposed here by SessionUtil is useful *here* and in very few other places.

As you can see, the SessionUtil class does nothing we haven't done so far; it just does it in a class with general visibility. We can add a dependency on this module to other projects and immediately have a clean way to acquire a session – and if need be, we can use this class as an abstraction for acquiring sessions through the Jakarta EE persistence mechanism, or via Spring,[12] for example.

Want to see the util project in more detail? We walk through it in Chapter 7.

Add a Ranking

The first thing we want to be able to do is add a Ranking. Let's do this first by creating our client code, which will give us an idea of what it is we need to write. See Listing 3-18.

Listing 3-18. src/test/java/chapter3/application/AddRankingTest.java

```
package chapter03.application;

import org.testng.annotations.Test;

import static org.testng.Assert.assertEquals;

public class AddRankingTest {
  RankingService service = new HibernateRankingService();

  @Test
  public void addRanking() {
    service.addRanking("J. C. Smell", "Drew Lombardo", "Mule", 8);
    assertEquals(service.getRankingFor("J. C. Smell", "Mule"), 8);
  }
}
```

We haven't written the interface or its implementation yet – which we'll rectify in the next listing. Here, we're just trying out the API to see how it looks and if it seems to fit what we need to do.

[12] Note that Spring has its own ways to manage Hibernate Session references; using this in a Spring application would be ill-advised.

Looking at the code in Listing 3-19, we can fairly easily say that `addRanking()` logically adds a ranking to J. C. Smell, as observed by Drew Lombardo, about Mule, with a skill level of 8. It'd be easy to confuse the parameters; we'll have to be sure to name them clearly, but even with clear names, there's a possibility for confusion.

Likewise, we can say that `getRankingFor()` fairly clearly retrieves a ranking for J. C. Smell's skill at Mule. Again, the possibility lurks for type confusion; the compiler wouldn't be able to tell us offhand if we called `getRankingFor("Mule", "J. C. Smell");`, and while we might be able to mitigate this in code,[13] with this structure there's always going to be the possibility for confusion.

It's fair to say that this aspect of the API is clear enough and easily tested; let's get to writing some code.

The test code shown in Listing 3-19 gives us the structure of the RankingService, with at least these two methods.

Listing 3-19. `src/main/java/chapter3/application/RankingService.java`

```
package chapter03.application;

import chapter03.hibernate.Person;

import java.util.Map;

public interface RankingService {
  int getRankingFor(String subject, String skill);

  void addRanking(String subject, String observer, String skill, int
  ranking);

}
```

[13] The solution to string confusion is... unpleasant. We could pollute our type system with types like `PersonName` and `SkillName`, such that we had to pass in a `PersonName` when referring to J. C., but this tends to make theorists very happy - because it's not possible to pass in a `SkillName` by accident - but it makes people who have to program with the API rather upset because they end up having to work with all of these types that are semantically similar but contribute little actual *value* to the product. It's "more type-safe" but also a bear to use day after day.

The full RankingService in the sample code has more methods. As usual, we'll see them and add them as needed, and we'll see the full class soon.

Now let's look at some of the HibernateRankingService, which will reuse much of the code we've written in order to test our data model.

What we're doing in this class is fairly simple: we have a top-level method (the one that's publicly visible) that acquires a session, then delegates the session along with the rest of the data to a worker method. The worker method handles the data manipulation, and is for the most part a copy of the createData() method from the RankingTest, and uses the other utility methods we'd written for RankingTest, too.

Why are we doing this? Mostly, we're anticipating other methods that might need to use addRanking() in such a way that it participates with an existing session. See Listing 3-20, which is another partial listing only.

Listing 3-20. src/main/java/chapter3/application/HibernateRankingService.java

```
@Override
public void addRanking(String subjectName,
                       String observerName,
                       String skillName,
                       int rank) {
  try (Session session = SessionUtil.getSession()) {
    Transaction tx = session.beginTransaction();

    addRanking(session, subjectName, observerName,
        skillName, rank);

    tx.commit();
  }
}

private void addRanking(Session session,
                        String subjectName,
                        String observerName,
                        String skillName,
                        int rank) {
  Person subject = savePerson(session, subjectName);
  Person observer = savePerson(session, observerName);
```

```
    Skill skill = saveSkill(session, skillName);

    Ranking ranking = new Ranking();
    ranking.setSubject(subject);
    ranking.setObserver(observer);
    ranking.setSkill(skill);
    ranking.setRanking(rank);
    session.save(ranking);
  }
```

This leaves our `getRankingFor()` method unimplemented; however, just as `addRanking()` was lifted nearly complete from `RankingTest`, we can copy the code for `getAverage()` and change how the `Session` is acquired, as shown in Listing 3-21.

Listing 3-21. `src/main/java/chapter3/application/HibernateRankingService.java`

```
  @Override
  public int getRankingFor(String subject, String skill) {
    try (Session session = SessionUtil.getSession()) {
      Transaction tx = session.beginTransaction();

      int average = getRankingFor(session, subject, skill);
      tx.commit();
      return average;
    }
  }

  private int getRankingFor(Session session, String subject,
                            String skill) {
    Query<Ranking> query = session.createQuery(
        "from Ranking r "
            + "where r.subject.name=:name "
            + "and r.skill.name=:skill", Ranking.class);
    query.setParameter("name", subject);
    query.setParameter("skill", skill);

    IntSummaryStatistics stats = query
        .list()
```

```
        .stream()
        .collect(
            Collectors.summarizingInt(Ranking::getRanking)
        );

    return (int) stats.getAverage();
}
```

Just as with the addRanking() method, the publicly visible method allocates a Session and then delegates to an internal method, and it's for the same reason: we may want to calculate the average in an existing session. (We'll see this in action in the next section, when we want to update a Ranking.)

For the record, this internal method is still awful. It works, but we can optimize it quite a bit. However, our datasets have been so small that there's been no point. We'll get there.

Now, when we run the test (with mvn test in the top-level directory, or via your IDE, if you're using one), the AddRankingTest passes, with no drama - which is exactly what we want. Even more satisfying, if we want to play around with the internals of HibernateRankingService, we can; we will be able to tell as soon as something breaks because our tests require that things work.

Also, if you look very carefully - okay, not that carefully, because it's rather obvious - you'll see that we've also managed to go down the path of fulfilling another of our requirements: determining the average ranking for a given subject's skill. With that said, though, we don't have a rigorous test in place yet. We'll get there, too.

Update a Ranking

Next, we handle the (not very likely) situation of updating a Ranking. This is potentially very simple, but we need to think about what happens if a preexisting Ranking doesn't exist. Imagine Drew Lombardo trying to change J. C. Smell's mastery of Mule to 8, when he's not bothered to offer any prior Ranking for J. C. and Mule yet.

We probably don't need to think about it too much, because in this situation it's likely that we'd just add the Ranking, but other more mission-critical applications may want the extra time spent in thought.

As it is, let's create two tests: one that uses an existing Ranking and another using a nonexistent Ranking; see Listing 3-22.

Listing 3-22. src/test/java/chapter3/application/UpdateRankingTest.java

```
package chapter03.application;

import org.testng.annotations.Test;

import static org.testng.Assert.assertEquals;

public class UpdateRankingTest {
  RankingService service = new HibernateRankingService();
  static final String SCOTT = "Scotball Most";
  static final String GENE = "Gene Showrama";
  static final String CEYLON = "Ceylon";

  @Test
  public void updateExistingRanking() {
    service.addRanking(GENE, SCOTT, CEYLON, 6);
    assertEquals(service.getRankingFor(GENE, CEYLON), 6);
    service.updateRanking(GENE, SCOTT, CEYLON, 7);
    assertEquals(service.getRankingFor(GENE, CEYLON), 7);
  }

  @Test
  public void updateNonexistentRanking() {
    assertEquals(service.getRankingFor(SCOTT, CEYLON), 0);
    service.updateRanking(SCOTT, GENE, CEYLON, 7);
    assertEquals(service.getRankingFor(SCOTT, CEYLON), 7);
  }
}
```

These two tests are very simple.

updateExistingRanking() first adds a Ranking, then checks to verify that it was added properly; it updates that same Ranking, then determines if the average has changed. Since this is the only Ranking for this subject and this Skill, the average should match the changed Ranking.

updateNonExistentRanking() does almost the same thing: it makes sure that we have nothing for this subject and skill (i.e., it checks for 0, our signal value for "no rankings exist"), then "updates" that Ranking (which, according to our requirements, should add the Ranking), and then checks the resulting average.

Now let's look at the service's code used to put this into effect, as shown in Listing 3-23.[14]

Listing 3-23. src/main/java/chapter3/application/HibernateRankingService.java

```
@Override
public void updateRanking(String subject,
                          String observer,
                          String skill,
                          int rank) {
  try (Session session = SessionUtil.getSession()) {
    Transaction tx = session.beginTransaction();

    Ranking ranking = findRanking(session, subject,
        observer, skill);
    if (ranking == null) {
      addRanking(session, subject, observer, skill, rank);
    } else {
      ranking.setRanking(rank);
    }
    tx.commit();
  }
}
```

It's worth considering that this code could be more efficient for what it does. Since there's no state to be preserved from the record that's been changed, we *could* feasibly delete the record outright if it exists, then add a new record.

[14] We're adding a lot of methods to our RankingService, and unless you modify the RankingService interface, some of this code won't compile yet, because we're using @Override to make sure that method signatures match. We're going to include the full RankingService source in a few sections, along with the *full and complete* HibernateRankingService source, and *those* full listings will have been successfully compiled when this chapter was written, guaranteed.

However, if the rankings had a timestamp of sorts - perhaps `createTimestamp` and `lastUpdatedTimestamp` attributes - then in this scenario an update (as we do here) makes more sense. Our data model isn't complete;[15] we could anticipate adding fields like these at some point.

Remove a Ranking

Removing a `Ranking` has two conditions to consider: one is that the `Ranking` exists (of course!), and the other is that it does not exist. It might be that our architectural requirements mandate that removal of a `Ranking` that isn't actually present is an error; but for this case, we'll assume that the removal merely attempts to validate that the `Ranking` doesn't exist.

Our test code is shown in Listing 3-24.

Listing 3-24. `src/test/java/chapter3/application/RemoveRankingTest.java`

```
package chapter03.application;

import org.testng.annotations.Test;

import static org.testng.Assert.assertEquals;

public class RemoveRankingTest {
  RankingService service = new HibernateRankingService();

  @Test
  public void removeRanking() {
    service.addRanking("R1", "R2", "RS1", 8);
    assertEquals(service.getRankingFor("R1", "RS1"), 8);
    service.removeRanking("R1", "R2", "RS1");
    assertEquals(service.getRankingFor("R1", "RS1"), 0);
  }
```

[15] This isn't a "real application," although it could be; however, it's being implemented here solely for the purpose of serving as a crude example.

```
  @Test
  public void removeNonexistentRanking() {
    service.removeRanking("R3", "R4", "RS2");
  }
}
```

The tests should be fairly easy to step through.

The first test (removeRanking()) creates a Ranking and validates that it gives us a known average, then removes it, which should change the average back to 0 (which indicates that no data exists for that Ranking, as already stated).

The second test calls removeRanking() that should not exist (because we don't create it anywhere); it should change nothing about the subject.

It's worth pointing out that our tests are fairly complete, but not as complete as they could be. For example, some of our tests might inadvertently be adding data to the database, depending on how the services are written. While that's not very important for this application, it's worth thinking about how to validate the entire database state after a test is run.

Application frameworks like Spring Boot and Quarkus automate the database initialization mechanism. There are also libraries such as Flyway and Liquibase that can populate databases for you on demand.

Of course, we need the code for removeRanking.

Listing 3-25. src/main/java/chapter3/application/HibernateRankingService.java

```
@Override
public void removeRanking(String subject,
                          String observer,
                          String skill) {
  try (Session session = SessionUtil.getSession()) {
    Transaction tx = session.beginTransaction();

    removeRanking(session, subject, observer, skill);

    tx.commit();
  }
}
```

```
private void removeRanking(Session session,
                           String subject,
                           String observer,
                           String skill) {
  Ranking ranking = findRanking(session, subject,
      observer, skill);
  if (ranking != null) {
    session.delete(ranking);
  }
}
```

Find Average Ranking for a Subject's Skill

We're nearing the point where we're starting to exhaust the codebase written to test our data model. It's time to verify the code that calculates the average ranking for a given skill for a given subject. We've already used this code to verify some of our other requirements (all of them so far, in fact), but we've done so with limited data. Let's throw more data at the `getRankingFor()` method to validate that it's actually doing what it's supposed to do.

Our test code is shown in Listing 3-26.

Listing 3-26. `src/test/java/chapter3/application/FindAverageRankingTest.java`

```
package chapter03.application;

import org.testng.annotations.Test;

import static org.testng.Assert.assertEquals;

public class FindAverageRankingTest {
  RankingService service = new HibernateRankingService();

  @Test
  public void validateRankingAverage() {
    service.addRanking("A", "B", "C", 4);
    service.addRanking("A", "B", "C", 5);
    service.addRanking("A", "B", "C", 6);
```

```
    assertEquals(service.getRankingFor("A", "C"), 5);
    service.addRanking("A", "B", "C", 7);
    service.addRanking("A", "B", "C", 8);
    assertEquals(service.getRankingFor("A", "C"), 6);
  }
}
```

We actually don't have any changes for the service – it's using the `getRankingFor()` method we've already seen from the "Add a Ranking" section.

Find All Rankings for a Subject

What we're looking for here is a list of skills, with their averages, for a given subject.

We have a few options as to how we can represent this data; do we want a `Map<String, Integer>`, so that we can easily locate what skill level goes with a skill? Do we want a queue, so that the skill levels are ranked in order?

This will depend on the architectural requirements for interaction. At this level (and for this particular application design), we'll use a `Map<String, Integer>`; it gives us the data we need (a set of skills with their average rankings) with a simple data structure. Eventually, we may revisit this requirement and fulfill it more efficiently.

As per usual, let's write our test code and then make it run properly; see Listing 3-27.

Listing 3-27. `src/test/java/chapter3/application/FindAllRankingsTest.java`

```
package chapter03.application;

import org.testng.annotations.Test;

import java.util.Map;

import static org.testng.Assert.assertEquals;
import static org.testng.Assert.assertNotNull;

public class FindAllRankingsTest {
  RankingService service = new HibernateRankingService();

  @Test
  public void findAllRankingsEmptySet() {
    assertEquals(service.getRankingFor("Nobody", "Java"), 0);
```

```
    assertEquals(service.getRankingFor("Nobody", "Python"), 0);
    Map<String, Integer> rankings = service.findRankingsFor("Nobody");

    // make sure our dataset size is what we expect: empty
    assertEquals(rankings.size(), 0);
  }

  @Test
  public void findAllRankings() {
    assertEquals(service.getRankingFor("Somebody", "Java"), 0);
    assertEquals(service.getRankingFor("Somebody", "Python"), 0);
    service.addRanking("Somebody", "Nobody", "Java", 9);
    service.addRanking("Somebody", "Nobody", "Java", 7);
    service.addRanking("Somebody", "Nobody", "Python", 7);
    service.addRanking("Somebody", "Nobody", "Python", 5);
    Map<String, Integer> rankings = service.findRankingsFor("Somebody");

    assertEquals(rankings.size(), 2);
    assertNotNull(rankings.get("Java"));
    assertEquals(rankings.get("Java"), new Integer(8));
    assertNotNull(rankings.get("Python"));
    assertEquals(rankings.get("Python"), new Integer(6));
  }
}
```

We have two tests here, of course: the first looks for a subject for whom there should be no data, and it validates that we got an empty dataset in return.

The second validates that we have no data for the subject, populates some data, and then looks for the set of ranking averages. It then makes sure we have the count of averages we expect and validates that the rankings themselves are what we expect.

Again, it's doable to write more complete tests, perhaps, but these tests do validate whether our simple requirements are fulfilled. We're still not checking for side effects, but that's outside of the scope of this chapter.[16]

[16] One possibility for checking for side effects might be clearing the entire dataset (as we did in the RankingTest code, by closing the SessionFactory down every test), then clearing the data we expected to write and looking for any extraneous data. There are certainly other possibilities, but all of these are out of our scope here.

So let's look at the code for findRankingsFor(). As usual, we'll have a public method and then an internal method that participates in an existing Session, as shown in Listing 3-28.

Listing 3-28. src/main/java/chapter3/application/HibernateRankingService.java

```
@Override
public Map<String, Integer> findRankingsFor(String subject) {
  Map<String, Integer> results;
  try (Session session = SessionUtil.getSession()) {
    return findRankingsFor(session, subject);
  }
}

private Map<String, Integer> findRankingsFor(Session session,
                                             String subject) {
  Map<String, Integer> results = new HashMap<>();

  Query<Ranking> query = session.createQuery(
      "from Ranking r where "
          + "r.subject.name=:subject order by r.skill.name",
      Ranking.class);
  query.setParameter("subject", subject);
  List<Ranking> rankings = query.list();
  String lastSkillName = "";
  int sum = 0;
  int count = 0;
  for (Ranking r : rankings) {
    if (!lastSkillName.equals(r.getSkill().getName())) {
      sum = 0;
      count = 0;
      lastSkillName = r.getSkill().getName();
    }
    sum += r.getRanking();
```

```
        count++;
        results.put(lastSkillName, sum / count);
    }
    return results;
}
```

The internal `findRankingsFor()` method (as with all of our methods that calculate averages) is really not very attractive. It uses a control-break mechanism to calculate the averages as we iterate through the rankings.[17]

According to the Wikipedia page on control break (`https://en.wikipedia.org/wiki/Control_break`), "[w]ith fourth generation languages such as SQL, the programming language should handle most of the details of control breaks automatically." That's absolutely correct, and it's also why I've been pointing out the inefficiency of all of these routines. We're manually doing something that the database (and Hibernate) should be able to do for us - and it can. We're just not using that capability yet. We will finally get there when we look at the next application requirement.

It's possible to use the Streams API in Java to convert the list of rankings to a map of skills and the average of that skill. However, it's almost as contrived as the control break used here and is harder to read for most people. In the end, since the average should be calculated by the database anyway, using the Streams API for this is overkill.

In any event, the new tests should be able to pass (perhaps not with flying colors, because the actual underlying services aren't done with an eye for efficiency), which allows us to move to the last (and probably most complicated) requirement.

Find the Highest-Ranked Subject for a Skill

With this requirement, we want to find out who is ranked highest for a given skill; if we have three people ranked for Java, we want the one whose average score is best. If there are no rankings for this skill, we want a null response as a signal value. Off to the tests; let's look at Listing 3-29.

[17] Pretty much everyone who knows SQL moderately well has probably been fuming about how we're pulling data from the database. That's okay - the way it's being done here *is* pretty lame. It's straightforward and easy to understand, which serves the purpose of explanation... but it's not very efficient from the CPU's side of things.

Listing 3-29. src/test/java/chapter3/application/FindBestRankingTest.java

```
package chapter03.application;

import chapter03.hibernate.Person;
import org.testng.annotations.Test;

import static org.testng.Assert.assertEquals;
import static org.testng.Assert.assertNull;

public class FindBestRankingTest {
  RankingService service = new HibernateRankingService();

  @Test
  public void findBestForNonexistentSkill() {
    Person p = service.findBestPersonFor("no skill");
    assertNull(p);
  }

  @Test
  public void findBestForSkill() {
    service.addRanking("S1", "01", "Sk1", 6);
    service.addRanking("S1", "02", "Sk1", 8);
    service.addRanking("S2", "01", "Sk1", 5);
    service.addRanking("S2", "02", "Sk1", 7);
    service.addRanking("S3", "01", "Sk1", 7);
    service.addRanking("S3", "02", "Sk1", 9);
    // data that should not factor in!
    service.addRanking("S1", "02", "Sk2", 2);

    Person p = service.findBestPersonFor("Sk1");
    assertEquals(p.getName(), "S3");
  }
}
```

Our first test should be obvious: given a nonexistent skill, we shouldn't get a `Person` back. (This follows our established convention that suggests the use of a signal value rather than an exception.)

Our second test creates three subjects, each with skills in "Sk1," whatever that is. (It's "the ability to serve as test data.") S1 has an average of 7, S2 has an average of 6, and S3 has an average of 8. We should therefore expect S3 as the owner of the best ranking. We're throwing in some outlier data just to make sure that our service is limited to the actual data it's trying to find.

Note that we're not actually returning the skill's average! For an actual application, that's very likely to be a requirement; it could easily be fulfilled by immediately calling `getRankingFor()`, but given that method's design so far, that's a very expensive operation (involving a series of database round trips). We'll revisit this before too long; here, we're using as few object types as we can.

So let's look at some code in Listing 3-30. And we're finally going to get into a more capable query (and see how we might have been writing some of our other queries more efficiently).

Listing 3-30. `src/main/java/chapter3/application/HibernateRankingService.java`

```
@Override
public Person findBestPersonFor(String skill) {
  Person person = null;
  try (Session session = SessionUtil.getSession()) {
    Transaction tx = session.beginTransaction();

    person = findBestPersonFor(session, skill);

    tx.commit();
  }
  return person;
}

private Person findBestPersonFor(Session session, String skill) {
  Query<Object[]> query = session.createQuery(
      "select r.subject.name, avg(r.ranking)"
          + " from Ranking r where "
          + "r.skill.name=:skill "
          + "group by r.subject.name "
          + "order by avg(r.ranking) desc", Object[].class);
```

```
  query.setParameter("skill", skill);
  query.setMaxResults(1);
  List<Object[]> result = query.list();
  if (result.size() > 0) {
    // we want the first (and only) row
    Object[] row=result.get(0);
    String personName=row[0].toString();

    return findPerson(session, personName);
  }
  return null;
}
```

Our public method follows the convention we've established so far: creating a session and then delegating to an internal method.

The internal method, though, does some things we've not seen yet so far, starting with a different type of query.

Most of our queries have been of the "FROM class alias WHERE condition" form, which is fairly simple. Hibernate is generating SQL that uses a table name and can do joins automatically to iterate over a tree of data ("r.skillname", for example), but the overall form is very simple.

Here, we have an actual SELECT clause. Here's the full query as written in the code:

```
select r.subject.name, avg(r.ranking)
  from Ranking r
  where r.skill.name=:skill
  group by r.subject.name
  order by avg(r.ranking)
  desc
```

This actually returns tuples, which are sets of arrays of objects. (This is called a "projection," and we can actually create a class that represents a projection, but we'll demonstrate that in a later chapter.)

Our "select" clause specifies that the tuple will have two values: pulled from the subject name associated with the Ranking and a calculated value which, in this case, is the average of all of the Rankings in a particular group.

The "where" clause limits the overall dataset to those rankings where the skill name matches the parameter.

The "group by" clause means that sets of values are handled together, which in turn means that the average ranking (the second value of the tuple that the query returns) will be limited to each subject.

The "order by" clause means that Hibernate is going to give us the highest-ranked subjects before the lower-ranked subjects.

We also set the maximum number of results from the query to ... one, because we're only interested in the top-ranked person for a given skill; if a skill is popular (like "Java"), there might be hundreds of thousands of rankings, and we're looking for *the best person* - so we'd only want one element returned.

In practice, setting the maximum row count here is of limited application; the query returns a stream of bytes and will not transfer the entire dataset on the first request; it'll retrieve blocks of information as needed, so even if the query result is many megabytes, it'll only deliver what we use. However, using the maximum row count can also tell the *database* possible optimization parameters.

Could we do all of this programmatically? Of course, we could; that's pretty much what we've seen in most of our code, where we calculate values like the average skill manually. However, this saves round-trip data time; the database actually performs the calculations and returns a dataset that's exactly large enough to fulfill its role. Databases are normally tuned for efficiency in this kind of calculation, so we're probably saving time as well, provided we're not using an embedded database as we do in this example.[18]

Putting It All Together

As promised, here are the full listings for the `RankingService` and `HibernateRankingService` for this chapter. The `//tag::` and `//end::` comments are for the purposes of publication; when this chapter is rendered, it's using the actual example source, not being copied from the source into the chapter. (Therefore, if the author notices something and fixes it in the "live source code," the chapter is automatically corrected.)

[18] Even with an embedded database, though, it can be faster; an embedded database can use internal access to the data to which our application code normally has no access, even before we consider the possibility of efficient queries through the use of indexes.

Listing 3-31. src/main/java/chapter3/application/RankingService.java

```
//tag::preamble[]
package chapter03.application;

import chapter03.hibernate.Person;

import java.util.Map;

public interface RankingService {
  int getRankingFor(String subject, String skill);

  void addRanking(String subject, String observer, String skill, int
  ranking);

  //end::preamble[]
  void updateRanking(String subject, String observer, String skill, int
  ranking);

  void removeRanking(String subject, String observer, String skill);

  Map<String, Integer> findRankingsFor(String subject);

  Person findBestPersonFor(String skill);
}
```

Listing 3-32. src/main/java/chapter3/application/HibernateRankingService.java

```
package chapter03.application;

import chapter03.hibernate.Person;
import chapter03.hibernate.Ranking;
import chapter03.hibernate.Skill;
import com.autumncode.hibernate.util.SessionUtil;
import org.hibernate.Session;
import org.hibernate.Transaction;
import org.hibernate.query.Query;

import java.util.HashMap;
import java.util.IntSummaryStatistics;
```

```
import java.util.List;
import java.util.Map;
import java.util.stream.Collectors;

public class HibernateRankingService implements RankingService {
  //tag::getRankingFor[]
  @Override
  public int getRankingFor(String subject, String skill) {
    try (Session session = SessionUtil.getSession()) {
      Transaction tx = session.beginTransaction();

      int average = getRankingFor(session, subject, skill);
      tx.commit();
      return average;
    }
  }

  private int getRankingFor(Session session, String subject,
                            String skill) {
    Query<Ranking> query = session.createQuery(
        "from Ranking r "
            + "where r.subject.name=:name "
            + "and r.skill.name=:skill", Ranking.class);
    query.setParameter("name", subject);
    query.setParameter("skill", skill);

    IntSummaryStatistics stats = query
        .list()
        .stream()
        .collect(
            Collectors.summarizingInt(Ranking::getRanking)
        );

    return (int) stats.getAverage();
  }
  //end::getRankingFor[]

  //tag::addRanking[]
```

```
@Override
public void addRanking(String subjectName,
                       String observerName,
                       String skillName,
                       int rank) {
  try (Session session = SessionUtil.getSession()) {
    Transaction tx = session.beginTransaction();

    addRanking(session, subjectName, observerName,
        skillName, rank);

    tx.commit();
  }
}

private void addRanking(Session session,
                        String subjectName,
                        String observerName,
                        String skillName,
                        int rank) {
  Person subject = savePerson(session, subjectName);
  Person observer = savePerson(session, observerName);
  Skill skill = saveSkill(session, skillName);

  Ranking ranking = new Ranking();
  ranking.setSubject(subject);
  ranking.setObserver(observer);
  ranking.setSkill(skill);
  ranking.setRanking(rank);
  session.save(ranking);
}
//end::addRanking[]

//tag::updateRanking[]
@Override
public void updateRanking(String subject,
                          String observer,
                          String skill,
```

```
                              int rank) {
  try (Session session = SessionUtil.getSession()) {
    Transaction tx = session.beginTransaction();

    Ranking ranking = findRanking(session, subject,
        observer, skill);
    if (ranking == null) {
      addRanking(session, subject, observer, skill, rank);
    } else {
      ranking.setRanking(rank);
    }
    tx.commit();
  }
}
//end::updateRanking[]

//tag::removeRanking[]
@Override
public void removeRanking(String subject,
                          String observer,
                          String skill) {
  try (Session session = SessionUtil.getSession()) {
    Transaction tx = session.beginTransaction();

    removeRanking(session, subject, observer, skill);

    tx.commit();
  }
}

private void removeRanking(Session session,
                           String subject,
                           String observer,
                           String skill) {
  Ranking ranking = findRanking(session, subject,
      observer, skill);
```

```
    if (ranking != null) {
      session.delete(ranking);
    }
  }
  //end::removeRanking[]

  //tag::findRankingsFor[]
  @Override
  public Map<String, Integer> findRankingsFor(String subject) {
    Map<String, Integer> results;
    try (Session session = SessionUtil.getSession()) {
      return findRankingsFor(session, subject);
    }
  }

  private Map<String, Integer> findRankingsFor(Session session,
                                                String subject) {
    Map<String, Integer> results = new HashMap<>();

    Query<Ranking> query = session.createQuery(
        "from Ranking r where "
            + "r.subject.name=:subject order by r.skill.name",
        Ranking.class);
    query.setParameter("subject", subject);
    List<Ranking> rankings = query.list();
    String lastSkillName = "";
    int sum = 0;
    int count = 0;
    for (Ranking r : rankings) {
      if (!lastSkillName.equals(r.getSkill().getName())) {
        sum = 0;
        count = 0;
        lastSkillName = r.getSkill().getName();
      }
      sum += r.getRanking();
```

```
      count++;
      results.put(lastSkillName, sum / count);
    }
    return results;
  }
  //end::findRankingsFor[]

  //tag::findBestPersonFor[]
  @Override
  public Person findBestPersonFor(String skill) {
    Person person = null;
    try (Session session = SessionUtil.getSession()) {
      Transaction tx = session.beginTransaction();

      person = findBestPersonFor(session, skill);

      tx.commit();
    }
    return person;
  }

  private Person findBestPersonFor(Session session, String skill) {
    Query<Object[]> query = session.createQuery(
        "select r.subject.name, avg(r.ranking)"
            + " from Ranking r where "
            + "r.skill.name=:skill "
            + "group by r.subject.name "
            + "order by avg(r.ranking) desc", Object[].class);
    query.setParameter("skill", skill);
    query.setMaxResults(1);
    List<Object[]> result = query.list();
    if (result.size() > 0) {
      // we want the first (and only) row
      Object[] row=result.get(0);
      String personName=row[0].toString();
```

```
      return findPerson(session, personName);
    }
    return null;
  }
  //end::findBestPersonFor[]

  private Ranking findRanking(Session session, String subject,
                              String observer, String skill) {
    Query<Ranking> query = session.createQuery(
        "from Ranking r where "
            + "r.subject.name=:subject and "
            + "r.observer.name=:observer and "
            + "r.skill.name=:skill", Ranking.class);
    query.setParameter("subject", subject);
    query.setParameter("observer", observer);
    query.setParameter("skill", skill);
    Ranking ranking = query.uniqueResult();
    return ranking;
  }

  private Person findPerson(Session session, String name) {
    Query<Person> query = session.createQuery(
        "from Person p where p.name=:name",
        Person.class);
    query.setParameter("name", name);
    Person person = query.uniqueResult();
    return person;
  }

  private Skill findSkill(Session session, String name) {
    Query<Skill> query = session.createQuery(
        "from Skill s where s.name=:name", Skill.class);
    query.setParameter("name", name);
    Skill skill = query.uniqueResult();
    return skill;
  }
```

```
  private Skill saveSkill(Session session, String skillName) {
    Skill skill = findSkill(session, skillName);
    if (skill == null) {
      skill = new Skill();
      skill.setName(skillName);
      session.save(skill);
    }
    return skill;
  }

  private Person savePerson(Session session, String name) {
    Person person = findPerson(session, name);
    if (person == null) {
      person = new Person();
      person.setName(name);
      session.save(person);
    }
    return person;
  }
}
```

Summary

In this chapter, we've seen how to go from a problem definition to an object model, along with an example of test-driven design to test the model. We've also lightly covered the concepts of object state with respect to persistence and transactions.

We then focused on the application requirements, building a series of actions through which those requirements could be fulfilled. We covered how to create, read, update, and delete data, along with using Hibernate's query language to perform a fairly complex query with calculated data.

In the next chapter, we will look at the architecture of Hibernate and the lifecycle of a Hibernate-based application.

CHAPTER 4

The Persistence LifeCycle

In this chapter, we discuss the lifecycle of persistent objects in Hibernate. These persistent objects can be POJOs without any special marker interfaces or inheritance related to Hibernate. Part of Hibernate's popularity comes from its ability to work with a normal object model.

We are also going to cover some of the methods of the `Session` interface that are used for creating, retrieving, updating, and deleting persistent objects from Hibernate.

Introducing the Lifecycle

After adding Hibernate to your application, you do not need to change your existing Java object model to add persistence marker interfaces or any other type of hint for Hibernate. Instead, Hibernate works with normal Java objects that your application creates with the `new` operator or that other objects create.

For Hibernate's purposes, these can be drawn up into two categories: objects for which Hibernate has entity mappings and objects that are not directly recognized by Hibernate. A correctly mapped entity object will consist of fields and properties that are mapped and that are themselves either references to correctly mapped entities, references to collections of such entities, or "value" types (primitives, primitive wrappers, strings, or arrays of these).

Given an instance of an object that is mapped to Hibernate, it can be in any one of four different states: transient, persistent, detached, or removed.[1]

Transient objects exist in memory only. Hibernate does not manage transient objects or persist changes to transient objects. If you have a `Person` POJO, and you create an instance with `new Person()`, that object is *transient* and there's no expectation that it's somehow represented in a database as long as it's in *transient* state.

[1] If these terms feel vaguely familiar, you may have read Chapter 3.

J. B. Ottinger et al., *Beginning Hibernate 6*, https://doi.org/10.1007/978-1-4842-7337-1_4

To persist the changes to a transient object, you would have to ask the session to save the transient object to the database, at which point Hibernate assigns the object an identifier and marks the object as being in *persistent* state.

Persistent objects exist in the database, and Hibernate manages the persistence for persistent objects. We show this relationship between the objects and the database in Figure 4-1. If fields or properties change on a persistent object, Hibernate will keep the database representation up to date when the application marks the changes as to be committed.

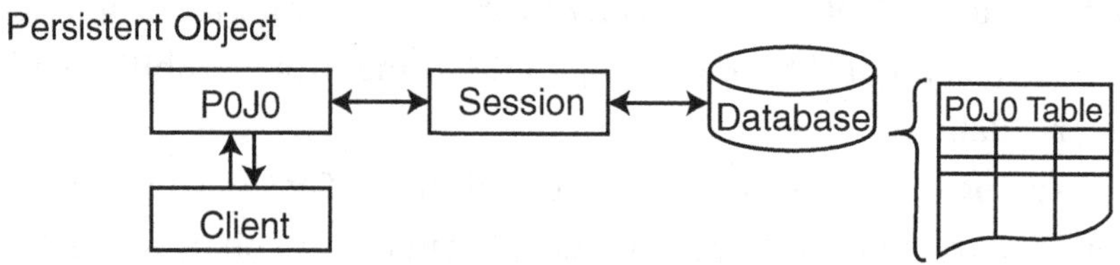

Figure 4-1. *Persistent objects are maintained by Hibernate*

Detached objects have a representation in the database, but changes to the object will not be reflected in the database, and vice versa. This temporary separation of the object and the database is shown in Figure 4-2. A detached object can be created by closing the session that it was associated with or by evicting it from the session with a call to the session's `evict()` method.

One reason you might consider detaching an entity would be to read an object out of the database, modify the properties of the object in memory, and then store the results someplace other than your database. This would be an alternative to doing a deep copy of the object.

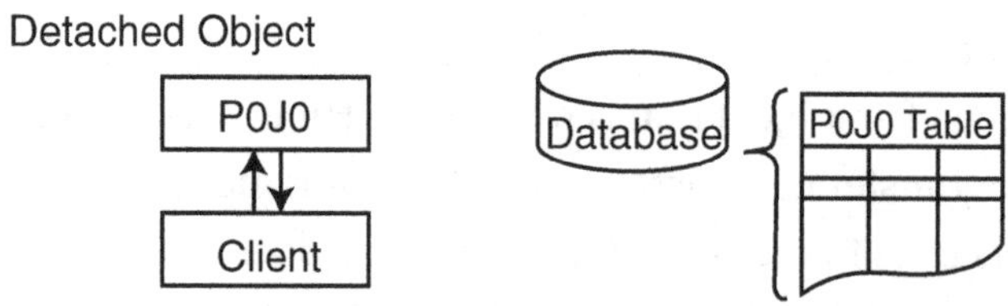

Figure 4-2. *Detached objects exist in the database, unmaintained by Hibernate*

In order to persist changes made to a detached object, the application must reattach it to a valid Hibernate session. A detached instance can be associated with a new Hibernate session when your application calls one of the `load()`, `refresh()`, `merge()`, `update()`, or `save()` methods on the new session with a reference to the detached object. After the call, the detached object would be a persistent object managed by the new Hibernate session.

Removed objects are objects that are being managed by Hibernate (persistent objects, in other words) that have been passed to the session's `remove()` method. When the application marks the changes held in the session as to be committed, the entries in the database that correspond to removed objects are deleted.

Versions prior to Hibernate 3 had support for the Lifecycle and Validatable interfaces. These allowed your objects to listen for save, update, delete, load, and validate events using methods on the object. In Hibernate 3, this function moved into events and interceptors, and the old interfaces were removed. Since Hibernate 4, the JPA persistence lifecycle is also supported, so events can be embedded into the objects and marked with annotations.

Entities, Classes, and Names

Entities represent Java objects with mappings that permit them to be stored in the database. The mappings indicate how the fields and properties of the object should be stored in the database tables. However, it is possible that you will want objects of a particular type to be represented in two different ways in the database. For instance, you could have one Java class for users, but two different tables in the database that store users. This may not be the best database design, but similar problems are common in legacy systems. Other systems that can't be easily modified may depend on the existing database design, and Hibernate is powerful enough to cover this scenario. In this case, how does Hibernate choose which to use?

An object representing an entity will be a normal Java class. It will also have an entity name. By default, the name of the entity will be the same as the name of the class type.[2] You have the option, however, to change this via the mappings or annotations and thus distinguish between objects of the same type that are mapped to different tables. There

[2] As we saw in Chapter 3, HQL uses the entity name, not the class name; but because we didn't specify any custom entity names, the class name and the entity name were the same.

are, therefore, methods in the `Session` API that require an entity name to be provided to determine the appropriate mapping. If this is omitted, it will either be because no such distinction is needed or because, for convenience, the method assumes the most common case - that the entity name is the same as the class name - and duplicates the function of another, more specific method that permits the entity name to be specified explicitly.

Identifiers

An identifier, or identity column, maps to the concept of a primary key in relational databases. A primary key is a unique set of one or more columns that can be used to specify a particular collection of data.

There are two types of identifiers: natural and artificial.

A *natural* identifier is something that the application finds meaningful - a user ID, for example, or a Social Security number[3] or equivalent.

An *artificial* identifier is one whose value is arbitrary. Our code so far uses values generated by the database (identity columns) that have no relation whatsoever with the data associated with that identifier. This tends to yield more flexibility with respect to associations and other such interactions, because the artificial identifier can be smaller than a natural identifier in many cases.

Why would artificial identifiers be better than natural identifiers? Well, there are a few possible reasons. One reason artificial identifiers might be better than natural identifiers is that an artificial identifier might be a smaller type (in memory) than a natural identifier.

Consider a user email. In most cases, user email addresses won't change, and they tend to be unique for a given user; however, the email addresses might be at least 20 bytes long[4] (and could be much longer). An integral user ID (a long or an int) might be 4 or 8 bytes long, and no longer.

[3] The US Social Security Administration says that they have enough Social Security numbers to assign unique identification for "several generations." (See `www.ssa.gov/history/hfaq.html`, Q20.) That may be good enough for a natural identifier, although privacy advocates would rightfully complain; also, note that "several generations" might not be enough. Programmers were absolutely sure that nobody would still have data with two-digit years in them ... until Y2K, which took a lot of man-hours to fix.

[4] In earlier printings, the number here was "ten." But `"@gmail.com"` is ten characters long, all by itself. To be fair, worrying about dozens of bytes is probably unwise, but so is profligate wasting of memory.

Another more compelling reason is that artificial identifiers won't change with the data's natural lifecycle. An email address, for example, might change over time; someone might abandon an old email address and prefer a new one.[5] Anything that relied on that email address as a natural identifier would have to be changed synchronously to allow updates.

Yet another reason is that artificial identifiers are simple. Databases (and Hibernate) allow the use of composite identifiers - identifiers built up from more than one property in an object. However, this means that when you refer to a specific object or row in the database, you have to include *all columns in that identifier*, whether as an embedded object or as a set of individual columns. It's doable, certainly; some data models require it (for legacy or other business reasons, for example). However, for efficiency's sake, most would normally prefer artificial keys.

In Hibernate, an object attribute is marked as an identifier with the @Id annotation, as shown in Listing 4-1.

Listing 4-1. A Typical Identifier Field

```
@Id
public Long id;
```

In Listing 4-1, you see a `Long` - a "big integer" for H2 - that's marked as a presumably artificial identifier. This value will need to be assigned before the object with this attribute can be persisted.

In our example code so far, though, we've assigned no identifiers manually. We've used another annotation, `@GeneratedValue`, which tells Hibernate that it is responsible for assigning and maintaining the identifier. The mechanism through which this happens depends quite a bit on the Hibernate configuration and the database in use.

You may have missed it, but `@Id` doesn't mean an identifier is automatically assigned. You must use a `@GeneratedValue` annotation if you don't want to assign identifier values yourself!

There are five different generation possibilities: identity, sequence, table, auto, and none. Identity generation relies on a natural table sequencing. This is requested in the `@GeneratedValue` annotation by using the `GenerationType.IDENTITY` option, as shown in Listing 4-2.

[5] Your author has at least seven "primary email addresses" to choose from, for example.

Listing 4-2. An Autogenerated Identity Field

```
@Id
@GeneratedValue(strategy=GenerationType.IDENTITY)
public Long id;
```

Identity generation is awfully convenient, and it feels very natural to use. However, it requires actual insertion of the data into the database before an identifier is known, and the use of IDENTITY disables JDBC batching of inserts (again, because the identifiers are detected *after* the row is inserted). The Hibernate documentation suggests the use of other generation strategies, and it's hard to argue with it.

The *sequence* mechanism depends on the database's ability to create table sequences (which tends to limit it to PostgreSQL, Oracle, and a few others). It corresponds to the GenerationType.SEQUENCE strategy.

The *table* mechanism uses a table whose purpose is to store blocks of artificial identifiers; you can let Hibernate generate this for you, or you can specify all of the table's specifics with an additional @TableGenerator annotation. To use artificial key generation via table, use the GenerationType.TABLE strategy.

The fourth artificial key generation strategy is *auto*, which normally maps to the IDENTITY strategy, but depends on the database in question. (It's supposed to default to something that's efficient for the database in question.) To use this, use the GenerationType.AUTO strategy.

The fifth strategy isn't actually a strategy at all: it relies on manual assignment of an identifier. If Session.persist() is called with an empty identifier, you'll have an IdentifierGenerationException thrown.

Entities and Associations

Entities can contain references to other entities, either directly as an embedded property or field or indirectly via a collection of some sort (arrays, sets, lists, etc.). These associations are represented using foreign key relationships in the underlying tables. These foreign keys will rely on the identifiers used by participating tables, which is another reason to prefer small (and artificial) keys.

When only one of the pair of entities contains a reference to the other, the association is *unidirectional*. If the association is mutual, then it is referred to as being *bidirectional*.

A common mistake when designing entity models is to try to make all associations bidirectional. Associations that are not a natural part of the object model should not be forced into it. Hibernate Query Language often presents a more natural way to access the same information.

In associations, one (and only one) of the participating classes is referred to as "managing the relationship." If both ends of the association manage the relationship, then we would encounter a problem when client code called the appropriate set method on both ends of the association. Should two foreign key columns be maintained - one in each direction (risking circular dependencies) - or only one?

Ideally, we would like to dictate that only changes to one end of the relationship will result in any updates to the foreign key; and indeed, Hibernate allows us to do this by marking one end of the association as being managed by the other (marked by the `mappedBy` attribute of the association annotation).

`mappedBy` is purely about how the foreign key relationships between entities are saved. It has nothing to do with saving the entities themselves. Despite this, they are often confused with the entirely orthogonal cascade functionality (described in the "Cascading Operations" section of this chapter).

While Hibernate lets us specify that changes to one association will result in changes to the database, it does not allow us to cause changes to one end of the association to be automatically reflected in the other end in the Java POJOs.

Let's jump in to see some code. Here's Chapter 4's `pom.xml`, from the source code for the book; it's not particularly enlightening, as it's largely a straight copy of other chapters' project models, but it's good to be thorough.

Listing 4-3. `pom.xml`

```
<?xml version="1.0" encoding="UTF-8"?>
<project xmlns:xsi="http://www.w3.org/2001/XMLSchema-instance"
         xmlns="http://maven.apache.org/POM/4.0.0"
         xsi:schemaLocation="http://maven.apache.org/POM/4.0.0
         http://maven.apache.org/xsd/maven-4.0.0.xsd">
    <parent>
        <artifactId>hibernate-6-parent</artifactId>
        <groupId>com.autumncode.books.hibernate</groupId>
        <version>5.0</version>
    </parent>
```

```
    <modelVersion>4.0.0</modelVersion>
    <artifactId>chapter04</artifactId>

    <dependencies>
        <dependency>
            <groupId>com.autumncode.books.hibernate</groupId>
            <artifactId>util</artifactId>
            <version>${project.version}</version>
        </dependency>
    </dependencies>
</project>
```

Let's create an example, in the chapter04.broken package, of a Message and an Email association, without an "owning object." First is the Message class, as shown in Listing 4-4.

Listing 4-4. A Broken Model, Beginning with Message

```
package chapter04.broken;

import javax.persistence.*;

@Entity
public class Message {
  @Id
  @GeneratedValue(strategy = GenerationType.AUTO)
  Long id;

  @Column
  String content;

  @OneToOne
  Email email;

  public Message() {
  }

  public Message(String content) {
    setContent(content);
  }
```

```
  // accessors and mutators ignored for brevity

  @Override
  public String toString() {
    // note use of email.subject because otherwise properly constructed
    // relationships would cause an endless loop that never ends
    // and therefore runs endlessly.
    return String.format(
        "Message{id=%d, content='%s', email.subject='%s'}",
        id,
        content,
        (email != null ? email.getSubject() : "null")
    );
  }
}
```

Listing 4-5 is the Email class.

Listing 4-5. A Broken Model's Email Class

```
package chapter04.broken;

import javax.persistence.*;

@Entity
public class Email {
  @Id
  @GeneratedValue(strategy = GenerationType.AUTO)
  Long id;
  @Column
  String subject;
  @OneToOne
  // (mappedBy = "email")
  Message message;

  public Email() {
  }
```

```
  public Email(String subject) {
    setSubject(subject);
  }

  // accessors and mutators ignored for brevity

  @Override
  public String toString() {
    // note use of message.content because otherwise properly constructed
    // relationships would cause an endless loop that never ends
    // and therefore runs endlessly.
    return String.format(
        "Email{id=%s, subject=`%s`, message.content=%s}",
        id,
        subject,
        (message != null ? message.getContent() : "null")
    );
  }
}
```

With these classes, there's no "owning relation"; the mappedBy attribute in Email is commented out. This means that we need to update both the Email and the Message in order to have our relationship properly modeled in both directions. Let's see the full chapter04.broken.BrokenInversionTest class, and we'll break it down after we see the source.

Listing 4-6. src/main/java/chapter04/broken/BrokenInversionTest.java

```
package chapter04.broken;

import com.autumncode.hibernate.util.SessionUtil;
import org.hibernate.Session;
import org.hibernate.Transaction;
import org.testng.annotations.Test;

import static org.testng.Assert.*;

public class BrokenInversionTest {
  @Test()
```

```
  public void testBrokenInversionCode() {
    Long emailId;
    Long messageId;
    Email email;
    Message message;

    try (Session session = SessionUtil.getSession()) {
      Transaction tx = session.beginTransaction();

      email = new Email("Broken");
      message = new Message("Broken");

      email.setMessage(message);
      // message.setEmail(email);

      session.save(email);
      session.save(message);

      emailId = email.getId();
      messageId = message.getId();

      tx.commit();
    }

    assertNotNull(email.getMessage());
    assertNull(message.getEmail());

    try (Session session = SessionUtil.getSession()) {
      email = session.get(Email.class, emailId);
      System.out.println(email);
      message = session.get(Message.class, messageId);
      System.out.println(message);
    }

    assertNotNull(email.getMessage());
    assertNull(message.getEmail());
  }
}
```

The final call to `message.getEmail()` will return `null` (assuming simple accessors and mutators are used). To get the desired effect, both entities must be updated. If the `Email` entity owns the association, this merely ensures the proper assignment of a foreign key column value. There is *no implicit call* of `message.setEmail(email)`. This must be explicitly given, as in Listing 4-7.

Listing 4-7. `src/main/java/chapter04/broken/ProperSimpleInversionTest.java`

```
package chapter04.broken;

import com.autumncode.hibernate.util.SessionUtil;
import org.hibernate.Session;
import org.hibernate.Transaction;
import org.testng.annotations.Test;

import static org.testng.Assert.assertNotNull;

public class ProperSimpleInversionTest {
  @Test
  public void testProperSimpleInversionCode() {
    Long emailId;
    Long messageId;
    Email email;
    Message message;

    try (Session session = SessionUtil.getSession()) {
      Transaction tx = session.beginTransaction();

      email = new Email("Proper");
      message = new Message("Proper");

      email.setMessage(message);
      message.setEmail(email);

      session.save(email);
      session.save(message);

      emailId = email.getId();
      messageId = message.getId();
```

```
      tx.commit();
    }

    assertNotNull(email.getMessage());
    assertNotNull(message.getEmail());

    try (Session session = SessionUtil.getSession()) {
      email = session.get(Email.class, emailId);
      System.out.println(email);
      message = session.get(Message.class, messageId);
      System.out.println(message);
    }

    assertNotNull(email.getMessage());
    assertNotNull(message.getEmail());
  }
}
```

The last assertion is `assertNotNull()`, where in the `BrokenInversionTest` it was `assertNull()`.

It is common for users new to Hibernate to get confused about this point. The reason it occurs is that Hibernate is using the actual current state of the entities. In `BrokenInversionTest.java`, when you set the message in the email, but not the email in the message, Hibernate persists the actual relationships in the object model, instead of trying to infer a relationship, even when that relationship would be expected. The extra relationship would be an unexpected side effect, even if it might be useful in this particular case.

If we include the mapping (the mappedBy attribute), we get a different result. We're going to modify `Message` (by moving it to a new package, `chapter04.mapped`) and `Email` (by moving it and including the `mappedBy` attribute, commented out in the prior listing).

The `Message` code is identical to the "broken" version, except for the package and the entity name (which means Hibernate will use "Message2" as the table name for this type), as shown in Listing 4-8.

Listing 4-8. src/main/java/chapter04/mapped/Message.java

```
package chapter04.mapped;

import javax.persistence.*;

@Entity(name = "Message2")
public class Message {
  @Id
  @GeneratedValue(strategy = GenerationType.AUTO)
  Long id;

  @Column
  String content;

  @OneToOne
  Email email;

  public Message() {
  }

  public Message(String content) {
    setContent(content);
  }

  // accessors and mutators omitted

  @Override
  public String toString() {
    // note use of email.subject because otherwise properly constructed
    // relationships would cause an endless loop that never ends
    // and therefore runs endlessly.
    return String.format(
        "Message{id=%d, content='%s', email.subject='%s'}",
        id,
        content,
        (email != null ? email.getSubject() : "null")
    );
  }
}
```

The Email code, in addition to changing the entity name and package, adds the mappedBy attribute. This actually adds a column to the Message database representation, representing the email ID. See Listing 4-9.

Listing 4-9. src/main/java/chapter04/mapped/Email.java

```
package chapter04.mapped;

import javax.persistence.*;

@Entity(name = "Email2")
public class Email {
  @Id
  @GeneratedValue(strategy = GenerationType.AUTO)
  Long id;
  @Column
  String subject;
  @OneToOne(mappedBy = "email")
  Message message;

  public Email() {
  }

  public Email(String subject) {
    setSubject(subject);
  }

  // accessors and mutators omitted

  @Override
  public String toString() {
    // note use of message.content because otherwise properly constructed
    // relationships would cause an endless loop that never ends
    // and therefore runs endlessly.
    return String.format(
        "Email{id=%s, subject=`%s`, message.content=%s}",
        id,
        subject,
```

```
            (message != null ? message.getContent() : "null")
        );
    }
}
```

With the mapping contained in the Message, there are some unexpected results. Our prior test failed to reestablish some relationships, requiring them to be set in both Email and Message. Here, we have nearly the same construct, but without the same result: we only have to set one side of the relationship instead of manually maintaining both references.

First, let's see the test code, as shown in Listing 4-10; note that this test is using the chapter04.mapped package, so it's getting the Email and Message classes we just saw.

Listing 4-10. src/test/java/chapter04/mapped/ImplicitRelationshipTest.java

```
package chapter04.mapped;

import com.autumncode.hibernate.util.SessionUtil;
import org.hibernate.Session;
import org.hibernate.Transaction;
import org.testng.annotations.Test;

import static org.testng.Assert.*;
import static org.testng.Assert.assertNotNull;

public class ImplicitRelationshipTest {
  @Test
  public void testImpliedRelationship() {
    Long emailId;
    Long messageId;
    Email email;
    Message message;

    try (Session session = SessionUtil.getSession()) {
      Transaction tx = session.beginTransaction();

      email = new Email("Inverse Email");
      message = new Message("Inverse Message");
```

```
      // email.setMessage(message);
      message.setEmail(email);

      session.save(email);
      session.save(message);

      emailId = email.getId();
      messageId = message.getId();

      tx.commit();
    }

    assertEquals(email.getSubject(), "Inverse Email");
    assertEquals(message.getContent(), "Inverse Message");
    assertNull(email.getMessage());
    assertNotNull(message.getEmail());

    try (Session session = SessionUtil.getSession()) {
      email = session.get(Email.class, emailId);
      System.out.println(email);
      message = session.get(Message.class, messageId);
      System.out.println(message);
    }

    assertNotNull(email.getMessage());
    assertNotNull(message.getEmail());
  }
}
```

This test passes, even though we didn't set the `Email's Message`.

That `mappingBy` attribute is the cause. In the database, the `Message2` table will have a column called "email_id," which is set to the `Email's` unique identifier when we update the `Message's email` property. When we close the session and reload, the relationship is set only through that column, which means the relationship is set "correctly" even though we didn't create the relationship properly when we first created the data.

If we were to manage the relationship in the `Email` entity (i.e., setting the `mappedBy` attribute in `Message.java` instead of `Email.java`), the situation would be reversed: setting the `Message's email` attribute wouldn't be reflected in the database, but setting the `Email's message` attribute would.

Here's a summary of the points made:

1. You must explicitly manage both ends of an association.
2. Only changes to the owner of an association will be honored in the database.
3. When you load a detached entity from the database, it will reflect the foreign key relationships persisted into the database.

Table 4-1 shows how you can select the side of the relationship that should be made the owner of a bidirectional association. Remember that to make an association the owner, you must mark the other end as being mapped by the other.

Table 4-1. *Marking the Owner of an Association*

One-to-one	Either end can be made the owner, but one (and only one) of them should be; if you don't specify this, you will end up with a circular dependency.
One-to-many	The "one" end must be made the owner of the association.
Many-to-one	This is the same as the one-to-many relationship viewed from the opposite perspective, so the same rule applies: the many end must be made the owner of the association.
Many-to-many	Either end of the association can be made the owner.

If this all seems rather confusing, just remember that association ownership is concerned exclusively with the management of the foreign keys in the database, and things should become clearer as you use Hibernate further. Associations and mappings are discussed in detail in the next few chapters.

Saving Entities

Creating an instance of a class you mapped with a Hibernate mapping does not automatically persist the object to the database. Until you explicitly associate the object with a valid Hibernate session, the object is *transient*, like any other Java object. In Hibernate, we use one of the `save()` – or `persist()`, which is a synonym for `save()` – methods on the `Session` interface to store a transient object in the database, as follows:

```
public Serializable save(Object object)
public Serializable save(String entityName, Object object)
```

Both `save()` methods take a transient object reference (which must not be `null`) as an argument. Hibernate expects to find a mapping (either annotations or an XML mapping) for the transient object's class; Hibernate cannot[6] persist arbitrary unmapped objects. If you have mapped multiple entities to a Java class, you can specify which entity you are saving (Hibernate wouldn't know from just the Java class name) with the `entityName` argument.

The `save()` methods all create a new `org.hibernate.event.spi.SaveOrUpdateEvent` event. Events are a fairly advanced subject in Hibernate that most readers won't need, but interested readers can read more at `https://red.ht/3iGN7tZ`, the "events" chapter from the Hibernate 6 documentation.

At its simplest, we create a new object in Java, set a few of its properties, and then save it through the session. Here's a simple object, shown in Listing 4-11.

Listing 4-11. `src/main/java/chapter04/model/SimpleObject.java`

```
package chapter04.model;

import javax.persistence.*;

@Entity
public class SimpleObject {
  @Id
  @GeneratedValue(strategy = GenerationType.AUTO)
  Long id;
  @Column
  String key;
```

[6] Correction: Hibernate *does not* persist arbitrary unmapped objects. This is a good thing.

```
  @Column
  Long value;

  public SimpleObject() {
  }

  // mutators and accessors not included for brevity
  // equals() and hashCode() will be covered later in this chapter
}
```

Listing 4-12 shows how this object is saved, as shown in chapter04.general.SaveLoadTest, in the testSaveLoad() method.

Listing 4-12. src/test/java/chapter04/general/SaveLoadTest.java

```
package chapter04.general;

import chapter04.model.SimpleObject;
import com.autumncode.hibernate.util.SessionUtil;
import org.hibernate.Session;
import org.hibernate.Transaction;
import org.testng.annotations.Test;

import static org.testng.Assert.*;

public class SaveLoadTest {
  @Test
  public void testSaveLoad() {
    Long id = null;
    SimpleObject obj;

    try (Session session = SessionUtil.getSession()) {
      Transaction tx = session.beginTransaction();

      obj = new SimpleObject();
      obj.setKey("sl");
      obj.setValue(10L);

      session.save(obj);
      assertNotNull(obj.getId());
      // we should have an id now, set by Session.save()
```

```
      id = obj.getId();

      tx.commit();
    }

    try (Session session = SessionUtil.getSession()) {
      // we're loading the object by id
      SimpleObject o2 = session.load(SimpleObject.class, id);
      assertEquals(o2.getKey(), "s1");
      assertNotNull(o2.getValue());
      assertEquals(o2.getValue().longValue(), 10L);

      SimpleObject o3 = session.load(SimpleObject.class, id);

      // since o3 and o2 were loaded in the same session, they're not only
      // equivalent - as shown by equals() - but equal, as shown by ==.
      // since obj was NOT loaded in this session, it's equivalent but
      // not ==.
      assertEquals(o2, o3);
      assertEquals(obj, o2);
      assertEquals(obj, o3);

      assertSame(o2, o3);
      assertFalse(o2 == obj);

      assertSame(obj, o3);
      assertFalse(obj == o3);
    }
  }
}
```

It is not appropriate to save an object that has already been persisted. Doing so will update the object, which will actually end up creating a duplicate with a new identifier. This can be seen in DuplicateSaveTest, in Listing 4-13.

Listing 4-13. src/test/java/chapter04/general/DuplicateSaveTest.java

```
package chapter04.general;

import chapter04.model.SimpleObject;
import com.autumncode.hibernate.util.SessionUtil;
import org.hibernate.Session;
import org.hibernate.Transaction;
import org.testng.annotations.Test;

import java.util.List;

import static org.testng.Assert.*;

public class DuplicateSaveTest {
  @Test
  public void duplicateSaveTest() {
    Long id;
    SimpleObject obj;

    try (Session session = SessionUtil.getSession()) {
      Transaction tx = session.beginTransaction();

      obj = new SimpleObject();

      obj.setKey("Open Source and Standards");
      obj.setValue(10L);

      session.save(obj);
      assertNotNull(obj.getId());

      id = obj.getId();

      tx.commit();
    }

    try (Session session = SessionUtil.getSession()) {
      Transaction tx = session.beginTransaction();

      obj.setValue(12L);

      // this is not good behavior!
```

```
      session.save(obj);

      tx.commit();
    }

    // note that save() creates a new row in the database!
    // this is wrong behavior. Don't do this!
    assertNotEquals(id, obj.getId());

    try (Session session = SessionUtil.getSession()) {
      List<SimpleObject> objects=session
          .createQuery("from SimpleObject", SimpleObject.class)
          .list();

      // again, this is a value we DO NOT WANT.
      assertEquals(objects.size(), 2);
    }
  }
}
```

When this test is run, the two identifiers would be expected to be equal but they're not; examining the values yielded equivalent objects, except for the IDs, which were sequentially assigned as the `SimpleObject @Id` generation specified.

You can, however, update an object with `Session.saveOrUpdate()` (or `Session.update()`, of course).

`saveOrUpdate()` will call `save()` if the object doesn't exist properly, whereas `update()` will not; `saveOrUpdate()`, then, is a little safer if your goal is to make sure an object exists in the database; `update()` would fail with an exception if the object didn't exist in the database already. This would be appropriate if you're trying to update an order invoice, for example; you wouldn't want to create one if it didn't exist already.

Listing 4-14 shows another class, `SaveOrUpdateTest`.

Listing 4-14. `src/test/java/chapter04/general/SaveOrUpdateTest.java`

```
package chapter04.general;

import chapter04.model.SimpleObject;
import com.autumncode.hibernate.util.SessionUtil;
import org.hibernate.Session;
```

```
import org.hibernate.Transaction;
import org.testng.annotations.Test;

import java.util.List;

import static org.testng.Assert.*;

public class SaveOrUpdateTest {
  @Test
  public void testSaveOrUpdateEntity() {
    Long id;
    SimpleObject obj;
    try (Session session=SessionUtil.getSession()) {
      Transaction tx = session.beginTransaction();
      // this only works for simple objects
      session
          .createQuery("delete from SimpleObject")
          .executeUpdate();
      tx.commit();
    }

    try (Session session = SessionUtil.getSession()) {
      Transaction tx = session.beginTransaction();

      obj = new SimpleObject();

      obj.setKey("Open Source and Standards");
      obj.setValue(14L);

      session.save(obj);
      assertNotNull(obj.getId());

      id = obj.getId();

      tx.commit();
    }

    try (Session session = SessionUtil.getSession()) {
      Transaction tx = session.beginTransaction();
```

```
      obj.setValue(12L);

      // if the key didn't exist in the database,
      // it would after this call.
      session.saveOrUpdate(obj);

      tx.commit();
    }

    // saveOrUpdate() will update a row in the database
    // if one matches. This is what one usually expects.
    assertEquals(id, obj.getId());

    try (Session session = SessionUtil.getSession()) {
      List<SimpleObject> objects=session
          .createQuery("from SimpleObject", SimpleObject.class)
          .list();

      assertEquals(objects.size(), 1);
    }
  }
}
```

It wouldn't be advisable to try to match this code construction in production code.

The object goes from transient state (when it's created) to persistent state (when it's first saved), then back to transient state (when the session is closed). We then update the object while it's in transient state and move it back to persistent state when we call `Session.saveOrUpdate()`.

Ideally, what you would do is load the object from the session in the first place (as we've done in most of our other examples where we show updates); this means that the updates take place on a persistent object, and we don't actually have to call `Session.save()`, `Session.update()`, or `Session.saveOrUpdate()` at all.[7] It's not an error to explicitly call one of the update methods, but it's not necessary.

Once an object is in a persistent state, Hibernate manages updates to the database itself as you change the fields and properties of the object.

---

[7] We saw Hibernate update an object without calling `save()` in Chapter 3: `chapter03.hibernate.RankingTest's changeRanking()` method does an in-place update of a persistent object.

Hibernate is pretty efficient about tracking changes, and it tracks only changed fields. If you have an entity with 30 attributes and change *one*, Hibernate will issue a fairly minimal SQL `UPDATE` to modify the database record, under normal circumstances.

Object Equality and Identity

When we discuss persistent objects in Hibernate, we also need to consider the role that object equality and identity play with Hibernate. When we have a persistent object in Hibernate, that object represents both an instance of a class in a particular Java virtual machine (JVM) and a row (or rows) in a database table (or tables).

Requesting a persistent object again from the same Hibernate session returns the same Java instance of a class, which means that you can compare the objects using the standard Java == equality syntax. If, however, you request a persistent object from more than one Hibernate session, Hibernate will provide distinct instances from each session, and the == operator will return `false` if you compare these object instances.

Taking this into account, if you are comparing objects in two different sessions, you will need to implement the `equals()` method on your Java persistence objects, which you should probably do as a regular occurrence anyway. (Just don't forget to implement `hashCode()` along with it.)

Implementing `equals()` can be interesting. Hibernate wraps the actual object in a proxy (for various performance-enhancing reasons, like loading data on demand), so you need to factor in a class hierarchy for equivalency; don't check actual type equivalency but check if the types are *assignable* or *compatible*. It's also typically more efficient to use accessors in your `equals()` and `hashCode()` methods, as opposed to the actual fields.

Most IDEs will generate `equals()` and `hashCode()` to use the instance references themselves instead of accessors. This is pretty efficient for most objects and is correct behavior; after all, an accessor is usually a one-line method that returns a reference. However, an accessor doesn't *have* to be a one-line method; it might create a copy of the reference or calculate a value, both of which may or may not be expensive operations. In the case of Hibernate, though, calling the accessor also gives the proxy a chance to load the attribute from the database if it's not already present, which is an important, and useful, feature in most cases.

Listing 4-15 is an implementation of equals() and hashCode() for the SimpleObject entity we've been using, generated by IntelliJ IDEA[8] and modified to use accessors.

Listing 4-15. src/main/java/chapter04/model/SimpleObject.java

```
package chapter04.model;

import javax.persistence.*;

@Entity
public class SimpleObject {
  @Id
  @GeneratedValue(strategy = GenerationType.AUTO)
  Long id;
  @Column
  String key;
  @Column
  Long value;

  public SimpleObject() {
  }

  // mutators and accessors not included for brevity

  @Override
  public boolean equals(Object o) {
    if (this == o) return true;
    if (!(o instanceof SimpleObject)) return false;

    SimpleObject that = (SimpleObject) o;

    // we prefer the method versions of accessors, because of Hibernate's
    proxies.
    if (getId() != null
        ? !getId().equals(that.getId())
        : that.getId() != null)
      return false;
```

[8] Just in case you're unaware: IDEA is an IDE for Java. It has a free community edition and a commercial "ultimate" edition. It can be found at http://jetbrains.com/idea.

```
    if (getKey() != null
        ? !getKey().equals(that.getKey())
        : that.getKey() != null)
      return false;
    return getValue() != null
        ? getValue().equals(that.getValue())
        : that.getValue() == null;
  }

  @Override
  public int hashCode() {
    int result = getId() != null ? getId().hashCode() : 0;
    result = 31 * result + (getKey() != null ? getKey().hashCode() : 0);
    result = 31 * result + (getValue() != null ? getValue().hashCode() : 0);
    return result;
  }
}
```

The `TestSaveLoad.java` class shows off the various possibilities and conditions for equality, as shown in Listing 4-12, which we saw earlier.

Note that in that code, `o2` and `o3` are *equal* (they hold the same reference), while `o2` and `obj` are *equivalent* (the references are different but hold equivalent data). Again, you shouldn't rely on this in production code; object equivalence should always be tested with `equals()`.

Loading Entities

Hibernate's `Session` interface provides several `load()` methods for loading entities from your database. Each `load()` method requires the object's primary key as an identifier.[9]

[9] As usual, there's more to `load()` than we're discussing here. We'll add more methods to this list as we keep going through Hibernate's capabilities. We're keeping the list small for simplicity's sake.

In addition to the ID, Hibernate also needs to know which class or entity name to use to find the object with that ID. If you don't pass in the class type to `load()`, you'll also need to cast the result to the correct type. The basic `load()` methods are as follows:

```
public <T> T load(Class<T> theClass, Object id)
public Object load(String entityName, Object id)
public void load(Object object, Object id)
```

The last `load()` method takes an `Object` as the first argument. This object should be of the same class type as the object you would like loaded, and it should be empty (i.e., constructed but with values that lack meaning for your app - consider using an object constructed with a default constructor, for example). Hibernate will populate that object with the object you requested. While this is similar to other library calls in Java - namely, `java.util.List.toArray()` - this syntax can be without much of an actual benefit.

The other `load()` methods take a lock mode as an argument.[10] The lock mode specifies whether Hibernate should look into the cache for the object and which database lock level Hibernate should use for the row (or rows) of data that represent this object. The Hibernate developers claim that Hibernate will usually pick the correct lock mode for you, although we have seen situations in which it is important to manually choose the correct lock. In addition, your database may choose its own locking strategy - for instance, locking down an entire table rather than multiple rows within a table. In order of least restrictive to most restrictive, the various lock modes you can use are the following:[11]

- `NONE`: Uses no row-level locking and uses a cached object if available; this is the Hibernate default.
- `READ`: Prevents other `SELECT` queries from reading data that is in the middle of a transaction (and thus possibly invalid) until it is committed.
- `UPGRADE`: Uses the `SELECT FOR UPDATE` SQL syntax (or equivalent) to lock the data until the transaction is finished. (This is actually deprecated; use `PESSIMISTIC_WRITE` instead.)

---

[10] There are also forms that take `LockOption` arguments, but the `LockMode` form is described even in Hibernate's documentation as being a convenient way to specify lock options.

[11] You can see the documentation for `LockMode` at `https://docs.jboss.org/hibernate/orm/6.0/javadocs/org/hibernate/LockMode.html`.

- UPGRADE_NOWAIT: Uses the NOWAIT keyword (for Oracle), which returns an error immediately if there is another thread using that row; otherwise, this is similar to UPGRADE.
- UPGRADE_SKIPLOCKED: Skips locks for rows already locked by other updates, but otherwise this is similar to UPGRADE.
- OPTIMISTIC: This mode assumes that updates will not experience contention. The entity's contents will be verified near the transaction's end.
- OPTIMISTIC_FORCE_INCREMENT: This is like OPTIMISTIC, except it forces the version of the object to be incremented near the transaction's end.
- PESSIMISTIC_READ and PESSIMISTIC_WRITE: Both of these obtain a lock immediately on row access.
- PESSIMISTIC_FORCE_INCREMENT: This obtains the lock immediately on row access and also immediately updates the entity version.

All of these lock modes are static fields on the org.hibernate.LockMode enum. (We discuss locking and deadlocks with respect to transactions in more detail in Chapter 8.) The load() methods that use lock modes are as follows:

```
public <T> T load(Class<T> theClass, Object id, LockMode lockMode)
public Object load(String entityName, Object id, LockMode lockMode)
```

You should not use a load() method unless you are sure that the object exists. If you are not certain, then use one of the get() methods. The load() methods will throw an exception if the unique ID is not found in the database, whereas the get() methods will merely return a null reference.

Much like load(), the get() methods take an identifier and either an entity name or a class. There are also two get() methods that take a lock mode as an argument. The get() methods are as follows:

```
public <T> T get(Class<T> entityType, Object id)
public Object get(String entityName, Object id)
public <T> T get(Class<T> entityType, Object id, LockMode lockMode)
public Object get(String entityName, Object id, LockMode lockMode)
```

There are also load and get variants that use LockOption instead, but most users will end up specifying combinations that map to LockMode features.

If you need to determine the entity name for a given object (by default, this is the same as the class name), you can call the getEntityName() method on the Session interface, as follows:

```
public String getEntityName(Object object)
```

Using the get() and load() methods is straightforward. For instance, through a web application, someone may select a Supplier details page[12] for the supplier with the ID 1. If we are not sure that the supplier exists, we use the get() method, with which we could check for null, as follows:

```
// get an id from some other Java class, for instance, through a web
application
Supplier supplier = session.get(Supplier.class,id);
if (supplier == null) {
    System.out.println("Supplier not found for id " + id);
    return;
}
```

We can also retrieve the entity name from Hibernate and use it with either the get() or load() method. As stated, the load() method will throw an exception if an object with that ID cannot be found.

```
String entityName = session.getEntityName(supplier);
Supplier secondarySupplier = (Supplier) session.load(entityName,id);
```

It's also worth pointing out that you can query for an entity, which allows you to look for objects with a specific identifier, as well as sets of objects that match other criteria. There's also a Criteria API that allows you to use a declarative mechanism to build queries. These topics will be covered in later chapters.

[12] Not the java.util.function.Supplier but a *business entity* named Supplier.

Merging Entities

Merging is performed when you desire to have a detached entity changed to persistent state again, with the detached entity's changes migrated to (or overriding) the database. The method signatures for the merge operations are the following:

```
Object merge(Object object)
Object merge(String entityName, Object object)
```

Merging is the inverse of `refresh()`, which overrides the detached entity's values with the values from the database. First, let's build a utility method (in its own class) to help us validate an object's values.

Listing 4-16. `src/test/java/chapter04/general/ValidateSimpleObject.java`

```java
package chapter04.general;

import chapter04.model.SimpleObject;
import com.autumncode.hibernate.util.SessionUtil;
import org.hibernate.Session;

import static org.testng.Assert.assertEquals;

public class ValidateSimpleObject {
  public static SimpleObject validate(
      Long id,
      Long expectedValue,
      String expectedKey) {
    SimpleObject so = null;
    try (Session session = SessionUtil.getSession()) {
      // will throw an Exception if the id isn't found
      // in the database
      so = session.load(SimpleObject.class, id);

      assertEquals(so.getKey(), expectedKey);
      assertEquals(so.getValue(), expectedValue);
    }
```

```
    return so;
  }
}
```

Now we can take a look at MergeTest.

Listing 4-17. src/test/java/chapter04/general/MergeTest.java

```
package chapter04.general;

import chapter04.model.SimpleObject;
import com.autumncode.hibernate.util.SessionUtil;
import org.hibernate.Session;
import org.hibernate.Transaction;
import org.testng.annotations.Test;

public class MergeTest {
  @Test
  public void testMerge() {
    Long id;
    try (Session session = SessionUtil.getSession()) {
      Transaction tx = session.beginTransaction();

      SimpleObject simpleObject = new SimpleObject();

      simpleObject.setKey("testMerge");
      simpleObject.setValue(1L);

      session.save(simpleObject);

      id = simpleObject.getId();

      tx.commit();
    }

    SimpleObject so = ValidateSimpleObject.validate(id, 1L, "testMerge");

    // the 'so' object is detached here.
    so.setValue(2L);
```

```
    try (Session session = SessionUtil.getSession()) {
      // merge is potentially an update, so we need a TX
      Transaction tx = session.beginTransaction();

      session.merge(so);

      tx.commit();
    }

    ValidateSimpleObject.validate(id, 2L, "testMerge");
  }
}
```

This code creates an entity (a `SimpleObject`) and then saves it; it then verifies the object's values (with the `validate()` method from `ValidateSimpleObject`), which itself returns a detached entity. We update the detached object and `merge()` it – which should update the value as written in the database, which we verify.

Refreshing Entities

Hibernate provides a mechanism to refresh persistent objects from their database representation, overwriting the values that the in-memory object might have. Use one of the `refresh()` methods on the Session interface to refresh an instance of a persistent object, as follows:

```
public void refresh(Object object)
public void refresh(Object object, LockMode lockMode)
```

As stated, these methods will reload the properties of the object from the database, overwriting them; thus, `refresh()` is the inverse of `merge()`. Merging overrides the database with the values held by the previously transient object, and `refresh()` overrides the values in the transient object with the values in the database.

Hibernate usually does a very good job of taking care of this for you, so you do not have to use the `refresh()` method very often. There are instances where the Java object representation will be out of sync with the database representation of an object, however. For example, if you use SQL to update the database, Hibernate will not be aware that the representation changed. You do not need to use this method regularly, though.[13] Similar to the load() method, the refresh() method can take a lock mode as an argument; see the discussion of lock modes in the previous "Loading Entities" section.

Let's take a look at code in Listing 4-18 that uses refresh() - basically an inverse of the code we saw that demonstrated merge().

Listing 4-18. src/test/java/chapter04/general/RefreshTest.java

```
package chapter04.general;

import chapter04.model.SimpleObject;
import com.autumncode.hibernate.util.SessionUtil;
import org.hibernate.Session;
import org.hibernate.Transaction;
import org.testng.annotations.Test;

public class RefreshTest {
  @Test
  public void testRefresh() {
    Long id;
    try (Session session = SessionUtil.getSession()) {
      Transaction tx = session.beginTransaction();

      SimpleObject simpleObject = new SimpleObject();

      simpleObject.setKey("testMerge");
      simpleObject.setValue(1L);

      session.save(simpleObject);

      id = simpleObject.getId();

      tx.commit();
    }
```

[13] If you do find yourself using refresh() often, you may want to look for ways to eliminate the reasons you're having to use refresh(). It's not that refresh() is bad, it's that it's a corrective measure that should not have to be used very often.

```
    SimpleObject so = ValidateSimpleObject.validate(id, 1L, "testMerge");

    // the 'so' object is detached here
    so.setValue(2L);

    try (Session session = SessionUtil.getSession()) {
      // note that refresh is a read,
      // so no TX is necessary unless an update occurs later
      session.refresh(so);
    }

    ValidateSimpleObject.validate(id, 1L, "testMerge");
  }
}
```

This code is the same as the `merge()` test, with two changes: the first is that it calls `refresh()` rather than `merge()` (surprise!); and the other is that it expects the object's data to revert to the original state from the database, verifying that `refresh()` overrides the transient object's data.

In prior editions of this book, the `merge()` and `refresh()` tests – and the `validate()` method they use – were all in a single class. Here, they're split out, mostly because that allows full source listings to be used.

Updating Entities

Hibernate automatically persists changes made to persistent objects into the database.[14] If a property changes on a persistent object, the associated Hibernate session will queue the change for persistence to the database using SQL. From a developer's perspective, you do not have to do any work to store these changes, unless you would like to force Hibernate to commit all of its changes in the queue. You can also determine whether the session is dirty and changes need to be committed. When you commit a Hibernate transaction, Hibernate will take care of these details for you.

The `flush()` method forces Hibernate to flush the session, as follows:

```
public void flush() throws HibernateException
```

[14] We've mentioned Hibernate updating objects attached to a `Session` a few times now, along with test code.

You can determine if the session is dirty with the isDirty() method, as follows:

```
public boolean isDirty() throws HibernateException
```

You can also instruct Hibernate to use a flushing mode for the session with the `setHibernateFlushMode()`[15] method. The `getHibernateFlushMode()` method returns the flush mode for the current session, as follows:

```
public void setHibernateFlushMode(FlushMode flushMode)
public FlushMode getHibernateFlushMode()
```

The possible flush modes are the following:

- `ALWAYS`: Every query flushes the session before the query is executed. This is going to be very slow.
- `AUTO`: Hibernate manages the query flushing to guarantee that the data returned by a query is up to date.
- `COMMIT`: Hibernate flushes the session on transaction commits.
- `MANUAL`: Your application needs to manage the session flushing with the flush() method. Hibernate never flushes the session itself.

By default, Hibernate uses the `AUTO` flush mode. Generally, you should use transaction boundaries to ensure that appropriate flushing is taking place, rather than trying to "manually" flush at the appropriate times.

Deleting Entities

In order to allow convenient removal of entities from the database, the `Session` interface provides a `delete()` method, as follows:

```
public void delete(Object object)
public void delete (String entityName, Object object)
```

This method takes a persistent object as an argument. The argument can also be a transient object with the identifier set to the ID of the object that needs to be erased.

[15] The name for `setHibernateFlushMode()` has changed from earlier versions of Hibernate, to avoid the definition and meaning from the Java Persistence API standard.

In the simplest form, in which you are simply deleting an object with no associations to other objects, this is straightforward; but many objects do have associations with other objects. To allow for this, Hibernate can be configured to allow deletes to cascade from one object to its associated objects.

For instance, consider the situation in which you have a parent with a collection of child objects, and you would like to delete them all. The easiest way to handle this is to use the cascade attribute on the collection's element in the Hibernate mapping. If you set the cascade attribute to delete or all, the delete will be cascaded to all of the associated objects. Hibernate will take care of deleting these for you: deleting the parent erases the associated objects.

Hibernate also supports bulk deletes, where your application executes a DELETE HQL statement against the database. These are very useful for deleting more than one object at a time because each object does not need to be loaded into memory just to be deleted, as shown here:

```
session.createQuery("delete from User").executeUpdate();
```

Network traffic is greatly reduced, as are the memory requirements compared to those for individually issuing a `delete()` call against each entity identifier.

Bulk deletes do not cause cascade operations to be carried out. If cascade behavior is needed, you will need to carry out the appropriate deletions yourself (as you would with SQL) or use the session's `delete()` method.

Cascading Operations

When you perform one of the operations described in this chapter on an entity, the operations will not be performed on the associated entities unless you explicitly tell Hibernate to perform them. When operations affect associated entities, they're referred to as "cascading" operations, because actions flow from one object to another.

For example, the code in Listing 4-19 will fail when we try to commit the transaction, because the `Message` entity that is associated with the `Email` entity has not been persisted into the database, so the `Email` entity cannot be accurately represented (with its foreign key onto the appropriate message row) in its table.

Listing 4-19. A Failed `save()` Due to Cascading

```
try(Session session = SessionUtil.getSession()) {
  Transaction tx=session.beginTransaction();
  Email email = new Email("Email title");
  Message message = new Message("Message content");
  email.setMessage(message);
  message.setEmail(email);
  session.save(email);
  tx.commit();
}
```

Ideally, we would like the save operation to be propagated from the Email entity to its associated Message object. We do this by setting the cascade operations for the properties and fields of the entity (or assigning an appropriate default value for the entity as a whole). So, the code in Listing 4-19 will perform correctly if at least the `PERSIST` cascade operation is set for the Email entity's message property. The cascade types supported by the Java Persistence API are as follows:

- `PERSIST`
- `MERGE`
- `REFRESH`
- `REMOVE`
- `DETACH`
- `ALL`

It's worth pointing out that Hibernate has its own configuration options for cascading,[16] which represent a superset of these; however, we're largely following the Java Persistence API specification for modeling, as this will typically be more common by far than the Hibernate-specific modeling:[17]

[16] If you want to see the full list of Hibernate's cascading options, see `https://docs.jboss.org/hibernate/orm/6.0/javadocs/org/hibernate/annotations/CascadeType.html`.

[17] That's the thing about standards: they're standard.

- CascadeType.PERSIST means that save() or persist() operations cascade to related entities; for our Email and Message example, if Email's @OneToOne annotation includes PERSIST, saving the Email would save the Message as well.
- CascadeType.MERGE means that related entities are merged into managed state when the owning entity is merged.
- CascadeType.REFRESH does the same thing for the refresh() operation.
- CascadeType.REMOVE removes all related entities association with this setting when the owning entity is deleted.
- CascadeType.DETACH detaches all related entities if a manual detach were to occur.
- CascadeType.ALL is shorthand for all of the cascade operations.

The cascade configuration option accepts an array of CascadeType references; thus, to include only refreshes and merges in the cascade operation for a one-to-one relationship, you might see the following:

```
@OneToOne(cascade={CascadeType.REFRESH, CascadeType.MERGE})
EntityType otherSide;
```

There's one more cascading operation that's not part of the normal set, called orphan removal, which removes an owned object from the database when it's removed from its owning relationship. However, it's not recommended to use this as a cascade type; it's recommended instead to use an annotation option, orphanRemoval, so that the annotation for @OneToMany might look like OneToMany(orphanRemoval=true) instead.

Let's suppose we have a Library entity, which contains a list of Book entities. Here are our listings for Library and Book.

Listing 4-20. src/main/java/chapter04/orphan/Library.java

```
package chapter04.orphan;

import javax.persistence.*;
import java.util.ArrayList;
import java.util.List;
```

```
@Entity
public class Library {
  @Id
  @GeneratedValue(strategy = GenerationType.AUTO)
  Long id;
  @Column
  String name;
  @OneToMany(orphanRemoval = true, mappedBy = "library")
  List<Book> books = new ArrayList<>();

  public Library() {
  }

  public Long getId() {
    return id;
  }

  public void setId(Long id) {
    this.id = id;
  }

  public String getName() {
    return name;
  }

  public void setName(String name) {
    this.name = name;
  }

  public List<Book> getBooks() {
    return books;
  }

  public void setBooks(List<Book> books) {
    this.books = books;
  }
}
```

Listing 4-21. src/main/java/chapter04/orphan/Book.java

```
package chapter04.orphan;

import javax.persistence.*;

@Entity
public class Book {
  @Id
  @GeneratedValue(strategy = GenerationType.AUTO)
  Long id;
  @Column
  String title;
  @ManyToOne
  Library library;

  public Book() {
  }

  public Long getId() {
    return id;
  }

  public void setId(Long id) {
    this.id = id;
  }

  public String getTitle() {
    return title;
  }

  public void setTitle(String title) {
    this.title = title;
  }

  public Library getLibrary() {
    return library;
  }
```

```
  public void setLibrary(Library library) {
    this.library = library;
  }
}
```

Note the use of orphanRemoval in the @OneToMany annotation. Now let's take a look at some test code, which will be fairly verbose since we need to validate our initial dataset, change it, and then revalidate; see Listing 4-22.

Listing 4-22. src/test/java/chapter04/orphan/OrphanRemovalTest.java

```
package chapter04.orphan;

import com.autumncode.hibernate.util.SessionUtil;
import org.hibernate.Session;
import org.hibernate.Transaction;
import org.hibernate.query.Query;
import org.testng.annotations.Test;

import java.util.List;

import static org.testng.Assert.assertEquals;
import static org.testng.Assert.assertNull;

public class OrphanRemovalTest {
  @Test
  public void orphanRemovalTest() {
    Long id = createLibrary();

    try (Session session = SessionUtil.getSession()) {
      Transaction tx = session.beginTransaction();

      Library library = session.load(Library.class, id);
      assertEquals(library.getBooks().size(), 3);

      library.getBooks().remove(0);
      assertEquals(library.getBooks().size(), 2);

      tx.commit();
    }
```

```
    try (Session session = SessionUtil.getSession()) {
      Transaction tx = session.beginTransaction();

      Library l2 = session.load(Library.class, id);
      assertEquals(l2.getBooks().size(), 2);

      Query<Book> query = session
        .createQuery("from Book b", Book.class);
      List<Book> books = query.list();
      assertEquals(books.size(), 2);

      tx.commit();
    }
  }

  @Test
  public void deleteLibrary() {
    Long id = createLibrary();
    try (Session session = SessionUtil.getSession()) {
      Transaction tx = session.beginTransaction();
      Library library = session.load(Library.class, id);
      assertEquals(library.getBooks().size(), 3);
      session.delete(library);
      tx.commit();
    }

    try (Session session = SessionUtil.getSession()) {
      Transaction tx = session.beginTransaction();
      Library library = session.get(Library.class, id);
      assertNull(library);
      List<Book> books=session
        .createQuery("from Book b", Book.class)
        .list();
      assertEquals(books.size(), 0);
    }
  }
```

```
  private Long createLibrary() {
    Library library = null;
    try (Session session = SessionUtil.getSession()) {
      Transaction tx = session.beginTransaction();

      library = new Library();
      library.setName("orphanLib");
      session.save(library);

      Book book = new Book();
      book.setLibrary(library);
      book.setTitle("book 1");
      session.save(book);
      library.getBooks().add(book);

      book = new Book();
      book.setLibrary(library);
      book.setTitle("book 2");
      session.save(book);
      library.getBooks().add(book);

      book = new Book();
      book.setLibrary(library);
      book.setTitle("book 3");
      session.save(book);
      library.getBooks().add(book);

      tx.commit();
    }

    return library.getId();
  }
}
```

What this does is not complicated: it builds a library with three books associated with it. Then it loads the library from the database, validates that it looks like it's supposed to ("a library with three books"), and removes one from the library. It does not delete the Book entity being removed; it only removes it from the Library's set of books, which makes it an orphan.

After committing the Library object's new state – via `tx.commit()` – we reload the Library from the database and validate that it now has only two books. The book we removed is gone from the library.

That doesn't mean it's actually been removed, though, so we then query the database for all `Book` entities to see if we have two or three. We should have only two, and so it is. We removed the orphan object when updating the library.

If you wanted the book to be present *after* removal, to be assigned to some other library, perhaps, then the `orphanRemoval` is incorrect; you'd *want* the book to be able to exist as an orphan.

Lazy Loading, Proxies, and Collection Wrappers

Consider the quintessential Internet web application: the online store. The store maintains a catalog of products. At the crudest level, this can be modeled as a catalog entity managing a series of product entities. In a large store, there may be tens of thousands of products grouped into various overlapping categories.

When a customer visits the store, the catalog must be loaded from the database. We probably don't want the implementation to load every single one of the entities representing the tens of thousands of products to be loaded into memory. For a sufficiently large retailer, this might not even be possible, given the amount of physical memory available on the machine. Even if this were possible, it would probably cripple the performance of the site.

Instead, we want only the catalog to load, possibly with the categories as well. Only when the user drills down into the categories should a subset of the products in that category be loaded from the database.

To manage this problem, Hibernate provides a facility called *lazy loading*. When enabled (this is the default using XML mappings, but not when using annotations, which default to *eager loading*), an entity's associated entities will be loaded only when they are directly requested, which can provide quite measurable performance benefits, as can be imagined. For example, the following code loads only a single entity from the database:

```
Email email = session.get(Email.class,new Integer(42));
```

However, if an association of the class is accessed, and lazy loading is in effect, the association is pulled from the database only as needed. For instance, in the following snippet, the associated Message object will be loaded since it is explicitly referenced:

```
// surely this email is about the meaning of life, the universe, and
everything
Email email = session.get(Email.class,new Integer(42));
String text = email.getMessage().getContent();
```

The simplest way that Hibernate can force this behavior upon your entities is by providing a proxy implementation of them.[18] Hibernate intercepts calls to the entity by substituting a proxy for it derived from the entity's class. Where the requested information is missing, it will be loaded from the database before control is given to the parent entity's implementation. Where the association is represented as a collection class, a wrapper (essentially a proxy for the collection, rather than for the entities that it contains) is created and substituted for the original collection.

Hibernate can only access the database via a session. If an entity is detached from the session when we try to access an association (via a proxy or collection wrapper) that has not yet been loaded, Hibernate throws a `LazyInitializationException`. The cure is to ensure either that the entity is made persistent again by attaching it to a session or that all of the fields that will be required are accessed before the entity is detached from the session.

If you need to determine whether a proxy, a persistence collection, or an attribute has been lazy loaded, you can call the `isInitialized(Object proxy)` and `isPropertyInitialized(Object proxy, String propertyName)` methods on the `org.hibernate.Hibernate` class. You can also force a proxy or collection to become fully populated by calling the `initialize(Object proxy)` method on the `org.hibernate.Hibernate` class. If you initialize a collection using this method, you will also need to initialize each object contained in the collection, as only the collection is guaranteed to be initialized.

---

[18] Proxies are why we use accessors in our `equals()` and `hashCode()` examples. Using the accessors gives the proxy a chance to load information if it's needed.

Querying Objects

Hibernate provides several different ways to query for objects stored in the database. You can obviously use the identifier of an object to load it from the database if you know the identifier already. The Criteria Query API is a Java API for constructing a query as an object. HQL is an object-oriented query language, similar to SQL, which you may use to retrieve objects that match the query. We discuss these further in Chapters 9 and 10. Hibernate provides a way to execute SQL directly (via a "native query") against the database to retrieve objects, should you have legacy applications that use SQL or if you need to use SQL features that are not supported through HQL and the Criteria Query API.

Summary

Hibernate provides a simple API for creating, retrieving, updating, and deleting objects from a relational database through the Session interface. Understanding the differences between transient, persistent, and detached objects in Hibernate will allow you to understand how changes to the objects update the database tables.

We have touched upon the need to create mappings to correlate the database tables with the fields and properties of the Java objects that you want to persist. The next chapter covers these in detail, and it discusses why they are required and what they can contain.

CHAPTER 5

An Overview of Mapping

The purpose of Hibernate is to allow you to treat your database as if it stores Java objects. However, in practice, relational databases do not store objects – they store data in tables and columns. Unfortunately, there is no simple way to consistently correlate the data stored in a relational database with the data represented by Java objects.[1]

The difference between an object-oriented association and a relational one is fundamental. Consider a simple class to represent a user and another to represent an email address, as shown in Figure 5-1.

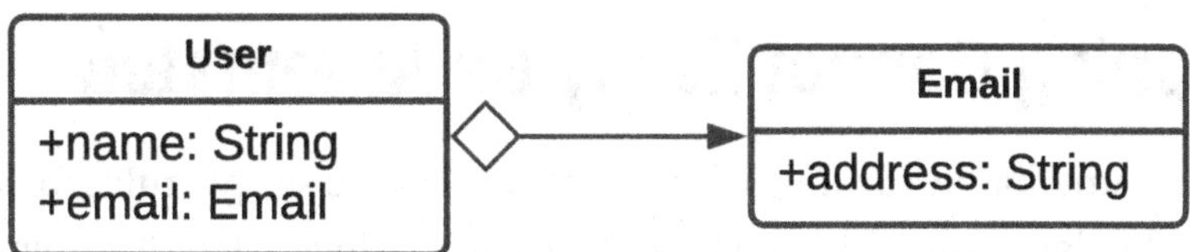

Figure 5-1. *A simple entity relationship diagram*

Here, `User` objects contain fields referring to `Email` objects. The association has a direction; given a `User` object, you can determine its associated `Email` object. For example, consider Listing 5-1.

Listing 5-1. Acquiring the `Email` Object from `User`

```
User user = getUserSomehow();
Email email = user.email;
```

The reverse, however, is not true. The natural way to represent this relationship in the database, as illustrated in Figure 5-2, is superficially similar.

[1] If there were simple, consistent, and accurate ways to correlate object structures and relational databases, books like this one probably wouldn't exist.

J. B. Ottinger et al., *Beginning Hibernate 6*, https://doi.org/10.1007/978-1-4842-7337-1_5

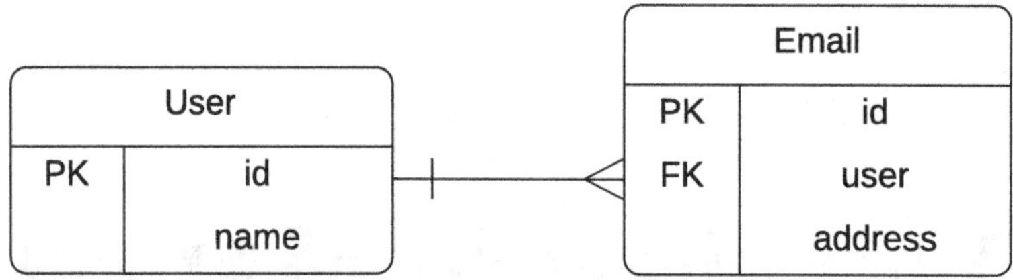

Figure 5-2. *A relational association*

Despite that similarity, the direction of the association is effectively reversed. Given an `Email` row, you can immediately determine which user row it belongs to in the database; this relationship is mandated by a foreign key constraint. It is possible to reverse the relationship in the database world through the suitable use of SQL - another difference.

Given the differences between the two worlds, it is necessary to manually intervene to determine how your Java classes should be represented in database tables.

Why Mapping Cannot Easily Be Automated

It is not always immediately obvious why you cannot create simple rules for storing your Java objects in the database so that they can be easily retrieved. For example, the most immediately obvious rule would be that a Java class must correlate to a single table. For example, instances of the `User` class defined in Figure 5-2 could surely be represented by a simple table like the one for a user, shown in Listing 5-2.

Listing 5-2. A Simple `User` Class with a Password

```
public class User {
  String name;
  String password;
}
```

And indeed it could, but some questions present themselves:

- How many rows should you end up with if you save a user twice?
- Are you allowed to save a user without a name?
- Are you allowed to save a user without a password?

When you start to think about classes that refer to other classes, there are additional questions to consider. Have a look at the Customer and Email classes shown in Listing 5-3.

Listing 5-3. Customer and Email Classes

```
public class Customer {
  int customerId;
  int customerReference;
  String name;
  Email email;
}

public class Email {
  String address;
}
```

Based on this, the following questions arise:

- Is a unique customer identified by its customer ID or its customer reference?
- Can an email address be used by more than one customer?
- Can a customer have more than one email ID?
- Should the relationship be represented in the Customer table?
- Should the relationship be represented in the Email table?
- Should the relationship be represented in some third (link) table?

Depending upon the answers to these questions, your database tables could vary considerably. You could take a stab at a reasonable design, such as that given in Figure 5-3, based upon your intuition about likely scenarios in the real world.

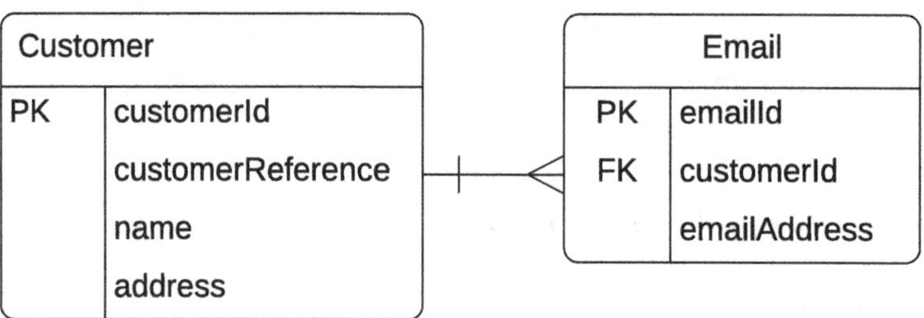

Figure 5-3. *A relational association*

Here, we have a table in which a customer has an artificial customer Id; email addresses can be used only by a single customer, and the relationship is maintained by the `Email` table.

It's entirely possible (and actually fairly common) to have tools like JBoss Tools or IDEA Ultimate generate Hibernate entities from database tables, because the tooling has access to the actual database structure; a tool can see that `customerId` is a foreign key for `Email` expecting a corresponding value in the `Customer` table, and can figure out decent names (the column names) that fit what might be an idiomatic mapping.

But Hibernate doesn't mandate any of that; you can have multiple layers of schema relationships that Hibernate **can** map but that a tool might design… badly.

Primary Keys

Most relational databases that provide SQL access are prepared to accept tables that have no predefined primary key. Hibernate is not so tolerant; even if your table has been created without a primary key, Hibernate will require you to specify one. This often seems perverse to users who are familiar with SQL and databases but not familiar with ORM tools. As such, let's examine in more depth the problems that arise when there's no primary key.

To begin, without a primary key it is impossible to (easily) uniquely identify a row in a table. For example, consider Table 5-1.

Table 5-1. *A Table in Which Rows Cannot Easily Be Uniquely Identified*

User	Age
dminter	35
dminter	40
dminter	55
dminter	40
jlinwood	57

This table clearly contains information about users and their respective ages. However, there are four users with the same identifier (*Dave* Minter, *Denise* Minter, *Daniel* Minter, and *Dashiel* Minter). There is probably a way of distinguishing them somewhere else in the system – perhaps by an email address or a user number. But if, for example, you want to know the age of Dashiel Minter with user ID 32, there is no way to obtain it from Table 5-1.

While Hibernate will not let you omit the primary key, it will permit you to form the primary key from a collection of columns, forming a "composite key." For example, Table 5-2 could be identified with a composite key of `usernumber` and `user`.

Table 5-2. *A Table in Which a Composite Primary Key Might Exist*

User	Usernumber	Age
dminter	1	35
dminter	2	40
dminter	3	55
dminter	32	40
jlinwood	1	57

Neither `User` nor `Usernumber` contains unique entries, but in combination they uniquely identify the age of a particular user, and so they are acceptable to Hibernate as a primary key.

Why does Hibernate need to uniquely identify entries when SQL doesn't? Because Hibernate is representing Java objects, which are always uniquely identifiable. The classic mistake made by new Java developers is to compare strings using the == operator instead of the `equals()` method. You can distinguish between references to two String objects that represent the same text and two references to the same `String` object.[2] SQL has no such obligation, and there are arguably cases in which it is desirable to give up the ability to make the distinction.

For example, if Hibernate could not uniquely identify an object with a primary key, then the following code could have several possible outcomes in the underlying table:

```
String customer = getCustomerFromHibernate("dcminter");
customer.setAge(10);
saveCustomerToHibernate(customer);
```

Let's say the table originally contains the data shown in Table 5-3.

Table 5-3. *Updating an Ambiguous Table*

User	Age
dminter	35
dminter	40

Which of the following should be contained in the resulting table?

- A single row for the user dcminter, with the age set to 10
- Two rows for the user, with both ages set to 10
- Two rows for the user, with one age set to 10 and the other to 40 (update the first `dminter` record)

[2] When comparing objects for equivalence, use `equals()`. It's like comparing two doorknobs: are the two *like* each other, or are they the *same doorknob*? The `equals()` method checks to see if they're alike. The == operator checks to see if they're the same actual doorknob.

- Two rows for the user, with one age set to 10 and the other to 30 (update the *second* `dminter` record)
- Three rows for the user, with one age set to 10 and the others to 35 and 40 (create a new `dminter` record altogether)

There are a lot of assumptions about what our mythical `saveCustomerToHibernate()` is doing here, some of which sound absolutely mad on the surface... but the idea being considered here is that if we say to "set *the* age of *a* record to a given value," what might the state of the database be?

In short, the Hibernate developers made a decision to enforce the use of primary keys when creating mappings so that this problem does not arise. Hibernate does provide facilities that will allow you to work around this if it is absolutely necessary (you can create views or stored procedures to "fake" the appropriate key, or you can use conventional JDBC to access the table data), but when using Hibernate, it is always more desirable to work with tables that have correctly specified primary keys, if at all possible.

Lazy Loading

When you load classes into memory from the database, you don't necessarily want *all* of the information to actually be loaded. To take a (fairly) extreme example, loading a list of emails should not cause the full body text and attachments of every email to be loaded into memory.

First, the full content of the emails might demand more memory than is actually available.

Second, even if the emails fit in memory, it would probably take a long time for all of this information to be obtained. (Remember, data normally goes from a database process to an application over the network, and even if your network is fast, data still takes time to transfer.)

If you were to tackle this problem in SQL, you would probably select a subset of the appropriate fields for the query to obtain the list, or limit the range of the data. Here's an example of selecting a subset of data:

```
SELECT from, to, date, subject FROM email WHERE username = 'dcminter';
```

Hibernate will allow you to fashion queries that are rather similar to this, but it also offers a more flexible approach, known as lazy loading. Certain relationships can be marked as being "lazy," and they will not be loaded from the database until they are actually required.

The default in Hibernate is that classes (including collections like Set and List) should be lazily loaded. For example, when an instance of the User class given in the next listing is loaded from the database, the only fields initialized immediately after load will be userId and username:[3]

```
public class User {
    int userId;
    String username;
    EmailAddress emailAddress;
    Set<Role> roles;
}
```

With this definition, the appropriate objects for emailAddress and roles will be loaded from the database if and when they are accessed, provided the session is still active.

This is the default behavior only; mappings can be used to specify which classes and fields should behave in this way.

Associations

When we looked at why the mapping process could not be automated, we discussed classes that might look like this, in Java:

```
public class Customer {
    int customerId;
    int customerReference;
    String name;
    StreetAddress address;
}
```

[3] There are conditions for this. In most of the examples we've seen, where the majority of columns are accessed directly via their attribute references, lazy loading is very much the norm regardless of type. When in doubt, specify and test.

```
public class StreetAddress {
   String address;
}
```

We also gave the following five questions that it raised:

- Is a unique customer identified by its customer ID or its customer reference?
- Can a given email address be used by more than one customer?
- Should the relationship be represented in the Customer table?
- Should the relationship be represented in the Email table?
- Should the relationship be represented in some third (link) table?

The first question can be answered simply; it depends on what column you specify as the primary key. The remaining four questions are related, and their answers depend on the object relationships. Furthermore, if your Customer class represents the relationship with the EmailAddress using a Collection class or an array, it would be possible for a user to have multiple email addresses:[4]

```
public class Customer {
   int customerId;
   int customerReference;
   String name;
   Set<EmailAddress> email;
}
```

So, you should add another question: Can a customer have more than one email address? The set could contain a single entry, so you can't automatically infer that this is the case.

The key questions from the previous options are as follows:

- Q1: Can an email address belong to more than one user?
- Q2: Can a customer have more than one email address?

[4] In fact, our ERD indicated that a `Customer` could in fact have multiple email addresses, with the crow's feet; the "crow's foot" on the `Email` table indicates a one-to-many relationship.

The answers to these questions can be formed into a truth table, as shown in Table 5-4.

Table 5-4. *Deciding the Cardinality of an Entity Relationship*

Q1 Answer	Q2 Answer	Relationship Between `Customer` and `Email`
No	No	One-to-one
Yes	No	Many-to-one
No	Yes	One-to-many
Yes	Yes	Many-to-many

These are the four ways in which the cardinality[5] of the relationship between the objects can be expressed. Each relationship can then be represented within the mapping table(s) in various ways.

The One-to-One Association

A one-to-one association between classes can be represented in a variety of ways. At its simplest, the properties of both classes are maintained in the same table. For example, a one-to-one association between a User and an Email class might be represented as a single table, as in Table 5-5.

Table 5-5. *A Combined* `User/Email` *Table*

ID	Username	Email
1	dminter	dminter@example.com
2	jlinwood	jlinwood@example.com
3	jbo	whackadoodle@example.com

[5] *Cardinality* refers to numbering, so cardinality in relationships indicates how many of each participant is being referred to by either side of the relationship.

Alternatively, the entities can be maintained in distinct tables with identical primary keys (as shown here) or with a key maintained from one of the entities into the other, as in Tables 5-6 and 5-7.

Table 5-6. *The `User` Table in a One-to-One*

ID	Username
1	dminter
2	jlinwood
3	jbo

Table 5-7. *The `Email` Table in a One-to-One*

ID	Email
1	dminter@example.com
2	jlinwood@example.com
3	whackadoodle@example.com

It is possible to create a mandatory foreign key relationship from one of the entities to the other, but this should not be applied in both directions because a circular dependency would then be created. It is also possible to omit the foreign key relationships entirely and rely on Hibernate to manage the key selection and assignment.

Use foreign key relationships! If your dataset is very, very small, they may not help much – but in any real database environment, they can prevent some really frustrating delays in processing data.

If it is not appropriate for the tables to share primary keys, then a foreign key relationship between the two tables can be maintained, with a `UNIQUE` constraint applied to the foreign key column. For example, reusing the `User` table we just saw, the `Email` table can be suitably populated, as shown in Table 5-8.

Table 5-8. The `Email` Table in a One-to-One with a Secondary Foreign Key

ID	UserID	Email
34	1	dminter@example.com
37	2	jlinwood@example.com
639	3	whackadoodle@example.com

This has the advantage that the association can easily be changed from one-to-one to many-to-one by removing the unique constraint on the foreign key column.

The One-to-Many and Many-to-One Associations

A one-to-many association (or from the perspective of the other class, a many-to-one association) can most simply be represented by the use of a foreign key, with no additional constraints.

The relationship can also be maintained by the use of a link table. This will maintain a foreign key into each of the associated tables, which will itself form the primary key of the link table. A link table is effectively mandatory for many-to-many relationships, but for relationships that have a cardinality of one on one side of the relationship, link tables tend to be used when the relationship has a state that isn't reflected in the objects themselves (like where in a `List` something might be), or when the objects should not have an explicit reference to another entity.

Table 5-9. A Simple User Table

ID	Username
1	dcminter
2	jlinwood

Table 5-10. A Simple Email Table

ID	Email
1	dcminter@example.com
2	dave@example.com
3	jlinwood@example.com
4	jeff@example.com

Table 5-11. A Link Table Joining Email and User in a 1:M Relationship

UserID	EmailId
1	1
1	2
2	3
2	4

Additional columns can be added to the link table to maintain information on the ordering of the entities in the association.

A unique constraint must be applied to the "one" side of the relationship (the `UserID` column of the User-Email table in Table 5-11); otherwise, the link table can represent the set of all possible relationships between `User` and `Email` entities, which is a many-to-many set association.

The Many-to-Many Association

As noted at the end of the previous section, if a unique constraint is not applied to the "one" end of the relationship when using a link table, it becomes a limited sort of many-to-many relationship. All of the possible combinations of `User` and `Email` can be represented, but it is not possible for the same user to have the same email address entity associated twice, because that would require the compound primary key to be duplicated.

If instead of using the foreign keys together as a compound primary key, we give the link table its own primary key (usually a surrogate key), the association between the two entities can be transformed into a full many-to-many relationship, as shown in Table 5-12.

Table 5-12. *A Many-to-Many User/Email Link Table*

ID	UserID	EmailId
1	1	1
2	1	2
3	1	3
4	1	4
5	2	1
6	2	2

Table 5-12 might describe a situation in which the user `dcminter` receives all email sent to any of the four addresses, whereas `jlinwood` receives only email sent to his own accounts. (The "EmailId" is the incoming email address, and both user ids have references to email addresses numbered 1 and 2; only `dcminter` has references for email addresses with ids 3 and 4.)

When the link table has its own independent primary key, thought should be given to the possibility that a new class needs to be created to represent the contents of the link table as an entity in its own right. This allows you to embed an additional state with the linking object (such as "how many times was this email address used?").

Applying Mappings to Associations

The mappings are applied to express the various different ways of forming associations in the underlying tables; there is no absolutely correct way to represent them.[6]

[6] The fact that there's no perfect, correct way to generalize relationships between entities is why otherwise fantastic tools like Hibernate haven't replaced good database analysts.

In addition to the basic choice of approach to take, the mappings are used to specify the minutiae of the tables' representations. While Hibernate tends to use sensible default values when possible, it is often desirable to override these. For example, the foreign key names generated automatically by Hibernate will be effectively random, whereas an informed developer can apply a name (e.g., `FK_USER_EMAIL_LINK`) to aid in the debugging of constraint violations at runtime.

Other Supported Features

While Hibernate can determine a lot of sensible default values for the mappings, most of these can be overridden by one or both of the annotation- and XML-based[7] approaches. Some apply directly to mappings; others, such as the foreign key names, are really only pertinent when the mapping is used to create the database schema. Lastly, some mappings can also provide a place to configure some features that are perhaps not "mappings" in the purest sense.

The final sections of this chapter discuss the features that Hibernate supports in addition to those already mentioned.

Specification of (Database) Column Types and Sizes

Java provides the primitive types and allows user declaration of interfaces and classes to extend these. Relational databases generally provide a small subset of "standard" types and then offer additional proprietary types.

Restricting yourself to the proprietary types will still cause problems, as there are only approximate correspondences between these and the Java primitive types.

A typical example of a problematic type is `java.lang.String` (treated by Hibernate as if it were a primitive type since it is used so frequently), which by default will be mapped to a fixed-size character data database type. Typically, the database would perform poorly if a character field of unlimited size was chosen, but lengthy `String` fields will be truncated as they are persisted into the database. In most databases, you

[7] We haven't actually spent much time in XML configuration for a very good reason: most people don't use it in the real world unless they absolutely have to. It's also excessively verbose, especially compared to the annotations.

would choose to represent a lengthy `String` field as a `TEXT`, `CLOB`, or long `VARCHAR` type (assuming the database supports the specific type). This is one of the reasons why Hibernate can't do all of the mapping for you and why you still need to understand some database fundamentals when you create an application that uses ORM.

By specifying mapping details, the developer can make appropriate trade-offs among storage space, performance, and fidelity to the original Java representation.

The Mapping of Inheritance Relationships to the Database

There is no SQL standard for representing inheritance relationships for the data in tables; and while some database implementations provide a proprietary syntax for this, not all do. Hibernate offers several configurable ways in which to represent inheritance relationships, and the mapping permits users to select a suitable approach for their model.

Primary Key

As stated earlier in this chapter (in the section entitled "Primary Keys," of all things), Hibernate demands that a primary key be used to identify entities. The choice of a surrogate key, a key chosen from the business data, and/or a compound primary key can be made via configuration.

When a surrogate key is used, Hibernate also permits the key generation technique to be selected from a range of techniques that vary in portability and efficiency. (This was shown in Chapter 4, in the "Identifiers" section.)

The Use of SQL Formula–Based Properties

It is sometimes desirable that a property of an entity be maintained not as data directly stored in the database but, rather, as a function performed on that data - for example, a subtotal field should not be managed directly by the Java logic, but instead be maintained as an aggregate function of some other property.

Mandatory and Unique Constraints

As well as the implicit constraints of a primary or foreign key relationship, you can specify that a field must not be duplicated - for example, a `username` field should often be unique.[8]

Fields can also be made mandatory - for example, requiring a message entity to have both a subject and message text. The generated database schema will contain corresponding `NOT NULL` and `UNIQUE` constraints so that it is very, very difficult to corrupt the table with invalid data (rather, the application logic will throw an exception if any attempt to do so is made).

Note that primary keys are implicitly both mandatory and unique.

Summary

This chapter has given you an overview of the reason why mappings are needed and what features they support beyond these absolute requirements. It has discussed the various types of associations and the circumstances under which you would choose to use them. The next chapter looks at how mappings are specified.

[8] As your author rereads "a `username` field should often be unique," the thought occurs: when would one *ever* want that to not be the case?

CHAPTER 6

Mapping with Annotations

In Chapter 5, we discussed the need to create mappings between the database model and the object model. Mappings can be created in two different ways: via inline annotations (as we've done through the book so far) or as separate XML files in one of two primary formats (Hibernate's internal XML format and JPA's mapping format, both of which have value but are not suggested for most applications).

The XML-based mapping is rarely used outside of situations where mapping an object model to a preexisting schema is required; even then, adept use of the annotations can match the XML configuration's features.

Creating Hibernate Mappings with Annotations

Prior to the inline annotations, the only way to create mappings was through XML files – although tools from Hibernate and third-party projects[1] allowed part or all of these to be generated from Java source code. Although using annotations is the newest way to define mappings, it is not automatically the best way to do so. We will briefly discuss the drawbacks and benefits of annotations before discussing when and how to apply them.

The Drawbacks of Annotations

If you are upgrading from an earlier Hibernate environment, you may already have XML-based mapping files to support your code base. All else being equal, you will not want to reexpress these mappings using annotations just for the sake of doing so.

[1] Most IDEs can generate XML mappings for you; also, see JBoss Tools (`https://tools.jboss.org/`), XDoclet (`http://xdoclet.sourceforge.net/xdoclet/index.html`), and MyEclipse (`www.genuitec.com/products/myeclipse/`) for other possibilities. With that said, most people prefer the annotations, for good reason.

J. B. Ottinger et al., *Beginning Hibernate 6*, https://doi.org/10.1007/978-1-4842-7337-1_6

If you are migrating from a legacy environment, you may not want to alter the preexisting POJO source code, lest you contaminate known good code with possible bugs.[2] Annotations are compiled into the class files, after all, and therefore might be considered to be changes to source or delivered artifacts.

If you do not have the source code to your POJOs (because it was generated by an automated tool or something similar), you may prefer the use of external XML-based mappings to the decompilation of class files to obtain Java source code for alteration.

Maintaining the mapping information as external XML files allows that mapping information to be modified to reflect business changes or schema alterations without forcing you to rebuild the application as a whole. However, building an application when you have a build system in place (Maven or Gradle, along with any continuous integration tools you might have) is usually pretty easy, so this isn't much of a convincing argument either way.

The Benefits of Annotations

Having considered the drawbacks, there are some powerful benefits to using annotations.

First, and perhaps most persuasively, we find annotations-based mappings to be far more intuitive than their XML-based alternatives, as they are immediately in the source code along with the properties with which they are associated. Most coders tend to prefer the annotations because fewer files have to be kept synchronized with each other.

Partly as a result of this, annotations are less verbose than their XML equivalents, as evidenced by the contrast between Listings 6-1 and 6-2, both of which would create a `Sample` entity in the database. The XML here maps directly to the annotations in use.

[2] There's probably value in creating tests for your object model, which would, one hopes, eliminate this as a concern, but there's no point in creating extra work for its own sake.

Listing 6-1. A Minimal Class Mapped with Annotations

```
import javax.persistence.* ;
@Entity
public class Sample {
  @Id
  @GeneratedValue(strategy = GenerationType.IDENTITY)
  public Integer id;
  public String name;
}
```

Listing 6-2. An Equivalent Mapping with XML

```
<?xml version='1.0' encoding='utf-8'?>
<!DOCTYPE
   hibernate-mapping
   PUBLIC
   "-//Hibernate/Hibernate Mapping DTD//EN"
   "http://hibernate.sourceforge.net/hibernate-mapping-3.0.dtd">
<hibernate-mapping default-access="field">
   <class name="Sample">
      <id type="int" column="id">
         <generator class="native"/>
      </id>
      <property name="name" type="string"/>
   </class>
</hibernate-mapping>
```

Some of the latter listing's verbosity is in the nature of XML itself (the tag names and the boilerplate document type declaration), and some of it is due to the closer integration of annotations with the source code. Here, for example, the XML file must explicitly declare that field access is used in place of property access (i.e., the fields are accessed directly rather than through their get/set methods); but the annotation infers this from the fact that it has been applied to the `id` field rather than the `getId()` method.

Hibernate uses and supports the JPA 2 persistence annotations. If you elect not to use Hibernate-specific features in your code and annotations, you will have the freedom to deploy your entities to environments using other ORM tools that support JPA 2.

Finally – and perhaps a minor point – because the annotations are compiled directly into the appropriate class files, there is less risk that a missing or stale mapping file will cause problems at deployment (this point will perhaps prove most persuasive to those who already have some experience with this hazard of the XML technique).

Choosing Which Mapping Mechanism to Use

In general, prefer annotations; the annotations themselves are portable across JPA implementations, and they're well known. Tools can create the annotated source code directly from a database, so synchronization is less of an issue than it could be, even with a preexisting schema.

The XML mapping can be done either in Hibernate's proprietary format or JPA's standard XML configuration, which is similar but not identical; if you somehow find XML to be a preferable configuration format, you're probably better off using the XML format from the industry standard JPA configuration.[3]

JPA 2 Persistence Annotations

When you develop using annotations, you start with a Java class and then annotate the source code listing with metadata notations. Hibernate uses reflection at runtime to read the annotations and apply the mapping information. If you want to use the Hibernate tools to generate your database schema, you must first compile your entity classes containing their annotations. In this section, we are going to introduce the significant core of the JPA 2 annotations alongside a simple set of classes to illustrate how they are applied.

The most common annotations, just for reference's sake, are `@Entity`, `@Id`, and `@Column`; other common ones we'll encounter often are `@GenerationStrategy` (associated with `@Id`) and the association-related annotations like `@OneToOne`, `@ManyToOne`, `@OneToMany`, and `@ManyToMany`.

[3] The JPA configuration was largely derived from Hibernate's configuration specification, which preceded JPA.

The set of example classes represents a publisher's catalog of books. You start with a single class, Book, which has no annotations or mapping information. We'll add Author as an entity as we go, too. For the purposes of this example, you do not have an existing database schema to work with, so you need to define your relational database schema as you go.

The Book class is very simple, as we get started. It has two fields, title and pages, and an identifier, id, which is an integer. The title is a String object, and pages is an integer. As we go through this example, we will add annotations, fields, and methods to the Book class. The complete source code listings for the Book and Author classes are given at the end of this chapter; the source files for the rest are available in the source code download for this chapter on the Apress website (www.apress.com).

Listing 6-3 gives a basic shell for source code of the Book class, in its unannotated form, as a starting point for the example.

Listing 6-3. src/main/java/chapter06/primarykey/before/Book.java

```
package chapter06.primarykey.before;

public class Book {
  String title;
  int pages;
  int id;

  public Book() {
  }

  public String getTitle() {
    return title;
  }

  public void setTitle(String title) {
    this.title = title;
  }

  public int getPages() {
    return pages;
  }
```

```
  public void setPages(int pages) {
    this.pages = pages;
  }

  public int getId() {
    return id;
  }

  public void setId(int id) {
    this.id = id;
  }
}
```

As you can see, this is a POJO, albeit without some of the things we'd probably want it to have, like `equals()`, `hashCode()`, and `toString()`. We are going to annotate this class as we go along, explaining the concepts behind annotation. In the end, we'll move it to a different package so that we'll have a good before-and-after picture of what the entity should be.

Entity Beans with `@Entity`

The first step is to annotate the `Book` class as a JPA 2 entity bean. We add the `@Entity` annotation to the `Book` class, as follows:

```
import javax.persistence.Entity;

@Entity
public class Book
  // Declaration of instance variables goes here
  public Book() {
  }
  // .. the rest of the class
```

These source listings are "in progress," so they don't have separate files in the book's source code. The actual source code for the class will differ from the code as we develop it in this chapter. We'll be able to see the "final product" later on in the chapter, too.

The JPA 2 standard annotations are contained in the `javax.persistence` package, so we import the appropriate annotations. Some IDEs will use specific imports, as opposed to "star imports," in situations where a few classes in a given package are imported; typically, an entity will use quite a few annotations from this package, so chances are it'll end up with star imports in any event.[4]

The `@Entity` annotation marks this class as an entity bean, so it must have a no-argument constructor that is visible with at least a `protected` scope.[5] Hibernate supports package scope as the minimum, but you lose portability to other JPA implementations if you take advantage of this. Other JPA 2 rules for an entity bean class are (a) that the class must not be final and (b) that the entity bean class must be concrete. Many of the rules for JPA 2 entity bean classes and Hibernate's persistent objects are the same - partly because the Hibernate team had much input into the JPA 2 design process and partly because there are only so many ways to design a relatively unobtrusive object-relational persistence solution.

So far, we've added the Entity annotation, a constructor, and an import statement. The rest of the POJO has been left alone.

Primary Keys with @Id and @GeneratedValue

Each entity bean has to have a primary key, which you annotate on the class with the `@Id` annotation. Typically, the primary key will be a single field, though it can also be a composite of multiple fields.

The placement of the `@Id` annotation determines the default access strategy that Hibernate will use for the mapping. If the annotation is applied to a field as shown in our next snippet, then field access will be used via reflection:

```
import javax.persistence.Entity;
import javax.persistence.Id;
```

[4] My IDE switches to using star imports instead of individual classes when the number of classes imported from a given package is greater than five. This is usually configurable per IDE, and whether it's desirable or not is entirely up to the reader.

[5] Naturally, there's a way around this. The normal requirement is to have a no-argument constructor; interceptors allow you to not have to do this.

```
@Entity
public class Sample {
  @Id
  int id;
  public int getId() {
     return this.id;
  }
  public void setId(int id) {
     this.id = id;
  }
  // .. the rest of the class
}
```

If, instead, the annotation is applied to the accessor for the field, as shown in our next snippet, then property access will be used. Property access means that Hibernate will call the mutator instead of actually setting the field directly; this also means the mutator can alter the value as it's being set or change other states available in the object. Which one you choose depends on your preference and need; usually field access is enough.[6]

Why wouldn't you just use field access all the time? Consider something like the United State's Social Security numbers: they're actually three sets of information - an *area number*, which is three digits; a *group number*, which is two digits; and a *serial number*. While the numbers don't have absolute meaning, you might want to separate them out into different attributes of a class even if it's stored in the database as a single element; with property access, you could use a method to split the three elements apart for your program while leaving the database structure alone.

```
import javax.persistence.Entity;
import javax.persistence.Id;

@Entity
public class Sample {
  int id;
```

[6] The reasoning behind "field access is enough" is that if you needed something to be part of the object's state, you'd include it in the database, which would mean you wouldn't need to set it when the object was instantiated. With that said, your mileage may vary; do what works for you.

```
    // note that we've moved the @Id annotation to the accessor
    @Id
    public int getId() {
        return this.id;
    }
    public void setId(int id) {
        this.id = id;
    }
    // .. the rest of the class
}
```

Here, you can see one of the strengths of the annotations approach. Because the annotations are placed inline with the source code, information can be extracted from the context of the mapping in the code, allowing many mapping decisions to be inferred rather than stated explicitly - which helps to further reduce the verbosity of the annotations.

By default, the @Id annotation will not create a primary key generation strategy,[7] which means that you, as the code's author, need to determine what valid primary keys are. You can have Hibernate determine primary keys for you through the use of the @GeneratedValue annotation. This takes a pair of attributes: strategy and generator.

The strategy attribute must be a value from the javax.persistence.GenerationType enumeration. If you do not specify a generator type, the default is AUTO. There are four different types of primary key generators on GenerationType, as shown in Table 6-1.

[7] Actually, the default generator is the "assigned" generator, which means the application is responsible for assigning the primary key before save() is called. This ends up having the same effect as if no key generation is specified.

Table 6-1. The GenerationType Options

Strategy	Description
AUTO	Hibernate decides which generator type to use, based on the database's support for primary key generation.
IDENTITY	The database is responsible for determining and assigning the next primary key. This is not recommended, because it has implications for transactions and batching.
SEQUENCE	Some databases support a SEQUENCE column type. See the "Generating Primary Key Values with @SequenceGenerator" section later in this chapter.
TABLE	This type keeps a separate table with the primary key values. See the "Generating Primary Key Values with @TableGenerator" section later in this chapter.

The generator attribute allows the use of a custom generation mechanism. Hibernate provides named generators for each of the four strategies in addition to others, such as "hilo," "uuid," and "guid." If you need to use Hibernate-specific primary key generators like hilo, you risk forfeiting portability of your application to other JPA 2 environments; that said, the Hibernate generators provide more flexibility and control.

For the Book class, we are going to use the AUTO key generation strategy. Letting Hibernate determine which generator type to use makes your code portable between different databases.

```
@Id
@GeneratedValue(strategy=GenerationType.AUTO)
int id;
```

Generating Primary Key Values with @SequenceGenerator

As noted in the section on the @Id tag, we can declare the primary key property as being generated by a database sequence. A sequence is a database object that can be used as a source of primary key values. It is similar to the use of an identity column type, except that a sequence is independent of any particular table and can therefore be used by multiple tables.

Is the ability of a sequence table to be used for multiple identifiers useful? It depends. The sequence generator is at its best under heavy access, because it allocates identifiers in blocks, so there's no chance for collision when new keys are allocated, though, so under *many* circumstances it's an excellent choice. It does not, however, guarantee that you'll get a series of predictable identifiers, because once a block has been allocated, that block of numbers is no longer available for *any* other identifier generation.

To declare the specific sequence object to use and its properties, you must include the @SequenceGenerator annotation on the annotated field. Here's an example:

```
@Id
@SequenceGenerator(name="seq1",sequenceName="HIB_SEQ")
@GeneratedValue(strategy=SEQUENCE,generator="seq1")
int id;
```

Here, a sequence generation annotation named seq1 has been declared. This refers to the database sequence object called HIB_SEQ. The name seq1 is then referenced as the generator attribute of the @GeneratedValue annotation.

Only the sequence generator name is mandatory; the other attributes will take sensible default values, but you should provide an explicit value for the sequenceName attribute as a matter of good practice anyway. If not specified, the sequenceName value to be used is selected by the persistence provider (in this case, Hibernate). The other (optional) attributes are initialValue (the generator starts with this number) and allocationSize (the number of ids in the sequence reserved at a time); the initialValue defaults to 1, and the block size of new allocations defaults to 50, which works out well for most applications. If your application ends up generating more than 50 identifiers in a few milliseconds, it's probably not a bad idea to use a larger allocation size, as Hibernate will generate a query to get new blocks when it needs more identifiers.

Generating Primary Key Values with @TableGenerator

The @TableGenerator annotation is used in a very similar way to the @SequenceGenerator annotation, but because @TableGenerator manipulates a standard database table to obtain its primary key values, instead of using a vendor-specific sequence object, it is guaranteed to be portable between database platforms.

For optimal portability and optimal performance, you should not specify the use of a table generator, but instead use the @GeneratorValue(strategy=GeneratorType.AUTO) configuration, which allows the persistence provider to select the most appropriate strategy for the database in use.

As with the sequence generator, the name attributes of `@TableGenerator` are mandatory and the other attributes are optional, with the table details being selected by the persistence provider:

```
@Id
@TableGenerator(name="tablegen",
                table="ID_TABLE",
                pkColumnName="ID",
                valueColumnName="NEXT_ID")
@GeneratedValue(strategy=TABLE,generator="tablegen")
int id;
```

The optional attributes are shown in Table 6-2.

Table 6-2. *`@TableGenerator` Optional Attributes*

Attribute Name	Meaning
allocationSize	Allows the number of primary keys set aside at one time to be tuned for performance. Defaults to 50. When Hibernate needs to assign a primary key, it will grab a "block" of keys from the key table and allocate keys in sequence until the block is used, so it would update the block every `allocationSize` assignment.
catalog	Allows the database catalog that the table resides within to be specified.
indexes	This is a list of `javax.persistence.Index` annotations that represent explicit indexes for the table that can't be derived from `@Column` specifiers, typically compound indexes.
initialValue	Allows the starting primary key value to be specified. Defaults to 1.
pkColumnName	Allows the primary key column of the table to be identified. The table can contain the details necessary for generating primary key values for multiple entities.
pkColumnValue	Allows the primary key for the row containing the primary key generation information to be identified.
schema	Allows the schema that the table resides within to be specified.

(continued)

Table 6-2. (*continued*)

Attribute Name	Meaning
`table`	The name of the table containing the primary key values.
`uniqueConstraints`	Allows additional constraints to be applied to the table for schema generation.
`valueColumnName`	Allows the column containing the primary key generation information for the current entity to be identified.

Because the table can be used to contain the primary key values for a variety of entries, it is likely to have a single row for each of the entities using it. It therefore needs its own primary key (`pkColumnName`), as well as a column containing the next primary key value to be used (`pkColumnValue`) for any of the entities obtaining their primary keys from it.

Compound Primary Keys with @Id, @IdClass, or @EmbeddedId

While the use of single-column surrogate keys is advantageous for various reasons, you may sometimes be forced to work with business keys. When these are contained in a single column, you can use `@Id` without specifying a generation strategy (forcing the user to assign a primary key value before the entity can be persisted). However, when the primary key consists of multiple columns, you need to take a different strategy to group these together in a way that allows the persistence engine to manipulate the key values as a single object.

You must create a class to represent this primary key. It will not require a primary key of its own, of course, but it must be a public class, must have a default constructor, must be serializable, and must implement `hashCode()` and `equals()` methods to allow the Hibernate code to test for primary key collisions (i.e., they must be implemented with the appropriate database semantics for the primary key values).

Your three strategies for using this primary key class once it has been created are as follows:

1. Mark it as `@Embeddable` and add it to your entity class as if it were a normal attribute, marked with `@Id`.
2. Add it to your entity class as if it were a normal attribute, marked with `@EmbeddableId`.
3. Add properties to your entity class for all of its fields, mark them with `@Id`, and mark your entity class with `@IdClass`, supplying the class of your primary key class.

All these techniques require the use of an `id` class because Hibernate must be supplied with a primary key object when various parts of its persistence API are invoked. For example, you can retrieve an instance of an entity by invoking the `Session` object's `get()` method, which takes as its parameter a single serializable object representing the entity's primary key.

The use of `@Id` with a class marked as `@Embeddable`, as shown in our next listings, is the most natural approach. The `@Embeddable` annotation can be used for nonprimary key embeddable values anyway (`@Embeddable` is discussed in more detail later in the chapter). It allows you to treat the compound primary key as a single property, and it permits the reuse of the `@Embeddable` class in other tables.

The embedded primary key classes must be serializable (i.e., they must implement `java.io.Serializable`, although it's possible you could use `java.io.Externalizable` as well[8]).

First, let's take a look at the key itself, an ISBN, or International Standard Book Number. ISBNs make sense as natural unique identifiers for books, because that's literally what they're for; they're intended to be unique across all literature, such that every printing and cover type of a given book has its own ISBN. (In other words, not only do different revisions of each book have their own ISBNs, the electronic form of the book you're reading and the paperback form of the exact same content are both intended to have their own unique ISBNs.)

[8] Serializable relies on Java's introspection to serialize and deserialize data. Externalizable forces the author to implement explicit serialization mechanisms. Externalizable can be far faster, but this doesn't give you any real benefits in this case.

Listing 6-4. src/main/java/chapter06/compoundpk/ISBN.java

```
package chapter06.compoundpk;

import javax.persistence.Column;
import javax.persistence.Embeddable;
import java.io.Serializable;

@Embeddable
public class ISBN implements Serializable {
  @Column(name = "group_number")
  int group;
  int publisher;
  int title;
  int checkDigit;

  public ISBN() {
  }

  public int getGroup() {
    return group;
  }

  public void setGroup(int group) {
    this.group = group;
  }

  public int getPublisher() {
    return publisher;
  }

  public void setPublisher(int publisher) {
    this.publisher = publisher;
  }

  public int getTitle() {
    return title;
  }
```

```
  public void setTitle(int title) {
    this.title = title;
  }

  public int getCheckDigit() {
    return checkDigit;
  }

  public void setCheckDigit(int checkdigit) {
    this.checkDigit = checkdigit;
  }

  @Override
  public boolean equals(Object o) {
    if (this == o) return true;
    if (!(o instanceof ISBN)) return false;

    ISBN isbn = (ISBN) o;

    if (checkDigit != isbn.checkDigit) return false;
    if (group != isbn.group) return false;
    if (publisher != isbn.publisher) return false;
    if (title != isbn.title) return false;

    return true;
  }

  @Override
  public int hashCode() {
    int result = group;
    result = 31 * result + publisher;
    result = 31 * result + title;
    result = 31 * result + checkDigit;
    return result;
  }
}
```

The @Embeddable annotation here means that it's meant to be, rather literally, embedded as an entity in the containing class; for ISBN, group, publisher, title, and checkDigit are all exported as columns for the containing class.

The group field actually uses a different name for the database column, because group is a reserved word in SQL. Here, we're preferring our own mapping to group_number instead of whatever the database dialect might prefer.

The class that *uses* this embeddable key, CPKBook – where CPK means "compound primary key" – might look like the one shown in Listing 6-5.

Listing 6-5. src/main/java/chapter06/compoundpk/CPKBook.java

```
package chapter06.compoundpk;

import javax.persistence.Column;
import javax.persistence.Entity;
import javax.persistence.Id;

@Entity
public class CPKBook {
  @Id
  ISBN id;
  @Column
  String name;

  public CPKBook() {
  }

  public ISBN getId() {
    return id;
  }

  public void setId(ISBN id) {
    this.id = id;
  }

  public String getName() {
    return name;
  }
```

```
  public void setName(String title) {
    this.name = title;
  }
}
```

This Book is awfully sparse, of course, as a simple example. But given that it has an embeddable identifier class - the ISBN - the SQL to create the cpkbook table would look like the one shown in Listing 6-6.

Listing 6-6. The Generated DDL for CPKBook

```
create table CPKBook (
    checkDigit integer not null,
    group_number integer not null,
    publisher integer not null,
    title integer not null,
    name varchar(255),
    primary key (checkDigit, group_number, publisher, title)
    );
```

Our next example uses an @EmbeddedId annotation to create effectively the exact same DDL as in Listing 6-6, except in the table name. An embedded id mainly differs in the accessibility and scope of the embedded key; here, we're basically describing EmbeddedISBN as a class in the *scope* of an EmbeddedPKBook. Our example here is contrived, since an ISBN has a common and accepted meaning (when you see "ISBN," you typically think of books rather than wonder what domain the term comes from), but you'd use this if you *did* have a constrained meaning for the key somehow.

Listing 6-7 is very short, mostly because the EmbeddedISBN has effectively the exact same class definition as the ISBN class that we'd marked as @Embeddable.

Listing 6-7. src/main/java/chapter06/compoundpk/EmbeddedPKBook.java

```
package chapter06.compoundpk;

import javax.persistence.Column;
import javax.persistence.EmbeddedId;
import javax.persistence.Entity;
import java.io.Serializable;
```

```
@Entity
public class EmbeddedPKBook {
  @EmbeddedId
  EmbeddedISBN id;
  @Column
  String name;

  static class EmbeddedISBN implements Serializable {
    // source matches the listing for ISBN.java
  }
}
```

Our last example uses the `@IdClass`, which is very similar to the `@EmbeddedId` example. With `@IdClass`, the entity has fields that **match** the id class' definition, all marked with `@Id` in the entity; the key class is used for `Session` methods like `get()` and `load()`, which require single objects to look up classes by key.

The DDL for this class looks exactly the same as with `CPKBook` and `EmbeddedPKBook`, except for the table name.

Listing 6-8. `src/main/java/chapter06/compoundpk/IdClassBook.java`

```
package chapter06.compoundpk;

import javax.persistence.Column;
import javax.persistence.Entity;
import javax.persistence.Id;
import javax.persistence.IdClass;
import java.io.Serializable;

@Entity
@IdClass(IdClassBook.EmbeddedISBN.class)
public class IdClassBook {
  @Id
  @Column(name = "group_number")
  int group;
  @Id
  int publisher;
  @Id
```

```
  int title;
  @Id
  int checkdigit;
  String name;

  public IdClassBook() {
  }

  static class EmbeddedISBN implements Serializable {
    int group;
    int publisher;
    int title;
    int checkdigit;

    public EmbeddedISBN() {
    }
    // source matches the listing for ISBN.java
  }
}
```

The @IdClass annotation uses the fully scoped name for the EmbeddedISBN class, whose simple name matches the EmbeddedISBN class from EmbeddedPKBook. This is an example of the scoping of the class name in question; the fully qualified names of the key classes are different even though the simple names are not.

The key class' fields *must* match the entity to which they apply; you can't use different names or types here. (The order of those fields, however, is not relevant.) The entity class' fields are marked with @Id, which feels somewhat natural when creating a compound primary key.

So why, then, would you use an id class when there are more rules that apply to using it? Primarily, natural object reference. The existence of the id class does not affect the entity definition, as fields like publisher are top-level attributes of the containing entity rather than being part of the ISBN. Whether *that* is a desirable attribute of your object model is up to you.[9]

[9] It's probably *wiser* to keep attributes as close to their defining entity as possible. If a publisher reference is part of an ISBN, it's probably best to have an ISBN class that contains publisher rather than having publisher be part of a book itself. However, the argument could also be made that the publisher key used as part of an ISBN might serve as a natural primary key for a Publisher table.

Is there a preference as to which one is "best?" The short answer is "yes," the *real* answer is "no." Based on anecdotal experience, the `@Embeddable` approach feels most natural, but the specific requirements of each application and problem domain really help determine your object model; it's easy to have keys composed of foreign key relationships with `@IdClass`, and both `@IdClass` and `@EmbeddedId` allow you to limit the effective visibility of the key types, for when you want an ISBN that's used as a primary key *but* you have another thing that you manage to call an ISBN type that had other uses or meanings in the same package.

Do what works best for your code, always.

Database Table Mapping with `@Table` and `@SecondaryTable`

By default, table names are derived from the entity names. Therefore, given a class `Book` with a simple `@Entity` annotation, the table name would be "`book`," adjusted for the database's configuration.

If the entity name is changed for some reason (by providing a different name in the `@Entity` annotation, such as `@Entity("BookThing")`), the new name will be used for the entity name. (Queries would need to use the entity name; from the user's perspective, the table name would be irrelevant.)

The table name can be customized further, and other database-related attributes can be configured via the `@Table` annotation. This annotation allows you to specify many of the details of the table that will be used to persist the entity in the database. As already pointed out, if you omit the annotation, Hibernate will default to using the class name for the table name, normalized by the database dialect, so you need only provide this annotation if you want to override that behavior.

The `@Table` annotation provides four attributes, allowing you to override the name of the table, its catalog, and its schema and to enforce unique constraints on columns in the table. Typically, you would only provide a substitute table name, thus `@Table(name="ORDER_HISTORY")`. The unique constraints will be applied if the database schema is generated from the annotated classes and will supplement any column-specific constraints (see discussions of `@Column` and `@JoinColumn` later in this chapter). They are not otherwise enforced.

The @SecondaryTable annotation provides a way to model an entity bean that is persisted across several different database tables.[10] Here, in addition to providing a @Table annotation for the primary database table, your entity can have a @SecondaryTable annotation, or a @SecondaryTables annotation, in turn, containing zero or more @SecondaryTable annotations. The @SecondaryTable annotation takes the same basic attributes as the @Table annotation, with the addition of the pkJoinColumns attribute. The pkJoinColumns attribute defines the join columns for the primary database table. It accepts an array of javax.persistence.PrimaryKeyJoinColumn objects. If you omit the pkJoinColumns attribute, then it will be assumed that the tables are joined on identically named primary key columns.

When an attribute in the entity is drawn from the secondary table, it must be marked with the @Column annotation, with a table attribute identifying the appropriate table; otherwise, it will be taken from the "main" database table. Listing 6-9 shows how a property of a Customer entity could be drawn from a second table mapped in this way.

Listing 6-9. src/main/java/chapter06/twotables/Customer.java

```
package chapter06.twotables;

import javax.persistence.*;

@Entity
@Table(
    name = "customer",
    uniqueConstraints = {@UniqueConstraint(columnNames = "name")}
)
@SecondaryTable(name = "customer_details")
public class Customer {
  @Id
  public int id;
  public String name;
```

[10] This isn't especially common if you're building an object model in Hibernate first; it would mostly occur when you're building an object model from a preexisting database that had a single entity in multiple tables for some reason. There *are* reasons, to be sure, related to issues that a database analyst and system administrator care about more than application programmers - like where tables are allocated on a disk - but they're not common.

```
    @Column(table = "customer_details")
    public String address;

    public Customer() {
    }
}
```

This class can be modeled in an H2 database with the following SQL:

```
create table customer
   (id integer not null, name varchar(255), primary key (id));
create table customer_details
   (address varchar(255), id integer not null, primary key (id));
alter table if exists customer
   add constraint UKcrkjmjk1oj8gb6j6t5kt7gcxm unique (name);
alter table if exists customer_details
   add constraint FK4g7jhj0n6g33lh0ar8ii6c9to foreign key (id) references
   customer;
```

Columns in the primary or secondary tables can be marked as having unique values within their tables by adding one or more appropriate `@UniqueConstraint` annotations to `@Table` or `@SecondaryTable`'s `uniqueConstraints` attribute, as shown with `name`. You may also set uniqueness at the field level with the unique attribute on the `@Column` attribute.

Persisting Basic Types with @Basic

By default, properties and instance variables in your POJO are persistent; Hibernate will store their values for you. The simplest mappings are therefore for the "basic" types. These include primitives, primitive wrappers, arrays of primitives or wrappers, enumerations, and any types that implement `Serializable` but are not themselves mapped entities. These are all mapped implicitly - no annotation is needed. By default, such fields are mapped to a single column, and eager fetching is used to retrieve them (i.e., when the entity is retrieved from the database, all the basic fields and properties are retrieved[11]). Also, when the field or property is not a primitive, it can be stored and retrieved as a `null` value.

This default behavior can be overridden by applying the `@Basic` annotation to the appropriate class member. The annotation takes two optional attributes and is itself entirely optional. The first attribute is named `optional` and takes a `Boolean`. Defaulting to `true`, this can be set to `false` to provide a hint to schema generation (or schema *usage* if you don't let Hibernate manage the schema) that the associated column should be created `NOT NULL`.[12] The second is named `fetch` and takes a member of the enumeration `FetchType`. This is `EAGER` by default, but can be set to `LAZY` to permit loading on access of the value.

Lazy loading means that the values of the references aren't actually necessarily initialized when the object is loaded by the `Session`. This has the potential advantage of performance - you can see if an object is persisted or not, without having to set all of its attributes - but it also means that your object might not be initialized fully at any given moment. (It's initialized when you actually start accessing the data.) This means that for lazily loaded data, the originating `Session` has to be active when you access the data, or else you will get a `LazyInitializationException` exception.

Lazy initialization is most valuable when you're actually loading relationships from the database. If you had a `PublishingHouse` object, with thousands of books having been published, you wouldn't necessarily want to load all of the books just because you are working with the `PublishingHouse` reference. Therefore, you'd want the books loaded lazily (because they probably have their own references to `Author` objects, and those authors might have more than one book, and so on and so forth, ad infinitum).

The `@Basic` attribute is usually omitted, with the `@Column` annotation's `nullable` attribute being used where the `@Basic` annotation's optional attribute might otherwise be used to provide the `NOT NULL` behavior.

---

[11] Note that even if data has been retrieved from a database, the class' attributes might not be initialized yet. When an instance is loaded from the session, the data might have been retrieved eagerly, but the object won't be initialized until something in it has been requested. This can yield some "interesting" behaviors, some of which were exposed in the previous chapters.

[12] Having non-nullability indicated in the schema is also useful for validation, even if you don't use it for schema generation.

Omitting Persistence with @Transient

Some fields, such as calculated values, may be used at runtime only, and they should be discarded from objects as when the entities are persisted into the database. The JPA specification provides the `@Transient` annotation for these transient fields. The @Transient annotation does not have any attributes - you just add it to the instance variable or the getter method as appropriate for the entity bean's property access strategy.

The `@Transient` annotation highlights one of the more important differences between using annotations with Hibernate and using XML mapping documents. With annotations, Hibernate will default to persisting all of the fields on a mapped object. When using XML mapping documents, Hibernate requires you to tell it explicitly which fields will be persisted.[13]

For our example, if we wanted to add a `Date` field named `publicationDate`, not be stored in the database to our Book class, we could mark this field transient thus:

```
@Transient
Date publicationDate;
```

If we are using a property access strategy for our `Book` class, we would need to put the `@Transient` annotation on the accessor instead.

Mapping Properties and Fields with @Column

The `@Column` annotation is used to specify the details of the column to which a field or property will be mapped. Some of the details are schema related and therefore apply only if the schema is generated from the annotated files. Others apply and are enforced at runtime by Hibernate (or the JPA 2 persistence engine). It is optional, with an appropriate set of default behaviors, but is often useful when overriding default behavior or when you need to fit your object model into a preexisting schema. It is more commonly used than the similar `@Basic` annotation, with the attributes in Table 6-3 commonly being overridden.

[13] This is not an endorsement of XML configuration. Use `@Transient` instead.

Table 6-3. @Column Attributes

Attribute	Description
name	This permits the name of the column to be explicitly specified – by default, this would be the name of the property. However, it is often necessary to override the default behavior when it would otherwise result in an SQL keyword being used as the column name (e.g., `user` or `group`, both of which are SQL keywords; you could replace `user` with `user_name`, for example).
length	`length` permits the size of the column used to map a value (particularly a `String` value) to be explicitly defined. The column size defaults to 255, which might otherwise result in truncated `String` data, for example.
nullable	This controls the nullability of a column. If the schema is generated by Hibernate, the column will be marked as `NOT NULL`; otherwise, the value here affects validation of the object. The default is that fields should be permitted to be `null`; however, it is common to override this when a field is, or ought to be, mandatory.
unique	This marks the field containing only unique values. This defaults to false, but commonly would be set for a value that might not be a primary key but would still cause problems if duplicated (such as username). This has little effect if Hibernate does not manage the schema.
table	This attribute is used when the owning entity has been mapped across one or more secondary tables. By default, the value is assumed to be drawn from the primary table, but the name of one of the secondary tables can be substituted here (see the `@SecondaryTable` annotation example earlier in this chapter).
insertable	This value controls whether Hibernate will **create** values for this field. It defaults to true, but if set to false, the annotated field will be omitted from insert statements generated by Hibernate (i.e., it won't be persisted initially by Hibernate, but might be updated; see the `updatable` attribute, next.)

(continued)

Table 6-3. (*continued*)

Attribute	Description
updatable	This defaults to true, but if set to false, the annotated field will be omitted from update statements generated by Hibernate (i.e., it won't be altered once it has been persisted).
columnDefinition	This value can be set to an appropriate DDL fragment to be used when generating the column in the database. This can only be used during schema generation from the annotated entity and should be avoided if possible, since it is likely to reduce the portability of your application between database dialects.
precision	precision permits the precision of decimal numeric columns to be specified for schema generation and will be ignored when a nondecimal value is persisted. The value given represents the number of digits in the number (usually requiring a minimum length of n+1, where n is the scale, covered next in this table).
scale	This permits the scale of decimal numeric columns to be specified for schema generation and will be ignored where a nondecimal value is persisted. The value given represents the number of places after the decimal point.

Here's a (short) example of how some of these attributes might be applied to a title field for a Book class:

```
@Column(name="working_title",length=200,nullable=false)
String title;
```

Likewise, for a class representing a decimal number, you might have something like this:

```
@Column(scale=2,precision=5,nullable=false)
double royalty;
```

This would persist a number like 10.2385 as 10.24 if the database supports trimming precision of decimal values. The corollary here is fairly obvious: your database might not support this feature. H2, for example, stores a full floating-point value for royalty even with the precision and scale being set.

Modeling Entity Relationships

Naturally, annotations also allow you to model associations between entities. JPA 2 supports one-to-one, one-to-many, many-to-one, and many-to-many associations. Each of these has its corresponding annotation.

We discussed the various ways in which these mappings can be established in the tables in Chapter 5. In this section, we will show how the various mappings are requested using the annotations.

Mapping an Embedded (Component) One-to-One Association

When all the fields of one entity are maintained within the same table as another, the enclosed entity is referred to in Hibernate as a *component*. The JPA standard refers to such an entity as being *embedded*.

This works for id classes, too, and the naming used is very similar.

The `@Embedded` and `@Embeddable` attributes are used to manage this relationship. In this chapter's example of primary keys, we associate an `ISBN` class with a `Book` class in this way.

The `ISBN` class is marked with the `@Embeddable` annotation. An embeddable entity must be composed entirely of basic fields and attributes. An embeddable entity can only use the `@Basic`, `@Column`, `@Lob`, `@Temporal`, and `@Enumerated` annotations. It cannot maintain its own primary key with the `@Id` annotation because its primary key is the primary key of the enclosing entity.

The `@Embeddable` annotation itself is purely a marker annotation, and it takes no additional attributes, as follows. Typically, the fields and properties of the embeddable entity need no further markup.

```
@Embeddable
public class AuthorAddress {
...
}
```

The enclosing entity then marks appropriate fields or getters in entities, making use of the embeddable class with the `@Embedded` annotation, as shown here:

```
@Embedded
AuthorAddress address;
```

The @Embedded annotation draws its column information from the embedded type, but permits the overriding of a specific column or columns with the @AttributeOverride and @AttributeOverrides annotations (the latter to enclose an array of the former if multiple columns are being overridden). For example, here we see how to override the default column names of the address and country attributes of AuthorAddress with columns named ADDR and NATION, names surely chosen by a slightly malicious database analyst:

```
@Embedded
@AttributeOverrides({
    @AttributeOverride(name="address",column=@Column(name="ADDR")),
    @AttributeOverride(name="country",column=@Column(name="NATION"))
})
AuthorAddress address;
```

Neither Hibernate nor the JPA standard supports mapping an embedded object across more than one table. In practice, if you want this sort of persistence for your embedded entity, you will usually be better off making it a first-class entity (i.e., not embedded) with its own @Entity marker and @Id annotations and then mapping it via a conventional one-to-one association, as explained in the next section.[14]

Mapping a Conventional One-to-One Association

There is nothing intrinsically wrong with mapping a one-to-one association between two entities where one is not a component of (i.e., embedded into) the other. The relationship is often somewhat suspect, however. You should give some thought to using the embedded technique described previously before using the @OneToOne annotation.

Why would you want a one-to-one association, then? Well, consider the situation where you have entities that are closely related, but still retain the ability to be accessed independently: a Home, perhaps, which has an address, and a Homeowner, the entity whose name is on the deed to that Home.

[14] You could also use this situation - where you want an embedded object spread across multiple tables - as a sign that maybe you're not meant to use object-relational mapping for those entities. But the truth is that you're probably mapping it incorrectly. *Probably.*

You can have a bidirectional relationship with a one-to-one association. One side will need to own the relationship and be responsible for updating a join column with a foreign key to the other side. The nonowning side will need to use the mappedBy attribute to indicate the entity that owns the relationship.

Assuming that you are resolute on declaring the association in this way (perhaps because you anticipate converting it to a one-to-many or many-to-one relationship in the foreseeable future), applying the annotation is quite simple – all of the attributes are optional. Here's how simply a relationship like this might be declared:

```
@OneToOne
Address address;
```

The `@OneToOne` annotation permits the optional attributes to be specified (Table 6-4).

Table 6-4. *The OneToOne Annotation Attributes*

Attribute	Description
`targetEntity`	This can be set to the class of an entity storing the association. If left unset, the appropriate type will be inferred from the field type or the return type of the property's getter.
`cascade`	This value can be set to any of the members of the `javax.persistence.CascadeType` enumeration. It defaults to none being set. See the "Cascading Operations" section for a discussion of these values.
`fetch`	This can be set to the `EAGER` or `LAZY` members of `FetchType`. (It defaults to `EAGER`.)
`optional`	This indicates whether the value being mapped can be `null`.
`orphanRemoval`	This attribute indicates that if the value being mapped is deleted, this entity will also be deleted.
`mappedBy`	This value indicates that a bidirectional one-to-one relationship is owned by the named entity.[15] The owning entity contains the primary key of the subordinate entity.

[15] An association is bidirectional if each entity maintains a property or field representing its end of the same relationship. For example, if our Address class maintained a reference to the Publisher located there, and the Publisher class maintained a reference to its Address, then the association would be bidirectional.

Mapping a Many-to-One or One-to-Many Association

A many-to-one association and a one-to-many association are the same association seen from the perspective of the owning and subordinate entities, respectively.

The simplest way to maintain a many-to-one relationship between two entities is by managing the foreign key of the entity at the "one" end of the one-to-many relationship as a column in the "many" entity's table.

The @OneToMany annotation can be applied to a field or property value for a collection or an array representing the mapped "many" end of the association:

```
@OneToMany(cascade = ALL,mappedBy = "publisher")
Set<Book> books;
```

The many-to-one end of this relationship is expressed in similar terms to the one-to-many end, as shown here:

```
@ManyToOne
@JoinColumn(name = "publisher_id")
Publisher publisher;
```

The @ManyToOne annotation takes a similar set of attributes to @OneToMany. The list in Table 6-5 describes the attributes, all of which are optional.

Table 6-5. *@ManyToOne Attributes*

Attribute	Description
cascade	This indicates the appropriate cascade policy for operations on the association; it defaults to none.
fetch	This attribute indicates the fetch strategy to use; it defaults to LAZY.
optional	This indicates whether the value can be null; it defaults to true.
targetEntity	This value indicates the entity that stores the primary key – this is normally inferred from the type of the field or property (Publisher, in the preceding example).

We have also supplied the optional `@JoinColumn` attribute to name the foreign key column required by the association something other than the default (publisher) - this is not necessary, but it illustrates the use of the annotation. (Hibernate will derive a foreign key column name from the "owning type" if it is not specified.)

When a unidirectional one-to-many association is to be formed, it is possible to express the relationship using a link table. This is achieved by adding the `@JoinTable` annotation, as shown here:[16]

```
@OneToMany(cascade = ALL)
@JoinTable
Set<Book> books;
```

The `@JoinTable` annotation provides attributes that allow various aspects of the link table to be controlled. These attributes are shown in Table 6-6.

Table 6-6. *The `@JoinTable` Attributes*

Attribute	Description
`name`	This is the name of the join table to be used to represent the association.
`catalog`	This is the name of the catalog containing the join table.
`schema`	This is the name of the schema containing the join table.
`joinColumns`	This reference is an array of `@JoinColumn` attributes representing the primary key of the entity at the "one" end of the association. You'd use multiple values if the "one" end had a composite primary key.
`inverseJoinColumns`	This is an array of `@JoinColumn` attributes representing the primary key of the entity at the "many" end of the association.

[16] When a join table is being used, the foreign key relationship is maintained within the join table itself - it is therefore not appropriate to combine the mappedBy attribute of the @OneToMany annotation with the use of a @JoinTable annotation.

Here, we see a fairly typical application of the @JoinTable annotation to specify the name of the join table and its foreign keys into the associated entities:

```
@OneToMany(cascade = ALL)
@JoinTable(
  name="PublishedBooks",
  joinColumns = { @JoinColumn( name = "publisher_id") },
  inverseJoinColumns = @JoinColumn( name = "book_id")
)
Set<Book> books;
```

Mapping a Many-to-Many Association

When a many-to-many association does not involve a first-class entity joining the two sides of the relationship, a link table must be used to maintain the relationship. This can be generated automatically, or the details can be established in much the same way as with the link table described in the earlier "Mapping a Many-to-One or One-to-Many Association" section of the chapter.

The appropriate annotation is naturally @ManyToMany and takes the attributes shown in Table 6-7.

Table 6-7. *The @ManyToMany Attributes*

Attribute	Description
mappedBy	This refers to the field that owns the relationship – this is only required if the association is bidirectional. If an entity provides this attribute, then the other end of the association is the owner of the association, and the attribute must name a field or property of that entity.
targetEntity	This is the entity class that is the target of the association. Again, this may be inferred from the generic or array declaration and only needs to be specified if this inference is not possible. (You'll get an error on schema generation if the schema can't be fully inferred by Hibernate.)
cascade	This indicates the cascade behavior of the association, which defaults to none.
fetch	This indicates the fetch behavior of the association, which defaults to LAZY.

This example maintains a many-to-many association between the Book entity and the Author entity. The Book entity owns the association, so its getAuthors() method must be marked with an appropriate @ManyToMany attribute, as shown here:

```
@ManyToMany(cascade = ALL)
Set<Author> authors;
```

Here, the Author entity is *managed by* the Book entity. The link table is not explicitly managed, so, as shown in the following snippet, we mark it with a @ManyToMany annotation and indicate that the foreign key is managed by the author's attribute of the associated Book entity:

```
@ManyToMany(mappedBy = "authors")
Set<Book> books;
```

Alternatively, we could specify the link table in full:

```
@ManyToMany(cascade = ALL)
@JoinTable(
   name="Books_to_Author",
   joinColumns={@JoinColumn(name="book_ident")},
   inverseJoinColumns={@JoinColumn(name="author_ident")}
)
Set<Author> authors;
```

Cascading Operations

When an association between two entities is established (such as a one-to-one association between Human and Pet or a one-to-many association between Customer and Orders), it is common to want certain persistence operations on one entity to also be applied to the entity that it is linked to. Take, for example, the following code:

```
Human dave = new Human("dave");
Pet cat = new PetCat("Tibbles");
dave.setPet(cat);
session.save(dave);
```

In the last line, we are likely to want to save the `Pet` object associated with the Human object. In a one-to-one relationship, we usually expect all operations on the owning entity to be propagated through – that is, to be cascaded to – the dependent entity. In other associations, this is not true, and even in a one-to-one relationship, we may have special reasons for wanting to spare the dependent entity from delete operations (perhaps for auditing reasons).

We are therefore able to specify the types of operations that should be cascaded through an association to another entity using the `cascade` attribute, which takes an array of members of the `CascadeType` enumeration. The members correspond with the names of the key methods of the `EntityManager` class used for EJB 3 persistence and have the following rough correspondence with operations on entities:

- `ALL` requires all operations to be cascaded to dependent entities. This is the same as including `MERGE`, `PERSIST`, `REFRESH`, `DETACH`, and `REMOVE`.
- `MERGE` cascades updates to the entity's state in the database (i.e., `UPDATE...`).
- `PERSIST` cascades the initial storing of the entity's state in the database (i.e., `INSERT...`).
- `REFRESH` cascades the updating of the entity's state from the database (i.e., `SELECT...`).
- `DETACH` cascades the removal of the entity from the managed persistence context.
- `REMOVE` cascades deletion of the entity from the database (i.e., `DELETE...`).
- If no cascade type is specified, no operations will be cascaded through the association.

In the light of these options, the appropriate annotation for the relationship between a publisher and its address would be as follows:

```
@OneToOne(cascade=CascadeType.ALL)
Address address;
```

Collection Ordering

An ordered collection can be persisted in Hibernate or JPA 2 using the @OrderColumn annotation to maintain the order of the collection. You can also order the collection at retrieval time by means of the @OrderBy annotation. For example, if you were to retrieve a list ordered by the books' names in ascending order, you could annotate a suitable method.

The following code snippet specifies a retrieval order for an ordered collection:

```
@OneToMany(cascade = ALL, mappedBy = "publisher")
@OrderBy("name ASC")
List<Book> books;
```

Why is books not a Set, since you'd want a given book only once in a given collection? This is because in Java, Set is unordered and unique, while List is ordered (and not unique). We're relying on the database for uniqueness (by presumption, since we can't tell from the data model here), but we definitely want ordered results; there are certainly ordered Set types in Java, but if you want to access the fifth book in a collection, for example, you want a List. Which type you choose depends heavily on how you use the data.

The value of the @OrderBy annotation is an ordered list of the field names to sort by, each one optionally appended with ASC (for ascending order, as in the preceding code) or DESC (for descending order). If neither ASC nor DESC is appended to one of the field names, the order will default to ascending. @OrderBy can be applied to any collection-valued association.

Inheritance

The JPA 2 standard and Hibernate both support three approaches to mapping inheritance hierarchies into the database. These are as follows:

- Single table (SINGLE_TABLE): One table for each class hierarchy
- Joined (JOINED): One table for each subclass (including interfaces and abstract classes)
- Table per class (TABLE_PER_CLASS): One table for each concrete class implementation

Persistent entities that are related by inheritance must be marked up with the @Inheritance annotation. This takes a single strategy attribute, which is set to one of three `javax.persistence.InheritanceType` enumeration values corresponding to `SINGLE_TABLE`, `JOINED`, or `TABLE_PER_CLASS`.

Single Table

The single-table approach manages one database table for the superclass and all its subtypes. There are columns for each mapped field or property of the superclass and for each distinct field or property of the derived types. When following this strategy, you will need to ensure that columns are appropriately renamed when any field or property names collide in the hierarchy.

Listing 6-10. The Root of a `SINGLE_TABLE` Inheritance Tree

```
package chapter06.single;

import javax.persistence.Entity;
import javax.persistence.Id;
import javax.persistence.Inheritance;
import javax.persistence.InheritanceType;

@Entity(name="SingleBook")
@Inheritance(strategy = InheritanceType.SINGLE_TABLE)
public class Book {
  // contents common to all Books go here
  @Id
  Long bookId;
  String title;
  // imagine many more
}
```

Listing 6-11. A Derived Entity in a `SINGLE_TABLE` Inheritance Tree

```
package chapter06.single;

import javax.persistence.Entity;

@Entity(name="SingleCBook")
public class ComputerBook extends Book {
  String primaryLanguage;
}
```

This structure would create a single table, called `SingleBook`, with the following fields: `bookId`, `title`, `DTYPE`, and `primaryLanguage`, with `primaryLanguage` being left at `NULL` for books that weren't assignable to a `ComputerBook`. Here's what this looks like, with the H2 database:

```
create table SingleBook (
   DTYPE varchar(31) not null,
   bookId bigint not null,
   title varchar(255),
   primaryLanguage varchar(255),
   primary key (bookId)
   );
```

Joined Table

An alternative to the monolithic single-table approach is the otherwise similar joined-table approach. Here, a discriminator column is used, but the fields of the various derived types are stored in distinct tables. (In other words, you get a "main table" with common attributes, but attributes that belong to subclasses get their own tables.) Other than the differing strategy, this inheritance type is specified in the same way (as shown in Listing 6-12).

Listing 6-12. The Root of a JOINED Inheritance Tree

```
package chapter06.joined;

import javax.persistence.*;

@Entity(name="JoinedBook")
@Inheritance(strategy = InheritanceType.JOINED)
public class Book {
  // contents common to all Books go here
  @Id
  Long bookId;
  String title;
  // imagine many more
}
```

Listing 6-13. A Leaf on a JOINED Inheritance Tree

```
package chapter06.joined;

import javax.persistence.Entity;

@Entity(name="JoinedCBook")
public class ComputerBook extends Book{
  String primaryLanguage;
}
```

With H2, this structure can be seen with the following SQL:

```
create table JoinedBook
   (bookId bigint not null, title varchar(255), primary key (bookId));
create table JoinedCBook
   (primaryLanguage varchar(255), bookId bigint not null, primary key (bookId));
alter table if exists JoinedCBook
   add constraint FK62rdg2vgeqlpviherbmj5b1su foreign key (bookId)
   references JoinedBook;
```

In this case, if we assume ComputerBook looks the same, we have *two* tables: JoinedBook and JoinedCBook. The JoinedBook table has bookId and title, and the JoinedCBook table would have bookId (which is how it knows how the data is associated) and primaryLanguage. Hibernate will query both tables to determine the appropriate entity type on retrieval.

Table per Class

Finally, there is the table-per-class approach, in which all of the fields of each type in the inheritance hierarchy are stored in distinct tables. Because of the close correspondence between the entity and its table, the `@DiscriminatorColumn` annotation is not applicable to this inheritance strategy. Listing 6-14 shows how our Book class could be mapped in this way.

Listing 6-14. The Root of a `TABLE_PER_CLASS` Inheritance Tree

```
package chapter06.perclass;

import javax.persistence.Entity;
import javax.persistence.Id;
import javax.persistence.Inheritance;
import javax.persistence.InheritanceType;

@Entity(name="PerClassBook")
@Inheritance(strategy = InheritanceType.TABLE_PER_CLASS)
public class Book {
  // contents common to all Books go here
  @Id
  Long bookId;
  String title;
  // imagine many more
}
```

Listing 6-15. A Leaf on a `TABLE_PER_CLASS` Inheritance Tree

```
package chapter06.perclass;

import javax.persistence.Entity;

@Entity(name="PerClassCBook")
public class ComputerBook extends Book {
  String primaryLanguage;
}
```

Here, we have two tables (again), PerClassBook and PerClassCBook, but PerClassBook has bookId and title, while PerClassCBook has *three* columns now: bookId and title (just like PerClassBook) and primaryLanguage. In the table-per-class strategy, every entity is stored completely in its own table and has no database-enforced relationship to other tables in its hierarchy.

Here's the SQL generated for H2:

```
create table PerClassBook (
   bookId bigint not null,
   title varchar(255),
   primary key (bookId)
   );
create table PerClassCBook (
   bookId bigint not null,
   title varchar(255),
   primaryLanguage varchar(255),
   primary key (bookId)
   );
```

Choosing Between Inheritance Types When Modeling Inheritance

Each of these different inheritance types has trade-offs. When you create a database schema that models a class hierarchy, you have to weigh performance and database maintainability to decide which inheritance type to use.

It is easiest to maintain your database when using the joined-table approach. If fields are added or removed from any class in the class hierarchy, only one database table needs to be altered to reflect the changes. In addition, adding new classes to the class hierarchy only requires that a new table be added, eliminating the performance problems of adding database columns to large datasets. With the table-per-class approach, a change to a column in a parent class requires that the column change be made in all child tables. The single-table approach can be messy, leading to many columns in the table that aren't used in every row, as well as a rapidly horizontally growing table.

Read performance will be best with the single-table approach. A select query for any class in the hierarchy will only read from one table, with no joins necessary, with single-table. The table-per-class type has great performance if you only work with the leaf nodes in the class hierarchy (i.e., if you work specifically with `ComputerBook` entities, and not `Book` types). Any queries related to the parent classes will require joins on a number of tables to get results. The joined-table approach will also require joins for any select query, so this will affect performance. The number of joins will be related to the size of the class hierarchy - large, deep class hierarchies may not be good candidates for the joined-table approach.

We recommend using the joined-table approach unless performance could be a problem because of the size of the dataset and the depth of the class hierarchy, but this decision is entirely based on the type and volume of data you're working with. Measure.

Other JPA 2 Persistence Annotations

Although we have now covered most of the core JPA 2 persistence annotations, there are a few others that you will encounter fairly frequently. We cover some of these in passing in the following sections.

Temporal Data

Fields or properties of an entity that have `java.util.Date` or `java.util.Calendar` types represent temporal data. By default, these will be stored in a column with the `TIMESTAMP` data type, but this default behavior can be overridden with the `@Temporal` annotation.

The annotation accepts a single value attribute from the `javax.persistence.TemporalType` enumeration. This offers three possible values: `DATE`, `TIME`, and `TIMESTAMP`. These correspond, respectively, to `java.sql.Date`, `java.sql.Time`, and `java.sql.Timestamp`. The table column is given the appropriate data type at schema generation time. The next listing shows an example mapping a `java.util.Date` property as a `TIME` type - the `java.sql.Date` and `java.sql.Time` classes are both derived from the `java.util.Date` class, so, confusingly, both are capable of representing dates and times in the database! (The java.sql.Date class only exposes date-related information, so no times, and the java.sql.Time class represents only times, no dates, whereas a Timestamp is more of an analog to the old java.util.Date.)

```
@Temporal(TemporalType.TIME)
java.util.Date startingTime;
```

Astute readers are also thinking of the java.time package, which *also* represents temporal data, albeit with far more detail than the rather coarse java.util.Date class. The java.time classes are actually innately supported as temporal types and don't need the @Temporal annotation to specify the nature of the field; Hibernate will map them appropriately by default, so all you would need to do is allow them to be persisted at all.

Of these, LocalDate is mapped to a SQL DATE type, LocalTime and OffsetTime are mapped to the TIME type, and Instant, LocalDateTime, OffsetDateTime, and ZonedDateTime are all mapped to TIMESTAMP.

If you can, use the java.time classes over the java.util classes for dates and times. They are far better defined and specified than the older java.util.Date and java.util.Calendar classes and thus involve far fewer assumptions about what the actual value is and how to convert it to other types.

Element Collections

In addition to mapping collections using one-to-many mappings, JPA 2 introduced an @ElementCollection annotation for mapping collections of basic or embeddable classes, like List or Set. You can use the @ElementCollection annotation to simplify your mappings. Listing 6-16 shows an example where you use the @ElementCollection annotation to map a java.util.List collection of string objects.

Listing 6-16. src/main/java/chapter06/embedded/User.java

```
package chapter06.embedded;

import javax.persistence.ElementCollection;
import javax.persistence.Entity;
import javax.persistence.GeneratedValue;
import javax.persistence.Id;
import java.util.List;
```

```
@Entity
public class User {
  @Id
  @GeneratedValue
  Long id;
  String name;
  // this is... not wise from a security perspective
  String password;
  @ElementCollection
  List<String> passwordHints;
}
```

This class actually creates two tables. The DDL looks like this, for H2:

```
create table User (
   id bigint not null,
   name varchar(255),
   password varchar(255),
   primary key (id)
   );
create table User_passwordHints (
   User_id bigint not null,
   passwordHints varchar(255)
   );
```

`User` is getting its primary key from a `hibernate_sequence` table in the preceding DDL.

Do not use a `User` *class like this without a lot of caution!* The use of `password` here implies that the *actual password* is being stored in the table in plaintext. In real life, that's basically inviting your user authentication to be hacked. You need to use hashed passwords, or encoded passwords, or certificates, or ... pretty much anything other than plaintext in your passwords. There's nothing in that class definition that says the code does *not* hash the password, but there's nothing saying it *does*, either.

You can embed more complex types, as well, using the `@Embeddable` annotation on the types. It's *probably* more useful to map complex types as actual entities rather than embedded types, but it's doable. (If the type is complicated enough to be queried specifically, it probably wants to be an entity, whereas if you only care about data in the context of an *owning* entity, an embedded type might be appropriate.) Here's an example of an EBook (for "Embedded Book," to prevent the reuse of "Book" 40 times in this chapter) and an embedded Author type.

There are two attributes on the @ElementCollection annotation: targetClass and fetch. The targetClass attribute tells Hibernate which class is stored in the collection. If you use generics on your collection, you do not need to specify targetClass because Hibernate will infer the correct class.[17] The fetch attribute takes a member of the enumeration, FetchType. This is EAGER by default, but can be set to LAZY to permit loading when the value is accessed.

Listing 6-17. src/main/java/chapter06/embedded/EBook.java

```
package chapter06.embedded;

import javax.persistence.ElementCollection;
import javax.persistence.Entity;
import javax.persistence.GeneratedValue;
import javax.persistence.Id;
import java.util.Set;

@Entity
public class EBook {
  @Id
  @GeneratedValue
  Long id;
  String name;
  @ElementCollection
  Set<Author> authors;
}
```

[17] The moral, as always: use generics on your collection. There's absolutely no reason not to.

Listing 6-18. `src/main/java/chapter06/embedded/Author.java`

```
package chapter06.embedded;

import javax.persistence.Embeddable;
import java.time.LocalDate;

@Embeddable
public class Author {
  String name;
  LocalDate dateOfBirth;
}
```

The generated SQL (again for H2) looks like this:

```
create table EBook (
   id bigint not null,
   name varchar(255),
   primary key (id)
);
create table EBook_authors (
   EBook_id bigint not null,
   dateOfBirth date,
   name varchar(255)
);
```

Note how a given author can appear multiple times in a given book (there's no restriction on any attribute of a given `Author` from a database perspective[18]) - again, `@ElementCollection` isn't meant to replace `@OneToMany` or its ilk, and it's entirely reasonable to consider using the relationship annotations instead of the embedded annotations if the data has any complexity at all.

[18] You could use a `List<Author>` instead of a `Set<Author>`, but the semantics of the `Set` are enforced by Java, and not the database. The database schema would look the same.

Large Objects

A persistent property or field can be marked for persistence as a database-supported large object type by applying the @Lob annotation.

The annotation takes no attributes, but the underlying large object type to be used will be inferred from the type of the field or parameter. `String`- and character-based types will be stored in an appropriate character-based type. All other objects, like `byte[]`, would be stored in a BLOB. Here, we see a `String` – a title of some kind[19] – mapped into a large object column type:

```
@Lob
String title; // a very, very long title indeed
```

The `@Lob` annotation can be used in combination with the `@Basic` or the `@ElementCollection` annotation. How this type is referenced in a specific database depends very much on the database dialect in use.

Mapped Superclasses

A special case of inheritance occurs when the root of the hierarchy is not itself a persistent entity, but various classes derived from it are. Such a class can be abstract or concrete. The @MappedSuperclass annotation allows you to take advantage of this circumstance.

The class marked with `@MappedSuperclass` is not an entity and is not queryable (it cannot be passed to methods that expect an entity in the `Session` or `EntityManager` objects). It cannot be the target of an association.

The mapping information for the columns of the superclass will be stored in the same table as the details of the derived class (in this way, the annotation resembles the use of the `@Inheritance` annotation with the `SINGLE_TABLE` strategy).

In other respects, the superclass can be mapped as a normal entity, but the mappings will apply to the derived classes only (since the superclass itself does not have

[19] Before you think this example is entirely contrived, some titles can be amazingly long. Check out `https://bookstr.com/list/5-books-with-hilariously-long-titles/` for some examples that might not fit in traditional-size columns.

an associated table in the database). When a derived class needs to deviate from the superclass' behavior, the @AttributeOverride annotation can be used (much as with the use of an embeddable entity).

For example, if Book was a superclass of ComputerBook, but Book objects themselves were never persisted directly, then Book could be marked as @MappedSuperclass, as shown in Listing 6-19.

Listing 6-19. src/main/java/chapter06/mapped/Book.java

```
package chapter06.mapped;

import javax.persistence.GeneratedValue;
import javax.persistence.Id;
import javax.persistence.MappedSuperclass;

@MappedSuperclass
public class Book {
    @Id
    @GeneratedValue
    Integer id;
    String name;

    public Book() {
    }

    public Integer getId() {
        return id;
    }

    public void setId(Integer id) {
        this.id = id;
    }

    public String getName() {
        return name;
    }
```

```
    public void setName(String name) {
        this.name = name;
    }
}
```

It's worth noting that the superclass can be marked as `abstract` as well; it doesn't *have* to be concrete. The superclass also needs to specify the identifier for the subclasses.

Here's something derived from a Book (Listing 6-20).

Listing 6-20. `src/main/java/chapter06/mapped/ComputerBook.java`

```
package chapter06.mapped;

import javax.persistence.Entity;

@Entity
public class ComputerBook extends Book {
    String language;

    public ComputerBook() {
    }

    public String getLanguage() {
        return language;
    }

    public void setLanguage(String language) {
        this.language = language;
    }
}
```

With this structure, a single table is created:

```
create table ComputerBook (
   id integer not null,
   name varchar(255),
   language varchar(255),
   primary key (id)
   );
```

The fields of the ComputerBook entity derived from Book would then be stored in the ComputerBook entity class' table.

Mapped superclasses do *not* mark their subclasses as entities. Classes derived directly from Book but not mapped as entities in their own right, such as a hypothetical MarketingBook class, would not be persistable. In this respect alone, the mapped superclass approach behaves differently from the conventional @Inheritance approach with a SINGLE_TABLE strategy.

Ordering Collections with @OrderColumn

While @OrderBy allows data to be ordered once it has been retrieved from the database, JPA 2 also provides an annotation that allows the ordering of appropriate collection types (e.g., List) to be maintained in the database, as opposed to being ordered **at retrieval**; it does so by maintaining an order column to represent that order. Here's an example:

```
@OneToMany
@OrderColumn(
   name="employeeNumber"
)
List<Employee> employees;
```

Here, we are declaring that an employeeNumber column will maintain a value, starting at zero and incrementing as each entry is added to the list. The default starting value can be overridden by the base attribute. By default, the column can contain null (unordered) values. The nullability can be overridden by setting the nullable attribute to false. By default, when the schema is generated from the annotations, the column is assumed to be an integer type; however, this can be overridden by supplying a columnDefinition attribute specifying a different column definition string. (There are more options for @OrderColumn, but they're not used very often.)

Using a Set here makes little sense, semantically; a Set is inherently unordered.

Named Queries (HQL or JPQL)

`@NamedQuery` and `@NamedQueries` allow one or more Hibernate Query Language or Java Persistence Query Language (JPQL) queries to be associated with an entity. The required attributes are as follows:

- `name` is the name by which the query is retrieved.
- `query` is the JPQL (or HQL) query associated with the name.

Listing 6-21 shows an example associating a named query with the `Author` entity. The query would retrieve `Author` entities by name, so it is natural to associate it with that entity; however, there is no actual requirement that a named query be associated in this way with the entity that it concerns. (Hibernate builds a list of the named queries, and what they return is *not* associated with where they're declared.)

Listing 6-21. A JPQL Named Query Annotation

```
@Entity
@NamedQuery(
        name="findAuthorsByName",
        query="from Author where name = :author"
)
public class Author {
...
}
```

There is also a `hints` attribute, taking a `QueryHint` annotation name/value pair, which allows caching mode, timeout value, and a variety of other platform-specific tweaks to be applied (this can also be used to comment the SQL generated by the query).

You do not need to directly associate the query with the entity against which it is declared, but it is normal to do so. If a query has no natural association with any of the entity declarations, it is possible to make the `@NamedQuery` annotation at the package level.[20]

[20] Note that something being *possible* is very different from something being *preferable*. Your author knows of exactly zero instances of this feature having been used in production; this doesn't mean it's not ever been used, but it's far from common.

There is no natural place to put a package-level annotation, so Java annotations allow for a specific file, called package-info.java, to contain them.[21] Listing 6-22 gives an example of this.

Listing 6-22. A package-info.java File

```
@javax.annotations.NamedQuery(
    name="findBooksByAuthor",
    query="from Book b where b.author.name = :author"
)
package chapter06.annotations;
```

Hibernate's Session allows named queries to be accessed directly, as shown in Listing 6-23.

Listing 6-23. Invoking a Named Query via the Session

```
Query query = session.getNamedQuery("findBooksByAuthor", Book.class);
query.setParameter("author", "Dave");
List<Book> booksByDave = query.list();
System.out.println("There is/are " + booksByDave.size()
    + " books by Dave in the catalog");
```

If you have multiple @NamedQuery annotations to apply to an entity, they can be provided as an array of values of the @NamedQueries annotation, no matter *where* the @NamedQueries are declared.

Named Native Queries (SQL)

Hibernate also allows the database's native query language (usually a dialect of SQL) to be used in place of HQL or JPQL. You risk losing portability here if you use a database-specific feature, but as long as you choose reasonably generic SQL, you should be okay.

[21] Well, speaking literally, there *is* a place to put a package-level annotation: it's the package-info.java, after all.

The @NamedNativeQuery annotation is declared in almost exactly the same manner as the @NamedQuery annotation. The following block of code shows a simple example of the declaration of a named native query:

```
@NamedNativeQuery(
  name="nativeFindAuthorNames",
  query="select name from author"
)
```

All queries are used in the same way; the only difference is how they're accessed, whether by Session.getNamedQuery(), Session.createQuery(), or Session.createSQLQuery(); the results can be retrieved as a List through Query.list(), or a scrollable result set can be accessed via Query.scroll(), Query.iterate() provides an Iterator (surprise!), and if the Query has only one object returned, Query.uniqueResult() can be used.

Multiple @NamedNativeQuery annotations can be grouped with the @NamedNativeQueries annotation.

Configuring the Annotated Classes

Once you have an annotated class, you will need to provide the class to your application's Hibernate configuration, just as if it were an XML mapping. With annotations, you can either use the declarative configuration in the hibernate.cfg.xml XML configuration document, accessed via the classpath, or programmatically add annotated classes to Hibernate's org.hibernate.cfg.AnnotationConfiguration object. Your application may use both annotated entities and XML mapped entities in the same configuration.

To provide a declarative mapping, we use a normal hibernate.cfg.xml XML configuration file and add the annotated classes to the mapping using the mapping element (see Listing 6-24). Notice that we have specified the name of the annotated classes as mappings. This file is located in either src/main/resources or src/test/resources relative to the root directory of the project; in this case, it's chapter06/src/test/resources/hibernate.cfg.xml.

Listing 6-24. A Hibernate XML Configuration File

```
<?xml version="1.0"?>
<!DOCTYPE hibernate-configuration PUBLIC
    "-//Hibernate/Hibernate Configuration DTD 3.0//EN"
    "http://www.hibernate.org/dtd/hibernate-configuration-3.0.dtd">
<hibernate-configuration>
  <session-factory>
    <!--  Database connection settings  -->
    <property name="connection.driver_class">org.h2.Driver</property>
    <property name="connection.url">jdbc:h2:./db6</property>
    <property name="connection.username">sa</property>
    <property name="connection.password"/>
    <property name="dialect">org.hibernate.dialect.H2Dialect</property>
    <!-- set up c3p0 for use -->
    <property name="c3p0.max_size">10</property>
    <!--  Echo all executed SQL to stdout  -->
    <property name="show_sql">true</property>
    <!--  Drop and re-create the database schema on startup  -->
    <property name="hbm2ddl.auto">create</property>

    <mapping class="chapter06.primarykey.after.Book"/>
    <mapping class="chapter06.compoundpk.CPKBook"/>
    <mapping class="chapter06.compoundpk.EmbeddedPKBook"/>
    <mapping class="chapter06.compoundpk.IdClassBook"/>
    <mapping class="chapter06.twotables.Customer"/>

    <mapping class="chapter06.mapped.ComputerBook"/>

    <mapping class="chapter06.naturalid.Employee"/>
    <mapping class="chapter06.naturalid.SimpleNaturalIdEmployee"/>

    <mapping class="chapter06.embedded.User"/>
    <mapping class="chapter06.embedded.EBook"/>
    <mapping class="chapter06.embedded.Author"/>
```

```
    <mapping class="chapter06.single.Book"/>
    <mapping class="chapter06.single.ComputerBook"/>

    <mapping class="chapter06.joined.Book"/>
    <mapping class="chapter06.joined.ComputerBook"/>

    <mapping class="chapter06.perclass.Book"/>
    <mapping class="chapter06.perclass.ComputerBook"/>
  </session-factory>
</hibernate-configuration>
```

You can also add an annotated class to your Hibernate configuration programmatically. The annotation toolset comes with an org.hibernate.cfg.AnnotationConfiguration object that extends the base Hibernate Configuration object for adding mappings. The methods on AnnotationConfiguration for adding annotated classes to the configuration are as follows:

```
addAnnotatedClass(Class persistentClass) throws MappingException
addAnnotatedClasses(List<Class> classes)
addPackage(String packageName) throws MappingException
```

Using these methods, you can add one annotated class, a list of annotated classes, or an entire package (by name) of annotated classes. As with the Hibernate XML configuration file, the annotated entities are interoperable with XML mapped entities.[22]

Hibernate-Specific Persistence Annotations

Hibernate has various annotations that extend the standard persistence annotations. They can be very useful, but you should keep in mind that their use will constrict your application to Hibernate; this won't affect any of the code we've written so far, since most of it uses Hibernate-specific classes already.

[22] Again, this is not an endorsement of the Hibernate XML configuration. It's also not exactly a condemnation, but...

Tip It is possible to overstate the importance of portability – most bespoke applications are never deployed to an environment other than the one for which they were originally developed. As a mature product, Hibernate has numerous features to offer above and beyond the base JPA 2 specification. You should not waste too much time trying to achieve a portable solution in preference to these proprietary features unless you have a definite requirement for portability. If you need the features, use them.

@Immutable

The `@org.hibernate.annotations.Immutable` annotation marks an entity as being, well, immutable. This is useful for situations in which your entity represents reference data - things like lists of states, genders, or other rarely mutated data.

Since things like states (or countries) tend to be rarely changed, someone usually updates the data manually, via SQL or an administration application. Hibernate can cache this data aggressively, which needs to be taken into consideration; if the reference data changes, you'd want to make sure that the applications using it are notified or restarted somehow.

What the annotation tells Hibernate is that any updates to an immutable entity should not be passed on to the database. It's a "safe" object; one probably shouldn't update it very often, if only to avoid confusion.

`@Immutable` can be placed on a collection; in this case, changes to the collection (additions or removals) will cause a `HibernateException` to be thrown.

Natural IDs

The first part of this chapter spent a lot of pages discussing primary keys, including generated values. Generated values are referred to as "artificial primary keys" and are very much recommended[23] as a sort of shorthand reference for a given row.

However, there's also the concept of a "natural ID," which provides another convenient way to refer to an entity, apart from an artificial or composite primary key.

An example might be a Social Security number or a Tax Identification Number in the United States. An entity (being a person or a corporation) might have an artificial primary key generated by Hibernate, but it also might have a unique tax identifier. This might be annotated with `@Column(unique=true, nullable=false, updatable=false)`, which would create a unique, immutable index,[24] but a natural ID also provides a loadable mechanism that we've not seen yet in any of our previous code, plus an actual optimization.

The Session provides the concept of a loader mechanism, known as a "load access." There are three loaders contained in Hibernate: able to load by ID, natural ID, and simple natural ID.

Loading by ID refers to an internal reference for a given instance. For example, if an object with an ID of 1 is already referred to by Hibernate, Hibernate doesn't need to go to the database to load that object - it can look the object up through its ID and return that reference.

A natural ID is another form of that ID; in the case of a tax identifier, the system could look it up by the actual object ID (which would be an artificial key in most cases) or by the tax ID number itself - and if the tax ID is a "natural ID," then the library is able to look that object up internally instead of building a query for the database.

Just as there are simple identifiers and composite identifiers comprising single fields and multiple fields, respectively - there are two forms of natural ID, similarly being made up of single fields or multiple fields.

---

[23] Note that there are different views of this. Most anecdotal data would suggest artificial keys as primary keys because they're short and immutable by nature; however, you can find many who advocate natural keys because they naturally map to the data model instead of adding to it. With that said, there are some data-oriented applications (data warehousing, for example) in which artificial keys are advocated without opposition. With this in mind, the recommendation stands: use artificial keys. Your data is likely to be warehoused at some point.

[24] The @UniqueConstraints annotation, mentioned earlier in this chapter, can do the same for a compound index. With that said, we're trying to look at a better way to do at least some ordering and indexing.

In the case of the simple IDs, the load process provides a simple `load()` method, with the ID in question being the parameter. If no instance with the ID exists, `load()` returns `null`. The loader also provides an alternative, a `getReference()` method, which will throw an exception if no object with that natural ID is in the database.

For natural IDs, there are two forms of load mechanisms; one uses the simple natural ID (where the natural ID is one and only one field), and the other uses named attributes as part of a composite natural ID.

Now let's look at some actual code. First, let's create a class representing an employee in Listing 6-25; our employee will have a name (everyone has a name), an artificial ID (an employee number) assigned by the database, and a natural ID, representing a manually assigned badge number.

Listing 6-25. A `SimpleNaturalIdEmployee` Class

```
package chapter06.naturalid;

import org.hibernate.annotations.NaturalId;

import javax.persistence.*;

@Entity
public class SimpleNaturalIdEmployee {
  @Id
  @GeneratedValue(strategy = GenerationType.AUTO)
  Integer id;
  @NaturalId
  Integer badge;
  String name;
  @Column(scale=2,precision=5,nullable=false)
  double royalty;

  public SimpleNaturalIdEmployee() {
  }
  // extra housekeeping not echoed here
}
```

The simple natural ID is declared by annotating a single field, badge, with `@NaturalId`. This enables us to use the `byNaturalId()` to acquire the entity with that field.

To use the loader mechanism, you would get a reference through the use of `Session.byId()`, `Session.byNaturalId()`, or `Session.bySimpleNaturalId()`, with the type of the entity being passed in. The simple loaders (for the ID and for the simple natural ID) follow the same form: you acquire the loader, then either load or get the reference, using the key value as a parameter. Let's see how that would look. First, we create a test base class that gives us the ability to create test data easily.

Listing 6-26. `IdTestBase.java`

```
package chapter06.naturalid;

import com.autumncode.hibernate.util.SessionUtil;
import org.hibernate.Session;
import org.hibernate.Transaction;

public class IdTestBase {
  protected SimpleNaturalIdEmployee createSimpleEmployee(
      String name, int badge
  ) {
    SimpleNaturalIdEmployee employee = new SimpleNaturalIdEmployee();
    employee.setName(name);
    employee.setBadge(badge);
    employee.setRoyalty(10.2385);

    try (Session session = SessionUtil.getSession()) {
      Transaction tx = session.beginTransaction();
      session.save(employee);
      tx.commit();
    }
    return employee;
  }

  protected Employee createEmployee(
      String name,
      int section,
      int department
  ) {
```

```
    Employee employee = new Employee();
    employee.setName(name);
    employee.setDepartment(department);
    employee.setSection(section);
    try (Session session = SessionUtil.getSession()) {
      Transaction tx = session.beginTransaction();
      session.save(employee);
      tx.commit();
    }
    return employee;
  }
}
```

Now let's see a test that uses the bySimpleNaturalId() method.

Listing 6-27. IdTestSimple.java

```
package chapter06.naturalid;

import com.autumncode.hibernate.util.SessionUtil;
import org.hibernate.Session;
import org.hibernate.Transaction;
import org.testng.annotations.Test;

import static org.testng.Assert.assertEquals;
import static org.testng.Assert.assertNotNull;

public class IdTestSimple extends IdTestBase {
  @Test
  public void testSimpleNaturalId() {
    Integer id = createSimpleEmployee("Sorhed", 5401).getId();

    try (Session session = SessionUtil.getSession()) {
      Transaction tx = session.beginTransaction();
```

```
            SimpleNaturalIdEmployee employee =
                session
                    .byId(SimpleNaturalIdEmployee.class)
                    .load(id);
            assertNotNull(employee);
            SimpleNaturalIdEmployee badgedEmployee =
                session
                    .bySimpleNaturalId(SimpleNaturalIdEmployee.class)
                    .load(5401);
            assertEquals(badgedEmployee, employee);

            tx.commit();
        }
    }
}
```

This code creates a new employee, with a specific badge number (5401). It then uses `Session.byId(SimpleNaturalIdEmployee.class)` to acquire a loader for the entity and calls `load(id)`, with the ID returned by the `createSimpleEmployee()` method.

There's an interesting thing happening here, though, that the code demonstrates without it necessarily being obvious from the code level.

When we run this method, we actually load two references - or else the test for equivalency wouldn't make any sense.[25] However, if we look at the actual SQL executed in the `Session`, we see only one call being issued.

This is because Hibernate will cache the natural IDs in objects that it loads in a session. When we use the natural ID in the load accessor, Hibernate looks in the session cache and finds that natural ID - and knows that this is the reference for which we're asking. It doesn't need to go to the database because it already has it in memory.

This helps make the class more self-documenting, as well as slightly more efficient; it means that if we have a data about a person from the real world, the API is more efficient. We can find a given employee by using a naturally indexed badge number instead of relying on other indexes, even if at the database level the other indexes do come into play.

[25] Let's assume that we usually make sense, please.

An entity with a compound natural ID merely has more fields annotated with @NaturalId. Let's create an employee for whom a section and department are a natural ID,[26] as shown in Listing 6-28.

Listing 6-28. An Employee Class with a Compound Natural Id

```
package chapter06.naturalid;

import org.hibernate.annotations.NaturalId;

import javax.persistence.Entity;
import javax.persistence.GeneratedValue;
import javax.persistence.GenerationType;
import javax.persistence.Id;

@Entity
public class Employee {
  @Id
  @GeneratedValue(strategy = GenerationType.AUTO)
  Integer id;
  @NaturalId
  Integer section;
  @NaturalId
  Integer department;
  String name;

  public Employee() {
  }
  // extra housekeeping not echoed here
}
```

Next, let's look at a test that demonstrates the use of the natural ID loader, shown in Listing 6-29.[27]

[26] In the previous footnote, we said that we *usually* make sense. This is a good example of when we really don't; this is horribly contrived and would earn a solid scolding in an actual project. With that said, the code works and is fairly demonstrative of the concept.

[27] The "employee names" here are taken shamelessly - well, mostly shamelessly - from the Harvard Lampoon's book *Bored of the Rings.*

Listing 6-29. The Natural Id Loader in Action

```
package chapter06.naturalid;

import com.autumncode.hibernate.util.SessionUtil;
import org.hibernate.ObjectNotFoundException;
import org.hibernate.Session;
import org.hibernate.Transaction;
import org.testng.annotations.Test;

import static org.testng.Assert.*;

public class NaturalIdTest extends IdTestBase {
  @Test
  public void testSimpleNaturalId() {
    Integer id = createSimpleEmployee("Sorhed", 5401).getId();

    try (Session session = SessionUtil.getSession()) {
      Transaction tx = session.beginTransaction();

      SimpleNaturalIdEmployee employee =
          session
              .byId(SimpleNaturalIdEmployee.class)
              .load(id);
      assertNotNull(employee);
      SimpleNaturalIdEmployee badgedEmployee =
          session
              .bySimpleNaturalId(SimpleNaturalIdEmployee.class)
              .load(5401);
      assertEquals(badgedEmployee, employee);

      tx.commit();
    }
  }

  @Test
  public void testLoadByNaturalId() {
    Employee initial = createEmployee("Arrowroot", 11, 291);
    try (Session session = SessionUtil.getSession()) {
      Transaction tx = session.beginTransaction();
```

```
      Employee arrowroot = session
          .byNaturalId(Employee.class)
          .using("section", 11)
          .using("department", 291)
          .load();
      assertNotNull(arrowroot);
      assertEquals(initial, arrowroot);

      tx.commit();
    }
  }

  @Test
  public void testGetByNaturalId() {
    Employee initial = createEmployee("Eorwax", 11, 292);
    try (Session session = SessionUtil.getSession()) {
      Transaction tx = session.beginTransaction();

      Employee eorwax = session
          .byNaturalId(Employee.class)
          .using("section", 11)
          .using("department", 292)
          .getReference();
      System.out.println(initial.equals(eorwax));
      assertEquals(initial, eorwax);

      tx.commit();
    }
  }

  @Test
  public void testLoadById() {
    Integer id = createEmployee("Legolam", 10, 289).getId();
    try (Session session = SessionUtil.getSession()) {
      Transaction tx = session.beginTransaction();

      Employee boggit = session.byId(Employee.class).load(id);
      assertNotNull(boggit);
```

```
      /*
     load successful, let's delete it for the second half of the test
     */
    session.delete(boggit);

    tx.commit();
  }

  try (Session session = SessionUtil.getSession()) {
    Transaction tx = session.beginTransaction();

    Employee boggit = session.byId(Employee.class).load(id);
    assertNull(boggit);

    tx.commit();
  }
}

@Test
public void testGetById() {
  Integer id = createEmployee("Eorache", 10, 290).getId();
  try (Session session = SessionUtil.getSession()) {
    Transaction tx = session.beginTransaction();

    Employee boggit = session.byId(Employee.class)
        .getReference(id);
    assertNotNull(boggit);

    /*
     * load successful, let's delete it for the second half of the test
     */
    session.delete(boggit);

    tx.commit();
  }

  try (Session session = SessionUtil.getSession()) {
    Transaction tx = session.beginTransaction();
```

```
      try {
        Employee boggit = session.byId(Employee.class)
            .getReference(id);

        // trigger object initialization - which, with a nonexistent
           object,
        // will blow up.
        boggit.getDepartment();
        fail("Should have had an exception thrown!");
      } catch (ObjectNotFoundException ignored) {
      }

      tx.commit();
    }
  }
}
```

In `testLoadByNaturalId()`, we see something very similar to our previous test for natural ID usage: we create an employee and then search for the ID. The object returned by `Session.byNaturalId()` has a `using()` method that takes a field name and the field value, as opposed to using a single reference for the identifier. If we don't include every field making up the natural ID, we'll get an exception.

Note that we're using the `load()` method; if the natural ID is not present in the database, `load()` will return a signal value of null.

Another test method in `NaturalIdTest` is `testGetByNaturalId()`. This one, using `getReference()`, will throw an exception if the id value isn't present, so we don't need the check for `null`.

Summary

In this chapter, we used JPA 2 annotations to add metadata to our POJOs for Hibernate, and we looked at some Hibernate-specific annotations that can enhance these at the cost of reduced portability.

In the next chapter, we're going to discuss JPA configuration for Hibernate, more of the object lifecycle, and data validation.

CHAPTER 7

JPA Integration and Lifecycle Events

Hibernate provides a number of capabilities beyond the simple "native Hibernate API." In this chapter, we are going to discuss using the standard JPA configuration resource, Hibernate's object validation facilities, and object lifecycle events - along with a few other tricks.

The Java Persistence API

The Java Persistence API, or JPA, is a standard approved by the Java Community Process, with input from representatives of a number of projects and vendors - and very heavily influenced by Hibernate. It was created as part of a new Enterprise Java specification, largely because Entity Beans - the prior standard for enterprise persistence - were difficult to write and use and even more difficult to use well.[1]

Hibernate was represented in the community team that created JPA, and it's fair to say that the JPA specification bears a strong resemblance to Hibernate's API; and Hibernate has integrated many JPA practices itself, as the previous chapter on mapping shows. (Most of the mapping features and annotations are part of the JPA specification; now, the native Hibernate versions of those annotations are available but rarely used in practice.[2])

[1] An informal survey of developers from TheServerSide Symposium 2004 indicated that nearly 95% of entity beans were being used in a way that was inefficient or improper. While informal and therefore anecdotal, that's still a heck of a result.

[2] Statements like "X is rarely used in practice" are almost always anecdotal. This one certainly is; you can probably find projects that fanatically rely on the Hibernate-specific annotations. The anecdote stands.

J. B. Ottinger et al., *Beginning Hibernate 6*, https://doi.org/10.1007/978-1-4842-7337-1_7

Hibernate provides an implementation of the JPA specification. Therefore, you can use JPA directly, with a JPA-specific configuration file, and acquire an `EntityManager` instead of a `Session`.

There are a few reasons you might want to do this. For one thing, JPA is a standard, which means that code that conforms to the standard is generally portable, allowing for differences among varying implementations. You can use Hibernate for development, for example, and for production you could deploy into an application server that provides EclipseLink instead. (The opposite applies as well: you could develop with EclipseLink and deploy into an architecture that uses Hibernate.)

Another reason is the Java EE specification itself. Java EE containers are required to provide JPA, which means the container can manage and profile resources; leveraging a non-JPA configuration puts a larger burden on the application developer. However, it's worth pointing out that one can use Hibernate as the JPA implementation even in a container that defaults to a different JPA implementation, providing you the best of both worlds: a JPA standard for configuration (which has its own benefits, in some slight ways) and Hibernate's excellent performance and expanded feature set.[3]

So let's look at what we would need to do to support the JPA configuration file, as opposed to the Hibernate configuration process. We're going to walk through a series of simple steps to give us a working toolkit. They are the following:

1. Add Hibernate's JPA support to the `util` project, as a nontransitive dependency.[4]

2. Add a `JPASessionUtil` class, as a close analog to the `SessionUtil` utility. Much as `SessionUtil` provides a `Session` instance, `JPASessionUtil` will provide an `EntityManager` instance, and we will also add a mechanism by which it will provide a Hibernate `Session`; this way, we can use the JPA configuration with the Hibernate API.

---

[3] The mechanism for using Hibernate in an environment where it's not the default provider is fairly simple: in the persistence.xml, add `<provider>org.hibernate.ejb.HibernatePersistence</provider>`. You'll still want to look up how to install Hibernate into your application server, however.

[4] We want a nontransitive dependency because we don't want to force all of the modules that use the util project to include JPA support.

3. Write a JPA configuration and a test to show a functional operation; this will give us an idea of some of the differences between JPA and Hibernate.

The Project Object Model

Let's take a look at the `util` project's `pom.xml`. We mentioned it in Chapter 3, but skipped over the details for it, because the book's source code has it in full form (and – here's a secret – we knew we'd be going back over it in this chapter.)

Listing 7-1. `util/pom.xml`

```
<?xml version="1.0" encoding="UTF-8"?>
<project xmlns:xsi="http://www.w3.org/2001/XMLSchema-instance"
         xmlns="http://maven.apache.org/POM/4.0.0"
         xsi:schemaLocation="http://maven.apache.org/POM/4.0.0 http://
         maven.apache.org/xsd/maven-4.0.0.xsd">
  <parent>
    <artifactId>hibernate-6-parent</artifactId>
    <groupId>com.autumncode.books.hibernate</groupId>
    <version>5.0</version>
  </parent>
  <modelVersion>4.0.0</modelVersion>
  <artifactId>util</artifactId>

  <dependencies>
    <dependency>
      <groupId>org.hibernate.orm</groupId>
      <artifactId>hibernate-hikaricp</artifactId>
      <version>${hibernate.core.version}</version>
    </dependency>
    <dependency>
      <groupId>org.projectlombok</groupId>
      <artifactId>lombok</artifactId>
```

```
      <scope>test</scope>
    </dependency>
  </dependencies>
</project>
```

Most of this is pretty ordinary, but note the inclusion of lombok and at test scope. This dependency is used to autogenerate a boilerplate for Java classes - and we'll discuss it in depth in the next section of this chapter. We scope it as test because we want to be able to write code that uses it (and test it), but we do *not* want to force any project that uses this one to have lombok as an explicit dependency; we're basically marking this as a *nontransitive* dependency.

Transitive dependencies are carried from project to project, after all; if we say project A depends on dependency B, then any project that uses A must *also* depend on B. Nontransitive dependencies need to be explicitly included, so if A has a *nontransitive* dependency on artifact D - such as lombok, as shown here - a project that uses A must explicitly declare a dependency on D.

Now let's take a brief aside to talk about *boilerplate*, because it's time to get rid of a lot of it with Lombok.

Introducing Lombok

"Boilerplate," in our context, is something written that gets reused over and over and over without significant changes. We see it in simple accessors and mutators all the time; when we have a String name, we expect there to be two methods that go with it:

```
String getName() { return name; }
void setName(String name) { this.name=name; }
```

We see the same thing for equals() and hashCode() and, for that matter, toString() as well. These methods are different from field to field and from class to class, of course, but they're essentially *all the same* differing only in details - and often an IDE can generate them for us.

The problem with that is that it creates a "normalcy" to such methods. As long as they always do the exact same thing, that's probably okay; in this book, we tend not to print those methods in the source code, because they're very repetitive and offer no information that a reader would find useful.

The danger is when the implementations *do* vary from the standard; for example, if our accessor (the `getName()`) were to return a normalized version of the `name` field, we as readers and programmers are so used to the *boilerplate* that a method that didn't do the exact same thing as every other boilerplated method simply doesn't stand out.

Thus, while boilerplate code isn't *bad*, it would be better if we didn't have to include it.

Many languages, including later versions of Java (i.e., 15 or later), provide syntax for providing classes with this boilerplate. Java 14 introduced the `record`, which is an immutable class that provides accessors and other standard methods for you. However, records are not candidates for persistence with Hibernate or JPA (yet) because of the requirements that a class be proxied for update to data; a record can't be mutated by the framework (because they're immutable) and thus can't be lazily initialized, a feature that's actually very important for performance.

Records in Java are best suited for data transfer, not persistence.

However, Lombok (`https://projectlombok.org`) allows us to annotate an object simply and cleanly, such that we can display all of the code associated with the entity, with all of the boilerplate code removed even from the source.

Lombok provides a number of annotations that can generate all of the boilerplated methods we just mentioned, and more: `toString()`, `equals()`, `hashCode()`, mutators, accessors, and a no-argument constructor, among many others. Lombok is a compile-time dependency; we don't need the library to exist in anything that depends on the generated classes.

We already included it in our `pom.xml`, but here's the specific dependency; it's included here as a nontransitive dependency.

We *want* Lombok to be a nontransitive dependency. It's an annotation processor that runs at compile time only; there are no downstream dependencies on it in what it generates, so a transitive dependency makes no sense from a deployment perspective.

```
<dependency>
    <groupId>org.projectlombok</groupId>
    <artifactId>lombok</artifactId>
    <version>1.18.20</version>
    <scope>test</scope>
</dependency>
```

So what does Lombok do for us? It actually generates boilerplate code based on what we want it to do. We can annotate a field with `@Getter`, for example, and it will generate a proper JavaBean-compatible accessor method based on that field's name. There's even a sort of catch-all annotation, `@Data`, which will generate accessors and mutators for all fields, as well as good implementations for `equals()`, `hashCode()`, and `toString()`, such that we can have a *full* and complete entity with a listing like the one shown in Listing 7-2.

Listing 7-2. `util/src/test/java/com/autumncode/util/model/Thing.java`

```
package com.autumncode.util.model;

import lombok.Data;

import javax.persistence.*;

@Entity(name = "Thing")
@Data
public class Thing {
  @Id
  @GeneratedValue(strategy = GenerationType.AUTO)
  Integer id;
  @Column
  String name;
}
```

This class will, after compilation and processing through the Lombok annotation processor, have `setId(Integer)`, `getId()`, `setName(String)`, `getName()`, an `equals()` implementation that compares against `id` and `name`, as well as a compatible `hashCode()` implementation, and a `toString()` that includes all of the attributes as well. That source code is *literally* all we need – there's no more "code eliminated for brevity" like we've seen in prior listings.

We also have options in Lombok to specify different kinds of constructors; our `Thing` retains the default constructor for now.

We're going to use this class as we explore the rest of this chapter.

The JPASessionUtil Class

JPA uses the concept of "persistence units," which are named configurations. Every persistence configuration will have a unique name within a given deployment. Because the persistence units are named, we need to factor in the possibility of multiple persistence units for our utility class, as shown in Listing 7-3.

Listing 7-3. `util/src/main/java/com/autumncode/jpa/util/JPASessionUtil.java`

```
package com.autumncode.jpa.util;

import org.hibernate.Session;

import javax.persistence.EntityManager;
import javax.persistence.EntityManagerFactory;
import javax.persistence.Persistence;
import java.util.HashMap;
import java.util.Map;

public class JPASessionUtil {
  private static Map<String, EntityManagerFactory>
      persistenceUnits = new HashMap<>();

  @SuppressWarnings("WeakerAccess")
  public static synchronized EntityManager
  getEntityManager(String persistenceUnitName) {
    persistenceUnits
        .putIfAbsent(
            persistenceUnitName,
            Persistence
                .createEntityManagerFactory(
                    persistenceUnitName
                ));
    return persistenceUnits
        .get(persistenceUnitName)
        .createEntityManager();
  }
```

```
  public static Session getSession(String persistenceUnitName) {
    return getEntityManager(persistenceUnitName)
        .unwrap(Session.class);
  }
}
```

Pardon the formatting; these are long method calls and they're all chained, so while there's no additional *complexity* in making the chained calls, they end up looking much longer than they really are, conceptually speaking.

In this class, we're setting up a way to reuse `EntityManagerFactory` instances, looked up by name. If no `EntityManagerFactory` exists for a given name, we'll create it and save it. If no persistence unit exists for a given name, a `javax.persistence.PersistenceException` will be thrown.

This code isn't useful if you're using a framework that manages persistence units for you, like Jakarta EE or Spring. In fact, nearly any framework that provides JPA integration will make this class completely unnecessary, which is part of why it's not very long. We use it mainly to make writing example code in subsequent chapters more convenient.

The `getSession()` method provides access to the underlying implementation of the `EntityManager`. For Hibernate, this will be `org.hibernate.Session`; if the actual implementation isn't Hibernate, then you'll have a runtime exception thrown.

All this is useful, but let's get around to using it. Let's write some tests to show how this class should be used.

Testing JPASessionUtil

Our first tests simply try to acquire resources: one set of resources that are properly configured[5] and another set of resources that do not. This will allow us to validate that the utility returns what it's expected to return, even when badly configured. Listing 7-4 shows the code for our first suite of tests; we're going to follow that up with a JPA configuration that these tests will use.

[5] Including the Platonic quality of, well, "existence." Each of us can decide on our own if this is a compliment to *The Republic* or not.

Listing 7-4. util/src/test/java/com/autumncode/jpa/util/JPASessionUtilTest.java

```
package com.autumncode.jpa.util;

import com.autumncode.util.model.Thing;
import org.hibernate.Session;
import org.hibernate.Transaction;
import org.hibernate.query.Query;
import org.testng.annotations.Test;

import javax.persistence.EntityManager;
import javax.persistence.TypedQuery;

import static org.testng.Assert.*;

public class JPASessionUtilTest {
  @Test
  public void getEntityManager() {
    EntityManager em = JPASessionUtil
        .getEntityManager("utiljpa");
    em.close();
  }

  @Test(
      expectedExceptions = {javax.persistence.PersistenceException.class}
  )
  public void nonexistentEntityManagerName() {
    JPASessionUtil.getEntityManager("nonexistent");
    fail("We shouldn't be able to acquire an EntityManager here");
  }

  @Test
  public void getSession() {
    Session session = JPASessionUtil.getSession("utiljpa");
    session.close();
  }
```

```
@Test(
    expectedExceptions = {javax.persistence.PersistenceException.class}
)
public void nonexistentSessionName() {
  JPASessionUtil.getSession("nonexistent");
  fail("We shouldn't be able to acquire a Session here");
}

@Test
public void testEntityManager() {
  EntityManager em = JPASessionUtil.getEntityManager("utiljpa");
  em.getTransaction().begin();
  Thing t = new Thing();
  t.setName("Thing 1");
  em.persist(t);
  em.getTransaction().commit();
  em.close();

  em = JPASessionUtil.getEntityManager("utiljpa");
  em.getTransaction().begin();
  TypedQuery<Thing> q = em.createQuery(
      "from Thing t where t.name=:name",
      Thing.class);
  q.setParameter("name", "Thing 1");
  Thing result = q.getSingleResult();
  assertNotNull(result);
  assertEquals(result, t);
  em.remove(result);
  em.getTransaction().commit();
  em.close();
}

@Test
public void testSession() {
  Thing t = null;
  try (Session session = JPASessionUtil.getSession("utiljpa")) {
    Transaction tx = session.beginTransaction();
```

```
      t = new Thing();
      t.setName("Thing 2");
      session.persist(t);
      tx.commit();
    }

    try (Session session = JPASessionUtil.getSession("utiljpa")) {
      Transaction tx = session.beginTransaction();
      Query<Thing> q =
          session.createQuery(
              "from Thing t where t.name=:name",
              Thing.class);
      q.setParameter("name", "Thing 2");
      Thing result = q.uniqueResult();
      assertNotNull(result);
      assertEquals(result, t);
      session.delete(result);
      tx.commit();
    }
  }
}
```

You'll notice that the nonexistent tests do something odd: they declare expected `Exception` types. Ordinarily, exceptions mean that a test has failed; in this case, we're saying that the test has not failed if a matching exception is thrown.

However, "not failing" isn't the same as "passing." For these tests, we actually want to fail unless we get an exception; therefore, we try to acquire the resource and call `fail()` - and an exception will exit the method before `fail()` is executed, which means the test passes.

However, none of these tests will pass unless we include a JPA configuration file, which is required to be in the classpath at `/META-INF/persistence.xml`, as shown in Listing 7-5.

Listing 7-5. util/src/test/resources/META-INF/persistence.xml

```
<persistence
    xmlns:xsi="http://www.w3.org/2001/XMLSchema-instance"
    xmlns="http://java.sun.com/xml/ns/persistence"
    xsi:schemaLocation="
            http://java.sun.com/xml/ns/persistence
             http://java.sun.com/xml/ns/persistence/persistence_2_0.xsd"
    version="2.0">
  <persistence-unit name="utiljpa">
    <properties>
      <property name="javax.persistence.jdbc.driver" value="org.
      h2.Driver"/>
      <property name="javax.persistence.jdbc.url" value="jdbc:h2:./
      utiljpa"/>
      <property name="javax.persistence.jdbc.user" value="sa"/>
      <property name="javax.persistence.jdbc.password" value=""/>
      <property name="hibernate.dialect" value="org.hibernate.dialect.
      H2Dialect"/>
      <property name="hibernate.hbm2ddl.auto" value="update"/>
      <property name="hibernate.show_sql" value="true"/>
    </properties>
  </persistence-unit>
</persistence>
```

With this file created, we have a valid persistence unit, named utiljpa; we're now able to run our four tests. With their passing, you can see (and prove) that JPASessionUtil returns an instance of EntityManager and Session when requested and throws an exception when an invalid request is made.

As you can see in the testEntityManager() method, we use a Thing – our Lombok-annotated entity class – just as if it were a regular POJO, calling setName() explicitly (and equals() implicitly, via assertEquals()).

You'll also note the testSession() method. This and testEntityManager() are functionally equivalent tests.

In each one, we have two operations. In each, we acquire a class that offers persistence,[6] start a transaction, and persist a Thing entity, and then commit the transaction; then we repeat the process, querying and then deleting the entity. The only difference between the two methods is the persistence API used; the testEntityManager() test uses JPA, and the testSession() uses the Hibernate API.

Most differences are fairly simple: instead of Session.delete(), JPA uses EntityManager.remove(), for example. The query types are different (JPA's typed query is a javax.persistence.TypedQuery, whereas Hibernate's is an org.hibernate.query.Query), although they are still functionally equivalent. Probably the most relevant change is in the usage of transactions, and that's been entirely voluntary. You could, for example, use the block shown in Listing 7-6 in the testSession() method, which makes it almost entirely identical to the JPA version.

Listing 7-6. Mirroring the EntityManager API with Session

```
try(Session session = JPASessionUtil.getSession("utiljpa")) {
  session.getTransaction().begin();
  Thing t = new Thing();
  t.setName("Thing 2");
  session.persist(t);
  session.getTransaction().commit();
}
```

It's important to note, however, that Session and EntityManager are similar but not identical; while Listing 7-6 would work if you were using EntityManager instead of Session, even in the small block of testing code Session uses org.hibernate.query.Query instead of the javax.persistence.TypedQuery.

So which one should you use? Well, it depends on what you need. If you need JPA compatibility, then you'll have to restrict yourself to the EntityManager and its capabilities; otherwise, use the one you prefer. The Hibernate API provides some fine-tuning features that JPA cannot; if you want to use them, you will want to use Session, but apart from that, the two APIs will be equivalent for most intents and purposes.

[6] Your author calls a class that offers persistence services a "persistence actor," but that sounds irrepressibly stuffy.

Lifecycle Events

The Java Persistence API exposes certain events to a data model. These events allow the developer to implement additional functionality that the architecture itself might not easily offer. The events are specified through the use of annotations, and the event handlers can be embedded in an entity directly or can be held in a separate entity listener class.

You could use the lifecycle in a few different ways: you could manually update a timestamp, for example, or perhaps you could write audit data, initialize transient data, or validate data before persisting it.

There are lifecycle events corresponding to object creation, reads, updates, and deletes. For each event type that makes sense in a persistence context, there are callback hooks for before and after the event occurs.

The event handlers are simple methods corresponding to one of seven lifecycle phases.

Table 7-1. *The Entity Lifecycle Phases*

Lifecycle Annotation	When Methods Run
`@PrePersist`	Executes before the data is actually inserted into a database table. It is not used when an object exists in the database and an update occurs.
`@PostPersist`	Executes after the data is written to a database table.
`@PreUpdate`	Executes when a managed object is updated. This annotation is not used when an object is first persisted to a database.
`@PostUpdate`	Executes after an update for managed objects is written to the database.
`@PreRemove`	Executes before a managed object's data is removed from the database.
`@PostRemove`	Executes after a managed object's data is removed from the database.
`@PostLoad`	Executes after a managed object's data has been loaded from the database and the object has been initialized.

Listing 7-7 offers an entity, descriptively named "LifecycleThing," which offers hooks for the various lifecycle events. As with our earlier classes, this uses Lombok to hide the boilerplate, such that this is the actual entire source code listing.[7]

Listing 7-7. src/main/java/chapter07/lifecycle/LifeCycleThing.java

```
package chapter07.lifecycle;

import lombok.Data;
import org.slf4j.Logger;
import org.slf4j.LoggerFactory;

import javax.persistence.*;
import java.util.BitSet;

@Entity
@Data
public class LifecycleThing {
  static Logger logger = LoggerFactory.getLogger(LifecycleThing.class);
  static BitSet lifecycleCalls = new BitSet();

  @Id
  @GeneratedValue(strategy = GenerationType.AUTO)
  Integer id;
  @Column
  String name;

  @PostLoad
  public void postLoad() {
    log("postLoad", 0);
  }

  @PrePersist
  public void prePersist() {
    log("prePersist", 1);
  }

  @PostPersist
```

[7] This will also hopefully be the last time the use of Lombok is pointed out.

```
  public void postPersist() {
    log("postPersist", 2);
  }

  @PreUpdate
  public void preUpdate() {
    log("preUpdate", 3);
  }

  @PostUpdate
  public void postUpdate() {
    log("postUpdate", 4);
  }

  @PreRemove
  public void preRemove() {
    log("preRemove", 5);
  }

  @PostRemove
  public void postRemove() {
    log("postRemove", 6);
  }

  private void log(String method, int index) {
    lifecycleCalls.set(index, true);
    logger.info("{}: {} {}", method,
        this.getClass().getSimpleName(), this);
  }
}
```

This class keeps track of the lifecycle calls made in a BitSet. When a lifecycle event occurs, it sets a bit in the BitSet; a test can (and will) examine the BitSet to make sure there are no gaps, which will give us a clearer picture of whether we have successfully executed each callback.

We could, of course, just use our eyes and examine the results visually. This works, of course (and is the backbone of most user testing, sadly), but we want objective, repeatable, and more verifiable results.

Our lifecycle test is shown in Listing 7-8. All it needs to do is create, read, update, and remove an entity; that will fire off each of our event handlers, and we can see the sequencing (if we watch the application logs) and have the test validate that no tests have been skipped (because it checks the BitSet).

Listing 7-8. `src/test/java/chapter07/lifecycle/FirstLifecycleTest.java`

```
package chapter07.lifecycle;

import com.autumncode.jpa.util.JPASessionUtil;
import org.hibernate.Session;
import org.hibernate.Transaction;
import org.testng.Reporter;
import org.testng.annotations.Test;

import static org.testng.Assert.*;

public class FirstLifecycleTest {
  @Test
  public void testLifecycle() {
    Integer id;
    LifecycleThing thing1, thing2, thing3;
    try (Session session = JPASessionUtil.getSession("chapter07")) {
      Transaction tx = session.beginTransaction();
      thing1 = new LifecycleThing();
      thing1.setName("Thing 1");

      session.save(thing1);
      id = thing1.getId();
      System.out.println(thing1);
      tx.commit();
    }

    try (Session session = JPASessionUtil.getSession("chapter07")) {
      Transaction tx = session.beginTransaction();
      thing2 = session
          .byId(LifecycleThing.class)
          .load(-1);
      assertNull(thing2);
```

```
      Reporter.log("attempted to load nonexistent reference");

      thing2 = session.byId(LifecycleThing.class)
          .getReference(id);
      assertNotNull(thing2);
      assertEquals(thing1, thing2);

      thing2.setName("Thing 2");

      tx.commit();
    }
    try (Session session = JPASessionUtil.getSession("chapter07")) {
      Transaction tx = session.beginTransaction();

      thing3 = session
          .byId(LifecycleThing.class)
          .getReference(id);
      assertNotNull(thing3);
      assertEquals(thing2, thing3);

      session.delete(thing3);

      tx.commit();
    }
    assertEquals(LifecycleThing.lifecycleCalls.nextClearBit(0), 7);
  }
}
```

There are three sections to this test, each using its own session and transaction. The first creates a `LifecycleThing` and persists it. The second attempts to load a nonexistent entity and then an existing entity; it then updates the existing entity. The third section loads that same entity and removes it. This means we have every lifecycle event in an object represented: creation, reads, updates, and deletes.

For each lifecycle event, a log message is produced. At the same time, the internal `BitSet` is modified to track whether the lifecycle methods have been called; at the end of the test, the `BitSet` is checked to see that every bit up through 7 has been set. If the value is correct, then we know that every lifecycle method has been called at least once.

The result should be fairly obvious: in this case, `prePersist()` is called before the persistence takes place, and `postPersist()` runs after the persistence has occurred. Exceptions can be tricky in lifecycle handlers. If an exception occurs in a lifecycle listener before the event - that is, in `@PrePersist`, `@PreUpdate`, or `@PreRemove` - it will get passed to the caller for handling. The transaction, however, remains valid. With that said, you will invalidate the transaction if an error occurs in the `@PostPersist`, `@PostUpdate`, `@PostRemove`, or `@PostLoad` code.

An exception in a postloading operation would be ... interesting to have to handle. (It would indicate that the data in the database was invalid from the object's perspective; consider if a field in the database had a range of values from an Enum, e.g., and that this is checked programmatically **after** the load operation.) It would probably have to be handled in the database itself, and you'd be well advised to avoid this possibility at all costs.

External Entity Listeners

The greatest weakness of the `LifecycleThing` (apart from the fact that it's a class whose sole purpose is illustrating the persistence lifecycle) is that all of the event listeners are embedded in the class itself. We can, instead, designate an external class as an entity listener, with the same annotations, through the use of the `@EntityListeners` annotation. Listing 7-9 shows a simple entity with an external entity listener.

Listing 7-9. `src/main/java/chapter07/lifecycle/UserAccount.java`

```
package chapter07.lifecycle;

import lombok.*;

import javax.persistence.*;

@Entity
@NoArgsConstructor
@Data
@EntityListeners({UserAccountListener.class})
public class UserAccount {
  @Id
  @GeneratedValue(strategy = GenerationType.AUTO)
```

```
  Integer id;
  String name;
  @Transient
  String password;
  Integer salt;
  Integer passwordHash;

  public boolean validPassword(String newPass) {
    return newPass.hashCode() * salt == getPasswordHash();
  }
}
```

Listing 7-10 shows what a simple external listener might look like.

Listing 7-10. src/main/java/chapter07/lifecycle/UserAccountListener.java

```
package chapter07.lifecycle;

import javax.persistence.PrePersist;

public class UserAccountListener {
  @PrePersist
  void setPasswordHash(Object o) {
    UserAccount ua = (UserAccount) o;
    if (ua.getSalt() == null || ua.getSalt() == 0) {
      ua.setSalt((int) (Math.random() * 65535));
    }
    ua.setPasswordHash(
        ua.getPassword().hashCode() * ua.getSalt()
    );
  }
}
```

When the `UserAccount` is persisted, the `UserAccountListener` will set a hashed password, multiplied by a random salt; presumably, a user-supplied password could be tested by applying the same salt.[8] (This is not secure, by any means. Don't use this code as an example of security.)

In this case, the listener only watches for one object type; it does no error checking. (It will throw an error if the incorrect type is passed to it.)

Event listeners factor in conveniently anywhere where you actually need access to the persistence lifecycle, especially when considering data validation.

Data Validation

We're going to start seeing libraries that aren't the "current version" from here on, depending on whether they've updated to use the Jakarta EE packaging or not. Hibernate 6 is still using the `javax.persistence` packaging for JPA, not `jakarta.persistence`, and the versions of things like the Validator API are chosen to conform to the old `javax` prefix where possible. Hibernate *has* a `jakarta.persistence` migration, but it's not the "normal" approach yet, and until it is those migrations should be considered as being "under testing" and not "production ready," even though they *might* be fine. In the meantime, using both `jakarta` and `javax` is confusing, so until the migration to `jakarta` is complete, we'll stick with the `javax` prefix.

Hibernate also offers a validation API, presently the reference implementation of Java's Bean Validation specification, version 3.0.[9] The Bean Validation specification allows your data model to enforce its own constraints, as opposed to the coders having to add their own data value checks throughout the application code.

Model-based validation should have obvious value: it means that you are able to trust the state of your model, no matter at what stage you're accessing data.

Consider the situation where data validation is applied in a web service; accessing that data apart from the web service might not have the validation applied, which means that you can trust the data accessed via the web service more than you can trust it if it's accessed from other environments. This is a bad thing.

---

[8] For more information on cryptographic salt, see `https://en.wikipedia.org/wiki/Salt_(cryptography)`.

[9] `https://jakarta.ee/specifications/bean-validation/3.0/`.

Note that we already have some validation capabilities, as part of the JPA specification itself. We can, for example, specify that columns' values are unique (via `@Id` or `@Column(unique=true)`; we can also specify that columns not be null or empty via `@Column(nullable=false)`. Through the magic of the entity lifecycle, we can enforce data validation through callbacks and external listeners as well,[10] and it's worth noting that in some cases this is still a valuable, workable approach.

So let's see what we can do to try out some more powerful validation capabilities with Hibernate.

The first step is to add Hibernate Validator to our project. If you're using Validator in a Java SE project (a stand-alone application, e.g., like our tests), then you need to add four dependencies; if you're deploying your application into a Java EE application server like WildFly, you only need to add the Validator dependency itself.

Listing 7-11 shows the full `pom.xml` for this chapter. Note that it uses placeholders for the versions of its dependencies; the book's source code is organized as a single project, and these versions are specified as properties in the top-level project.

Listing 7-11. `chapter07/pom.xml`

```
<?xml version="1.0" encoding="UTF-8"?>
<project xmlns:xsi="http://www.w3.org/2001/XMLSchema-instance"
         xmlns="http://maven.apache.org/POM/4.0.0"
         xsi:schemaLocation="http://maven.apache.org/POM/4.0.0 http://
         maven.apache.org/xsd/maven-4.0.0.xsd">
    <parent>
        <artifactId>hibernate-6-parent</artifactId>
        <groupId>com.autumncode.books.hibernate</groupId>
        <version>5.0</version>
    </parent>
    <modelVersion>4.0.0</modelVersion>
    <artifactId>chapter07</artifactId>

    <dependencies>
        <dependency>
```

[10] A callback would be a validation applied through a lifecycle method; you might test a value in a method annotated with @PrePersist, for example. An external entity listener would do the same sort of thing.

```
            <groupId>com.autumncode.books.hibernate</groupId>
            <artifactId>util</artifactId>
            <version>${project.version}</version>
        </dependency>
        <dependency>
            <groupId>org.projectlombok</groupId>
            <artifactId>lombok</artifactId>
        </dependency>
        <dependency>
            <groupId>org.hibernate.validator</groupId>
            <artifactId>hibernate-validator</artifactId>
            <version>${hibernate.validator.version}</version>
        </dependency>
        <dependency>
            <groupId>org.hibernate.validator</groupId>
            <artifactId>hibernate-validator-cdi</artifactId>
            <version>${hibernate.validator.version}</version>
        </dependency>
        <dependency>
            <groupId>javax.el</groupId>
            <artifactId>javax.el-api</artifactId>
            <version>${javax.el-api.version}</version>
        </dependency>
        <dependency>
            <groupId>org.glassfish</groupId>
            <artifactId>javax.el</artifactId>
            <version>${javax.el-api.version}</version>
        </dependency>
    </dependencies>
</project>
```

Now let's look at a class and a test that uses validation to ensure the correctness of our data. First is the ValidatedPerson class, as shown in Listing 7-12.

Listing 7-12. src/main/java/chapter07/validated/ValidatedPerson.java

```
package chapter07.validated;

import lombok.*;

import javax.persistence.*;
import javax.validation.constraints.Min;
import javax.validation.constraints.NotNull;
import javax.validation.constraints.Size;

@Entity
@Data
@Builder
@AllArgsConstructor(access = AccessLevel.PACKAGE)
@NoArgsConstructor
public class ValidatedPerson {
  @Id
  @GeneratedValue(strategy = GenerationType.IDENTITY)
  Long id;
  @Column
  @NotNull
  @Size(min = 2, max = 60)
  String fname;
  @Column
  @NotNull
  @Size(min = 2, max = 60)
  String lname;
  @Column
  @Min(value = 13)
  Integer age;
}
```

We've actually added some things to this entity via Lombok. The first thing we should look into is the `@AllArgsConstructor` annotation, which creates a package-visible constructor with all attributes as parameters; it's as if we had created `ValidatedPerson(Long id, String fname, String lname, Integer age)`. We set it to package-visible because we don't want any other classes using it, mostly because we're using another Lombok annotation, `@Builder`.

The `@Builder` annotation creates an inner class, accessible via a `builder()` method.[11] This inner class uses a fluent API[12] to provide a convenient way to construct classes; with the builder, we can use the following code to construct a `ValidatedPerson`:

```
ValidatedPerson person=ValidatedPerson.builder()
    .age(15)
    .fname("Johnny")
    .lname("McYoungster")
    .build();
```

Now let's look at the validation annotations we're using, and why. It's worth noting that we're not using all of the annotations Validator makes available to us - there are more than 25 currently documented, not counting the possibility of custom validators. These are just some of the validation annotations in common use.

The first one that stands out is `@NotNull`, used on the `fname` attribute. This is an analog to the `@Column(nullable=false)` annotation we've mentioned earlier, but is applied at a different point in the persistence lifecycle; if `@NotNull` is used, the column will still be set the same way (to not allow null values), but the validation occurs before persistence. If we use `@Column(nullable=false)`, the validation occurs in the database and gives us a database constraint violation rather than a validation failure - which is a very slight semantic difference, but a difference nonetheless.

`@Size` can partially be emulated by using `@Column(length=60)`, but `@Column` has no way to enforce minimum size constraints, and again the validation phase takes place before the persistence phase.

`@Min(value=13)` specifies that the integral value has a minimum value, as one might expect; there's a corresponding `@Max` annotation for maximum values.

---

[11] As with most things, there's a limitation. Lombok cannot generate builders that are aware of a class hierarchy; this is caused by how Lombok works and is very difficult to get around.

[12] See `http://en.wikipedia.org/wiki/Fluent_interface` for more information on what a Fluent API is and what it can look like.

One interesting thing about each of these is that they can actually change the database definition.[13] @Min and @Max, for example, add table constraints if the database is able to support them, and @NotNull enforces the constraint both in code and at the database level. @Size will assign a maximum size to a database column, if the maximum size is given; minimum size isn't something the database can normally enforce.

Let's see what some of this looks like, in a test. What we'll do is write a series of objects into a Hibernate Session, most of which will fail validation in some way. The actual persistence mechanism sounds like something for which we can write a method, so without further ado,[14] let's look at Listing 7-13 for the entire set of tests so we can see how validation is applied.

Listing 7-13. src/test/java/chapter07/validator/ValidatorTest.java

```
package chapter07.validator;

import chapter07.unvalidated.UnvalidatedSimplePerson;
import chapter07.validated.ValidatedPerson;
import com.autumncode.hibernate.util.SessionUtil;

import javax.validation.ConstraintViolationException;

import org.hibernate.Session;
import org.hibernate.Transaction;
import org.testng.annotations.Test;

import static org.testng.Assert.fail;

public class ValidatorTest {
  private ValidatedPerson persist(ValidatedPerson person) {
    try (Session session = SessionUtil.getSession()) {
      Transaction tx = session.beginTransaction();
      session.persist(person);
      tx.commit();
    }
```

[13] The Validator documentation calls the level of effect on the database "Hibernate metadata impact," such that validations of which the database is unaware have no metadata impact, but validations like @NotNull are described as meaning "Column(s) are not nullable."

[14] Does *anyone* like lots of ado? Or even know, precisely, what a lot of ado would look like?

```
  return person;
}

@Test
public void createUnvalidatedUnderagePerson() {
  Long id = null;
  try (Session session = SessionUtil.getSession()) {
    Transaction transaction = session.beginTransaction();

    UnvalidatedSimplePerson person = new UnvalidatedSimplePerson();
    person.setAge(12); // underage for system
    person.setFname("Johnny");
    person.setLname("McYoungster");

    // this succeeds because the UnvalidatedSimplePerson
    // has no validation in place.
    session.persist(person);
    id = person.getId();
    transaction.commit();
  }
}

@Test
public void createValidPerson() {
  persist(ValidatedPerson.builder()
      .age(15)
      .fname("Johnny")
      .lname("McYoungster").build());
}

@Test(expectedExceptions = ConstraintViolationException.class)
public void createValidatedUnderagePerson() {
  persist(ValidatedPerson.builder()
      .age(12)
      .fname("Johnny")
      .lname("McYoungster").build());
  fail("Should have failed validation");
}
```

```
  @Test(expectedExceptions = ConstraintViolationException.class)
  public void createValidatedPoorFNamePerson2() {
    persist(ValidatedPerson.builder()
        .age(14)
        .fname("J")
        .lname("McYoungster2").build());
    fail("Should have failed validation");
  }

  @Test(expectedExceptions = ConstraintViolationException.class)
  public void createValidatedNoFNamePerson() {
    persist(ValidatedPerson.builder()
        .age(14)
        .lname("McYoungster2").build());
    fail("Should have failed validation");
  }
}
```

Our first method in this listing - persist() - exercises the persistence cycle, to save code. Our test methods will create an object and pass it to this to execute the validation lifecycle.

Our four other methods create entities that match various single criteria: a valid entity, an entity whose `fname` is too short, an entity whose `lname` is too short, an entity with no `fname`, and an entity that's `underage`. In the case of the tests where we expect validation failures, we mark the methods as accepting an exception - and failing if the `persist()` method executes successfully. This works for us since we expect the `persist()` method to fail in these cases.

One thing worth noting is how *repetitive* all of this code is: we have a number of tests that vary a field value, and thus our tests all look vaguely the same. We can do better than this - and the test frameworks in common use actually provide for this. We can *parameterize* our tests, where we declare a *data provider* method that generates inputs, and the test framework will call our parameterized test methods with all of the datasets, treating them as separate tests.

Listing 7-14 shows a parameterized version of the `ValidatorTest`.

Listing 7-14. src/test/java/chapter07/validator/ParameterizedTest.java

```
package chapter07.validator;

import chapter07.unvalidated.UnvalidatedSimplePerson;
import chapter07.validated.ValidatedPerson;
import com.autumncode.hibernate.util.SessionUtil;
import lombok.val;
import org.hibernate.Session;
import org.hibernate.Transaction;
import org.testng.IExpectedExceptionsHolder;
import org.testng.annotations.DataProvider;
import org.testng.annotations.Test;

import javax.validation.ConstraintViolationException;

import static org.testng.Assert.fail;

public class ParameterizedTest {
  private ValidatedPerson persist(ValidatedPerson person) {
    try (Session session = SessionUtil.getSession()) {
      Transaction tx = session.beginTransaction();
      session.persist(person);
      tx.commit();
    }
    return person;
  }

  @DataProvider
  Object[][] provider() {
    return new Object[][]{
        {"Johnny", "McYoungster", 15, false},
        {"Johnny", "McYoungster", 12, true},
        {"J", "McYoungster", 14, true},
        {"Johnny", "M", 14, true},
        {"Johnny", null, 14, true},
    };
  }
```

```
  @Test(dataProvider = "provider")
  void testValidations(String fname, String lname, Integer age, boolean
  expectException) {
    try {
      val builder=ValidatedPerson
          .builder()
          .age(age)
          .fname(fname);
      if(lname!=null) {
        builder.lname(lname);
      }
      persist(builder.build());
      if (expectException) {
        fail("should have caught an exception");
      }
    } catch (Exception ex) {
      if (!expectException) {
        fail("expected an exception");
      }
    }
  }
}
```

What we've done here is declared a method that returns an array of Object arrays - `provider()` - and given it four values: a first name, a last name, an age, and a boolean indicating whether the dataset is "valid" or not. These values will be set positionally in our test method, `testValidations()`.

The test method itself is a little more complex than the version in `ValidatorTest`, because we want to be able to test *missing* values. We're not actually being as complete as we *could* be here - we only have a check for a missing `lname` - but the concept would apply for every parameter. We're also using Java 11's `val` keyword, because we can let Java infer the type of the `builder` - it's actually `ValidatedPerson.ValidatedPersonBuilder`.

In each branch of the `try/catch` structure, we use the `expectException` value to determine if the result is what we wanted; if we reach the end of the `try` without an exception and we expected one, we fail the test, and we invert that mechanism for the `catch` clause. If you want to validate that this is working as expected, change the values in the `provider()` method, which also centralizes where all of your test data goes.[15]

One thing you might notice, though, is that we have validations that encompass only single attributes. We can use the entity lifecycle to create our own custom validations, but Validator allows us to create our own validation annotations - including single-field validations (as we've seen used) and class-level validations.

Let's create a coordinate entity - and let's use, for the sake of example, a validation that ensures that a valid Coordinate isn't allowed to be in quadrant III in the Cartesian quadrant system. (Coordinates in quadrant III have negative x- and y- attributes.) Single-field validations wouldn't work here, because -5 is valid as an x coordinate, as long as the y coordinate isn't negative as well.

We actually have a number of options we can choose to build the validation. The most flexible option is an annotation that looks up the dependent fields - so a validation on X would contain a reference to Y and the attendant acceptable criteria, and vice versa. With that said, let's choose a simpler option, one very specific to our Coordinate class.[16]

First, let's see the `Coordinate` class. Then we'll create the tests that we expect to pass; and last, we'll take a look at the annotation that applies the validation. Much like the `SimpleValidatedPerson` entity, we're going to use Lombok fairly heavily to eliminate boilerplate code.

Listing 7-15. `src/main/java/chapter07/validated/Coordinate.java`

```
package chapter07.validated;

import lombok.AllArgsConstructor;
import lombok.Builder;
import lombok.Data;
import lombok.NoArgsConstructor;
```

[15] The data provider mechanism is built-in in JUnit 5 and TestNG; earlier versions of JUnit have the feature as well, but through add-on libraries.

[16] If you're interested in more detail about custom constraints - and you probably should be, if Validator interests you - see `https://docs.jboss.org/hibernate/validator/6.2/reference/en-US/html_single/`.

```
import javax.persistence.Entity;
import javax.persistence.GeneratedValue;
import javax.persistence.GenerationType;
import javax.persistence.Id;
import javax.validation.constraints.NotNull;

@Entity
@Data
@Builder
@NoArgsConstructor
@AllArgsConstructor
@NoQuadrantIII
public class Coordinate {
  @Id
  @GeneratedValue(strategy = GenerationType.AUTO)
  Integer id;
  @NotNull
  Integer x;
  @NotNull
  Integer y;
}
```

This class won't compile without our annotation (the `@NoQuadrantIII` annotation) being defined fully; that's coming up very shortly.

Let's look at our test code, which creates nine coordinates and persists them all; the `Coordinate` objects that represent the origin as well as quadrants I, II, and IV should all persist successfully,[17] and the Coordinate for quadrant III should fail. We're going to use the data provider mechanism again to eliminate lots of repetitive code, but not for the failure condition, which is limited in scope. This time, we'll test the failure condition explicitly.

[17] Fun math fact: We're also testing coordinates that lie *between* quadrants. Point (1,0), e.g., lies between quadrants I and II, but we've decided our coordinates are allowed anywhere *but* quadrant III, so that's okay.

Listing 7-16. src/test/java/chapter07/validator/CoordinateTest.java

```
package chapter07.validator;

import chapter07.validated.Coordinate;
import com.autumncode.hibernate.util.SessionUtil;
import org.hibernate.Session;
import org.hibernate.Transaction;
import org.testng.annotations.DataProvider;
import org.testng.annotations.Test;

import javax.validation.ConstraintViolationException;

public class CoordinateTest {
  private void persist(Coordinate entity) {
    try (Session session = SessionUtil.getSession()) {
      Transaction tx = session.beginTransaction();
      session.persist(entity);
      tx.commit();
    }
  }

  @DataProvider(name = "validCoordinates")
  private Object[][] validCoordinates() {
    return new Object[][]{
        {1, 1},
        {-1, 1},
        {1, -1},
        {1, 0},
        {-1, 0},
        {0, -1},
        {0, 1},
        {0, 0},
      // trailing comma is valid: see JLS 10.6 https://bit.ly/3C3QNOJ
    };
  }
```

```
  @Test(dataProvider = "validCoordinates")
  public void testValidCoordinate(Integer x, Integer y) {
    Coordinate c = Coordinate.builder().x(x).y(y).build();
    persist(c);
    // has passed validation, if we reach this point.
  }

  @Test(expectedExceptions = ConstraintViolationException.class)
  public void testInvalidCoordinate() {
    testValidCoordinate(-1, -1);
  }
}
```

Creating a validation constraint involves two classes: one is the annotation itself, and the other is the implementation of the annotation.

Listing 7-17. src/main/java/chapter07/validated/NoQuadrantIII.java

```
package chapter07.validated;

import javax.validation.Constraint;
import javax.validation.Payload;
import java.lang.annotation.*;

@Target({ElementType.TYPE, ElementType.ANNOTATION_TYPE})
@Retention(RetentionPolicy.RUNTIME)
@Constraint(validatedBy = {QuadrantIIIValidator.class})
@Documented
public @interface NoQuadrantIII {
  String message() default "Failed quadrant III test";

  Class<?>[] groups() default {};

  Class<? extends Payload>[] payload() default {};
}
```

Listing 7-18. src/main/java/chapter07/validated/QuadrantIIIValidator.java

```
package chapter07.validated;

import javax.validation.ConstraintValidator;
import javax.validation.ConstraintValidatorContext;

public class QuadrantIIIValidator
    implements ConstraintValidator<NoQuadrantIII, Coordinate> {
  @Override
  public void initialize(NoQuadrantIII constraintAnnotation) {
  }

  @Override
  public boolean isValid(
      Coordinate value,
      ConstraintValidatorContext context
  ) {
    return !(value.getX() < 0 && value.getY() < 0);
  }
}
```

In this case, the `isValid()` method - which gets a `ConstraintValidatorContext` and a `Coordinate` to validate - we can simply use the `Coordinate` and check its attributes to see if it passes validation or not. More complex scenarios could exist; the annotation could include ranges of values to use, for example.

Summary

This chapter has covered the use of the standard Java Persistence API configuration file, as well as how to access the persistence lifecycle and validation before persistence. It has also discussed the use of Lombok to help avoid boilerplate code, and it has shown how to use a data provider in TestNG to eliminate extra test code as well.

In the next chapter, we will look at how a client application communicates with the database representation of the entities by using the `Session` object.

CHAPTER 8

Using the Session

You may have noticed that the Session is the central point of access to Hibernate functionality. We will now look at what it embodies and what that implies about how you should use it.

Sessions

From the examples in the earlier chapters, you will have noticed that a small number of classes dominate our interactions with Hibernate. Of these, Session, actually an interface, is the linchpin.

The Session object is used to create new database entities, read in objects from the database, update objects in the database, and delete objects from the database.[1] It allows you to manage the transaction boundaries of database access and (in a pinch) to obtain a traditional JDBC connection object so that you can do things to the database that the Hibernate developers have not already considered in their existing design.

If you are familiar with the JDBC approach, it helps to think of a Session object as somewhat like a JDBC connection and the SessionFactory, which provides Session objects, as somewhat like a connection pool which provides Connection objects. These similarities in roles are illustrated in Figure 8-1.

[1] In other words, the Session is used for almost everything, which makes it rather linchpin-like. Go figure.

J. B. Ottinger et al., *Beginning Hibernate 6*, https://doi.org/10.1007/978-1-4842-7337-1_8

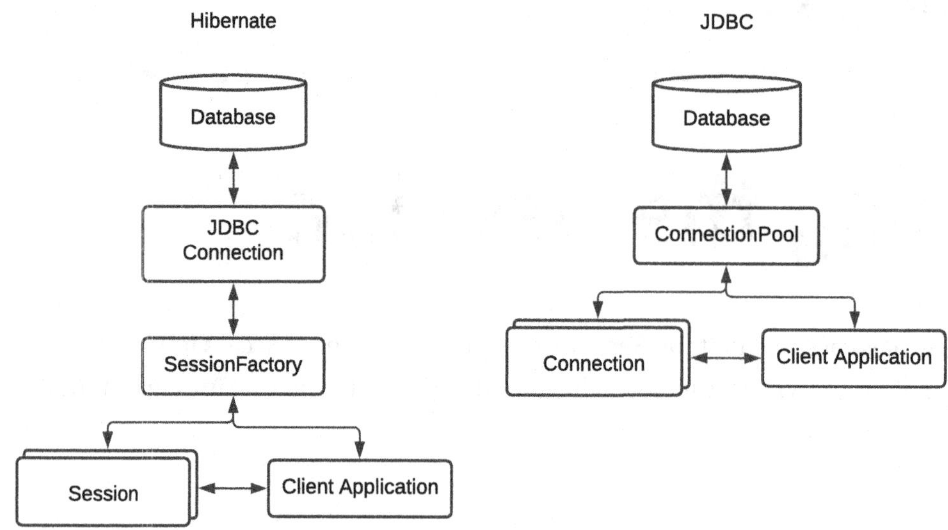

Figure 8-1. *Similarities between sessions and JDBC connections*

SessionFactory objects are expensive objects; needlessly duplicating them will cause problems quickly, and creating them is a relatively time-consuming process. Ideally, you should have a single SessionFactory for each database your application will access.

SessionFactory objects are also threadsafe, so it is not necessary to obtain one for each thread. However, you will create numerous Session objects – at least one for each thread using Hibernate. Sessions in Hibernate are *not* threadsafe, so sharing Session objects between threads could cause data loss or deadlock. In fact, you will often want to create multiple Session instances even during the lifetime of a specific thread (see the "Threads" section for concurrency issues).

The analogy between a Hibernate session and a JDBC connection only goes so far. One important difference is that if a Hibernate Session object throws an exception of any sort, you must discard it and obtain a new Session. This prevents data in the session's cache from becoming inconsistent with the database.

We've already covered the core methods in Chapter 4, so we won't discuss all the methods available to you through the Session interface. For an exhaustive look at what's available, you should read the API documentation on the Hibernate website or in the Hibernate 6 download. Tables 8-1 to 8-4 give a broad overview of the various categories of methods available to you; despite their lengths, this is not an exhaustive list.

Table 8-1. *Session Methods for Create, Read, Update, Delete*

Method	Description
`save()`	Saves an object to the database. This should not be called for an object that has already been saved to the database.
`saveOrUpdate()`	Saves an object to the database or updates the database if the object already exists. This method is slightly less efficient than the `save()` method since it may need to perform a `SELECT` statement to check whether the object already exists, but it will not fail if the object has already been saved.
`merge()`	Merges the fields of a nonpersistent object into the appropriate persistent object (determined by ID). If no such object exists in the database, then one is created and saved.
`persist()`	Reassociates an object with the session so that changes made to the object will be persisted.
`get()`	Retrieves a specific object from the database by the object's identifier.
`getEntityName()`	Retrieves the entity name (this will usually be the same as the fully qualified class name of the POJO).
`getIdentifier()`	Determines the identifier – the object(s) representing the primary key – for a specific object associated with the session.
`load()`	Loads an object from the database by the object's identifier (you should use the `get()` methods if you are not certain that the object is in the database and you don't want to trap an exception).
`refresh()`	Refreshes the state of an associated object from the database.
`update()`	Updates the database with changes to an object.
`delete()`	Deletes an object from the database.
`createFilter()`	Creates a filter (a selection criterion) to narrow operations on the database.
`enableFilter()`	Enables a named filter in queries produced by `createFilter()`.

(*continued*)

Table 8-1. *(continued)*

Method	Description
disableFilter()	Disables a named filter.
getEnabledFilter()	Retrieves a currently enabled filter object.
createQuery()	Creates a Hibernate query to be applied to the database.
getNamedQuery()	Retrieves a query from the mapping file.
cancelQuery()	Cancels execution of any query currently in progress from another thread. This does not necessarily dictate what resources are freed or when; the database might still attempt to fulfill the query despite cancellation, for example.
createCriteria()	Creates a criteria object for narrowing search results.

Table 8-2. *Session Methods for Transactions and Locking*

Method	Description
beginTransaction()	Begins a transaction.
getTransaction()	Retrieves the current transaction object. This does not return null when no transaction is in progress. Instead, the active property of the returned object is false.
lock()	Gets a database lock for an object (or can be used like merge() if LockMode.NONE is given). In effect, this method checks the status of an object in the database as compared to the object in memory.

Table 8-3. *Session Methods for Managing Resources*

Method	Description
contains()	Determines whether a specific object is associated with the database.
clear()	Clears the session of all loaded instances and cancels any saves, updates, or deletions that have not been completed. Retains any iterators that are in use.

(continued)

Table 8-3. (*continued*)

Method	Description
`evict()`	Disassociates an object from the session so that subsequent changes to it will not be persisted.
`flush()`	Flushes all pending changes into the database – all saves, updates, and deletions will be carried out; essentially, this synchronizes the session with the database. This still takes place in the context of a transaction, however, so its usefulness might be limited depending on the kinds of transactions in use.
`isOpen()`	Determines whether the session has been closed.
`isDirty()`	Determines whether the session is synchronized with the database; it will be `true` if the session has not written changes in memory to the database tables.
`getCacheMode()`	Determines the caching mode currently employed.
`setCacheMode()`	Changes the caching mode currently employed.
`getCurrentLockMode()`	Determines the locking mode currently employed for a specific object. (It can be set with the `lock()` method, e.g., among many other options.)
`setFlushMode()`	Determines the approach to flushing currently used. The options are to flush after every operation, flush when needed, never flush, or flush only on commit.
`setReadOnly()`	Marks a persistent object as read-only (or as writable). There are minor performance benefits from marking an object as read-only, but changes to its state will be ignored until it is marked as writable.
`close()`	Closes the session and, hence, the underlying database connection; releases other resources (such as the cache). You must not perform operations on the Session object after calling `close()`.
`getSessionFactory()`	Retrieves a reference to the `SessionFactory` object that created the current `Session` instance.

Table 8-4. *Session Methods Related to JDBC Connections*

Method	Description
connection()	Retrieves a reference to the underlying database connection.
disconnect()	Disconnects the underlying database connection.
reconnect()	Reconnects the underlying database connection.
isConnected()	Determines whether the underlying database connection is connected.

Transactions and Locking

Transactions and locking are intimately related: the locking techniques chosen to enforce a transaction can determine both the performance and the likelihood of success of the transaction. The type of transaction selected dictates, to some extent, the type of locking that it must use.

You are not obliged to use transactions if they do not suit your needs, but there is rarely a good reason to avoid them. If you decide to avoid them, you will need to invoke the `flush()` method on the session at appropriate points to ensure that your changes are persisted to the database.

Don't avoid transactions. It's very little code to acquire a transaction, and we've seen examples in our `SessionUtil` from earlier chapters that use lambdas to manage operations with an active `Session` and `Transaction` - and the benefits of knowing when and how things occur cannot be overstated. It bears repeating: just use transactions.

Transactions

A transaction is a unit of work guaranteed to behave as if you have exclusive use of the database. Generally speaking, if you wrap your work in a transaction, the behavior of other system users will not affect your data.[2] A transaction can be started, committed to write data to the database, or rolled back to remove all changes from the beginning onward (usually as the result of an error). To properly complete an operation, you obtain a `Transaction` object from the database (beginning the transaction) and manipulate the session as shown in the following code:

---

[2] Strictly speaking, transactions give you the *ability* to isolate from other simultaneous operations on the database.

```
try(Session session = factory.openSession()) {
  session.beginTransaction();
  // Normal session usage here?
  session.getTransaction().commit();
} catch (HibernateException e) {
  Transaction tx = session.getTransaction();
  if (tx.isActive()) tx.rollback();
}
```

In the real world, it's not actually desirable for all transactions to be fully ACID (see the next section!) because of the performance problems that this can cause.

Different database suppliers support and permit you, to a lesser or greater extent, to break the ACID rules, but the degree of control over the isolation rule is actually mandated by the SQL-92 standard. There are important reasons that you might want to break this rule, so both JDBC and Hibernate also make explicit allowances for it.

The ACID Tests

ACID is an acronym often associated with databases, standing for four attributes that a transaction represents. They are *atomicity*, *consistency*, *isolation*, and *durability*:

- Atomicity: A transaction should be all or nothing. If it fails to complete, the database will be left as if none of the operations had ever been performed – this is known as a `rollback`. Atomicity means that you can't get only part of a transaction's committed data; changes in a transaction are applied as a single unit.
- Consistency: A transaction should be incapable of breaking any rules defined for the database. For example, foreign key constraints must be obeyed. If for some reason this is impossible (i.e., you try to persist data that is inconsistent with the schema), the transaction will be rolled back.

- Isolation: The effects of the transaction will be completely invisible to all other transactions until it has completed successfully. This guarantees that the transaction will always see the data in a sensible state. For example, consider if an update to a user's address should only contain a correct address (i.e., it will never have the house name for one location but the ZIP code for another); without isolation, a transaction could easily see when another transaction had updated the first part but had not yet completed.
- Durability: The data should be retained intact. If the system fails for any reason, it should always be possible to retrieve the database up to the moment of the failure.

The isolation levels permitted by JDBC (and Hibernate) are listed in Table 8-5.

Table 8-5. *JDBC Isolation Levels*

Level	Name	Transactional Behavior
0	None	Anything is permitted; the database or driver does not support transactions.
1	Read Uncommitted	Dirty, nonrepeatable, and phantom reads are permitted.
2	Read Committed	Nonrepeatable reads and phantom reads are permitted.
4	Repeatable Read	Phantom reads are permitted.
8	Serializable	The rule must be obeyed absolutely.

A *dirty read* may see the in-progress changes of an uncommitted transaction. As with the isolation example discussed in the ACID list, it could see the wrong ZIP code for an address.

A *nonrepeatable read* can see different data over time for the same query. For example, it might determine a specific user's ZIP code at the beginning of the transaction and again at the end, and get a different answer both times without making any updates.

A *phantom read* sees different numbers of rows for the same query. For example, it might see 100 users in the database at the beginning of the query and 105 at the end without making any updates.

Hibernate treats the isolation as a global setting: you apply the configuration option `hibernate.connection.isolation` in the usual manner, setting it to one of the values permitted in Table 8-5.

Locking

A database can conform to these various levels of isolation in a number of ways, and you will need a working knowledge of locking to elicit the desired behavior and performance from your application in all circumstances.

To prevent simultaneous access to data, the database itself will acquire a lock on that data. This can be acquired for the momentary operation on the data only, or it can be retained until the end of the transaction. The former is called *optimistic locking*, and the latter is called *pessimistic locking*.

The Read Uncommitted isolation level always acquires optimistic locks, whereas the Serializable isolation level will only acquire pessimistic locks. Some databases offer a feature that allows you to append the `FOR UPDATE` query to a select operation, which requires the database to acquire a pessimistic lock even in the lower isolation levels.

Hibernate provides some support for this feature when it is available and takes it somewhat further by adding facilities that describe additional degrees of isolation obtainable from Hibernate's own cache.

The `LockMode` enum[3] controls this fine-grained isolation (see Table 8-6). It is only applicable to the `get()` methods, so it is limited; however, when possible, it is preferable to the direct control of isolation mentioned previously.

Table 8-6. *Lock Modes That Can Be Requested*

Mode	Description
NONE	Reads from the database only if the object is not available from the caches.
READ	Reads from the database regardless of the contents of the caches.
UPGRADE	Obtains a dialect-specific upgrade lock for the data to be accessed (if this is available from your database).
UPGRADE_NOWAIT	Behaves like UPGRADE, but when support is available from the database and dialect, the method will fail with an exception immediately. Without this option, or on databases for which it is not supported, the query must wait for a lock to be granted (or for a timeout to occur).

[3] See `https://docs.jboss.org/hibernate/orm/6.0/javadocs/org/hibernate/LockMode.html`.

An additional lock mode, `WRITE`, is acquired by Hibernate automatically when it has written to a row within the current transaction. This mode cannot be set explicitly, but calls to `getLockMode()` may return it.

Having discussed locking in general, we need to touch on some of the problems that locks can cause.

Deadlocks

Deadlocks occur when two resources compete for dependencies without resolution. For example, imagine you have two processes that need resources “A” and “B” - except the first process acquires resource A first and then accesses B, and the second process gets resource B first and then loads A. If the first process grabs A, and then waits to access B, but the second process loads B before process A grabs it, they will deadlock when trying to acquire their second resource.

It looks something like this:

Process One	Process Two
Lock resource A	
	Lock resource B
	Wait until A is available
Wait until B is available	

Hibernate can detect this kind of cycle and will throw an error (an `OptimisticLockException`, because we’re relying on optimistic locks) if it’s found. Let’s create one so we can see what happens. Our example will submit two `Runnable` instances into a `ServiceExecutor`, and each one will acquire (and modify, therefore locking) two resources, except in different orders, therefore creating our deadlock situation. Afterward, it will verify that both transactions failed, by determining if the data is back in its original (unmodified) condition.

First, we need our project model, of course.

There are elements in this project that apply to the caching section, which we’ll talk about later in this chapter.

Listing 8-1. chapter08/pom.xml

```
<?xml version="1.0" encoding="UTF-8"?>
<project xmlns:xsi="http://www.w3.org/2001/XMLSchema-instance"
         xmlns="http://maven.apache.org/POM/4.0.0"
         xsi:schemaLocation="http://maven.apache.org/POM/4.0.0
         http://maven.apache.org/xsd/maven-4.0.0.xsd">
    <parent>
        <artifactId>hibernate-6-parent</artifactId>
        <groupId>com.autumncode.books.hibernate</groupId>
        <version>5.0</version>
    </parent>

    <modelVersion>4.0.0</modelVersion>
    <artifactId>chapter08</artifactId>

    <dependencies>
        <dependency>
            <groupId>com.autumncode.books.hibernate</groupId>
            <artifactId>util</artifactId>
            <version>${project.version}</version>
        </dependency>
        <dependency>
            <groupId>org.projectlombok</groupId>
            <artifactId>lombok</artifactId>
        </dependency>
        <dependency>
            <groupId>org.apache.ignite</groupId>
            <artifactId>ignite-core</artifactId>
        </dependency>
        <dependency>
            <groupId>org.hibernate.orm</groupId>
            <artifactId>hibernate-jcache</artifactId>
        </dependency>
    </dependencies>
</project>
```

Next, we need an entity to work with.

Listing 8-2. chapter08/src/main/java/chapter08/model/Publisher.java

```
package chapter08.model;

import lombok.Data;

import javax.persistence.Entity;
import javax.persistence.GeneratedValue;
import javax.persistence.GenerationType;
import javax.persistence.Id;

@Entity
@Data
public class Publisher {
  @Id
  @GeneratedValue(strategy = GenerationType.AUTO)
  Long id;
  String name;
}
```

Here's the Hibernate configuration file. Note that it, like the pom.xml, has a few things related to caching; these will be used later in this chapter.

Listing 8-3. chapter08/src/test/resources/hibernate.cfg.xml

```
<!DOCTYPE hibernate-configuration PUBLIC
    "-//Hibernate/Hibernate Configuration DTD 3.0//EN"
    "http://www.hibernate.org/dtd/hibernate-configuration-3.0.dtd">
<hibernate-configuration>
  <session-factory>
    <!-- Database connection settings -->
    <property name="connection.driver_class">org.h2.Driver</property>
    <property name="connection.url">jdbc:h2:./db8</property>
    <property name="connection.username">sa</property>
    <property name="connection.password"/>
    <property name="dialect">org.hibernate.dialect.H2Dialect</property>

    <property name="hibernate.cache.region.factory_class">
      jcache
```

```
    </property>
    <property name="hibernate.javax.cache.missing_cache_strategy">
      create
    </property>

    <!--  Echo all executed SQL to stdout  -->
    <property name="show_sql">true</property>
    <property name="use_sql_comments">true</property>

    <!--  Drop and re-create the database schema on startup  -->
    <property name="hbm2ddl.auto">create-drop</property>

    <mapping class="chapter08.model.Publisher"/>
  </session-factory>
</hibernate-configuration>
```

And at last we get to our deadlock example itself. It looks long, but most of the complexity is in trying to ensure that the updates happen in the right order and at the right times. Let's take a look at the code and then unpack it.

Listing 8-4. chapter08/src/test/java/chapter08/DeadlockExample.java

```
package chapter08;

import chapter08.model.Publisher;
import com.autumncode.hibernate.util.SessionUtil;
import org.hibernate.PessimisticLockException;
import org.hibernate.Session;
import org.hibernate.Transaction;
import org.hibernate.query.Query;
import org.slf4j.Logger;
import org.slf4j.LoggerFactory;
import org.testng.annotations.Test;

import javax.persistence.OptimisticLockException;
import java.util.concurrent.ExecutorService;
import java.util.concurrent.Executors;
import java.util.concurrent.TimeUnit;
import java.util.stream.Collectors;
```

```
import static org.testng.Assert.assertEquals;

public class DeadlockExample {
  Logger logger= LoggerFactory.getLogger(this.getClass());

  private Long createPublisher(Session session, String name) {
    Publisher publisher = new Publisher();
    publisher.setName(name);
    session.save(publisher);
    return publisher.getId();
  }

  private void updatePublishers(String prefix, Long... ids) {
    try (Session session = SessionUtil.getSession()) {
      Transaction tx = session.beginTransaction();
      for (Long id : ids) {
        Thread.sleep(300);
        Publisher publisher = session
            .byId(Publisher.class)
            .load(id);
        publisher.setName(prefix + " " + publisher.getName());
      }
      tx.commit();
    } catch (OptimisticLockException e) {
      logger.error("lock exception with prefix "+ prefix);
    } catch(InterruptedException ignored) {
    }
  }

  @Test
  public void showDeadlock() throws InterruptedException {
    Long publisherAId;
    Long publisherBId;

    //clear out old data and populate tables
    try (Session session = SessionUtil.getSession()) {
      Transaction tx = session.beginTransaction();
      session
```

```
          .createQuery("delete from Publisher")
          .executeUpdate();

      publisherAId = createPublisher(session, "A");
      publisherBId = createPublisher(session, "B");
      tx.commit();
    }

    ExecutorService executor = Executors.newFixedThreadPool(2);
    executor.submit(
        () -> updatePublishers("session1", publisherAId, publisherBId));
    executor.submit(
        () -> updatePublishers("session2", publisherBId, publisherAId));
    executor.shutdown();

    if (!executor.awaitTermination(60, TimeUnit.SECONDS)) {
      executor.shutdownNow();
      if (!executor.awaitTermination(60, TimeUnit.SECONDS)) {
        System.out.println("Executor did not terminate");
      }
    }
    try (Session session = SessionUtil.getSession()) {
      Query<Publisher> query = session.createQuery(
          "from Publisher p order by p.name",
          Publisher.class
      );
      String result = query
          .list()
          .stream()
          .map(Publisher::getName)
          .collect(Collectors.joining(","));
      assertEquals(result, "A,B");
    }
  }
}
```

The first method we saw was `createPublisher()`, which takes an active `Session` and a "publisher name" - and returns an `id` of the `Publisher` it just saved for us. We'll be using that identifier to lock the `Publisher` when we try to update it.

The second method is `updatePublishers()`, which takes a "prefix" and a list of keys to update. The point of this method is nonsensical outside of the context of this test; it's simply to prepend the `prefix` to the name of every `Publisher` whose identifier is passed in, *in order*, with a fairly long delay between each update. We'll be executing this method from two different threads, each with a different order of identifiers, creating our deadlock situation.

It even helpfully tells us when it gets the lock exception - "just in case."

Why is the delay so long? Mostly because you can't guarantee when an executor will actually start. On most machines, a delay of 300 milliseconds here is gratuitous; however, note that your CPU may be different, and you may need to adjust the delay.

Lastly, we get to the actual test itself, `showDeadlock()`. It has three phases: the first sets up our data (using the `createPublisher()` method); the second creates an `ExecutorService` and submits two tasks, performed by `updatePublishers()`, inverting the order of identifiers: the first executor updates the first and then the second `Publisher`, and the other executor updates the *second* and then the *first* `Publisher`, which should create conflicting updates.

The last phase of `showDeadlock()` retrieves the set of `Publisher` entities, ordering them by `name` so the results are predictable, and validates that the names are "A" and "B," respectively, which is what we set them to when we first created them.

Remember, we're expecting them to be unchanged, as we deliberately created a deadlock situation, such that *both* sets of updates should fail.

On output, along with any other logging information, we should see the following messages, although their orders might differ for you (and I've truncated timestamps from the messages, too, as they're irrelevant):

```
[pool-1-thread-2] ERROR chapter08.DeadlockExample - lock exception with
prefix session2
[pool-1-thread-1] ERROR chapter08.DeadlockExample - lock exception with
prefix session1
```

Caching

Accessing a database is an expensive[4] operation, even for a simple query. The request has to be sent (usually over the network) to the server. The database server may have to compile the SQL into a query plan. The query plan has to be run and is limited largely by disk performance. The resulting data has to be shuttled back (again, usually across the network[5]) to the client, and only then can the application program begin to process the results.

Most good databases will cache the results of a query if it is run multiple times, eliminating the disk I/O and query compilation time. But this will be of limited value if there are large numbers of clients making substantially different requests. Even if the cache generally holds the results, the time taken to transmit the information across the network is often the larger part of the delay.

Some applications will be able to take advantage of in-process databases, but this is the exception rather than the rule - and such databases have their own limitations.

The natural and obvious answer is to have a cache at the client end of the database connection. This is not a feature provided or supported by JDBC directly, but Hibernate provides one cache (the first-level, or L1, cache) through which all requests must pass. A second-level cache (L2) is optional and configurable.

The L1 cache ensures that, within a session, requests for a given object from a database will always return the same object instance, thus preventing data from conflicting and preventing Hibernate from trying to load an object multiple times.

Items in the L1 cache can be individually discarded by invoking the `evict()` method on the session for the object that you wish to discard. To discard all items in the L1 cache, invoke the `clear()` method.

---

[4] "Expensive" is a relative term, and it's very dependent on what your comparison points are. As used here, accessing a database is "expensive" when compared to accessing data in memory - an in-memory operation, even over a large dataset, might take microseconds, while a database operation has to work with a networking, which adds *milliseconds*. That may not sound like much, but as R. Admiral Grace Hopper once pointed out, milliseconds add up... but compare the four-millisecond operation on a database to the three minutes it may take to load a physical tape, and databases look *awesome*.

[5] Note that since we're using an embedded database, most of our examples don't go across a physical network interface at all, because nothing makes a good point like irony.

In this way, Hibernate has a major advantage over the traditional JDBC approach: with no additional effort from the developer, a Hibernate application gains the benefits of a client-side database cache.

Figure 8-2 shows the two caches available to the session: the compulsory L1 cache, through which all requests must pass, and the optional L2 cache. The L1 cache will always be consulted before any attempt is made to locate an object in the L2 cache. You will notice that the L2 cache is external to Hibernate; and although it is accessed via the session in a way that is transparent to Hibernate users, it is a pluggable interface to any one of a variety of caches that are maintained on the same JVM as your Hibernate application or on an external JVM. This allows a cache to be shared between applications on the same machine or even among multiple applications on multiple machines.

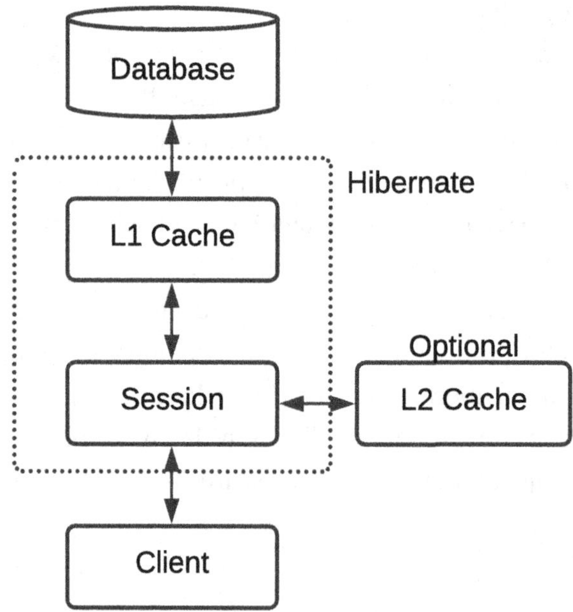

Figure 8-2. *The relationship between a `Session` and caches*

In principle, any third-party cache can be used with Hibernate. An `org.hibernate.Cache` interface is provided, which must be implemented to provide Hibernate with a handle to the cache implementation. The cache provider is then specified by giving the implementation class name as the value of the `hibernate.cache.provider_class` property.

With Hibernate 6, the **preferred** cache mechanism is to use a JCache-compatible provider. JCache is a specification governing the minimum features a cache should provide (much as JPA is a specification governing what minimum features a persistence framework should provide). There are a **lot** of JCache-compatible libraries out there; see `https://jcp.org/aboutJava/communityprocess/implementations/jsr107/index.html` for a list of known providers.

The type of access to the L2 cache can be configured on a per-session basis by selecting a `CacheMode` enum (see Table 8-7) and applying it with the `Session.setCacheMode()` method.

Table 8-7. *CacheMode Options*

Mode	Description
NORMAL	Data is read from and written to the cache as necessary.
GET	Data is never added to the cache (although cache entries are invalidated when updated by the session).
PUT	Data is never read from the cache, but cache entries will be updated as they are read from the database by the session.
REFRESH	This is the same as PUT, but the use_minimal_puts Hibernate configuration option will be ignored if it has been set.
IGNORE	Data is never read from or written to the cache (except that cache entries will still be invalidated when they are updated by the session, in case another `Session` has cached them somehow).

The `CacheMode` setting does not affect the way in which the L1 cache is accessed.

The decision to use an L2 cache is not clear-cut. Although it has the potential to greatly reduce access to the database, the benefits depend on the type of cache and the way in which it will be accessed.

A distributed cache will cause additional network traffic. Some types of database access may result in the contents of the cache being flushed before they are used; in this case, it will be adding unnecessary overhead to the transactions.

The L2 cache cannot account for the changes in the underlying data, which are the result of actions by an external program that is not cache aware. This could potentially lead to problems with stale data, which is not an issue with the L1 cache.

In practice, as with most optimization problems, it is best to carry out performance testing under realistic load conditions. This will let you determine if a cache is necessary and help you select which one will offer the greatest improvement.

Actually, configuring for cache usage is fairly simple. In order to set everything up, in this example, we will need to do the following:

1. Select a cache provider and add the dependency to Maven.
2. Configure Hibernate to use the cache provider for a second-level cache.
3. Alter our entities to mark them as cacheable.

We'll choose Apache Ignite as a cache provider, as it's trivial to set up in a Java SE environment. The dependency block for Maven will look like this:[6]

```
<dependency>
  <groupId>org.apache.ignite</groupId>
  <artifactId>ignite-core</artifactId>
  <version>2.10.0</version>
</dependency>
```

We can tell Hibernate to use our second-level cache by adding some properties to our configuration, as we've already seen earlier in the chapter:

```
<property
  name="hibernate.cache.region.factory_class">
  jcache
</property>
<property
  name="hibernate.javax.cache.missing_cache_strategy">
  create
</property>
```

The last thing we need to do is mark an entity as cacheable. In Listing 8-5, we'll create a simple `Supplier` entity (which we'll revisit in the next chapters) and mark it as being a candidate for the second-level cache.

[6] Actually, the dependency block used in the book's source code doesn't have the `<version>` tag, because the version is managed by the top-level project model.

Listing 8-5. chapter08/src/main/java/chapter08/model/Supplier.java

```
package chapter08.model;

import lombok.Data;
import org.hibernate.annotations.Cache;
import org.hibernate.annotations.CacheConcurrencyStrategy;

import javax.persistence.*;
import java.io.Serializable;

@Entity
@Cache(usage = CacheConcurrencyStrategy.NONSTRICT_READ_WRITE)
@Data
public class Supplier implements Serializable {
  @Id
  @GeneratedValue(strategy = GenerationType.AUTO)
  Integer id;
  @Column(unique = true)
  String name;

  public Supplier(String name) {
    this.name = name;
  }

  public Supplier() {
  }
}
```

If we load a specific Supplier in one session, then immediately load the same Supplier in another session, the database will not (necessarily) be queried because it's being pulled from the second-level cache instead of from the database each time. Using different sessions is necessary because the Supplier instance would be cached in the first-level cache of each Session; the sessions share a second-level cache and not a first-level cache.

Let's show this in action, with yet another test.

Listing 8-6. chapter08/src/test/java/chapter08/QueryTest.java

```
package chapter08;

import chapter08.model.Supplier;
import com.autumncode.hibernate.util.SessionUtil;
import org.hibernate.Session;
import org.hibernate.Transaction;
import org.testng.annotations.AfterMethod;
import org.testng.annotations.BeforeMethod;
import org.testng.annotations.Test;

import java.util.ArrayList;
import java.util.List;

public class QueryTest {
  List<Integer> keys = new ArrayList<>();

  @BeforeMethod
  public void populateData() {
    clearSuppliers();
    Session session = SessionUtil.getSession();
    Transaction tx = session.beginTransaction();
    for (int i = 0; i < 10; i++) {
      Supplier supplier = new Supplier("Supplier " + (i + 1));
      session.save(supplier);
      keys.add(supplier.getId());
    }
    tx.commit();
    session.close();
  }

  @AfterMethod
  public void clearSuppliers() {
    Session session = SessionUtil.getSession();
    Transaction tx = session.beginTransaction();

    session.createQuery("delete from Supplier")
        .executeUpdate();
```

```
    tx.commit();
    session.close();
  }

  @Test
  public void testSuppliers() {
    for(int i=0;i<100; i++) {
      // create a new Session every loop...
      try(Session session=SessionUtil.getSession()) {
        Transaction tx = session.beginTransaction();
        Integer key=keys.get((int)(Math.random()*keys.size()));
        Supplier supplier = session.get(Supplier.class,key);
        System.out.println(supplier.getName());
        tx.commit();
      }
    }
  }
}
```

Here, we start our test by creating a set of `Supplier` instances in the database. (There are a lot of ways we could do this, of course, but this is very simple.)

The actual test itself - `testSuppliers` - simply does a large number of loads against our set of `Supplier` instances, using a random key. It then prints out the supplier name for every load, so it will generate a fairly long output. If you **run** this test, the output looks something like this, because we have "show SQL" on in our configuration in `hibernate.cfg.xml`:

```
Hibernate: select s1_0.id, s1_0.name from Supplier as s1_0 where s1_0.id = ?
Supplier 9
Hibernate: select s1_0.id, s1_0.name from Supplier as s1_0 where s1_0.id = ?
Supplier 2
Supplier 2
Hibernate: select s1_0.id, s1_0.name from Supplier as s1_0 where s1_0.id = ?
Supplier 7
Hibernate: select s1_0.id, s1_0.name from Supplier as s1_0 where s1_0.id = ?
Supplier 5
Hibernate: select s1_0.id, s1_0.name from Supplier as s1_0 where s1_0.id = ?
```

```
Supplier 6
Hibernate: select s1_0.id, s1_0.name from Supplier as s1_0 where s1_0.id = ?
Supplier 10
Supplier 7
Hibernate: select s1_0.id, s1_0.name from Supplier as s1_0 where s1_0.id = ?
Supplier 1
Hibernate: select s1_0.id, s1_0.name from Supplier as s1_0 where s1_0.id = ?
Supplier 8
Supplier 10
Supplier 9
```

You'll note that the database isn't actually being queried very often; we will see ten SQL statements issued (after a while, as that's not a complete run of the output) with a *lot* of repetitive supplier names; this is because the sessions are loading the suppliers from the Ignite cache.

Is this useful? It's hard to say. In this case, it's certainly useful for demonstrating the function of the cache, but is it actually a performance improvement? Not enough to matter; for our test, generating the console output is the most expensive part of the entire test, and the cache saves us very little. For a *real* application, the advice is *always* to test thoroughly, under realistic read and write conditions, and measure the results of different configurations.

Second-level caches *can* improve performance dramatically, but only if the conditions are right and it's applied wisely.

Threads

Having considered the caches available to a Hibernate application, you may now be concerned about the risk of a conventional Java deadlock if two threads of execution were to contend for the same object in the Hibernate session cache.

In principle, this is possible, and unlike database deadlocks, Java thread deadlocks do not time out with an error message. Fortunately, there is a very simple solution:

```
Patient: Doctor, it hurts when I do this.
Doctor: Don't do that, then.
```

Do not share the `Session` object between threads. This will eliminate any risk of deadlocking on objects contained within the session cache.

The easiest way to ensure that you do not use the same Session object outside the current thread is to use an instance local to the current method or create a session and pass it to a number of "worker methods," closing the session when the operation is done:

```
try(Session session=SessionUtil.getSession()) {
  Transaction tx=session.beginTransaction();
  operationOne(session);
  operationTwo(session);
  operationThree(session);
  tx.commit();
}
```

If you absolutely must maintain an instance for a longer duration, maintain the instance within a ThreadLocal object. For most purposes, however, the lightweight nature of the Session object makes it more practical to construct, use, and destroy an instance, rather than to store a session.

Summary

In this chapter, we have discussed the nature of Session objects and how they can be used to obtain and manage transactions. We have looked at the two levels of caching that are available to applications and how concurrent threads should manage sessions.

In the next chapter, we discuss the various ways in which you can retrieve objects from the database. We also show you how to perform more complicated queries against the database using HQL.

CHAPTER 9

Searches and Queries

In the last chapter, we discussed how the Hibernate session is used to interact with the database. Some of the session's methods take query strings in their parameter lists or return `Query` objects. These methods are used to request arbitrary information from the database. In order to fully show how they're used, we must introduce the Hibernate Query Language (HQL), used to phrase these requests. As well as extracting information (with `SELECT`), HQL can be used to alter the information in the database (with `INSERT`, `UPDATE`, and `DELETE`). We cover all of this basic functionality in this chapter.

HQL is an object-oriented query language, similar to SQL, but instead of operating on tables and columns, HQL works with persistent objects and their properties. It is a superset of the JPQL, the Java Persistence Query Language; a JPQL query is a valid HQL query, but not all HQL queries are valid JPQL queries.

HQL is a language with its own syntax and grammar. HQL queries are expressed much as SQL itself is, as a string, like `from Product p`. Ultimately, your HQL queries are translated by Hibernate into conventional SQL queries; Hibernate also provides an API that allows you to directly issue SQL queries.

Hibernate Query Language (HQL)

While most ORM tools and object databases offer an object query language, Hibernate's HQL stands out as complete and easy to use. Although you can use SQL statements directly with Hibernate (which is covered in detail in the "Using Native SQL" section of this chapter), we recommend that you use HQL (or criteria) whenever possible to avoid database portability hassles, as well as to take advantage of Hibernate's SQL generation and caching strategies. In addition to its technical advantages over traditional SQL, HQL is a more compact query language than SQL because it can make use of the relationship information defined in the Hibernate mappings.

J. B. Ottinger et al., *Beginning Hibernate 6*, https://doi.org/10.1007/978-1-4842-7337-1_9

We realize that not every developer trusts Hibernate's generated SQL to be perfectly optimized. If you do encounter a performance bottleneck in your queries, we recommend that you use SQL tracing on your database during performance testing of your critical components. If you see an area that needs optimization, first try to optimize using HQL, and only later drop into native SQL. Hibernate provides statistics information through a JMX MBean, which you can use for analyzing Hibernate's performance. Hibernate's statistics also give you insight into how caching is performing.

If you would like to execute HQL statements through a GUI-based tool, the Hibernate team provides a Hibernate console for Eclipse in the Hibernate Tools subproject. This console is a plug-in for recent versions of Eclipse; see `https://tools.jboss.org/` for more information. Other IDEs have similar functionality available.

Syntax Basics

HQL was inspired by SQL and is a major inspiration for the Java Persistence Query Language (JPQL). The JPQL specification is included in the standard for JPA available from the Java Community Process website (`www.jcp.org/en/jsr/detail?id=338`). HQL's syntax is defined as an ANTLR grammar; the grammar files are included in the grammar directory of the Hibernate core download. (ANTLR is a tool for building language parsers.)

As the ANTLR grammar files are somewhat cryptic, and as not every statement that is permissible according to the ANTLR grammar's rules can be used in Hibernate, we outline the syntax for the four fundamental HQL operations in this section. Note that the following descriptions of syntax are not comprehensive; there are some deprecated or more obscure usages (particularly for `SELECT` statements) that are not covered here.

UPDATE

`UPDATE` alters the details of existing objects in the database. This is an operation going from memory *to* database - an update doesn't affect anything you've already loaded. (You can, of course, update objects you've loaded, and when a transaction is committed, any changes will be written to the database; this does not, however, require an HQL `UPDATE`.) Here's the syntax of the `UPDATE` statement:

```
UPDATE [VERSIONED]
   [FROM] path [[AS] alias] [, ...]
   SET property = value [, ...]
   [WHERE logicalExpression]
```

The “path” refers to the fully qualified name of the entity or entities. The alias names may be used to abbreviate references to specific entities or their properties and must be used when property names in the query would otherwise be ambiguous.

`VERSIONED` means that the update will update timestamps, if any, that are part of the entity being updated.

The property names are the names of properties of entities listed in the FROM path.

The syntax of logical expressions is discussed later, in the “Using Restrictions with HQL” section.

An example of the update in action might look like this:

```
Query query=session.createQuery(
    "update Person p set p.creditscore=:creditscore where p.name=:name"
    );
query.setInteger("creditscore", 612);
query.setString("name", "John Q. Public");
int modifications=query.executeUpdate();
```

`Query` is normally typed; the actual type is `Query<R>`, and we’re not showing an `R` here! That’s okay, because we’re issuing an `UPDATE`, not a selection; the `executeUpdate()` call returns a count of modified records, and we’re discarding the type that might have been returned from a `list()` operation.

DELETE

`DELETE` removes the details of existing objects from the database. As with updates, objects you’ve already loaded aren’t affected by an HQL `DELETE`. This also means that Hibernate’s cascade rules will not be followed for deletions carried out using HQL. However, if you have specified cascading deletes at the database level (either directly or through Hibernate), the database will still remove the child rows. This approach to deletion is commonly referred to as “bulk deletion,” since it is the most efficient way to remove large numbers of entities from the database. Here’s the syntax of the `DELETE` statement:

```
DELETE
   [FROM] path [[AS] alias]
   [WHERE logicalExpression]
```

As with UPDATE, path is the fully qualified name of an entity. The alias names may be used to abbreviate references to specific entities or their properties and must be used when property names in the query would otherwise be ambiguous.

In practice, deletes might look like this:

```
Query query=session.createQuery(
    "delete from Person p where p.accountstatus=:status
    ");
query.setString("status", "toBePurged");
int rowsDeleted=query.executeUpdate();
```

As with the UPDATE example, we're discarding the type we might have specified with the Query because we're only interested in the number of entities deleted; we're not using the typed query.

INSERT

An HQL INSERT cannot be used to directly insert arbitrary entities – it can only be used to insert entities constructed from information obtained from SELECT queries (unlike ordinary SQL, in which an INSERT command can be used to insert arbitrary data into a table, as well as insert values selected from other tables). Basically, an HQL INSERT uses data from the database to construct entities, rather than using data supplied to it. Here's the syntax of the INSERT statement:

```
INSERT
   INTO path ( property [, ...])
   select
```

The name of an entity is represented by path. The property names are the names of properties of entities listed in the FROM path of the incorporated SELECT query.

The select query is an HQL SELECT query (as described in the next section).

As this HQL statement can only use data provided by an HQL select, its application can be limited. Suppose we wanted to copy records to be deleted from a USERS table to a PURGED_USERS table, for archival purposes.[1] We could manually copy the records from the USERS table to a PURGED_USERS table, thus meeting the requirement for HQL INSERT, like so:

```
Query query=session.createQuery(
    "insert into purged_users(id, name, status) "+
    "select id, name, status from users where status=:status"
    );
query.setString("status", "toBePurged");
int rowsCopied=query.executeUpdate();
```

As with UPDATE and DELETE in HQL, we're ignoring the type for the Query, because we're not requesting typed information back, only the count of modified rows.

SELECT

An HQL SELECT is used to query the database for classes and their properties. As noted previously, this is very much a short summary of the full expressive power of HQL SELECT queries. Here's the syntax of the SELECT statement:

```
[SELECT [DISTINCT] property [, ...]]
   FROM path [[AS] alias] [, ...] [FETCH ALL PROPERTIES]
   WHERE logicalExpression
   GROUP BY property [, ...]
   HAVING logicalExpression
   ORDER BY property [ASC | DESC] [, ...]
```

The fully qualified name of an entity is path. The alias names may be used to abbreviate references to specific entities or their properties and must be used when property names used in the query would otherwise be ambiguous.

The property names are the names of properties of entities listed in the FROM path.

If FETCH ALL PROPERTIES is used, then lazy loading semantics will be ignored, and all the immediate properties of the retrieved object(s) will be actively loaded (this does not apply recursively; entities loaded this way may or may not have *their* nested data retrieved).

[1] This example is contrived; why wouldn't you just set a status on the USERS table to indicate that the user records in question were inactive?

When the properties listed consist only of the names of aliases in the FROM clause, the SELECT clause can be omitted in HQL. If you are using the JPA with JPQL, one of the differences between HQL and JPQL is that the SELECT clause is required in JPQL.

Thus, in HQL, it's acceptable to use "FROM USERS U" as a query, whereas in JPQL the equivalent would be SELECT U FROM USERS U.

Named Queries

Hibernate (and JPA) provides named queries. Named queries are created via class-level annotations on entities; normally, the queries apply to the entity in whose source file they occur, but there's no absolute requirement for this to be true.

Named queries are created with the @NamedQueries annotation, which contains an array of @NamedQuery sets; each has query content (the query itself) and a name.

First, let's take a look at the project model, the framework under which we can build our project.

Listing 9-1. chapter09/pom.xml

```
<?xml version="1.0" encoding="UTF-8"?>
<project xmlns:xsi="http://www.w3.org/2001/XMLSchema-instance"
         xmlns="http://maven.apache.org/POM/4.0.0"
         xsi:schemaLocation="http://maven.apache.org/POM/4.0.0
         http://maven.apache.org/xsd/maven-4.0.0.xsd">
    <parent>
        <artifactId>hibernate-6-parent</artifactId>
        <groupId>com.autumncode.books.hibernate</groupId>
        <version>5.0</version>
    </parent>

    <modelVersion>4.0.0</modelVersion>
    <artifactId>chapter09</artifactId>

    <dependencies>
        <dependency>
            <groupId>com.autumncode.books.hibernate</groupId>
            <artifactId>util</artifactId>
            <version>${project.version}</version>
```

```
        </dependency>
        <dependency>
            <groupId>org.hibernate.validator</groupId>
            <artifactId>hibernate-validator</artifactId>
            <version>${hibernate.validator.version}</version>
        </dependency>
        <dependency>
            <groupId>org.hibernate.validator</groupId>
            <artifactId>hibernate-validator-cdi</artifactId>
            <version>${hibernate.validator.version}</version>
        </dependency>
        <dependency>
            <groupId>javax.el</groupId>
            <artifactId>javax.el-api</artifactId>
            <version>${javax.el-api.version}</version>
        </dependency>
        <dependency>
            <groupId>org.glassfish</groupId>
            <artifactId>javax.el</artifactId>
            <version>${javax.el-api.version}</version>
        </dependency>
    </dependencies>
</project>
```

Next, let's create an object model we can use as an example. Our object model will contain products and suppliers; it will also contain a specialized product ("Software") that adds an attribute to `Product`. One effect of the hierarchy we use here is that Lombok is no longer as usable as it has been,[2] so we're going to eliminate some of the boilerplate from the source code – namely, constructors, mutators, accessors, `equals()`, `hashCode()`, and `toString()`. The source code download for the book will have all of these methods, of course.

[2] Lombok works by analyzing Java source code. It does not walk a hierarchy; while this would be very useful, there are some real technical challenges to implementation. While someday Lombok may indeed be able to handle object hierarchies as conveniently as it handles simple objects, as of this writing it doesn't work well for object hierarchies, so we're not going to use it in this chapter.

Listing 9-2. chapter09/src/main/java/chapter09/model/Product.java

```
package chapter09.model;

import javax.persistence.*;
import javax.validation.constraints.NotNull;
import java.io.Serializable;
import java.util.Objects;

@Entity
@Inheritance(strategy = InheritanceType.JOINED)
public class Product implements Serializable {
  @Id
  @GeneratedValue(strategy = GenerationType.AUTO)
  Integer id;
  @ManyToOne(optional = false, fetch = FetchType.LAZY)
  Supplier supplier;
  @Column
  @NotNull
  String name;
  @Column
  @NotNull
  String description;
  @Column
  @NotNull
  Double price;

  public Product() {
  }

  public Product(Supplier supplier,
                 String name,
                 String description,
                 Double price) {
    this.supplier = supplier;
```

```
    this.name = name;
    this.description = description;
    this.price = price;
  }
}
```

Listing 9-3. chapter09/src/main/java/chapter09/model/Supplier.java

```
package chapter09.model;

import javax.persistence.*;
import javax.validation.constraints.NotNull;
import java.io.Serializable;
import java.util.ArrayList;
import java.util.List;

@Entity
public class Supplier implements Serializable {
  @Id
  @GeneratedValue(strategy = GenerationType.AUTO)
  Integer id;
  @Column(unique = true)
  @NotNull
  String name;
  @OneToMany(cascade = CascadeType.ALL, orphanRemoval = true,
      mappedBy = "supplier", targetEntity = Product.class)
  List<Product> products = new ArrayList<>();

  public Supplier(String name) {
    this.name = name;
  }

  public Supplier() {
  }
}
```

Listing 9-4. chapter09/src/main/java/chapter09/model/Software.java

```
package chapter09.model;

import javax.persistence.Column;
import javax.persistence.Entity;
import javax.validation.constraints.NotNull;
import java.io.Serializable;
import java.util.Objects;

@Entity
public class Software extends Product implements Serializable {
  @Column
  @NotNull
  String version;

  public Software() {
  }

  public Software(Supplier supplier,
                  String name,
                  String description,
                  Double price,
                  String version) {
    super(supplier, name, description, price);
    this.version = version;
  }
}
```

We also need the Hibernate configuration, of course.

Listing 9-5. chapter09/src/test/resources/hibernate.cfg.xml

```
<?xml version="1.0"?>
<!DOCTYPE hibernate-configuration PUBLIC
    "-//Hibernate/Hibernate Configuration DTD 3.0//EN"
    "http://www.hibernate.org/dtd/hibernate-configuration-3.0.dtd">
<hibernate-configuration>
  <session-factory>
```

```
    <!-- Database connection settings -->
    <property name="connection.driver_class">org.h2.Driver</property>
    <property name="connection.url">jdbc:h2:./db9</property>
    <property name="connection.username">sa</property>
    <property name="connection.password"/>
    <property name="dialect">org.hibernate.dialect.H2Dialect</property>
    <!-- set up c3p0 for use -->
    <property name="c3p0.max_size">10</property>
    <!-- Echo all executed SQL to stdout -->
    <property name="show_sql">true</property>
    <property name="use_sql_comments">true</property>

    <!-- Drop and re-create the database schema on startup -->
    <property name="hbm2ddl.auto">create-drop</property>

    <mapping class="chapter09.model.Software"/>
    <mapping class="chapter09.model.Product"/>
    <mapping class="chapter09.model.Supplier"/>
  </session-factory>
</hibernate-configuration>
```

Adding a named query is as simple as adding an annotation to one of the entities. For example, if we wanted to add a named query to retrieve all Supplier entities, we could do so by adding a @NamedQuery annotation to any of the entities, although it makes the most sense to put the query in the source code for Supplier:

```
@NamedQuery(name = "supplier.findAll", query = "from Supplier s")
```

Of course, for such a simple query, there's no real need for a named query *at all* – you'd just use the query text. You might, however, use a named query for consistency's sake or to allow for ease of future maintenance. Imagine adding a field to Supplier that indicated whether the Supplier was active or not; you could then easily update the query to include where active=true, without having to hunt down every place in your code where you queried Supplier sets.

You can group queries together by adding a @NamedQueries annotation and then embedding the named queries in an array as part of that annotation. This would look like the one shown in Listing 9-6.

Listing 9-6. chapter09/src/main/java/chapter09/model/Supplier.java

```
@NamedQueries({
    @NamedQuery(name = "supplier.findAll",
        query = "from Supplier s"),
    @NamedQuery(name = "supplier.findByName",
        query = "from Supplier s where s.name=:name"),
    @NamedQuery(name = "supplier.averagePrice",
        query = "select p.supplier.id, avg(p.price) " +
            "from Product p " +
            "GROUP BY p.supplier.id"),
})
@NamedNativeQueries({
    @NamedNativeQuery(name = "supplier.findAverage",
        query = "SELECT p.supplier_id, avg(p.price) "
            + "FROM Product p GROUP BY p.supplier_id"
    )
})
```

Astute readers will see `@NamedNativeQueries` in use. This will be explained later, but a native query is an SQL query issued through Hibernate. Native queries are fantastically useful if you know SQL well and you're targeting a specific database; here, we're actually building a projection from the `Product` table, using simple SQL.

Using the named queries is very simple. Let's create a `TestBase` class that populates and clears out data for every test, and then we'll create a test that uses our `supplier.findAll` query.[3]

Using `TestBase` is very simple, although it's probably not the *best* class ever written; before it runs a test, it populates a dataset and initializes a `Session`; after the test, it closes the `Session` and cleans up. (The way it uses a `Session` is mostly to help shorten classes that *use* TestBase.)

[3] There are a few ways we could have avoided the `TestBase` class. We could create a new `SessionFactory` for every test or use dbUnit (`https://dbunit.sourceforge.net`), but this seems more direct.

Listing 9-7. chapter09/src/test/java/chapter09/TestBase.java

```
package chapter09;

import chapter09.model.Product;
import chapter09.model.Software;
import chapter09.model.Supplier;
import com.autumncode.hibernate.util.SessionUtil;
import org.hibernate.Session;
import org.hibernate.Transaction;
import org.testng.annotations.AfterMethod;
import org.testng.annotations.BeforeMethod;

public class TestBase {
  Session session;
  Transaction tx;

  @BeforeMethod
  public void populateData() {
    try (Session session = SessionUtil.getSession()) {
      Transaction tx = session.beginTransaction();

      Supplier supplier = new Supplier("Hardware, Inc.");
      supplier.getProducts().add(
          new Product(supplier, "Optical Wheel Mouse", "Mouse", 5.00));
      supplier.getProducts().add(
          new Product(supplier, "Trackball Mouse", "Mouse", 22.00));
      session.save(supplier);

      supplier = new Supplier("Supplier 2");
      supplier.getProducts().add(
          new Software(supplier, "SuperDetect", "Antivirus", 14.95, "1.0"));
      supplier.getProducts().add(
          new Software(supplier, "Wildcat", "Browser", 19.95, "2.2"));
      supplier.getProducts().add(
          new Product(supplier, "AxeGrinder", "Gaming Mouse", 42.00));
```

```
      session.save(supplier);
      tx.commit();
    }

    this.session = SessionUtil.getSession();
    this.tx = this.session.beginTransaction();
  }

  @AfterMethod
  public void closeSession() {
    session.createQuery("delete from Product").executeUpdate();
    session.createQuery("delete from Supplier").executeUpdate();
    if (tx.isActive()) {
      tx.commit();
    }
    if (session.isOpen()) {
      session.close();
    }
  }
}
```

So here's a test that uses one of our named queries in `Supplier`. Since it's working with a known dataset, it can query the size of the returned list and validate that the query succeeded on that basis.

Listing 9-8. `chapter09/src/test/java/chapter09/TestNamedQuery.java`

```
package chapter09;

import chapter09.model.Supplier;
import org.hibernate.query.Query;
import org.testng.annotations.Test;

import java.util.List;

import static org.testng.Assert.assertEquals;

public class TestNamedQuery extends TestBase{
  @Test
```

```
  public void testNamedQuery() {
    Query<Supplier> query = session.getNamedQuery("supplier.findAll");
    List<Supplier> suppliers = query.list();
    assertEquals(suppliers.size(), 2);
  }
}
```

Of course, we can always create queries on the fly, as we've shown many times through this book so far.

Listing 9-9. `chapter09/src/test/java/chapter09/TestSimpleQuery.java`

```
package chapter09;

import chapter09.model.Product;
import org.hibernate.query.Query;
import org.testng.annotations.Test;

import java.util.List;

import static org.testng.Assert.assertEquals;

public class TestSimpleQuery extends TestBase{
  @Test
  public void testSimpleQuery() {
    Query<Product> query = session.createQuery(
        "from Product",
        Product.class);

    query.setComment("This is only a query for product");
    List<Product> products = query.list();
    assertEquals(products.size(), 5);
  }
}
```

The `createQuery()` method takes a valid HQL statement (and, if desired, a Java type reference, like `Supplier.class`) and returns an `org.hibernate.query.Query` object. The `Query` interface provides methods for returning the query results as a Java `List`, as an `Iterator`, or as a unique result. If you provide a type reference, many operations will use that type for the returned values, so if you were looking for a list of `Supplier` entities, you could use `createQuery("from Supplier s", Supplier.class)`, and the `list()` would return a `List<Supplier>` instead of a `List<Object>`. Other functionality includes named parameters, results scrolling, JDBC fetch sizes, and JDBC timeouts. You can also add a comment to the SQL that Hibernate creates, which is useful for tracing which HQL statements correspond to which SQL statements, as shown in the next section.

Like all SQL syntax, you can write from in lowercase or uppercase (or mixed case). However, any Java classes or properties that you reference in an HQL query have to be specified in the proper case. For example, when you query for instances of a Java class named Product, the HQL query `"from Product"` is the equivalent of `"FROM Product"`. However, the HQL query "from product" is not the same as the HQL query `"from Product"`. Because Java class names are case sensitive, Hibernate is case sensitive about class names as well.

Logging and Commenting the Underlying SQL

Hibernate can output the underlying SQL behind your HQL queries into your application's log file. This is especially useful if the HQL query does not give the results you expect or if the query takes longer than you wanted. You can run the SQL that Hibernate generates directly against your database in the database's query analyzer at a later date to determine the causes of the problem. This is not a feature you will have to use frequently, but it is useful should you have to turn to your database administrators for help in tuning your Hibernate application.

Logging the SQL

The easiest way to see the SQL for a Hibernate HQL query is to enable SQL output in the logs with the show_sql property. Set this property to true in your `hibernate.cfg.xml` configuration file,[4] and Hibernate will output the SQL into the logs. You do not need to enable any other logging settings, although setting logging for Hibernate to debug also outputs the generated SQL statements, along with a lot of other verbiage.

After enabling SQL output in Hibernate, you should rerun the previous example (the `TestSimpleQuery` test, from Listing 9-9). Here is the generated SQL statement for the HQL statement from Product:

[4] If you're using the JPA configuration, the property name is "`hibernate.show_sql`."

```
Hibernate: /* This is only a query for product */ select p1_0.id, p1_1.id,
case when p1_1.id is not null then 1 when p1_0.id is not null then 0 end,
p1_0.description, p1_0.name, p1_0.price, p1_0.supplier_id, p1_1.version
from Product as p1_0 left outer join Software as p1_1 on p1_0.id = p1_1.id
```

As an aside, remember that the Software class inherits from Product, which complicates Hibernate's generated SQL for this simple query. When we select all objects from our simple Supplier class, the generated SQL for the HQL query "from Supplier" is much simpler:

```
Hibernate: /* dynamic native SQL query */ select s1_0.id, s1_0.name from
Supplier as s1_0
```

If you turn your logging level up to debug[5] for the Hibernate classes, you will see SQL statements in your log files, along with lots of information about how Hibernate parsed your HQL query and translated it into SQL.

Commenting the Generated SQL

Tracing your HQL statements through to the generated SQL can be difficult, so Hibernate provides a commenting facility on the Query object that lets you apply a comment to a specific query. The Query<R> interface has a setComment() method that takes a String object as an argument, as follows:

```
public Query<R> setComment(String comment)
```

Hibernate will not add comments to your SQL statements without some additional configuration, even if you use the setComment() method. You will also need to set a Hibernate property, use_sql_comments, to true in your Hibernate configuration, as shown in the listing earlier in the chapter. If you set this property but do not set a comment on the query programmatically, Hibernate will include the HQL used to generate the SQL call in the comment. We find this to be very useful for debugging HQL.

Use commenting to identify the SQL output in your application's logs if SQL logging is enabled. For instance, if we add a comment to this example, the Java code would look like this:

[5] Well, debug or "whatever equivalent your logging library might use", although it'd be surprising to see something sufficiently divergent such that debug wasn't workable.

```
String hql = "from Supplier";
Query<Supplier> query = session.createQuery(hql, Supplier.class);
query.setComment("My HQL: " + hql);
List<Supplier> results = query.list();
```

The output in your application's log will have the comment in a Java-style comment before the SQL:

```
Hibernate: /*My HQL: from Supplier*/ select supplier0_.id as id,
supplier0_.name as name2_ from Supplier supplier0_
```

This can be useful for identifying SQL in your logs, especially because the generated SQL is a little difficult to follow when you are scanning large quantities of it. (Running the example code from this chapter's tests serves as a great example; it's hundreds of lines' worth of output.)

The `from` Clause and Aliases

We have already discussed the basics of the from clause in HQL in the earlier section, "SELECT." The most important feature to note is the alias. Hibernate allows you to assign aliases to the classes in your query with the as clause. Use the aliases to refer back to the class inside the query. For instance, our previous simple example would be the following:

```
from Product as p
```

or the following:

```
from Product as product
```

You'll see either alias naming convention in applications, although it's generally used to shorten long queries (and thus you'll see "`from Product as p`" more often than other such forms). The `as` keyword is optional - you can also specify the alias directly after the class name, as follows:

```
from Product product
```

If you need to fully qualify a class name in HQL, just specify the package and class name. Hibernate will take care of most of this behind the scenes, so you really need this only if you have classes with duplicate names in your application. If you have to do this in Hibernate, use syntax such as the following:

```
from chapter09.model.Product
```

The `from` clause is very basic and useful for working directly with objects. However, if you want to work with the object's properties without loading the full objects into memory, you must use the `select` clause.

The `select` Clause and Projection

The `select` clause provides more control over the result set than the `from` clause. If you want to obtain a subset of the properties of objects in the result set - and not the full objects themselves - use the `select` clause. For instance, we could run a projection[6] query on the products in the database that only returned the product names, instead of loading the full object into memory, as in the class shown in Listing 9-10.

Listing 9-10. chapter09/src/test/java/chapter09/TestSimpleProjection.java

```
package chapter09;

import org.hibernate.query.Query;
import org.testng.annotations.Test;

import java.util.List;

import static org.testng.Assert.assertEquals;

public class TestSimpleProjection extends TestBase {
  @Test
  public void testSimpleProjection() {
```

[6] A SQL projection is basically a subset of columns from a set of rows, in relational terms: if you have a table consisting of addresses, cities, and states, the address, city, and state make a list of columns. A "projection" of that table might consist of only the cities from that table, for example.

```
    Query<String> query = session.createQuery(
        "select p.name from Product p",
        String.class);
    List<String> suppliers = query.list();
    for (String s : suppliers) {
      System.out.println(s);
    }
    assertEquals(suppliers.size(), 5);
  }
}
```

The result set for this query will contain a `List` of Java String objects. Additionally, we can retrieve the prices and the names for each product in the database, as shown in Listing 9-11.

Listing 9-11. `chapter09/src/test/java/chapter09/TestBiggerProjection.java`

```
package chapter09;

import org.hibernate.query.Query;
import org.testng.annotations.Test;

import java.util.Arrays;
import java.util.List;

import static org.testng.Assert.assertEquals;

public class TestBiggerProjection extends TestBase {
  @Test
  public void testBiggerProjection() {
    Query<Object[]> query = session.createQuery(
        "select p.name, p.price from Product p");
    List<Object[]> products = query.list();
    for (Object[] data : products) {
      System.out.println(Arrays.toString(data));
    }
    assertEquals(products.size(), 5);
  }
}
```

We're going to revisit this idea, in slightly different ways, when we discuss "data transfer objects," or "DTOs," in a later chapter. A result of `Object[]` is not inherently useful.

This result set contains a `List` of Object arrays (therefore, `List<Object[]>`) - each array represents one set of properties (in this case, a name and price pair).

If you're only interested in a few properties, this approach can allow you to reduce network traffic to the database server and save memory on the application's machine.

Using Restrictions with HQL

As with SQL, you use the where clause to select results that match your query's expressions. HQL provides many different expressions that you can use to construct a query. In the HQL language grammar, there are many possible expressions,[7] including these:

- Logic operators: `OR`, `AND`, `NOT`
- Equality operators: `=` (for "equals"), `<>`, `!=`, `^=` (which mean "not equal")
- Comparison operators: `<`, `>`, `<=`, `>=`, `like`, `not like`, `between`, `not between`
- Math operators: `+`, `-`, `*`, `/`
- Concatenation operator: `||`
- Cases: `Case when <logical expression> then <unary expression> else <unary expression> end`
- Collection expressions: `some`, `exists`, `all`, `any`

[7] If you want to see them all and be amazed, see `https://docs.jboss.org/hibernate/orm/6.0/userguide/html_single/Hibernate_User_Guide.html#hql`. There are a lot of expressions available via JPA, and Hibernate adds a few itself.

In addition, you may also use the following expressions in the where clause:

- HQL named parameters, such as `:date` and `:quantity`
- JDBC query parameter: ? (used very rarely in HQL, and should probably be avoided in favor of named parameters)
- Date and time SQL-92 functional operators: `current_time()`, `current_date()`, `current_timestamp()`
- SQL functions (supported by the database): `length()`, `upper()`, `lower()`, `ltrim()`, `rtrim()`, etc.

Using Named Parameters

Hibernate supports named parameters in its HQL queries. This makes writing queries that accept input from the user easy – and you do not have to defend against SQL injection attacks.

SQL injection is an attack against applications that create SQL directly from user input with string concatenation. For instance, if we accept a name from the user through a web application form, then it would be a very bad form to construct an SQL (or HQL) query like this:

```
String sql = "select p from products where name = '" + name + "'";
```

A malicious user could pass a name to the application that contained a terminating quote and semicolon, followed by another SQL command (such as delete from products) that would let the user do whatever they wanted. They would just need to end with another command that matched the SQL statement's ending quote.[8] This is a very common attack, especially if the malicious user can guess details of your database structure.

[8] See `https://xkcd.com/327/`. You're welcome.

You could escape the user's input yourself for every query, but it is much less of a security risk[9] if you let Hibernate manage all of your input with named parameters. Hibernate's named parameters are similar to the JDBC query parameters (?) you may already be familiar with, but Hibernate's parameters are less confusing. It is also more straightforward to use Hibernate's named parameters if you have a query that uses the same parameter in multiple places.

When using JDBC query parameters, any time you add, change, or delete parts of the SQL statement, you need to update your Java code that sets its parameters, because the parameters are indexed based on the order in which they appear in the statement. Hibernate lets you provide names for the parameters in the HQL query, so you do not have to worry about accidentally moving parameters around in the query.

Listing 9-12. `chapter09/src/test/java/chapter09/TestNamedParams.java`

```
package chapter09;

import chapter09.model.Product;
import org.hibernate.query.Query;
import org.testng.annotations.Test;

import java.util.List;

import static org.testng.Assert.assertEquals;

public class TestNamedParams extends TestBase {
  @Test
  public void testNamedParams() {
    Query<Product> query = session.createQuery(
        "from Product where price >= :price",
        Product.class);
    query.setParameter("price",25.0);
    List<Product> products = query.list();
    assertEquals(products.size(), 1);
  }
}
```

[9] It's possible to triage queries yourself, of course; all you have to do is validate the query with a grammar to allow the expressions you want. In the real world, most of us can't justify the time and effort this entails. Don't do it. Use the facilities that Hibernate makes available to you.

You can even supply object references like this, as shown in Listing 9-13, where we see `query.setParameter("supplier", supplier);` - here, we have a "named parameter" that maps to an actual entity.

Listing 9-13. chapter09/src/test/java/chapter09/TestNamedEntity.java

```
package chapter09;

import chapter09.model.Product;
import chapter09.model.Supplier;
import org.hibernate.query.Query;
import org.testng.annotations.Test;

import java.util.List;

import static org.testng.Assert.assertEquals;
import static org.testng.Assert.assertNotNull;

public class TestNamedEntity extends TestBase {
  @Test
  public void testNamedEntity() {
    Query<Supplier> supplierQuery=session.createQuery(
            "from Supplier where name=:name",
        Supplier.class);
    supplierQuery.setParameter("name", "Supplier 2");
    Supplier supplier= supplierQuery.getSingleResult();
    assertNotNull(supplier);

    Query<Product> query = session.createQuery(
        "from Product where supplier = :supplier",
        Product.class);
    query.setParameter("supplier", supplier);

    List<Product> products = query.list();
    assertEquals(products.size(), 3);
  }
}
```

You can also use regular JDBC query parameters in your HQL queries. We do not particularly see any reason why you would want to, but they do work.

Paging Through the Result Set

Pagination through the result set of a database query is a very common application pattern. Typically, you would use pagination for a web application that returned a large set of data for a query, for example. The web application would page through the database query result set to build the appropriate page for the user. The application would be very slow if the web application loaded all of the data into memory for each user. Instead, you can page through the result set and retrieve the results you are going to display one chunk at a time.

There are two methods on the `Query<R>` interface for paging: `setFirstResult()` and `setMaxResults()`. The `setFirstResult()` method takes an integer that represents the first row in your result set, starting with row 0. You can tell Hibernate to only retrieve a fixed number of objects with the `setMaxResults()` method. Your HQL is unchanged - you need only to modify the Java code that executes the query. Here's a test that shows pagination in action to get the fifth through the eighth names of `Supplier` entities.

Listing 9-14. `chapter09/src/test/java/chapter09/TestPagination.java`

```java
package chapter09;

import chapter09.model.Supplier;
import com.autumncode.hibernate.util.SessionUtil;
import org.hibernate.Session;
import org.hibernate.Transaction;
import org.hibernate.query.Query;
import org.testng.annotations.Test;

import java.util.List;
import java.util.stream.Collectors;

import static org.testng.Assert.assertEquals;

public class TestPagination {
  @Test
  public void testPagination() {
    try (Session session = SessionUtil.getSession()) {
      Transaction tx = session.beginTransaction();
      session.createQuery("delete from Product").executeUpdate();
      session.createQuery("delete from Supplier").executeUpdate();
```

```
      for (int i = 0; i < 30; i++) {
        Supplier supplier = new Supplier();
        supplier.setName(String.format("supplier %02d", i));
        session.save(supplier);
      }

      tx.commit();
    }

    try (Session session = SessionUtil.getSession()) {
      Query<String> query = session.createQuery(
          "select s.name from Supplier s order by s.name",
          String.class);
      query.setFirstResult(4);
      query.setMaxResults(4);
      List<String> suppliers = query.list();
      String list = suppliers
          .stream()
          .collect(Collectors.joining(","));
      assertEquals(list,
          "supplier 04,supplier 05,supplier 06,supplier 07");
    }
  }
}
```

You can change the numbers around and play with the pagination. If you turn on SQL logging (as our sample configuration does), you can see which SQL commands Hibernate uses for pagination. For the open source H2 database, Hibernate uses `offset` and `fetch first ? rows only`. For other databases, Hibernate uses the appropriate commands for pagination. If your application is having performance problems with pagination, this can be very helpful for debugging.

Obtaining a Unique Result

As we saw in the TestNamedEntity.java source, HQL's Query<R> interface provides a getSingleResult() method for obtaining just one object from an HQL query. Although your query may yield only one object, you may also use the getSingleResult() method with other result sets if you limit the results to just the first result. You could use the setMaxResults() method discussed in the previous section. The getSingleResult() method on the Query<R> object returns a single object, or null if there are zero results. If there is more than one result, then the getSingleResult() method throws a NonUniqueResultException.

Listing 9-15. chapter09/src/test/java/chapter09/TestSingleResult.java

```
package chapter09;

import chapter09.model.Product;
import org.hibernate.NonUniqueResultException;
import org.hibernate.query.Query;
import org.testng.annotations.Test;

public class TestSingleResult extends TestBase {
  @Test(expectedExceptions = NonUniqueResultException.class)
  public void testGetSingleResultBad() {
    Query<Product> query = session.createQuery(
        "from Product",
        Product.class);

    Product products = query.getSingleResult();
  }

  @Test
  public void testGetSingleResultGood() {
    Query<Product> query = session.createQuery(
        "from Product",
        Product.class);
    query.setMaxResults(1);
    Product products = query.getSingleResult();
  }
}
```

This is not a good code! The example's very contrived, and the results are unordered; this example exists solely to illustrate the use of getSingleResult() in a few different ways.

Sorting Results with the order by Clause

To sort your HQL query's results, you will need to use the order by clause. You can order the results by any property on the objects in the result set: either ascending (asc) or descending (desc). You can use ordering on more than one property in the query, if you need to. A typical HQL query for sorting results looks like this:

```
from Product p where p.price>25.0 order by p.price desc
```

If you wanted to sort by more than one property, you would just add the additional properties to the end of the order by clause, separated by commas. For instance, you could sort by the supplier's name and then the product price, as follows:

```
from Product p order by p.supplier.name asc, p.price asc
```

HQL is more straightforward for ordering than the equivalent approach using the Criteria Query API.

Associations and Joins

In an object-relational mapper, joins are typically used in two ways. One is for querying objects based on joined criteria - which we saw in the "Using Named Parameters" section. The other way is to generate a "projection," a data structure whose only function is to serve as a way to refer to custom objects from a single query.

However, a projection can be more than just a subset of fields from a single object (which is what we saw in the "SELECT" section earlier in this chapter): it can be any type that Hibernate can represent.

This is the set of queries we have for Product.

Listing 9-16. chapter09/src/main/java/chapter09/model/Product.java

```
@NamedQueries({
    @NamedQuery(name = "product.searchByPhrase",
        query = "from Product p "
            + "where p.name like :text or p.description like :text"),
```

```
    @NamedQuery(name = "product.findProductAndSupplier",
        query = "from Product p, Supplier s where p.supplier=s"),
})
```

The query with the name `product.findProductAndSupplier` isn't especially useful on the surface, because we can get a product's supplier via an attribute in `Product`. However, for the sake of discussion, let's pretend that we have a use case where we'd like to have a product and its supplier as separate fields - possibly for the case where the product's supplier can't be eagerly fetched. (Again, this is entirely constructed for an example; in the real world, there's no need for such a query, given our data model.)

Note that we have two types being returned: `Product` and `Supplier`, with the join being on `p.supplier` - which means "return every product, and for every product, return the supplier referred to by that product."

The type of every row returned by such a query is `Object[]` - an array of objects.

Listing 9-17 shows what this looks like in action.

Listing 9-17. `chapter09/src/test/java/chapter09/TestJoinArray.java`

```java
package chapter09;

import chapter09.model.Product;
import chapter09.model.Supplier;
import org.hibernate.query.Query;
import org.testng.Assert;
import org.testng.annotations.Test;

import java.util.List;

import static org.testng.Assert.assertEquals;

public class TestJoinArray extends TestBase {
  @Test
  public void testJoinArray() {
    Query<Object[]> query = session.getNamedQuery(
        "product.findProductAndSupplier"
    );
    List<Object[]> suppliers = query.list();
```

```
    for (Object[] o : suppliers) {
      Assert.assertTrue(o[0] instanceof Product);
      Assert.assertTrue(o[1] instanceof Supplier);
    }
    assertEquals(suppliers.size(), 5);
  }
}
```

Of course, working with arrays of objects is not a lot of fun; it turns out we can actually specify the type of the object (and construct it) in the query.[10] Here, we have a `ProductAndSupplier` type that serves as an object - a tuple, an organization of data - and our query specifies how to create it. Note that we need to use the full package name, because Hibernate doesn't know about the type (it's not an entity) and must be told exactly how to create it.

Listing 9-18. chapter09/src/test/java/chapter09/TestJoinObject.java

```
package chapter09;

import chapter09.model.Product;
import chapter09.model.Supplier;
import org.hibernate.query.Query;
import org.testng.Assert;
import org.testng.annotations.Test;

import java.util.List;

import static org.testng.Assert.assertEquals;

class ProductAndSupplier {
  final Product p;
  final Supplier s;

  ProductAndSupplier(Product p, Supplier s) {
    this.p = p;
    this.s = s;
  }
```

[10] We'll revisit this idea in later chapters.

```
  @Override
  public String toString() {
    return "ProductAndSupplier{" +
        "p=" + p +
        ",\n   s=" + s +
        '}';
  }
}

public class TestJoinObject extends TestBase {
  @Test
  public void testJoinObject() {
    Query<ProductAndSupplier> query = session.createQuery(
        "select new chapter09.ProductAndSupplier(p,s) " +
            "from Product p, Supplier s where p.supplier=s",
        ProductAndSupplier.class);
    List<ProductAndSupplier> suppliers = query.list();
    for (ProductAndSupplier o : suppliers) {
      System.out.println(o);
    }
    assertEquals(suppliers.size(), 5);
  }
}
```

As we've said, this particular query example doesn't make a lot of sense, and the output from `TestJoinObject` validates that; the `Product` output actually represents the data we expect it to.

Aggregate Methods

HQL supports a range of aggregate methods, similar to SQL. They work the same way in HQL as in SQL, so you do not have to learn any specific Hibernate terminology. The difference is that in HQL, aggregate methods apply to the properties of persistent objects. The `count(...)` method returns the number of times the given column name appears in the result set. You may use the "count(*)" syntax to count all the objects in the result set or `count(product.name)` to count the number of objects in the result set with a `name` property. Here is an example using the `count(*)` method to count all products:

```
select count(*) from Product product
```

The `distinct` keyword only counts the unique values in the row set - for instance, if there are 100 products, but 10 have the same price as another product in the results, then a `select count(distinct product.price) from Product` query would return 90. In our database, the following query will return 2, one for each supplier:

```
select count(distinct product.supplier.name) from Product product
```

If we removed the `distinct` keyword, it would return 5, one for each product.

All of these queries return a `Long` object in the list. (The result is an integral value, in other words.) You could use the `getSingleResult()` method here to obtain the result.

The aggregate functions available through HQL include the following:

- `avg(property name)`: The average of a property's value
- `count(property name or *)`: The number of times a property occurs in the results
- `max(property name)`: The maximum value of the property values
- `min(property name)`: The minimum value of the property values
- `sum(property name)`: The sum total of the property values

If you have more than one aggregate method, the resulting `List` will contain an `Object` array with each of the aggregates you requested. Adding another aggregate to the select clause is straightforward:

```
select min(product.price), max(product.price) from Product product
```

You can also combine these with other projection properties in the result set.

Bulk Updates and Deletes with HQL

The Query<R> interface contains a method called executeUpdate() for executing HQL UPDATE or DELETE statements.[11] The executeUpdate() method returns an int that contains the number of rows affected by the update or delete, as follows:

```
public int executeUpdate() throws HibernateException
```

HQL updates look as you would expect them to, being based on SQL UPDATE statements. Do not include an alias with the update; instead, put the set keyword right after the class name, as follows:

```
String hql = "update Supplier set name = :newName where name = :name";
Query query = session.createQuery(hql);
query.setString("name","SuperCorp");
query.setString("newName","MegaCorp");
int rowCount = query.executeUpdate();
System.out.println("Rows affected: " + rowCount);
//See the results of the update
Query<Supplier> q = session.createQuery("from Supplier", Supplier.class);
List<Supplier> results = q.list();
```

After carrying out this query, any supplier previously named SuperCorp will be named MegaCorp. You may use a where clause with updates to control which rows get updated, or you may leave it off to update all rows. Notice that we printed out the number of rows affected by the query. We also used named parameters in our HQL for this bulk update.

Bulk deletes work in a similar way. Use the delete from clause with the class name you would like to delete from. Then use the where clause to narrow down which entries in the table you would like to delete. Use the executeUpdate() method to execute deletes against the database as well.

Be careful when you use bulk delete with objects that are in relationships. Hibernate will not know that you removed the underlying data in the database, and you can get foreign key integrity errors.

[11] Our test code uses a bulk delete to clear out the data, including the use of executeUpdate(), as mentioned earlier.

Our code surrounding the HQL DELETE statement is basically the same - we use named parameters, and we print out the number of rows affected by the delete:

```
String hql = "delete from Product where name = :name";
Query query = session.createQuery(hql);
query.setString("name","Mouse");
int rowCount = query.executeUpdate();
System.out.println("Rows affected: " + rowCount);
//See the results of the delete
Query<Product> prodQuery = session.createQuery("from Product", Product.class);
List results = prodQuery.list();
```

Using bulk updates and deletes in HQL works almost the same as in SQL, so keep in mind that these are powerful and can erase the data in your tables if you make a mistake with the where clause.

Using Native SQL

Although you should probably use HQL whenever possible, Hibernate does provide a way to use native SQL statements directly through Hibernate. One reason to use native SQL is that your database supports some special features through its dialect of SQL that are not supported in HQL. Another reason is that you may want to call stored procedures from your Hibernate application. Rather than just providing an interface to the underlying JDBC connection, like other Java ORM tools, Hibernate provides a way to define the entity (or join) that the query uses. This makes integration with the rest of your ORM-oriented application easy.

You can modify your SQL statements to make them work with Hibernate's ORM layer. You do need to modify your SQL to include Hibernate aliases that correspond to objects or object properties. You can specify all properties on an object with `objectname.*`, or you can specify the aliases directly with `objectname.property`. Hibernate uses the mappings to translate your object property names into their underlying SQL columns. This may not be the exact way you expect Hibernate to work, so be aware that you do need to modify your SQL statements for full ORM support. You will especially run into problems with native SQL on classes with subclasses - be sure you understand how you mapped the inheritance across either a single table or multiple tables, so that you select the right properties off the table.

Underlying Hibernate's native SQL support is the `org.hibernate.query.NativeQuery<T>` interface, which extends the `org.hibernate.query.Query<T>` interface. Your application will create a native SQL query from the session with the `createNativeQuery()` method on the Session interface (inherited from the QueryProducer interface, but that's probably more detail than we need).

```
public NativeQuery createNativeQuery(String sqlString)
```

You can also use named **native** queries. Here's an example using the named queries from `Supplier` to find the average product price for every `Supplier`.

Listing 9-19. chapter09/src/test/java/chapter09/TestNativeQuery.java

```
package chapter09;

import org.hibernate.query.Query;
import org.testng.annotations.Test;

import java.util.Arrays;
import java.util.List;

import static org.testng.Assert.assertEquals;

public class TestNativeQuery extends TestBase {
  @Test
  public void testNativeQuery() {
    Query query = session.getNamedQuery("supplier.findAverage");
    List<Object[]> suppliers = query.list();
    for (Object[] o : suppliers) {
      System.out.println(Arrays.toString(o));
    }
    assertEquals(suppliers.size(), 2);
  }

  @Test
  public void testHSQLAggregate() {
    Query query = session.getNamedQuery("supplier.averagePrice");
    List<Object[]> suppliers = query.list();
```

```
    for (Object[] o : suppliers) {
      System.out.println(Arrays.toString(o));
    }
    assertEquals(suppliers.size(), 2);
  }
}
```

The actual query being run in testNativeQuery() is this:

```
SELECT p.supplier_id, avg(p.price)
  FROM Product p
  GROUP BY p.supplier_id
```

Note, again, that this requires knowledge of the underlying database schema, and there's no reason you couldn't use HQL to get this same data, as the test code shows, with the equivalent HQL being

```
select p.supplier.id, avg(p.price)
  from Product p
  GROUP BY p.supplier.id
```

The only differences here are in the way the supplier identifier is accessed; in the first query, we use the actual underlying supplier_id column, and in the latter, we're walking the graph to get it. It'd be more effective to return the actual Supplier in the second query, but the focus here is on the native SQL execution.

Summary

HQL is a powerful object-oriented query language that provides the power of SQL while taking advantage of Hibernate's object-relational mapping and innate caching. If you are porting an existing application to Hibernate, you can use Hibernate's native SQL facilities to execute SQL against the database. The SQL functionality is also useful for executing SQL statements that are specific to a given database and have no equivalents in HQL. (It's also useful for executing stored procedures, a concept that relies on your specific database implementation.)

You can turn on SQL logging for Hibernate, and Hibernate will log the generated SQL that it executes against the database. If you add a comment to your HQL query object, Hibernate will display a comment in the log next to the SQL statement; this helps with tracing SQL statements back to HQL in your application.

Our next chapter explores filtering data trivially from Hibernate.

CHAPTER 10

Filtering the Results of Searches

Your application will often need to process only a subset of the data in the database tables. In these cases, you can create a Hibernate *filter* to cause queries to ignore the unwanted data. Filters provide a way for your application to limit the results of a query to data that passes the filter's criteria. Filters are not a new concept – you can achieve much the same effect using SQL database views or, well, named queries – but Hibernate offers a centralized management system for them.

Unlike database views,[1] Hibernate filters can be enabled or disabled during a Hibernate session. In addition, Hibernate filters are parameterized, which is particularly useful when you are building applications on top of Hibernate that use security roles or personalization.[2]

Filters are particularly useful when you have many similar queries with generalizable selection clauses. Filters allow you to use a generalized query, adding criteria for the query as needed.

[1] A database view is a view of a stored query, so one could have a users table with an "active" field, and a view might be defined as the result of `select * from users u where u.active=true`, for example. As you'll see, filters give you similar capabilities, but you can parameterize them, too, so they're quite flexible in practice.

[2] Security and personalization are not concepts that are tied to a database, but to user experience, and as such, they're not covered in this book.

J. B. Ottinger et al., *Beginning Hibernate 6*, https://doi.org/10.1007/978-1-4842-7337-1_10

When to Use Filters

As an example, consider an application that uses users and groups. A user has a status indicating whether that user is active or inactive and a set of memberships; if your application needs to manage users based on status and/or group membership, you're looking at four separate queries (or a wildcard query, which seems silly): one for *all* statuses and groups, one for a subset of statuses, one for a subset of groups, and one for a subset of both statuses and groups. The wildcard query could indeed work, but it would add a burden on the database that shouldn't be there, especially if one set of wildcards was very common.

If we were to use four different queries ("all users," "all users with **this** status," "all users in **that** group," and "all users with **this** status and in **that** group"), not only would we have four queries to test and maintain, but we'd also have to have a way of keeping track of which query we were supposed to be using at any given time.

We could also use custom queries for each execution (building the query as needed, instead of storing a set of queries). It's doable, but not entirely efficient, and it pollutes your services with query data.

Filters allow us to define sets of restrictions. Instead of custom queries or sets of similar queries, we can create a filter and apply it when we query the database, such that our actual query doesn't change, even though the dataset does.

The advantage to using Hibernate filters is that you can programmatically turn filters on or off in your application code, and your filters are defined in consistent locations for easy maintainability. The major disadvantage of filters is that you cannot create new filters at runtime. Instead, any filters your application requires need to be specified in the proper Hibernate annotations or mapping documents. Although this may sound somewhat limiting, the fact that filters can be parameterized makes them pretty flexible. For our user status filter example, only one filter would need to be defined in the mapping document (albeit in two parts). That filter would specify that the status column must match a named parameter. You would not need to define the possible values of the status column in the Hibernate annotations or mapping documents – the application can specify those parameters at runtime.

Although it is certainly possible to write applications with Hibernate that do not use filters, we find them to be an excellent solution to certain types of problems – notably security and personalization.

Getting Started

Before we go too much farther, we should take a look at the project model. For once, it's remarkably simple, as filters are very much part of Hibernate itself, and we have no external dependencies outside of what the `util` project will pull in.

Listing 10-1. `chapter10/pom.xml`

```
<?xml version="1.0" encoding="UTF-8"?>
<project xmlns:xsi="http://www.w3.org/2001/XMLSchema-instance"
         xmlns="http://maven.apache.org/POM/4.0.0"
         xsi:schemaLocation="http://maven.apache.org/POM/4.0.0
         http://maven.apache.org/xsd/maven-4.0.0.xsd">
    <parent>
        <artifactId>hibernate-6-parent</artifactId>
        <groupId>com.autumncode.books.hibernate</groupId>
        <version>5.0</version>
    </parent>
    <modelVersion>4.0.0</modelVersion>
    <artifactId>chapter10</artifactId>

    <dependencies>
        <dependency>
            <groupId>com.autumncode.books.hibernate</groupId>
            <artifactId>util</artifactId>
            <version>${project.parent.version}</version>
        </dependency>
        <dependency>
            <groupId>org.projectlombok</groupId>
            <artifactId>lombok</artifactId>
        </dependency>
    </dependencies>
</project>
```

Defining and Attaching Filters

Your first step is to create a filter definition. A filter definition is like metadata for a filter, including parameter definitions; it's not the filter itself, but it serves as a starting point.[3] After you have the filter definition, you create the filter itself; this contains the actual filter specification. Using the filter is a simple matter of enabling the filter by name and populating the parameters, if any.

What's the reason for having a filter definition separate from the filter itself? It's that the filter definitions are often written for a specific database, and thus they trend to being nonportable. If the filters and their definitions were unified, it'd be much more difficult to keep them portable; with a separated definition, it's easy to put a filter in a separately included resource.

Let's look at some filters, to make their usage clear.

Filters with Annotations

To use filters with annotations, you will need to use the `@FilterDef`, `@ParamDef`, and `@Filter` annotations. The `@FilterDef` annotation defines the filter and belongs to either the class or the package. To define a filter on a class, add a `@FilterDef` annotation alongside the `@Entity` annotation.

After you have defined your filters, you can attach them to classes or collections with the `@Filter` annotation. The `@Filter` annotation takes two parameters: name and condition. The name references a filter definition that we have previously described in an annotation. The condition parameter is an HQL `WHERE` clause. The parameters in the condition are denoted with colons, similar to named parameters in HQL. The parameters have to be defined on the filter definition. Here is a skeleton example of the filter annotations:

```
@Entity
@FilterDef(name = "byStatus", parameters = @ParamDef(name = "status",
type = "boolean"))
@Filter(name = "byStatus", condition = "status = :status")
```

[3] In this, it's like JNDI; you refer to a name in the filter definition, but the filter itself is defined elsewhere.

```
public class User {
   // other fields removed for brevity's sake
   boolean status;
}
```

Defining filters on each class is simple, but if you use a given filter for multiple entities, you will have a lot of duplication. For example, the byStatus filter might apply to things other than User entities. To define any annotation at a package level, you will need to create a Java source file named package-info.java in the package. The package-info.java should only include the package-level annotations and then declare the package immediately afterward. It is not meant to be a Java class. You will also need to tell Hibernate to map the package when you configure Hibernate, either through the addPackage() method on AnnotationConfiguration or in your Hibernate configuration XML:

```
SessionFactory factory = new MetadataSources(registry)
       .addPackage("com.autumncode.entities")
       .buildMetadata()
       .buildSessionFactory();
```

In XML, your mapping might look something like this:

```
<?xml version="1.0"?>
<!DOCTYPE hibernate-configuration PUBLIC
    "-//Hibernate/Hibernate Configuration DTD 3.0//EN"
    "http://www.hibernate.org/dtd/hibernate-configuration-3.0.dtd">
<hibernate-configuration>
  <session-factory>
    <!--  Database connection settings  -->
    <property name="connection.driver_class">org.h2.Driver</property>
    <property name="connection.url">jdbc:h2:file:./db10</property>
    <property name="connection.username">sa</property>
    <property name="connection.password"/>
    <property name="dialect">org.hibernate.dialect.H2Dialect</property>

    <mapping class="chapter10.model.User"/>
    <mapping package="chapter10.model" />
  </session-factory>
</hibernate-configuration>
```

Filters with XML Mapping Documents

For XML mapping documents, use the <filter-def> XML element, in an .hbm.xml file. These filter definitions must contain the name of the filter and the names and types of any filter parameters. You specify filter parameters with the <filter-param> XML element. Here is an excerpt from a mapping document with a filter called latePaymentFilter defined, in an Account.hbm.xml file that maps an Account entity:

```
<?xml version='1.0' encoding='utf-8'?>
<!DOCTYPE hibernate-mapping
   PUBLIC "-//Hibernate/Hibernate Mapping DTD//EN"
   "http://hibernate.sourceforge.net/hibernate-mapping-3.0.dtd">
<hibernate-mapping>
  <class name="Account" table="ACCOUNTS">
    <id name="id" type="int" column="id">
      <generator class="native" />
    </id>
    <property name="dueDate" column="dueDate" type="date" />
    <property name="dueAmount" column="dueAmount" type="double" />
  </class>
  <filter-def name="latePaymentFilter">
    <filter-param name="dueDate" type="date"/>
  </filter-def>
</hibernate-mapping>
```

Once you have created the filter definitions, you need to attach the filters to a class or a collection of mapping elements. You can attach a single filter to more than one class or collection. To do this, you add a <filter> XML element to each class and/or collection. The <filter> XML element has two attributes: name and condition. The name references a filter definition (for instance, latePaymentFilter). The condition represents a WHERE clause in HQL. Here's an example:

```
<class ...
  <filter name="latePaymentFilter" condition="paymentDate = :dueDate"/>
</class>
```

Each <filter> XML element must correspond to a <filter-def> element.

Prefer annotations to the XML, for most applications.

Using Filters in Your Application

Your application programmatically determines which filters to activate or deactivate for a given Hibernate session. Each Session can have a different set of filters with different parameter values. By default, sessions do not have any active filters – you must explicitly enable filters programmatically for each session. The Session interface contains several methods for working with filters, as follows:

```
public Filter enableFilter(String filterName)
public Filter getEnabledFilter(String filterName)
public void disableFilter(String filterName)
```

These are pretty self-explanatory – the enableFilter(String filterName) method activates the specified filter; the disableFilter(String filterName) method deactivates the filter; and if you have already activated a named filter, getEnabledFilter(String filterName) retrieves that filter (and returns null if the filter isn't enabled).

The org.hibernate.Filter interface has six methods. You are unlikely to use validate(); Hibernate uses that method when it processes the filters. The other five methods are as follows:

```
public Filter setParameter(String name, Object value)
public Filter setParameterList(String name, Collection values)
public Filter setParameterList(String name, Object[] values)
public String getName()
public FilterDefinition getFilterDefinition()
```

The setParameter() method is the most useful. You can substitute any Java object for the parameter, although its type should match the type you specified for the parameter when you defined the filter. The two setParameterList() methods are useful for using IN clauses in your filters. If you want to use BETWEEN clauses, use two different filter parameters with different names. Finally, the getFilterDefinition() method allows you to retrieve a FilterDefinition object representing the filter metadata (its name, its parameters' names, and the parameter types).

Once you have enabled a particular filter on the session, you do not have to do anything else to your application to take advantage of filters, as we demonstrate in the following example.

A Basic Filtering Example

Because filters are very straightforward, a basic example allows us to demonstrate most of the filter functionality, including activating filters and defining filters in mapping documents.

We're going to create a User entity, with an active status and membership in groups. We're going to define three filters: one very simple filter with no parameters (just to show how) and then two parameterized filters, which we'll apply in various combinations.

We're going to define *two* filters, to cover the four queries we mentioned earlier in the chapter, because filters are *additive* – if we need to filter by status, we enable a filter for status, and if we need to filter by group, we can enable that filter *separately*, and the two filters work in concert.

We're going to stick with the annotation configuration, as we're using a single database (H2), and it simplifies our example drastically. We're going to also revert to using Lombok, because that will shorten our example code by getting rid of a lot of boilerplate methods. Here's User.java.

Listing 10-2. chapter10/src/main/java/chapter10/model/User.java

```
package chapter10.model;

import lombok.Data;
import lombok.NoArgsConstructor;
import org.hibernate.annotations.*;

import javax.persistence.*;
import javax.persistence.Entity;
import java.util.Arrays;
import java.util.HashSet;
import java.util.Set;

@Entity
@Data
@NoArgsConstructor
@FilterDefs({
  @FilterDef(
    name = "byStatus",
    parameters = @ParamDef(name = "status", type = "boolean")),
```

```
  @FilterDef(
    name = "byGroup",
    parameters = @ParamDef(name = "group", type = "string")),
  @FilterDef(
    name = "userEndsWith1")
})
@Filters({
  @Filter(name = "byStatus", condition = "active = :status"),
  @Filter(name = "byGroup",
    condition =
      ":group in (select ug.groups from user_groups ug where ug.user_id = id)"),
  @Filter(name = "userEndsWith1", condition = "name like '%1'")
})
public class User {
  @Id
  @GeneratedValue(strategy = GenerationType.AUTO)
  Integer id;
  @Column(unique = true)
  String name;
  boolean active;
  @ElementCollection
  Set<String> groups;

  public User(String name, boolean active) {
    this.name = name;
    this.active = active;
  }

  public void addGroups(String... groupSet) {
    if (getGroups() == null) {
      setGroups(new HashSet<>());
    }
    getGroups().addAll(Arrays.asList(groupSet));
  }
}
```

There are a few things about this that stand out, especially with regard to groups.

First, groups are defined as a `Set`, annotated with `@ElementCollection`. This will create a table, `USER_GROUPS`, that will contain a user ID and a single column, with the various group names in a column named after the collection (thus, "groups" and not "group").

The SQL to represent this structure might look something like this, if we ignore the foreign keys Hibernate will create for us:

```
create table User (
  id integer not null,
  active boolean not null,
  name varchar(255),
  primary key (id)
  );
create table User_groups (
  User_id integer not null,
  groups varchar(255)
  );
```

Then, the filter that selects by group uses a subselect to limit the users returned. This condition is database specific and uses knowledge of the actual table structure; filters do some introspection, but not as much as they could. Be prepared to do some analysis to work out exactly what the filter condition should be.

We're also going to revise the `SessionUtil` class from our `util` module, to add two methods: `doWithSession()` and `returnFromSession()`. These methods are going to give us a chance to avoid some of the boilerplate around managing transactions and sessions.

Here's the *full* `SessionUtil.java` from the `util` module.

Listing 10-3. `util/src/main/java/com/autumncode/hibernate/util/SessionUtil.java`

```
//tag::preamble[]
package com.autumncode.hibernate.util;

import org.hibernate.Session;
import org.hibernate.SessionFactory;
import org.hibernate.Transaction;
import org.hibernate.boot.MetadataSources;
```

```
import org.hibernate.boot.registry.StandardServiceRegistry;
import org.hibernate.boot.registry.StandardServiceRegistryBuilder;
import org.slf4j.Logger;
import org.slf4j.LoggerFactory;

import java.util.function.Consumer;
import java.util.function.Function;

public class SessionUtil {
  private static final SessionUtil instance = new SessionUtil();
  private static final String CONFIG_NAME = "/configuration.properties";
  private SessionFactory factory;
  private Logger logger = LoggerFactory.getLogger(this.getClass());

  private SessionUtil() {
    initialize();
  }

  public static Session getSession() {
    return getInstance().factory.openSession();
  }

  public static void forceReload() {
    getInstance().initialize();
  }

  private static SessionUtil getInstance() {
    return instance;
  }

  private void initialize() {
    logger.info("reloading factory");
    StandardServiceRegistry registry =
      new StandardServiceRegistryBuilder()
        .configure()
        .build();
    factory = new MetadataSources(registry)
      .buildMetadata()
      .buildSessionFactory();
  }
```

```
  //end::preamble[]

  public static void doWithSession(Consumer<Session> command) {
    try (Session session = getSession()) {
      Transaction tx = session.beginTransaction();

      command.accept(session);
      if (tx.isActive() &&
        !tx.getRollbackOnly()) {
        tx.commit();
      } else {
        tx.rollback();
      }
    }
  }

  public static <T> T returnFromSession(Function<Session, T> command) {
    try (Session session = getSession()) {
      Transaction tx = null;
      try {
        tx = session.beginTransaction();

        return command.apply(session);
      } catch (Exception e) {
        throw new RuntimeException(e);
      } finally {
        if (tx != null) {
          if (tx.isActive() &&
            !tx.getRollbackOnly()) {
            tx.commit();
          } else {
            tx.rollback();
          }
        }
      }
    }
  }
}
```

Now let's get around to creating some tests. As we've done recently, let's create a chapter10.first.TestBase to build our test data.

Listing 10-4. chapter10/src/test/java/chapter10/first/TestBase.java

```
package chapter10.first;

import chapter10.model.User;
import com.autumncode.hibernate.util.SessionUtil;
import org.hibernate.query.Query;
import org.testng.annotations.AfterMethod;
import org.testng.annotations.BeforeMethod;

public class TestBase {
  @BeforeMethod
  public void setupTest() {
    SessionUtil.doWithSession((session) -> {
      User user = new User("user1", true);
      user.addGroups("group1", "group2");
      session.save(user);
      user = new User("user2", true);
      user.addGroups("group2", "group3");
      session.save(user);
      user = new User("user3", false);
      user.addGroups("group3", "group4");
      session.save(user);
      user = new User("user4", true);
      user.addGroups("group4", "group5");
      session.save(user);
    });
  }

  @AfterMethod
  public void endTest() {
    SessionUtil.doWithSession((session) -> {
      // need to manually delete all of the Users since
      // HQL delete doesn't cascade over element collections
```

```
      Query<User> query = session.createQuery("from User", User.class);
      for (User user : query.list()) {
        session.delete(user);
      }
    });
  }
}
```

Our first test doesn't use a filter at all. It's our baseline test and along the way demonstrates the usage of the doWithSession() method.

Listing 10-5. chapter10/src/test/java/chapter10/first/TestNoFilter.java

```
package chapter10.first;

import chapter10.model.User;
import com.autumncode.hibernate.util.SessionUtil;
import org.hibernate.query.Query;
import org.testng.annotations.Test;

import java.util.List;

import static org.testng.Assert.assertEquals;

public class TestNoFilter extends TestBase {
  @Test
  public void testSimpleQuery() {
    SessionUtil.doWithSession((session) -> {
      Query<User> query = session.createQuery("from User", User.class);
      List<User> users = query.list();
      assertEquals(users.size(), 4);
    });
  }
}
```

That's ... not really especially interesting, or fun. Let's try a test with our userEndsWith1 filter, which applies a very simple condition that accepts any user whose name ends with the digit 1.[4] This will show us how to enable a filter and validate the application of the filter.

Note that the query in both the `TestNoFilter` and `TestSimpleFilter` classes is the same: `"from User"`. Hibernate is applying the filter as an additional `where` clause when the query is executed. We'll be using this same query over and over again and using filters to modify the results.

Listing 10-6. chapter10/src/test/java/chapter10/first/TestSimpleFilter.java

```
package chapter10.first;

import chapter10.model.User;
import com.autumncode.hibernate.util.SessionUtil;
import org.hibernate.query.Query;
import org.testng.annotations.Test;

import java.util.List;

import static org.testng.Assert.assertEquals;

public class TestSimpleFilter extends TestBase {
  @Test
  public void testNoParameterFilter() {
    SessionUtil.doWithSession((session) -> {
      Query<User> query = session.createQuery("from User", User.class);

      session.enableFilter("userEndsWith1");
      List<User> users = query.list();
      assertEquals(users.size(), 1);
      assertEquals(users.get(0).getName(), "user1");
    });
  }
}
```

[4] A better example might have been a constant status, instead of "name ends with a 1," but the status is ideally parameterized as well. The data model would have been polluted without a contrived example, so that's what we have.

Now let's see how to set parameters with filters. Here, we're using a TestNG data provider to pass in a status and the count of users we expect to see *with* that status.

Listing 10-7. chapter10/src/test/java/chapter10/first/TestParameterFilter.java

```
package chapter10.first;

import chapter10.model.User;
import com.autumncode.hibernate.util.SessionUtil;
import org.hibernate.query.Query;
import org.testng.annotations.DataProvider;
import org.testng.annotations.Test;

import java.util.List;

import static org.testng.Assert.assertEquals;

public class TestParameterFilter extends TestBase {
  @DataProvider
  Object[][] statuses() {
    return new Object[][]{
      {true, 3},
      {false, 1}
    };
  }

  @Test(dataProvider = "statuses")
  public void testFilter(boolean status, int count) {
    SessionUtil.doWithSession((session) -> {
      Query<User> query = session.createQuery("from User", User.class);

      session
        .enableFilter("byStatus")
        .setParameter("status", status);

      List<User> users = query.list();
      assertEquals(users.size(), count);
    });
  }
}
```

You can *combine* filters, as well. Let's have one more test class, but this time it'll have two separate tests. The first one will exercise our byGroup filter, and the second one will use *two* filters - byGroup and byStatus.

Again, note that we're not changing our basic query - from User - at all. We could, if we chose to; the filters would simply add their criteria to the basic query.

This is the actual power of the filters. We have a basic query - from User - and we can programmatically decide to apply criteria to the query without having to do anything extra to the query itself.

Listing 10-8. chapter10/src/test/java/chapter10/first/TestMultipleFilters.java

```
package chapter10.first;

import chapter10.model.User;
import com.autumncode.hibernate.util.SessionUtil;
import org.hibernate.query.Query;
import org.testng.annotations.Test;

import java.util.List;

import static org.testng.Assert.assertEquals;

public class TestMultipleFilters extends TestBase {
  @Test
  public void testGroupFilter() {
    SessionUtil.doWithSession((session) -> {
      Query<User> query = session.createQuery("from User", User.class);

      session
        .enableFilter("byGroup")
        .setParameter("group", "group4");

      List<User> users = query.list();
      assertEquals(users.size(), 2);

      session
        .enableFilter("byGroup")
        .setParameter("group", "group1");
```

```
      users = (List<User>) query.list();
      assertEquals(users.size(), 1);

      // should be user 1
      assertEquals(users.get(0).getName(), "user1");
    });
  }

  @Test
  public void testBothFilters() {
    SessionUtil.doWithSession((session) -> {
      Query<User> query = session.createQuery("from User", User.class);

      session
        .enableFilter("byGroup")
        .setParameter("group", "group4");
      session
        .enableFilter("byStatus")
        .setParameter("status", Boolean.TRUE);

      List<User> users = query.list();

      assertEquals(users.size(), 1);
      assertEquals(users.get(0).getName(), "user4");
    });
  }
}
```

Summary

Filters are a useful way to separate some database concerns from the rest of your code. A set of filters can cut back on the complexity of the HQL queries used in the rest of your application, at the expense of some runtime flexibility. Instead of using views (which must be created at the database level), your applications can take advantage of dynamic filters that can be activated as and when they are required.

Next, let's take a look at integration into servlets, where we'll finally start to see the data transfer object pattern come into use.

CHAPTER 11

Integration into the Web

We've seen a lot about *how to use* Hibernate, including a series of example models, but none of this has really demonstrated how Hibernate would be used in the "real world." All of our running code has been embedded in tests, which isn't a bad thing for development, but this isn't a good way to make it clear how to integrate Hibernate into applications people are likely to use.

Tests are a good example of what you'd see in "deep code," back-end services, or embedded applications that don't expose the Hibernate objects directly to end users - and in fact, most modern developers would suggest that exposing Hibernate entities directly to users is a bad idea.[1]

So let's dive into a web application and show how Hibernate can actually be integrated.

There are *lots* of ways Hibernate can be integrated into a web application, and the best approach is dictated almost entirely by the choices made about deployment architecture. We're going to start with something very simple, where we control everything, and then we'll try to cover more complex scenarios that you'd encounter in "the real world."

Setting the Stage

Web applications in Java were originally built around the idea of "servlets," which are basically classes that generate responses to HTTP calls. That model still dominates the *design* of web applications, although the actual method of delivery has changed quite a bit and in various ways.

[1] I think I just spoiled the entire chapter by saying "exposing Hibernate entities directly is a bad idea." Whoops.

J. B. Ottinger et al., *Beginning Hibernate 6*, https://doi.org/10.1007/978-1-4842-7337-1_11

The idea was that systems would run a *container*, an application designed to manage modular applications, which used a specification called Java 2, Enterprise Edition,[2] and intended to provide services to those applications to support specific functionality. For example, a web container like Tomcat would provide an API to web *modules* such that they could be controlled with a centralized control panel, and resources like JDBC connections and other things could be provided to the modules at runtime.

The way those modules implemented the functionality was **originally** through servlets, which the modules would map to specific URLs. Web browsers (or any other app, really) would use those URLs and the various HTTP methods like `GET` and `POST` to run code in the servlets.

It was a simpler world back then, and while that mechanism worked (and well, for what it was), it was not the most appealing development process; if you wanted to look at a list of customers, your servlet had to render HTML, which is rather verbose and easy to get wrong.

Libraries popped up to make it a little easier (Apache ECS,[3] e.g., among others), but realistically there were too many concerns involved in building a web application; you had to understand the web module configuration, plus write the servlet's functionality, plus write the rendering into HTML... if you look at the process under a microscope, it's not that much of a burden, but in actuality it created a fairly heavy burden with relatively little value added for most developers; the majority of websites never reached the level of traffic required to justify the effort.

Naturally, the community responded in multiple beneficial ways (well, beneficial for the most part). The Model-View-Controller paradigm became very common, where servlets merely coordinated what views were rendered once data processing had occurred, with the aid of libraries like Struts and WebWork. Rendering engines like JavaServer Pages appeared, along with templating engines like Velocity and Thymeleaf, and this isn't even beginning to describe the massive proliferation of ideas and approaches; you could build a library solely out of books on web application programming using the JVM, with new frameworks popping up all the time, with all kinds of strengths.[4]

---

[2] Java 2, Enterprise Edition was commonly referred to as J2EE and eventually became Java EE because nobody really understood the reason for the "2" - and yes, there was one - and recently migrated to the "Jakarta EE" name.

[3] Apache ECS has been deprecated for many years, but if you're desperately interested in spelunking through history, it's still on the Web at `https://projects.apache.org/project.html?attic-ecs` - just be aware that there are better ways now.

[4] If you'd like to build a library out of books on web application programming on the JVM, see `www.apress.com` - plenty of references there!

Along with all of this, configuration got simpler, too. The Spring Framework took the rather heavyweight nature of Java EE and turned it on its head, emphasizing easier deployment, configuration, and development. What's more, since Java is largely community-driven, what Spring did for architecture fed into the Java EE specification just like Hibernate did with JPA,[5] and just as modeling Java classes to a database became much better with Hibernate influencing JPA, web application development became far, far easier with Spring and other libraries influencing the web-centric APIs in Java EE.

The Plan

This book is not, sadly, about web application development, and there's no rational way a single book could cover web development in Java very well anyway. With that said, however, there *are* common issues with using Hibernate in web applications that we can address.

We're going to develop a web application using Servlets, some aspects of which *will not work properly* because the intent is to show some of the problems and their solutions. We're not going to design a user interface, per se; not only is this not your author's skill area, but it's a secondary concern. The servlets we write here will generate JSON, which is suitable for rendering using a client application running in a browser; one could write such an app with Angular, React, or any number of other JavaScript frameworks.

The project will use an embedded servlet engine (Undertow, found at `https://undertow.io/`) for testing purposes, but will also be deployable in any compliant Java EE container - you should feel free to try it in Tomcat, WildFly, Open Liberty, or any other engine you like. Again, some parts of the app are expected to not work properly, but that's meant to be illustrative.

Again, this is not a chapter on web development, but a chapter on using Hibernate *in* web development. We're not going to be using the latest, hottest technologies in this chapter - when it comes to the Web, we're purposefully aiming low, because it's trivial to take the lessons we're going to learn and apply them to more advanced web frameworks, and by focusing on simplicity, we can avoid getting bogged down in lots of configuration or framework jargon.

[5] I bet you'd almost forgotten that this was a Hibernate book, didn't you?

The Application

We're going to design that most pedestrian of applications, a blog.

A blog is, of course, a "web log," a sort of online journal, and such applications dominate the Web. Most blogs these days are hosted on massive server farms like Medium (`https://medium.com`) and Substack (`https://substack.com`), and most individually hosted blogs are on software platforms like WordPress (`https://wordpress.org/`) or use static site generators like Jekyll or Hugo.[6]

We're not going to build a competitor for any of those. We are, however, going to be inspired by the model of authors writing posts that have comments. An enterprising reader could theoretically add security (a requirement) and a functional user interface (another requirement) and build something worthwhile, though.

So let's dive in.

The Project Model

First, we need to have our project model. This is going to include a lot of dependencies we've already seen, but the `packaging` will be `war` – as this is going to generate a "web archive" – and it will also include Undertow and Jackson.

Undertow is the servlet engine used in JBoss; Jackson (`https://github.com/FasterXML/jackson`) is a data processing library with which we'll read and write JSON. We will need `jackson-datatype-jsr310` as a dependency as well, because, as we'll see very soon, we're using some timestamp types from the Date and Time API.[7] We're also including our `util` library to handle `Session` acquisition and management, and Lombok will save us a lot of boilerplate.

[6] This book, of course, is written with AsciiDoctor – which can itself generate a static site.

[7] The Date and Time API is JSR-310, from `www.jcp.org/en/jsr/detail?id=310`, and has been part of the JVM's standard runtime library for quite a few versions. However, Jackson is compatible with *older* JVMs, too, and thus we need to enable support for JSR-310 types.

Listing 11-1. chapter11/pom.xml

```
<?xml version="1.0" encoding="UTF-8"?>
<project xmlns="http://maven.apache.org/POM/4.0.0"
         xmlns:xsi="http://www.w3.org/2001/XMLSchema-instance"
         xsi:schemaLocation="http://maven.apache.org/POM/4.0.0
          http://maven.apache.org/xsd/maven-4.0.0.xsd">
  <parent>
    <groupId>com.autumncode.books.hibernate</groupId>
    <artifactId>hibernate-6-parent</artifactId>
    <version>5.0</version>
  </parent>
  <modelVersion>4.0.0</modelVersion>
  <packaging>jar</packaging>

  <properties>
    <war.name>chapter11</war.name>
    <undertow.version>2.2.8.Final</undertow.version>
  </properties>

  <artifactId>chapter11</artifactId>

  <dependencies>
    <dependency>
      <groupId>org.projectlombok</groupId>
      <artifactId>lombok</artifactId>
    </dependency>
    <dependency>
      <groupId>com.autumncode.books.hibernate</groupId>
      <artifactId>util</artifactId>
      <version>${project.parent.version}</version>
    </dependency>
    <dependency>
      <groupId>io.undertow</groupId>
      <artifactId>undertow-core</artifactId>
      <version>${undertow.version}</version>
    </dependency>
```

```
    <dependency>
      <groupId>io.undertow</groupId>
      <artifactId>undertow-servlet</artifactId>
      <version>${undertow.version}</version>
    </dependency>
    <dependency>
      <groupId>com.h2database</groupId>
      <artifactId>h2</artifactId>
    </dependency>
    <dependency>
      <groupId>ch.qos.logback</groupId>
      <artifactId>logback-classic</artifactId>
    </dependency>
    <dependency>
      <groupId>com.fasterxml.jackson.core</groupId>
      <artifactId>jackson-databind</artifactId>
    </dependency>
    <dependency>
      <groupId>com.fasterxml.jackson.datatype</groupId>
      <artifactId>jackson-datatype-jsr310</artifactId>
    </dependency>
  </dependencies>
  <build>
    <finalName>${war.name}</finalName>
  </build>
</project>
```

The Data Model

We have three entities to work with, all in the `chapter11.model` package: `User`, `Post`, and `Comment`. A `User` can have many `Post` and `Comment` entries, and a `Post` has many `Comment` entities. In each one, we override Lombok's `toString()` because we want to make sure not to inadvertently refer to collections. (We don't want Lombok to output the collections at all.)

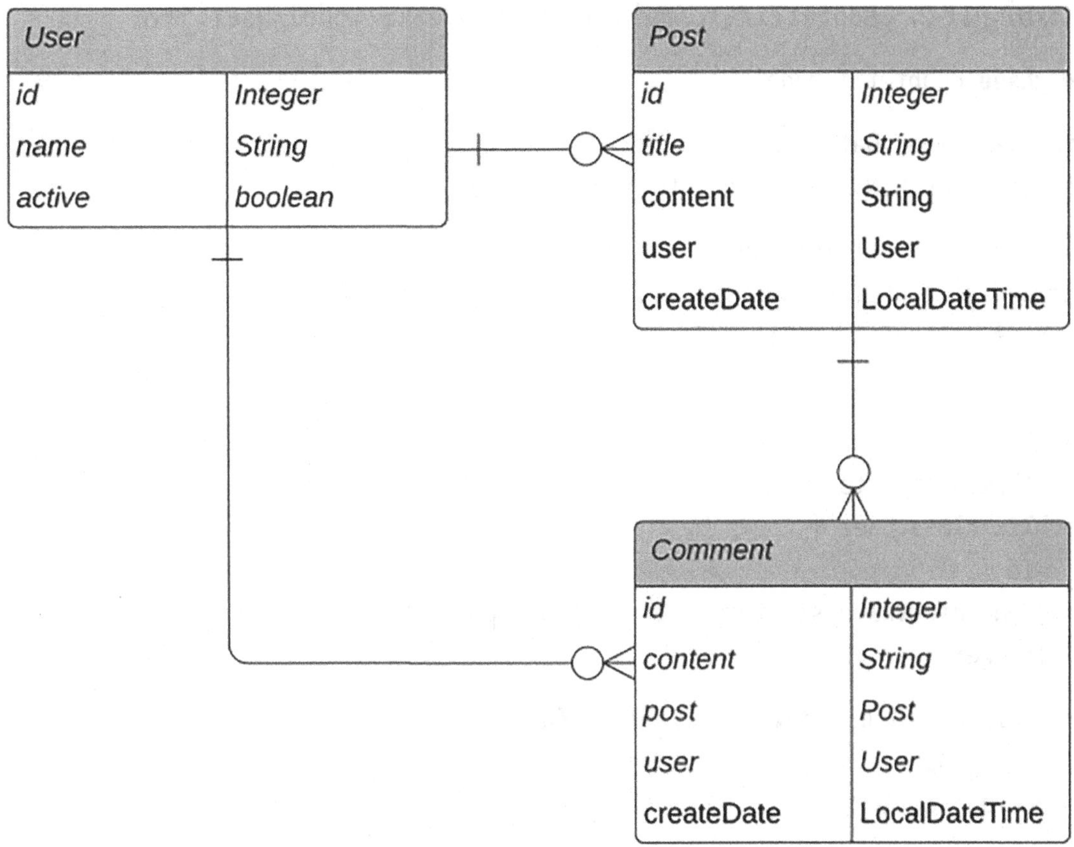

Figure 11-1. *The blog's entity relationship diagram*

We aren't likely to *use* `toString()` very much, but it's useful for "eye-checking" results. If you're following along in code, or as you develop your own models, chances are you'll do what your author does and use logging to take a look at values as you run your tests.

First, let's take a look at `User`. We initialize `posts` as an empty `ArrayList`; we probably don't need to do this, unless we find ourselves designing a process by which we add a `User` and posts to that user before the user is persisted, realistically, but initializing the list of posts this way is defensive in nature. (This prevents us from accidentally referring to a `null` in the list of posts before it's been saved, for example.)

Listing 11-2. chapter11/src/main/java/chapter11/model/User.java

```
package chapter11.model;

import lombok.Data;
import lombok.NoArgsConstructor;

import javax.persistence.*;
import java.util.ArrayList;
import java.util.List;

@Entity
@Data
@NoArgsConstructor
public class User {
  @Id
  @GeneratedValue(strategy = GenerationType.AUTO)
  Integer id;

  @Column(unique = true, nullable = false)
  String name;
  boolean active;

  @OneToMany(fetch = FetchType.LAZY)
  @JoinColumn(name = "user_id")
  @OrderBy("createDate")
  List<Post> posts = new ArrayList<>();

  public User(String name, boolean active) {
    this.name = name;
    this.active = active;
  }

  @Override
  public String toString() {
    return "User{" +
      "id=" + id +
      ", name='" + name + '\'' +
```

```
        ", active=" + active +
        '}';
  }
}
```

The toString() here is fairly vanilla, but we override it from Lombok's toString() because Lombok will include every attribute by default. Ordinarily, that'd be fine, but if we work with Hibernate entities - that is, objects loaded from Hibernate - then we end up running the risk of requiring initialization of lazy collections after a Session is closed, which means that accessing posts might cause us to get an org.hibernate.LazyInitializationException.

Requiring the Session to be in scope at all times - or, well, when we should be done accessing a Session - is one of the main concerns for this chapter.

Post is the most interesting one of the three entities we have, because it uses Hibernate filter definitions. Let's take a look at it and then wander through some interesting aspects.

Listing 11-3. chapter11/src/main/java/chapter11/model/Post.java

```
package chapter11.model;

import lombok.Data;
import lombok.NoArgsConstructor;
import org.hibernate.annotations.*;

import javax.persistence.*;
import javax.persistence.OrderBy;
import java.time.*;
import java.util.ArrayList;
import java.util.List;

@Entity
@Data
@NoArgsConstructor
@FilterDefs({
  @FilterDef(
    name = "byTerm",
    parameters = @ParamDef(name = "term", type = "string")),
```

```
  @FilterDef(
    name = "byName",
    parameters = @ParamDef(name = "name", type = "string")
  )
})
@Filters({
  @Filter(name = "byTerm",
    condition = "title like :term"),
  @Filter(name = "byName",
    condition = "user_id = (select u.id from User as u where u.name=:name)"),
})
public class Post {
  @Id
  @GeneratedValue(strategy = GenerationType.AUTO)
  Integer id;

  @Column(nullable = false)
  String title;

  @Column(nullable = false)
  @Lob
  String content;

  @ManyToOne
  User user;

  @OneToMany(fetch = FetchType.LAZY)
  @JoinColumn(name = "post_id")
  @OrderBy("createDate")
  List<Comment> comments = new ArrayList<>();

  @Temporal(TemporalType.TIMESTAMP)
  @Column(nullable = false)
  LocalDateTime createDate;
```

```
  @Override
  public String toString() {
    return "Post{" +
      "id=" + id +
      ", title='" + title + '\'' +
      ", content='" + content + '\'' +
      ", user=" + user +
      ", createDate=" + createDate +
      '}';
  }
}
```

We actually have two filters: byTerm and byName.

The first, byTerm, is a... rather simple word search filter, meant more as a placeholder than an actual search facility; it includes any Post whose title includes a wildcard, the "term" in the filter's name.

The byName filter is a little more interesting. It actually includes any Post whose user_id field matches a User with the given name - thus, it gives filters for any Post by a user's name. It's written the way it is because it's a *filter* and not a *query*; it might have been easier to write an HQL query to accomplish the same goal, but the reasons for filters will be made clear enough when we start to use them.

JPA has a Criteria Query API that provides similar features to Hibernate filters. However, as verbose as filters can become, they're still far, far less verbose than Criteria queries, and they require less work to set up.

Our last entity is the Comment, which seems faintly vanilla and boring after seeing Post and User.

Listing 11-4. chapter11/src/main/java/chapter11/model/Comment.java

```
package chapter11.model;

import lombok.Data;
import lombok.NoArgsConstructor;

import javax.persistence.*;
import java.time.LocalDateTime;
```

```
@Entity
@Data
@NoArgsConstructor
public class Comment {
  @Id
  @GeneratedValue(strategy = GenerationType.AUTO)
  Integer id;

  @Column(nullable = false)
  @Lob
  String content;

  @ManyToOne(fetch = FetchType.LAZY)
  @JoinColumn(name = "post_id")
  Post post;

  @ManyToOne(optional = false, fetch = FetchType.LAZY)
  @JoinColumn(name = "user_id")
  User user;

  @Temporal(TemporalType.TIMESTAMP)
  @Column(nullable = false)
  LocalDateTime createDate;

  @Override
  public String toString() {
    return "Comment{" +
      "id=" + id +
      ", content='" + content + '\'' +
      ", createDate=" + createDate +
      '}';
  }
}
```

We can't have a Hibernate application without a Hibernate configuration, so here it is; note that it's pretty much the same as all the others, except in the actual specific mappings. It's also located in `src/main/resources` instead of `src/test/resources` for once, mostly because we want our deployable artifact to be complete and deployable; if it were located in the `test` tree, the Hibernate configuration wouldn't be part of the deployable artifact.

Listing 11-5. chapter11/src/main/resources/hibernate.cfg.xml

```
<?xml version="1.0"?>
<!DOCTYPE hibernate-configuration PUBLIC
    "-//Hibernate/Hibernate Configuration DTD 3.0//EN"
    "http://www.hibernate.org/dtd/hibernate-configuration-3.0.dtd">
<hibernate-configuration>
  <session-factory>
    <!-- Database connection settings -->
    <property name="connection.driver_class">org.h2.Driver</property>
    <property name="connection.url">jdbc:h2:./db11</property>
    <property name="dialect">org.hibernate.dialect.H2Dialect</property>

    <!-- Echo all executed SQL to stdout -->
    <property name="show_sql">true</property>
    <property name="use_sql_comments">true</property>

    <!-- Drop and re-create the database schema on startup -->
    <property name="hbm2ddl.auto">create-drop</property>

    <mapping class="chapter11.model.User"/>
    <mapping class="chapter11.model.Post"/>
    <mapping class="chapter11.model.Comment"/>
  </session-factory>
</hibernate-configuration>
```

Building Our First Servlet Test

Next, we're going to look at probably the longest class in the entire chapter, our TestBase servlet.

There are actually a lot of ways to address writing code for web applications. The most preferred way is to write services that map to our user stories - functionality like "add user" or "add post" - and then use the servlets to call those services.

This model actually works remarkably well, but it does manage to naturally isolate you from some of the architectural concerns around using Hibernate in distributed applications. When you separate concerns like that - with "add user" being in a completely separate class - you have a natural transaction boundary, and it's rather easy to do things correctly and cleanly by accident. We'll use that model in subsequent chapters, but we need to understand why some of the choices we'll make then exist, so for now we're going to do things slightly suboptimally.

As a result, though, our tests can't focus solely on services - we need to set up an actual web server, with live servlets. It's not quite a full integration test,[8] but it *does* actually use a real HTTP client (the one included in Java 11) and issues real HTTP requests; if you wanted, you could manually do the exact same things the tests do.

Our `TestBase`, then, has a lot of roles: it needs to start (and stop) Undertow, along with registering a series of servlets. It also needs to provide an easy way to issue HTTP requests, along with building an easy way to map JSON into a navigable data structure.

We don't need to make it perfect, just good enough for our purposes. It wouldn't be an extraordinary amount of effort to make `TestBase` better in various ways, but it's already long enough.

Most of the complexity in `TestBase` is in the `populateServlets()` method, which cranks up a `DeploymentInfo`. It loads a JSON file called `servlets.json`, which contains a JSON dictionary; each entry is a Servlet, and it has data about each one such as the servlet's implementation class and URL, as well as any initialization parameters it might use.

Here's the `TestBase.java` class, and we'll include the `servlets.json` immediately thereafter so you can see the structure.[9]

Listing 11-6. `chapter11/src/test/java/chapter11/servlets/TestBase.java`

```
package chapter11.servlets;

import chapter11.model.Comment;
import chapter11.model.Post;
import chapter11.model.User;
import com.autumncode.hibernate.util.SessionUtil;
import com.fasterxml.jackson.annotation.JsonInclude;
import com.fasterxml.jackson.core.type.TypeReference;
```

[8] An integration test would involve a formal deployment into a container, or perhaps a primary entry point that included Undertow much as our test harness does, but we're not going to do that here. After all, we're still using embedded databases.

[9] Astute or experienced Java EE programmers will recognize that `servlets.json` is basically a replacement for `web.xml`, which Undertow does not use innately. We could have scanned for servlets in the classpath - after all, `@WebServlet` is an annotation that exists - but that's even more complicated.

```
import com.fasterxml.jackson.databind.ObjectMapper;
import com.fasterxml.jackson.databind.SerializationFeature;
import com.fasterxml.jackson.datatype.jsr310.JavaTimeModule;
import io.undertow.Handlers;
import io.undertow.Undertow;
import io.undertow.server.handlers.PathHandler;
import io.undertow.servlet.Servlets;
import io.undertow.servlet.api.DeploymentInfo;
import io.undertow.servlet.api.DeploymentManager;
import org.hibernate.query.Query;
import org.testng.annotations.AfterClass;
import org.testng.annotations.BeforeClass;
import org.testng.annotations.BeforeMethod;

import javax.servlet.Servlet;
import javax.servlet.ServletException;
import java.io.IOException;
import java.net.URI;
import java.net.http.HttpClient;
import java.net.http.HttpRequest;
import java.net.http.HttpResponse;
import java.time.Duration;
import java.util.Map;

public class TestBase {
  Undertow server;
  TypeReference<Map<String, Object>> mapOfMaps =
    new TypeReference<>() {
    };
  protected ObjectMapper mapper = new ObjectMapper()
    .setSerializationInclusion(JsonInclude.Include.NON_NULL)
    .disable(SerializationFeature.WRITE_DATES_AS_TIMESTAMPS);
  {
    mapper.registerModule(new JavaTimeModule());
  }
```

```
@BeforeClass
void start() throws ServletException, IOException {
  DeploymentInfo servletBuilder = Servlets.deployment()
    .setClassLoader(TestBase.class.getClassLoader())
    .setContextPath("/myapp")
    .setDeploymentName("test.war");
  populateServlets(servletBuilder);

  DeploymentManager manager = Servlets
    .defaultContainer()
    .addDeployment(servletBuilder);
  manager.deploy();
  PathHandler path = Handlers.path(Handlers.redirect("/myapp"))
    .addPrefixPath("/myapp", manager.start());
  server = Undertow.builder()
    .addHttpListener(8080, "localhost")
    .setHandler(path)
    .build();
  server.start();
}

private void populateServlets(DeploymentInfo servletBuilder)
  throws IOException {
  Map<String, Object> servlets = mapper
    .readValue(
      this
        .getClass()
        .getResourceAsStream("/servlets.json"
        ), mapOfMaps);
  servlets.entrySet().forEach(entry -> {
    Map<String, Object> data =
      (Map<String, Object>) entry.getValue();
    try {
      var servlet = Servlets.servlet(
        entry.getKey(),
```

```
        (Class<? extends Servlet>) Class.forName(
          data.get("class").toString()
        ));
      if (data.containsKey("initParams")) {
        Map<String, Object> params =
          (Map<String, Object>) data.get("initParams");
        params.entrySet().forEach(param -> {
          servlet.addInitParam(
            param.getKey(),
            param.getValue().toString()
          );
        });
      }
      servlet.addMapping(data.get("mapping").toString());
      servletBuilder.addServlets(servlet);
    } catch (ClassNotFoundException e) {
      e.printStackTrace();
    }
  });
}

@AfterClass
void stop() {
  server.stop();
}

@BeforeMethod
void clearAll() {
  SessionUtil.doWithSession(session -> {
    Query<Comment> commentQuery =
      session.createQuery("from Comment", Comment.class);
    for (var obj : commentQuery.list()) {
      session.delete(obj);
    }

    Query<Post> postQuery =
      session.createQuery("from Post", Post.class);
```

```
      for (Post post : postQuery.list()) {
        session.delete(post);
      }
      Query<User> query =
        session.createQuery("from User", User.class);
      for (User user : query.list()) {
        session.delete(user);
      }
    });
  }

  protected HttpResponse<String> issueRequest(String path)
    throws IOException, InterruptedException {
    HttpClient client = HttpClient.newBuilder().build();
    HttpRequest request = HttpRequest.newBuilder()
      .uri(URI.create("http://localhost:8080/myapp/" + path))
      .timeout(Duration.ofSeconds(3))
      .build();
    HttpResponse<String> response =
      client.send(request, HttpResponse.BodyHandlers.ofString());
    return response;
  }
}
```

This is a pretty big class, compared to a lot of the source files we've had so far, but it's not particularly complicated. Most of it is related to setting up our servlets, but it also cleans up the database and has a convenience method for issuing HTTP requests.

The `mapper` reference gives us an easy way to properly test serialized data with dates.

The `start()` method runs before every test class and cranks up the Undertow servlet engine, along with `populateServlets()`, which builds a list of entry points using a JSON file we'll see next. It uses the raw JSON structure, which isn't ideal; ordinarily, we'd construct an object model and use *that*, but we're trying to prefer fewer classes to more.

The `stop()` method runs after every test class' tests and shuts down the Undertow server.

The `clearAll()` method cleans up all data, and as it's marked with `@BeforeMethod`, it runs before every test; every test starts with a clean slate, from a data perspective.

Lastly, the `issueRequest()` provides an easy way to build an HTTP request for testing. It's absurdly simple; it only works with a request path, does no parameterization, and works only with HTTP `GET` requests. However, it *does* serve to remove a lot of boilerplate around issuing requests directly.

So why, then, even *have* `issueRequest()`? After all, we don't *need* HTTP to be the transport protocol; we could have classes that perform the actions that a servlet would provide and call those classes directly. There's no *need* for a server or protocol. With that said, though, the protocol barrier is something we're trying to demonstrate, so all of the setup is meant to illustrate architectural boundaries - like the use of HTTP - in a sort of "real-world" situation, even if in the "real world" nobody would rationally do any of this manually.

And here's the actual `servlets.json` file the chapter uses, as well, with every servlet included. (If you're manually building the chapter's codebase as you read, you'll want to refer to this listing, rather than using it wholesale, until you have all of the servlets implemented.)

Listing 11-7. `chapter11/src/test/resources/servlets.json`

```
{
  "HelloServlet": {
    "class": "chapter11.servlets.HelloWorld",
    "initParams": {
      "message": "Hello World"
    },
    "mapping": "/hello"
  },
  "BadAddUserServlet": {
    "class": "chapter11.servlets.BadAddUserServlet",
    "mapping": "/badadduser"
  },
  "AddUserServlet": {
    "class": "chapter11.servlets.AddUserServlet",
    "mapping": "/adduser"
  },
```

```
  "SimpleGetPostsServlet": {
    "class": "chapter11.servlets.SimpleGetPostsServlet",
    "mapping": "/simplegetposts"
  },
  "AddPostServlet": {
    "class": "chapter11.servlets.AddPostServlet",
    "mapping": "/addpost"
  },
  "GetPostsServlet": {
    "class": "chapter11.servlets.GetPostsServlet",
    "mapping": "/getposts"
  },
  "GetPostServlet": {
    "class": "chapter11.servlets.GetPostServlet",
    "mapping": "/getpost"
  },
  "AddCommentServlet": {
    "class": "chapter11.servlets.AddCommentServlet",
    "mapping": "/addcomment"
  }
}
```

Our servlets are designed to emit JSON, specifically, which sounds like an ideal reason to create a `ServletBase`, an abstract `HttpServlet` implementation that provides a convenient way to write an `Object` as JSON.

Listing 11-8. `chapter11/src/main/java/chapter11/servlets/ServletBase.java`

```java
package chapter11.servlets;

import com.fasterxml.jackson.annotation.JsonInclude;
import com.fasterxml.jackson.databind.ObjectMapper;
import com.fasterxml.jackson.databind.SerializationFeature;
import com.fasterxml.jackson.datatype.jsr310.JavaTimeModule;

import javax.servlet.http.HttpServlet;
import javax.servlet.http.HttpServletRequest;
```

```
import javax.servlet.http.HttpServletResponse;
import java.io.IOException;
import java.util.*;

abstract class ServletBase extends HttpServlet {
  protected ObjectMapper mapper = new ObjectMapper()
    .setSerializationInclusion(JsonInclude.Include.NON_NULL)
    .disable(SerializationFeature.WRITE_DATES_AS_TIMESTAMPS);
  {
    mapper.registerModule(new JavaTimeModule());
  }

  /* simple validation of parameters */
  protected Map<String, String> getValidatedParameters(
    HttpServletRequest req,
    String... fields
  ) {
    Map<String, String> map = new HashMap<>();
    List<String> badFields = new ArrayList<>();
    for (String fieldName : fields) {
      String value = req.getParameter(fieldName);
      if (value == null || value.isEmpty()) {
        badFields.add(fieldName);
      } else {
        map.put(fieldName, value);
      }
    }
    if (badFields.size() > 0) {
      throw new RuntimeException(
        "bad fields provided: " + badFields
      );
    }
    return map;
  }
```

```
  /* write out a valid response */
  protected void write(
    HttpServletResponse r,
    int code,
    Object entity
  ) throws IOException {
    r.setContentType("application/json");
    r.setStatus(code);
    r.getWriter().write(mapper
      .writerWithDefaultPrettyPrinter()
      .writeValueAsString(entity)
    );
  }

  /* write out an exception */
  protected final void writeError(
    HttpServletResponse resp,
    Throwable throwable
  ) throws IOException {
    write(resp,
      HttpServletResponse.SC_INTERNAL_SERVER_ERROR,
      Map.of("error", throwable.getMessage())
    );
  }
}
```

We use `setSerializationInclusion(JsonInclude.Include.NON_NULL)` because we want to ignore fields that have `null` in them when we serialize data. Is this *important*? Well, not here; we don't have an actual user interface, after all, and the number of *total* fields we have is so low that including a few references to empty data wouldn't matter in any event. With that said, though, this allows a *potential* user interface to check for field presence without having to then check for fields being *empty*. It's just defensive programming.

We also disable the `WRITE_DATES_AS_TIMESTAMPS` feature, because we use `LocalDateTime` and we really want this to be written in human-readable form. To do this, though, we need to register the `JavaTimeModule()` in Jackson, which is done with an initializer block.

We also have a getValidatedParameters() method, which returns a Map<String, String> of field names and their values - and throws a RuntimeException if a field hasn't been provided (and is required). This is done *very* primitively - there are far better ways to do this.

Next, we have write() and writeError() methods, which format output in a standard form for our output.

ServletBase is *functional* but not very *good*. You probably don't want to write servlets at this level, but it's important sometimes to understand what the underlying technology is doing.

The first servlet we see listed in servlets.json is a "Hello, World" servlet, named "HelloServlet" and implemented in a class called HelloWorld. This is a simple servlet that validates that our Undertow instance works, and it uses our ServletBase to write to the output.

Listing 11-9. chapter11/src/main/java/chapter11/servlets/HelloWorld.java

```
package chapter11.servlets;

import javax.servlet.http.HttpServletRequest;
import javax.servlet.http.HttpServletResponse;
import java.io.IOException;
import java.util.Map;

public class HelloWorld extends ServletBase {
  @Override
  protected void doGet(
    HttpServletRequest request,
    HttpServletResponse response)
    throws IOException {
    Map<String, String> data=Map.of(
      "response", this.getInitParameter("message")
    );
    write(response, HttpServletResponse.SC_OK, data);
  }
}
```

There are two interesting things here. One is the use of an "init parameter" to get the value of the response (provided in the `<initParams>` node in the `servlets.json`), and the other is the fact that we build a `Map<String, String>` to generate the response in the first place; JSON is a data structure, and we cannot write a simple string as output with JSON. We could have, of course, just written output directly, but we're trying to actually exercise the plumbing that our application will use.

We now need to *test* our `HelloWorld` servlet. Armed with `TestBase`, we can create a `HelloWorldTest` that looks like the one shown in Listing 11-10.

Listing 11-10. `chapter11/src/test/java/chapter11/servlets/HelloWorldTest.java`

```
package chapter11.servlets;

import org.testng.annotations.Test;

import javax.servlet.http.HttpServletResponse;
import java.io.IOException;
import java.net.http.HttpResponse;
import java.util.Map;

import static org.testng.Assert.assertEquals;

public class HelloWorldTest extends TestBase {
  @Test
  public void testHelloWorld()
    throws IOException, InterruptedException {
    HttpResponse<String> response =
      issueRequest("hello");

    Map<String, Object> data =
      mapper.readValue(response.body(), mapOfMaps);

    assertEquals(
      response.statusCode(),
      HttpServletResponse.SC_OK
    );
```

```
    assertEquals(
      data.get("response"),
      "Hello World"
    );
  }
}
```

Our `HelloWorldTest` is really pretty simple: after initialization through `TestBase`, it issues a request (through the obscurely named `issueRequest()` method, held in `TestBase`), which returns a `String` - a string that should contain JSON.

We then parse that through the `mapper` instance held in `TestBase` and validate that the response code is `SC_OK` (i.e., 200, the HTTP code that means the request was successful) and that the JSON map has a property called `response` with the value `Hello World`.

We *could* have created an object that had a `response` field in it and mapped our JSON to that, instead of using the "map of maps" approach we're demonstrating here. What's more, that's probably the "right way" to do it, and we'll see examples of that in practice in the next example; we avoided it here because it's just *one more thing* to explain. We're introducing enough new concepts already. It's better if we spread them out some.

This pattern, of issuing a request and examining the response, will repeat itself throughout our tests.

Our First (Wrong) Servlet: Adding a User

Let's create a servlet to add a new user to the system. In it, we're going to accept a username and check to see if the user exists already; if the user doesn't exist, we're going to create the user, and then we're going to return the user as JSON.

The process looks correct on the surface. This code is, however, wrong. We will see why very shortly.

Listing 11-11. `chapter11/src/main/java/chapter11/servlets/BadAddUserServlet.java`

```
package chapter11.servlets;

import chapter11.dto.UserDTO;
import chapter11.model.User;
import com.autumncode.hibernate.util.SessionUtil;
```

```
import org.hibernate.Session;
import org.hibernate.query.Query;

import javax.persistence.NoResultException;
import javax.servlet.ServletException;
import javax.servlet.http.HttpServletRequest;
import javax.servlet.http.HttpServletResponse;
import java.io.IOException;
import java.util.Map;

public class BadAddUserServlet extends ServletBase {
  @Override
  protected void doGet(
    HttpServletRequest req,
    HttpServletResponse resp
  )
    throws ServletException, IOException {
    try {
      Map<String, String> input =
        getValidatedParameters(req, "userName");

      User user = SessionUtil.returnFromSession(
        session -> createUser(session, input.get("userName"))
      );
      write(resp,
        HttpServletResponse.SC_OK,
        user);
    } catch (Exception e) {
      writeError(resp, e);
    }
  }

  private User createUser(Session session, String userName) {
    User entity;
    try {
```

```
      Query<User> query = session.createQuery(
        "from User u where u.name=:name",
        User.class);
      query.setParameter("name", userName);

      entity = query.getSingleResult();
    } catch (NoResultException nre) {
      entity = new User(userName, true);
      session.save(entity);
    }

    return entity;
  }
}
```

The entry point for the functionality for our servlet is `doGet()`, which maps to the HTTP method used to invoke the Servlet. (Therefore, it responds to `GET` requests, with other methods being ignored for our purposes.) It uses `getValidatedParameters()` to validate the parameters.

Then, it creates a `User` reference and calls `SessionUtil.returnFromSession()` with an invocation of `createUser()`. After that, there's really very little to do, outside of exception handling: it writes the `User` reference to the output.

However, the mechanism used to get the `User` is where this servlet fails.

Our design is to return the `User` that maps to a `userName`, period. If the `User` already exists, it loads the user from the database and returns *that*. (It's debatable whether that's actually wise, in the grand scheme of things; for a "real application," you wouldn't return an existing user like this, just in case someone's spamming the "add user" functionality to find existing usernames.)

The error is simple: Jackson, the JSON library we're using, will iterate through every attribute in the `User` and create a representation for it in JSON. However, the `posts` reference for the `User` is set to a simple `ArrayList` if the user is created by `createUser()` - but if it's loaded from the database, the `posts` reference is actually a proxied value, and the attempt to map the `User` will cause Hibernate to try to load the `Post` list from the database.

However, the mapping happens *after* the lambda exists: the Session is no longer active, and thus we'll get a LazyInitializationError.

Here's our test class, which actually exercises most of the code in the Servlet.

Listing 11-12. chapter11/src/test/java/chapter11/servlets/BadAddUserServletTest.java

```
package chapter11.servlets;

import org.testng.annotations.Test;

import javax.servlet.http.HttpServletResponse;
import java.io.IOException;
import java.net.http.HttpResponse;

import static org.testng.Assert.assertEquals;

public class BadAddUserServletTest extends TestBase{
  String getServletName() {
    return "badadduser";
  }

  @Test
  void emptyUserNameProvided()
    throws IOException, InterruptedException {
    HttpResponse<String> response =
      issueRequest(getServletName()+"?userName=");
    System.out.println(response.body());

    assertEquals(
      response.statusCode(),
      HttpServletResponse.SC_INTERNAL_SERVER_ERROR
    );
  }
```

```
  @Test
  void noUserNameProvided()
    throws IOException, InterruptedException {
    HttpResponse<String> response =
      issueRequest(getServletName());
    System.out.println(response.body());

    assertEquals(
      response.statusCode(),
      HttpServletResponse.SC_INTERNAL_SERVER_ERROR
    );
  }

  @Test
  void runAddUser()
    throws IOException, InterruptedException {
    HttpResponse<String> response =
      issueRequest(getServletName()+"?userName=ts");
    System.out.println(response.body());

    assertEquals(
      response.statusCode(),
      HttpServletResponse.SC_OK
    );

    response = issueRequest("badadduser?userName=ts");
    assertEquals(
      response.statusCode(),
      HttpServletResponse.SC_INTERNAL_SERVER_ERROR
    );
  }
}
```

First, it has an `emptyUserNameProvided` – which will fire off a validation error, as will providing no `userName` parameter at all, as shown by the `noUserNameProvided` test. (It uses `getServletName()` because we want to reuse some of these methods in another test, except with another servlet.)

Then we get to the runAddUser test, which calls our servlet *twice*: once to add the user in the first place, then to get the *same user* back... except the second call fails with an error, because of the lazy initialization. We don't test for the actual exception; we *could*, given that we control the source of the servlet, but in practice, one normally wouldn't expose the raw application exceptions to end users, and that wouldn't be a "testable result." (You'd translate exceptions like this to something more presentable for the user and test for *that* content.)

The AddUserServlet, Corrected

There are a few ways we could theoretically address the problem with BadAddUserServlet. One is to mark the posts element with @com.fasterxml.jackson.annotation.JsonIgnore, which tells Jackson to, well, ignore the attribute. However, there might be cases where we actually do want the entire user's history; marking the field as "ignored" feels a bit broad.

A better solution might be[10] to use something called a "data transfer object," a class whose purpose is purely dedicated to being transferred between architectural boundaries.

In this case, for example, we don't care about posts - and in fact, we don't want them, because loading an active user's set of posts might take quite a while. Therefore, our data transfer object, or DTO, would have only the fields we actually care about from User: id, name, and active. Listing 11-13 shows what it might look like.

Listing 11-13. chapter11/src/main/java/chapter11/dto/UserDTO.java

```
package chapter11.dto;

import lombok.Data;

@Data
public class UserDTO {
  int id;
  String name;
  boolean active;
```

[10] It's really hard, in programming, to say a solution is *definitely* better. I was going to take a few cheap shots at things I didn't like in this footnote, but held off because I was imagining my editor screaming at me in rage for not liking THIS HAS BEEN REDACTED, JOSEPH.

```
  public UserDTO() {
  }

  public UserDTO(
    int id,
    String name,
    boolean active
  ) {
    this.id = id;
    this.name = name;
    this.active = active;
  }
}
```

We give it a unique name of UserDTO because otherwise we might have to use the fully qualified class name (i.e., chapter11.dto.User) when we have the DTO and the entity in the same source file.

So how would we *use* it? Well, here's a working AddUserServlet, written with nearly the exact same structure as BadAddUserServlet, except using UserDTO to transfer data back and forth instead of User.

Listing 11-14. chapter11/src/main/java/chapter11/servlets/AddUserServlet.java

```
package chapter11.servlets;

import chapter11.dto.UserDTO;
import chapter11.model.User;
import com.autumncode.hibernate.util.SessionUtil;
import org.hibernate.Session;
import org.hibernate.query.Query;

import javax.persistence.NoResultException;
import javax.servlet.ServletException;
import javax.servlet.http.HttpServletRequest;
import javax.servlet.http.HttpServletResponse;
import java.io.IOException;
import java.util.Map;
```

```
public class AddUserServlet extends ServletBase {
  @Override
  protected void doGet(
    HttpServletRequest req,
    HttpServletResponse resp
  )
    throws ServletException, IOException {
    try {
      Map<String, String> input =
        getValidatedParameters(req, "userName");

      UserDTO user = SessionUtil.returnFromSession(
        session -> createUser(session, input.get("userName"))
      );
      write(resp,
        HttpServletResponse.SC_OK,
        user);
    } catch (Exception e) {
      writeError(resp, e);
    }
  }

  protected UserDTO createUser(Session session, String userName) {
    User entity;
    try {
      Query<User> query = session.createQuery(
        "from User u where u.name=:name",
        User.class);
      query.setParameter("name", userName);

      entity = query.getSingleResult();
    } catch (NoResultException nre) {
      entity = new User(userName, true);
      session.save(entity);
    }
```

```
        UserDTO dto = new UserDTO();
        dto.setId(entity.getId());
        dto.setName(entity.getName());
        dto.setActive(entity.isActive());

        return dto;
    }
}
```

We *could* use a different type of query to construct the DTO directly instead of going through a mapping of `User` to `UserDTO`. We'd still need to be able to **construct** a `User` entity, which means we'd still need to manually map to a `UserDTO` instance anyway. We won't follow this pattern for the rest of the chapter, but here's an example implementation that builds off of `AddUserServlet`, overriding `createUser()` to show the process.

Listing 11-15. `chapter11/src/main/java/chapter11/servlets/AddUserServletDTO.java`

```
package chapter11.servlets;

import chapter11.dto.UserDTO;
import chapter11.model.User;
import com.autumncode.hibernate.util.SessionUtil;
import org.hibernate.Session;
import org.hibernate.query.Query;

import javax.persistence.NoResultException;
import javax.servlet.ServletException;
import javax.servlet.http.HttpServletRequest;
import javax.servlet.http.HttpServletResponse;
import java.io.IOException;
import java.util.Map;
```

```
public class AddUserServletDTO extends AddUserServlet {
  protected UserDTO createUser(Session session, String userName) {
    UserDTO dto;
    try {
      Query<UserDTO> query = session.createQuery(
        "select new chapter11.dto.UserDTO(u.id, u.name,u.active) "
        +"from User u where u.name=:name",
        UserDTO.class);
      query.setParameter("name", userName);

      dto = query.getSingleResult();
    } catch (NoResultException nre) {
      User u = new User(userName, true);
      session.save(u);
      dto = new UserDTO(u.getId(), u.getName(), u.isActive());

    }
    return dto;
  }

}
```

If you wanted to use *this* class instead of the `AddUserServlet`, you'd modify `servlets.json` to simply refer to this class name instead.

Naturally, we should ask if it works. We'll inherit almost everything from `BadAddUserServletTest`, because we want to validate that using the incorrect parameters still causes an error, but we'll override `runAddUser` to actually validate that it gets an HTTP response code of 200 – which means a successful request – instead of expecting an error. Listing 11-16 shows the source.

Listing 11-16. `chapter11/src/test/java/chapter11/servlets/AddUserServletTest.java`

```
package chapter11.servlets;

import org.testng.annotations.Test;

import javax.servlet.http.HttpServletResponse;
import java.io.IOException;
```

```
import java.net.http.HttpResponse;
import java.util.Map;

import static org.testng.Assert.assertEquals;

public class AddUserServletTest
  extends BadAddUserServletTest {
  String getServletName() {
    return "adduser";
  }

  @Override
  @Test
  void runAddUser()
    throws IOException, InterruptedException {
    HttpResponse<String> response =
      issueRequest("adduser?userName=jbo");

    Map<String, Object> data =
      mapper.readValue(response.body(), mapOfMaps);

    assertEquals(
      response.statusCode(),
      HttpServletResponse.SC_OK
    );

    response = SimpleGetPostsService.getSimplePosts();

    assertEquals(
      response.statusCode(),
      HttpServletResponse.SC_OK
    );
  }
}
```

Now we can say that we can add users properly, using our definition of the "add user" process: it returns a User representation properly regardless of whether the database is modified or not.

Where DTOs Shine

The rule of thumb being displayed is simple and reinforces something we actually covered really early in the book, in Chapter 3. Entities loaded from Hibernate are actually *proxied* objects, and their data is populated as long as they're managed by a Session. Once the entities are detached from the Session, their state is fixed; if their data hasn't been loaded from the database, then their data *cannot* be loaded from the database until they're attached to a Session again somehow.

If you take nothing else from this chapter, take the lesson from the previous paragraph. There's a lot of really interesting code in the chapter, although most of it's of limited use for a "real application," but the prior paragraph is the primary takeaway. Everything else is proof and demonstration.

The two approaches, then, are to load entities **completely** before handing them back from when they're loaded and to create a detached version of the entity, which is what we did with the UserDTO. We could have done it with a copy of User, too:

```
User user=Session.load(userId, User.class);
// we never use clone() in Java, right?
User copy=new User();
copy.setId(user.getId());
copy.setName(user.getName());
return copy;
```

This would have avoided the lazy initialization issue just as easily as the use of UserDTO, by creating a *new* User and not making it a managed object.

If it involves fewer classes to maintain, why not use the strategy of creating an unmanaged instance of the entity? There's not really a good, solid answer, although there are contributing factors. Mostly it comes down to purpose, for me; I want classes to have a specific role. An entity class like User should be used for mapping data to and from the database; using it to transfer data between a servlet and a rich client is asking it to do double duty, and it's easy to forget what role a given class is playing, in that scenario; is this User instance managed, or is it being used to serialize to and from JSON?

If I use a UserDTO, then that's not a question that I have to ask; if I'm serializing to JSON, it's a UserDTO, period. If I'm reading from a database, it's a User entity, and I know that I need to convert back and forth if I'm crossing architectural boundaries like this.

What's more, I can create as many data transfer types as I like - if I want to have a DTO that includes the user's posts, I can create a `UserPostsDTO`, or if I want to include their comments, I can create a `UserCommentsDTO` and control the data precisely.[11]

Rounding Out the Application

So where does that leave us? The core aspects of the application's requirements might look something like

1. Create users (which we've shown already)
2. Create posts
3. Add comment to posts
4. Get posts by date
5. Get posts by user
6. Get posts by keyword

Most of these are pretty straightforward, although the last three are interesting because they'll use the filters we set up in our `Post` entity. There's even quite a possibility of abstracting a lot of the functionality into processes - after all, for each one we validate the input (in a fairly simple fashion) and then call a method to generate output.

It might be a worthwhile exercise for the reader to do this refactoring, actually, but our listings are going to be long enough without the refactoring, so we're just going to dive in. Let's take a look at how we create posts first.

Creating a Post

Creating a post for us involves the content and the title of the post as well as a valid user reference, according to our model. The actual code to accomplish this is fairly straightforward - it's the testing that's going to carry forward some pretty severe implications.

For example, consider the process of acquiring the valid user reference. Our `AddUserServlet` has code to do that, and it's not very long - 19 lines with a hard wrap for printing and a verbose conversion to `UserDTO`.

[11] What we do in this chapter is a balance of these approaches; we have a single DTO per entity, and the DTO is populated with "empty data" by default.

Under normal circumstances, we'd create a service class to hold that functionality for us, so we'd call out to a `getOrCreateUser()` method, either with or without a `Session` – a pattern we've seen in Chapter 3, for example. This gives us easily embedded functionality, without having to worry about session demarcation[12] – the places where objects leave the managed state.

The fact that service objects allow us to maintain the demarcation barriers almost without having to think about them is a great reason to use them. However, in this chapter, where the session begins and ends is a core lesson we're trying to examine – we're looking at the barriers and how to think about them, after all – so we're avoiding an obvious solution for the sake of learning why and how the solution works.

So, first, let's start building tools for our tests, such that we can build composable service calls to hide `issueRequest()` from us. We still want the `HttpResponse` objects, so we can test the body of the response and the response codes, but at least we can hide a lot of common aspects of making the service calls themselves.

We'll start with a class we'll call `BaseService`. We're going to design these as static classes, because they have absolutely no state to manage, and while this is an antipattern for actual implementations, the antipattern is limited to this chapter *and* our test structures. We're not designing these such that they'd replace an actual service call.[13]

Listing 11-17. `chapter11/src/test/java/chapter11/servlets/BaseService.java`

```
package chapter11.servlets;

import java.io.IOException;
import java.net.URI;
import java.net.URLEncoder;
import java.net.http.HttpClient;
```

[12] A "demarcation" is a dividing line between things, so when we refer to "session demarcation" for Hibernate, we're talking about when things become managed or unmanaged.

[13] To be honest: I wish there was a way to follow "good design without adding another hundred pages to the book. I drove myself crazy trying to figure out what compromises to make, to balance "teaching effectively" against "writing code I'd reject in the real world." If you want to complain about all the design shortcuts, I totally get it, believe me. But I would ask that you consider how you'd keep the content readable, along with illustrating the concepts we're trying to discuss; if you have a better solution that doesn't add unacceptable length, let me know and I'll use it for the next edition of the book.

```
import java.net.http.HttpRequest;
import java.net.http.HttpResponse;
import java.nio.charset.Charset;
import java.time.Duration;

public class BaseService {
  static String encode(String value) {
    return URLEncoder.encode(
      value,
      Charset.defaultCharset()
    );
  }

  static HttpResponse<String> issueRequest(String path)
    throws IOException, InterruptedException {
    HttpClient client = HttpClient.newBuilder().build();

    HttpRequest request = HttpRequest.newBuilder()
      .uri(URI.create("http://localhost:8080/myapp/" + path))
      .timeout(Duration.ofSeconds(3))
      .build();

    HttpResponse<String> response =
      client.send(request, HttpResponse.BodyHandlers.ofString());
    return response;
  }
}
```

As you can see, this class simply holds a simple `issueRequest()` along with a method to encode HTTP parameters. We can save *some* code by using this, but not a lot - after all, we already have a copy of `issueRequest()` in `TestBase`, as shown in our tests for the “add user” endpoints.

Let’s take a look at another service class, the `AddUserService`. This will extend `BaseService`, so it has access to `encode()` and `issueRequest()`, and returns the `HttpResponse` from calling the `AddUserServlet` endpoint.

Listing 11-18. chapter11/src/test/java/chapter11/servlets/AddUserService.java

```
package chapter11.servlets;

import java.io.IOException;
import java.net.http.HttpResponse;

public class AddUserService extends BaseService {
  static HttpResponse<String> addUser(
    String userName)
    throws IOException, InterruptedException {
    String path = String.format(
      "adduser?userName=%s",
      encode(userName)
    );
    return issueRequest(path);
  }
}
```

Our service to add a Post is very similar, although we haven't seen the endpoint to add a post yet.

Listing 11-19. chapter11/src/test/java/chapter11/servlets/AddPostService.java

```
package chapter11.servlets;

import java.io.IOException;
import java.net.http.HttpResponse;

public class AddPostService extends BaseService {
  static HttpResponse<String> addPost(
    String title,
    String content,
    String userName
  ) throws IOException, InterruptedException {
    String path = String.format(
      "addpost?title=%s&content=%s&userName=%s",
```

```
      encode(title),
      encode(content),
      encode(userName));
    return issueRequest(path);
  }
}
```

Lastly, we need one more service call, to *get* posts. This is a call that does a straightforward query - no parameters of any kind - and is used primarily for early testing. We haven't seen the endpoint for this either, but we will see it soon - and we'll make another "get posts" endpoint that has a lot more power to it not long after.

Listing 11-20. chapter11/src/test/java/chapter11/servlets/SimpleGetPostsService.java

```
package chapter11.servlets;

import java.io.IOException;
import java.net.http.HttpResponse;

public class SimpleGetPostsService extends BaseService{
  static HttpResponse<String> getSimplePosts()
    throws IOException, InterruptedException {
    return issueRequest("simplegetposts");
  }
}
```

Let's take a look at the two endpoints we've referred to - to "get posts simply" and "add posts" - and then we'll take a look at the test that brings all of this together for the first time. The SimpleGetPostsServlet is first, because it's so straightforward.

Listing 11-21. chapter11/src/main/java/chapter11/servlets/SimpleGetPostsServlet.java

```
package chapter11.servlets;

import chapter11.dto.PostDTO;
import chapter11.model.Post;
import com.autumncode.hibernate.util.SessionUtil;
```

```
import org.hibernate.Session;
import org.hibernate.query.Query;

import javax.servlet.ServletException;
import javax.servlet.http.HttpServletRequest;
import javax.servlet.http.HttpServletResponse;
import java.io.IOException;
import java.util.List;
import java.util.stream.Collectors;

public class SimpleGetPostsServlet extends ServletBase {
  @Override
  protected void doGet(
    HttpServletRequest req, HttpServletResponse resp
  ) throws ServletException, IOException {
    List<PostDTO> posts = SessionUtil.returnFromSession(session ->
      getPosts(session));
    write(
      resp,
      HttpServletResponse.SC_OK,
      posts
    );
  }

  private List<PostDTO> getPosts(Session session) {
    Query<Post> postQuery = session
      .createQuery("from Post p", Post.class);
    postQuery.setMaxResults(20);
    return postQuery.list().stream().map(post -> {
      PostDTO dto = new PostDTO();
      dto.setId(post.getId());
      dto.setUser(post.getUser().getName());
      dto.setContent(post.getContent());
      dto.setTitle(post.getTitle());
      dto.setCreatedDate(post.getCreateDate());
```

```
      return dto;
    }).collect(Collectors.toList());
  }
}
```

The only thing of note here is the streaming operation to convert a `Post` to a `PostDTO`. Of course, we can't have a `PostDTO` without source.

Listing 11-22. `chapter11/src/main/java/chapter11/servlets/PostDTO.java`

```
package chapter11.dto;

import lombok.Data;

import java.time.LocalDateTime;
import java.util.List;

@Data
public class PostDTO {
  int id;
  String user;
  String title;
  String content;
  List<CommentDTO> comments=List.of();
  LocalDateTime createdDate;
}
```

This class is, of course, a very simple representation of a `Post`. It initializes the `comments` attribute to an empty list, because we want to be able to use it to send back posts with comments… but we don't want to be forced to do so. With that said, though, we need to include our `CommentDTO` as well.

Listing 11-23. `chapter11/src/main/java/chapter11/servlets/CommentDTO.java`

```
package chapter11.dto;

import lombok.Data;

import java.time.LocalDateTime;
```

```
@Data
public class CommentDTO {
  String user;
  String content;
  LocalDateTime createdDate;
}
```

Now we can finally get to our AddPostServlet. This class looks fairly long - nearly 70 lines - but it's really quite straightforward. The code to get a User could have been abstracted away, but that code is only three statements (despite taking seven lines here[14]). After we get a User - and throw an implicit exception if the User doesn't exist - we create a Post, save it in the database with Session.save(), and then create a PostDTO to be serialized for the response.

And *finally* we get to a test to bring all of these parts together. First, let's take a look at the test class, and then we'll walk through what it does.

Listing 11-24. chapter11/src/test/java/chapter11/servlets/AddPostServletTest.java

```
package chapter11.servlets;

import chapter11.dto.PostDTO;
import com.fasterxml.jackson.core.type.TypeReference;
import org.testng.annotations.Test;

import javax.servlet.http.HttpServletResponse;
import java.io.IOException;
import java.net.http.HttpResponse;
import java.util.List;

import static org.testng.Assert.assertEquals;

public class AddPostServletTest
  extends TestBase {
```

[14] Again, there's a balance at work here; we could have created another class to encapsulate getting a User, but that means yet another code listing, along with every other similar call, and it's already likely to be overwhelming for many readers.

```
TypeReference<List<PostDTO>> listOfPosts =
  new TypeReference<>() {
  };

void addPost()
  throws IOException, InterruptedException {

  HttpResponse<String> response = AddPostService.addPost(
    "test post",
    "my test post",
    "jbo"
  );
  System.out.println(response.body());

  assertEquals(
    response.statusCode(),
    HttpServletResponse.SC_OK,
    "invalid user"
  );

  PostDTO data =
    mapper.readValue(
      response.body(),
      PostDTO.class
    );

  response = SimpleGetPostsService.getSimplePosts();

  assertEquals(
    response.statusCode(),
    HttpServletResponse.SC_OK
  );

  System.out.println(response.body());

  List<PostDTO> dtos=mapper.readValue(response.body(),
    listOfPosts);
  System.out.println(dtos);
  assertEquals(dtos.size(), 1);
}
```

```
  @Test(
    expectedExceptions = AssertionError.class,
    expectedExceptionsMessageRegExp = "invalid user.*"
  )
  void addPostNoUser() throws IOException, InterruptedException {
    addPost();
  }

  @Test
  void addPostWithValidUser()
    throws IOException, InterruptedException {

    HttpResponse<String> response =
      AddUserService.addUser("jbo");

    assertEquals(
      response.statusCode(),
      HttpServletResponse.SC_OK
    );

    addPost();
  }
}
```

There are four "pieces" to this class. The first is the declaration of a `TypeReference` so we can tell our `ObjectMapper` what types to use when deserializing JSON – we're basically telling Jackson how to create a `List` of `PostDTO` references. We saw the same thing in our `TestBase.java` class, except there we went with a `Map<String, Object>` as a more generalized form. (An equivalently generic – and unuseful – type reference here might be `TypeReference<List<Map<String, Object>>>`, but we obviously don't want *that*. We're not actually *using* the `PostDTO` references, but if we wanted to, we're ready to.)

The next method we see is a utility method to actually add a single post. It's pretty straightforward; it calls our `AddPostService.addPost()` method, then checks the response code via `assertEquals`, adding "invalid user" to the failure exception message should the assertion fail. (We'll see this used in our first test method.)

Assuming the assertion passes, it maps the JSON into a `PostDTO` – we don't *use* this, but if we wanted to validate the creation, we could. We don't do a full validation in the interests of space.

The addPost() method then calls GetSimplePostsServlet, because we want to make sure the post was actually created. (Otherwise, the AddPostServlet could return a new PostDTO and persist nothing - and yet still pass the test.) We make sure the call returns a status code of 200, and then we map the JSON into a list of PostDTO objects - and validate that the list has one post in it (the post we have just created).

The first test method we have is addPostNoUser(), which simply delegates to an addPost() method. As the name says, when addPost() is called, no user has been constructed, and we expect an exception. The actual exception type will be AssertionError (because it's triggered by assertEquals(), when we validate that the response status from adding a post is 200), and we also validate the exception *message* - because we want to pass the addPostNoUser() test *if and only if* the exception is thrown because no user was present.

The second test, addPostWithValidUser, is only slightly more than addPostNoUser: it adds the user *first* and then calls addPost() and expects no exception at all.

So what have we learned in this section? We've seen an awful lot - we're constructing classes to handle the actual calls to the servlets we build, although they're still pretty low level. We've also built out the rest of our DTOs, conceptually, and we've demonstrated that we can add posts properly - and we've also shown how to *get* the posts, although that's not done well yet.

Let's handle getting posts better next.

A Better "Get Posts" Servlet

If you look back at the Post entity, you'll notice that we have two filter definitions: byName and byTerm. It's time we used those to create a much, much better version of our SimpleGetPostsServlet. Structurally, it'll be just the same, but we're going to use two optional request parameters to specify a "name" - that is, an author for posts - or a "term," a simple wildcard for post titles.

Listing 11-25. chapter11/src/main/java/chapter11/servlets/GetPostsServlet.java

```
package chapter11.servlets;

import chapter11.dto.PostDTO;
import chapter11.model.Post;
import com.autumncode.hibernate.util.SessionUtil;
```

```
import org.hibernate.Session;
import org.hibernate.query.Query;

import javax.servlet.ServletException;
import javax.servlet.http.HttpServletRequest;
import javax.servlet.http.HttpServletResponse;
import java.io.IOException;
import java.util.List;
import java.util.stream.Collectors;

public class GetPostsServlet extends ServletBase {
  @Override
  protected void doGet(
    HttpServletRequest req, HttpServletResponse resp
  ) throws ServletException, IOException {
    List<PostDTO> posts = SessionUtil.returnFromSession(session ->
      getPosts(
        session,
        req.getParameter("userName"),
        req.getParameter("term"))
    );
    write(
      resp,
      HttpServletResponse.SC_OK,
      posts
    );
  }

  private List<PostDTO> getPosts(
    Session session,
    String userName,
    String term
  ) {
    if (userName != null && !userName.isEmpty()) {
      session
        .enableFilter("byName")
```

```
        .setParameter("name", userName);
    }

    if (term != null && !term.isEmpty()) {
      session
        .enableFilter("byTerm")
        .setParameter("term", "%" + term + "%");
    }

    Query<Post> postQuery = session
      .createQuery(
        "from Post p order by p.createDate ",
        Post.class
      );

    return postQuery.list().stream().map(post -> {
      PostDTO dto = new PostDTO();
      dto.setId(post.getId());
      dto.setUser(post.getUser().getName());
      dto.setContent(post.getContent());
      dto.setTitle(post.getTitle());
      dto.setCreatedDate(post.getCreateDate());
      return dto;
    }).collect(Collectors.toList());
  }
}
```

The `getPosts()` method is almost a clone of the `SimpleGetPostsServlet` version of the same method, with some extras thrown in. It accepts two parameters, which can be null or empty (thus we can't use our `ServletBase.getValidatedParameters()` call), along with the `Session`; it then enables the various filters based on the existence of those parameters.

Then it executes a straightforward query: `from Posts p order by p.createDate`, and the filters are applied by Hibernate based on whether they're active for this `Session` or not. We don't have to build a custom query or anything like that.

Of course, we can't have such a servlet without writing a test to show it in action. We have a matrix of possibilities to manage, so we'll use a DataProvider again.

First, we need a GetPostsService to match the service model we've used in our other tests.

Listing 11-26. chapter11/src/test/java/chapter11/servlets/GetPostsService.java

```
package chapter11.servlets;

import java.io.IOException;
import java.net.http.HttpResponse;

public class GetPostsService extends BaseService {
  static HttpResponse<String> getPosts(String userName, String term)
    throws IOException, InterruptedException {
    StringBuilder path = new StringBuilder("getposts");
    String separator = "?";
    if (userName != null && !userName.isEmpty()) {
      path
        .append(separator)
        .append("userName=")
        .append(userName);
      separator = "&";
    }
    if (term != null && !term.isEmpty()) {
      path
        .append(separator)
        .append("term=")
        .append(term);
    }
    return issueRequest(path.toString());
  }
}
```

This class is pretty straightforward; it basically builds a query based on the presence of our search terms and issues a request.

Our test is fairly straightforward as well: it has a `@BeforeMethod` included that populates our database with two users ("jbo" and "ts") and also adds five posts for those users, split out among them. The actual content's not especially important; we're just looking for a dataset that we can predict for our tests.

We then have a `searchCriteria()` method as a `@DataProvider`. Here, we're constructing a series of arrays of four elements:

1. A "search user" value
2. A "search title" value
3. A count of expected records given the search terms
4. A description of what the row describes

Our actual test *method* is pretty simple. It grabs a response from `GetPostsService.getPosts()` and validates that it responds with a successful status code, then converts the body of the response into a `List<PostDTO>` (just like our `AddPostServletTest` did), and validates that the count of responses matches what the data provider says it should be.

Listing 11-27. `chapter11/src/test/java/chapter11/servlets/GetPostsServletTest.java`

```
package chapter11.servlets;

import chapter11.dto.PostDTO;
import com.fasterxml.jackson.core.type.TypeReference;
import org.testng.annotations.BeforeMethod;
import org.testng.annotations.DataProvider;
import org.testng.annotations.Test;

import javax.servlet.http.HttpServletResponse;
import java.io.IOException;
import java.net.http.HttpResponse;
import java.util.List;
import java.util.stream.Collectors;

import static org.testng.Assert.assertEquals;
```

```
public class GetPostsServletTest
  extends TestBase {
  TypeReference<List<PostDTO>> listOfPosts =
    new TypeReference<>() {
    };

  @BeforeMethod
  void createUsersAndPosts() throws IOException, InterruptedException {
    List<Integer> errorCodes = List.of(
      AddUserService.addUser("jbo"),
      AddUserService.addUser("ts"),
      AddPostService.addPost("raccoons 1", "raccoons are cool", "jbo"),
      AddPostService.addPost("i like dogs", "see title", "jbo"),
      AddPostService.addPost("never seen no cat", "what are cats", "jbo"),
      AddPostService.addPost("raccoons 2", "raccoons are trash pandas", "ts"),
      AddPostService.addPost("dogs are good", "i named mine scooby", "ts")
    )
      .stream()
      .map(HttpResponse::statusCode)
      .filter(status -> status != 200)
      .collect(Collectors.toList());
    if (errorCodes.size() > 0) {
      throw new RuntimeException(
        "An error was encountered seeding data"
      );
    }
  }

  @DataProvider
  Object[][] searchCriteria() {
    return new Object[][]{
      {null, null, 5, "all posts"},
      {"jbo", null, 3, "jbo posts"},
      {"jbo", "cat", 1, "jbo cat posts"},
      {null, "raccoons", 2, "raccoon posts"},
      {"arl", null, 0, "invalid user posts"},
```

```
      {null, "crow", 0, "search term with no results"},
      {"ts", "cat", 0, "ts has no cat posts"}
    };
  }

  @Test(dataProvider = "searchCriteria")
  void getPosts(String userName, String term, int count, String desc)
    throws IOException, InterruptedException {
    HttpResponse<String> response =
      GetPostsService.getPosts(userName, term);

    assertEquals(
      response.statusCode(),
      HttpServletResponse.SC_OK
    );

    List<PostDTO> dtos = mapper.readValue(
      response.body(),
      listOfPosts);

    System.out.println(dtos);
    assertEquals(dtos.size(), count);
  }
}
```

Rounding Out the "Application"

There are two pieces of functionality that we've not written, and they're both related to specific posts. We haven't provided a way to retrieve a specific post, first, and we haven't provided a way to add comments to posts.

The processes for both mirror functionality we've already seen. We know how to get a `User`, after all, although we've not seen returning a `User` as a `UserDTO`, specifically; getting a `PostDTO` would be a matter of retrieving a `PostDTO` by the post's id and populating its set of comments appropriately. Adding a comment to a post would be much the same process as adding a post for a user.

Since these processes are so similar to what we've seen, we're going to implement the servlets and have *one* test that exercises the mechanisms of retrieving a given post and checking its comments.

We already have the data transfer objects, of course, so let's dive into the servlet to get a specific post. It's going to take one parameter, a post id, and return a fully populated PostDTO (including comments). Note that the name is very much like another Servlet of ours: this is GetPostServlet, not GetPostsServlet.

Listing 11-28. chapter11/src/main/java/chapter11/servlets/GetPostServlet.java

```
package chapter11.servlets;

import chapter11.dto.CommentDTO;
import chapter11.dto.PostDTO;
import chapter11.model.Post;
import com.autumncode.hibernate.util.SessionUtil;
import org.hibernate.ObjectNotFoundException;
import org.hibernate.Session;

import javax.servlet.ServletException;
import javax.servlet.http.HttpServletRequest;
import javax.servlet.http.HttpServletResponse;
import java.io.IOException;
import java.util.Map;
import java.util.stream.Collectors;

public class GetPostServlet extends ServletBase {
  @Override
  protected void doGet(
    HttpServletRequest req,
    HttpServletResponse resp)
    throws ServletException, IOException {
    try {
      Map<String, String> input = getValidatedParameters(req, "id");
      Integer id = Integer.parseInt(input.get("id"));

      PostDTO postDTO = SessionUtil
        .returnFromSession(session -> getPost(session, id));
```

```
    write(
      resp,
      HttpServletResponse.SC_OK,
      postDTO
    );
  } catch (Exception e) {
    handleException(resp, e);
  }
}

protected void handleException(
  HttpServletResponse resp,
  Exception e
) throws IOException {
  if (e.getCause() instanceof ObjectNotFoundException) {
    write(
      resp,
      HttpServletResponse.SC_NOT_FOUND,
      Map.of("error", e.getCause().getMessage())
    );
  } else {
    writeError(resp, e);
  }

}

protected PostDTO getPost(Session session, Integer id) {
  Post post = session.load(Post.class, id);
  PostDTO postDTO = new PostDTO();

  postDTO.setId(id);
  postDTO.setTitle(post.getTitle());
  postDTO.setContent(post.getContent());
  postDTO.setCreatedDate(post.getCreateDate());
  postDTO.setUser(post.getUser().getName());
```

```
    postDTO.setComments(
      post
        .getComments()
        .stream()
        .map(
          comment -> {
            CommentDTO commentDTO = new CommentDTO();
            commentDTO.setContent(comment.getContent());
            commentDTO.setCreatedDate(comment.getCreateDate());
            commentDTO.setUser(comment.getUser().getName());
            return commentDTO;
          })
        .collect(Collectors.toList())
    );
    return postDTO;
  }
}
```

Note the getPost() method, which is fairly straightforward but has a lot of code. All it's doing is loading a Post by id – and it will throw an exception if a Post given that id does not exist – and populating a PostDTO with the data, *including* the process of converting the set of comments to a list of CommentDTO objects.

The doGet() method deserves some discussion, though, in the catch() block. The handleException() method exists because the SessionUtil.returnFromSession() call doesn't return an ObjectNotFoundException from the lambda as one might hope; it actually throws a RuntimeException, with the actual underlying cause as part of the RuntimeException.

In this case, we actually want to return a 404 – an HTTP "not found" message – instead of a "server error" message, if the user submits a post id that **could** be correct but doesn't exist.[15]

So what we have to do is examine the cause of the exception when we catch it – if it's an ObjectNotFoundException, then the Session.load() for the Post failed, and we want to return a 404, and not a 500.

[15] The handleException() method would actually be a good candidate for a method in ServletBase, but we're trying to introduce complexity as we encounter it, instead of all at once.

The next servlet we want to take a look at is the AddCommentServlet, which *extends* GetPostServlet – because we want to reuse the getPost() method we just saw. It loads a User, then the Post by id, and then creates a simple Comment and adds it to the Post's existing list of comments; then it returns the value of getPost() from the GetPostServlet to return the populated PostDTO – which is largely loaded from cache at this point, because we're using the same Session throughout.

The key here is to note how we're managing Session; everything happens in the context of a lambda initialized with SessionUtil.returnFromSession(), so the cache is active, and we have full access to every object's data, because if it hasn't been populated when the call occurs – as with post.getComments().add(comment); – the Session can load whatever it needs on demand. What's more, since it all *is* happening within a single Session, our data is cached even if we try to fetch it *again.*

We can write code that is straightforward, and we get the benefits of the cache to make it all run quickly, although our tests aren't particularly fast due to setup and teardown time.

Here's our AddCommentServlet.

Listing 11-29. chapter11/src/main/java/chapter11/servlets/AddCommentServlet.java

```
package chapter11.servlets;

import chapter11.dto.CommentDTO;
import chapter11.dto.PostDTO;
import chapter11.model.Comment;
import chapter11.model.Post;
import chapter11.model.User;
import com.autumncode.hibernate.util.SessionUtil;
import org.hibernate.Session;
import org.hibernate.query.Query;

import javax.servlet.ServletException;
import javax.servlet.http.HttpServletRequest;
import javax.servlet.http.HttpServletResponse;
import java.io.IOException;
import java.time.LocalDateTime;
import java.util.Map;
import java.util.stream.Collectors;
```

```
public class AddCommentServlet extends GetPostServlet {
  @Override
  protected void doGet(
    HttpServletRequest req,
    HttpServletResponse resp)
    throws ServletException, IOException {
    try {
      Map<String, String> input = getValidatedParameters(
        req,
        "id",
        "userName",
        "content"
      );
      Integer id = Integer.parseInt(input.get("id"));

      PostDTO postDTO = SessionUtil
        .returnFromSession(session ->
          addComment(
            session,
            id,
            input.get("userName"),
            input.get("content")
          )
        );

      write
        (resp,
          HttpServletResponse.SC_OK,
          postDTO
        );
    } catch (Exception e) {
      handleException(resp, e);
    }
  }
```

```
  PostDTO addComment(
    Session session,
    Integer id,
    String userName,
    String content
  ) {
    Query<User> userQuery = session.createQuery(
      "from User u where u.name=:name",
      User.class
    );
    userQuery.setParameter("name", userName);
    User user = userQuery.getSingleResult();

    Post post = session.load(Post.class, id);

    Comment comment = new Comment();
    comment.setUser(user);
    comment.setPost(post);
    comment.setContent(content);
    comment.setCreateDate(LocalDateTime.now());

    session.save(comment);

    post.getComments().add(comment);

    return getPost(session, id);
  }
}
```

Of course, we need to have a test. That also implies that we have some service proxies to make the service calls much easier to read. Therefore, let's take a look at `GetPostService`, `AddCommentService`, and then `AddCommentServletTest`.

Thankfully, the services are rather short.

Listing 11-30. chapter11/src/test/java/chapter11/servlets/GetPostService.java

```
package chapter11.servlets;

import java.io.IOException;
import java.net.http.HttpResponse;

public class GetPostService extends BaseService {
  static HttpResponse<String> getPost(Integer id)
    throws IOException, InterruptedException {
    return issueRequest(
      String.format("getpost?id=%d", id)
    );
  }
}
```

Listing 11-31. chapter11/src/test/java/chapter11/servlets/AddCommentService.java

```
package chapter11.servlets;

import java.io.IOException;
import java.net.http.HttpResponse;

public class AddCommentService extends BaseService {
  static HttpResponse<String> addComment(
    Integer id,
    String content,
    String userName
  ) throws IOException, InterruptedException {
    String path = String.format(
      "addcomment?id=%s&content=%s&userName=%s",
      id,
      encode(content),
      encode(userName));
    return issueRequest(path);
  }
}
```

Now we get to the most fun of the tests (well, if such things can be fun): the AddCommentServletTest.

There are two tests. The setup is simple: the createUsersAndPosts() method sets up two users and a single post and saves the post so we can use its id to add a comment.

The first test, testAddComment(), loads the Post and verifies that it has no comments, because it shouldn't! Then it adds a comment and verifies that the PostDTO returned from AddCommentServlet has one comment; then it repeats the process to validate that we can add multiple comments in sequence.

Finally, it loads the Post again, through GetPostServlet, to make sure the results are the same as the call from AddCommentServlet.

The second test is a little simpler - it fetches a post that shouldn't exist, using the id of the post that *does* exist as a basis for deriving a new id.

Listing 11-32. chapter11/src/test/java/chapter11/servlets/AddCommentServletTest.java

```
package chapter11.servlets;

import chapter11.dto.PostDTO;
import org.testng.annotations.BeforeMethod;
import org.testng.annotations.Test;

import javax.servlet.http.HttpServletResponse;
import java.io.IOException;
import java.net.http.HttpResponse;

import static org.testng.Assert.assertEquals;

public class AddCommentServletTest extends TestBase {
  PostDTO post = null;

  @BeforeMethod
  void createUsersAndPosts()
    throws IOException, InterruptedException {
    AddUserService.addUser("jbo");
    AddUserService.addUser("ts");

    HttpResponse<String> postData =
      AddPostService.addPost("raccoons", "raccoons are neat", "jbo");
```

```
    // this is how we get the post's id.
    post = mapper.readValue(postData.body(), PostDTO.class);
  }

  @Test
  void testAddComment() throws IOException, InterruptedException {
    HttpResponse<String> response =
      GetPostService.getPost(post.getId());
    validatePost(response, 0);

    response = AddCommentService.addComment(
      post.getId(),
      "what's the deal with raccoons, really",
      "ts"
    );
    assertEquals(response.statusCode(), 200);
    validatePost(response, 1);

    response = AddCommentService.addComment(
      post.getId(),
      "they're the coolest",
      "jbo"
    );
    assertEquals(response.statusCode(), 200);
    validatePost(response, 2);

    response =
      GetPostService.getPost(post.getId());
    validatePost(response, 2);
  }

  @Test
  void testInvalidGetPost()
    throws IOException, InterruptedException {

    HttpResponse<String> response =
      GetPostService.getPost(post.getId() + 1);
```

```
    assertEquals(
      response.statusCode(),
      HttpServletResponse.SC_NOT_FOUND
    );
  }

  void validatePost(
    HttpResponse<String> response,
    int commentSize
  ) throws IOException {
    assertEquals(response.statusCode(), 200);

    PostDTO retrieved = mapper.readValue(response.body(), PostDTO.class);

    assertEquals(retrieved.getComments().size(), commentSize);
    assertEquals(retrieved.getTitle(), "raccoons");
  }
}
```

Summary

This has been a giant chapter! We've used it to demonstrate integrating Hibernate into a more or less working web application that manages a blog; it's not a *good* application, but could be used as the basis for one.

The lessons we've learned are many: we've seen how to set up an embedded servlet engine (Undertow), and we've learned about session demarcation and one approach for managing it well, and we've also seen a fairly exhaustive set of tests for the whole process.

It has to be said that most of the code in this chapter isn't *especially* useful; with enough effort and intent, it could be *made* useful, but what we're really looking for here is to understand some of the issues around passing data across architectural walls, from an entity to JSON, for example.

Our next chapters are going to focus on integrating Hibernate into frameworks that one is likely to *actually* encounter in the real world.

CHAPTER 12

Integrating Hibernate

In Chapter 11, we showed a technique for integrating Hibernate into a servlet application, but our application was very "bare-metal" for the JVM. Nobody writes applications like that.[1] Instead, people use application frameworks that take care of a lot of the concerns we had to deal with ourselves, like Quarkus, Spring Data (specifically the Spring Data JPA module, in our case), or ActiveJ. In this chapter, we're going to take a look at integrating Hibernate with those three platforms, which will give us a better idea of how Hibernate's used in the "real world," and we'll see how many of the lessons we've learned up to now still apply.

There's some difficulty here, though.

Hibernate 6 – the subject of this book – is, as of this writing, still *very* new, and the application framework authors have an implicit delay in integrating new releases. As such, then, framework support for Hibernate tends to lag behind Hibernate itself, and necessarily so.

Quarkus, for example, has a very tight binding with the internals of Hibernate, to provide optimization under many different circumstances (beyond the JVM, even). There's a lot of man-hours invested in the internal bindings, and if Hibernate 6 is still undergoing development, it's unwise of the Quarkus team to invest a lot of effort until there's a stable API to work against.

Therefore, in this chapter we're going to work against Hibernate 5 where necessary.

This is acceptable *mostly* because when the frameworks *do* get Hibernate 6 support – possibly by the time you read this – the integration will look nearly identical, if it's not exactly the same.

[1] Well, *someone* might write applications straight to the servlet API like we did in Chapter 11, but they're pouring a lot of effort into aspects of their applications that have much nicer alternatives.

J. B. Ottinger et al., *Beginning Hibernate 6*, https://doi.org/10.1007/978-1-4842-7337-1_12

This chapter is about integrating Hibernate, not Hibernate 6 – although we'll use Hibernate 6 where we can. We're going to see a lot of code and processes for generating projects, and our project structures are going to have a fair bit of duplication of effort, so be ready.

Spring

Our first integration is with Spring (`https://spring.io/projects/spring-framework`). Spring is a framework that provides services around *dependency injection*, an architectural design that encourages a clear separation of concerns: if a class requires a resource, it declares a dependency on it (based on interfaces, usually), and the framework provides an easy way to provide the dependency.

Imagine that we had a class that needed to access purchase orders to build a report, for example. That class wouldn't (or shouldn't) care where the purchase orders come from; it only needs to be able to access purchase orders. With dependency injection, we'd create an interface, a `PurchaseOrderAccessor`, perhaps, and declare a *dependency* on a `PurchaseOrderAccessor`.

During tests, we could provide an implementation that returned data populated from a JSON file, or constructed the data manually, for example, which means there's no Hibernate, no database, nothing that would be unpredictable, making an ideal test framework: you would be able to specify *exactly* what the data looked like, and thus the output from the purchase order report would be *absolutely* predictable. This is referred to as *functional* testing or *unit* testing.[2]

Of course, you'd also logically have a `PurchaseOrderAccessor` implementation that accessed a database. Here, Hibernate might be entirely appropriate, and this class also should be thoroughly tested, but this is an *integration* test, normally. (The lines here are usually quite blurred, and a lot of programmers will mix integration and functional testing.) Integration tests are tests that cross architectural boundaries, like between an application and its data storage mechanism.

[2] Terms like "functional testing" and "unit testing" are not defined in absolute terms. Some programmers will reject these definitions. Some won't. It's okay to be in either set; the most important thing is to get things done, not to argue about how clearly defined something might be, at least in *this* case.

This book has emphasized what would normally end up in integration testing, because it's focused on Hibernate. Databases go with the territory, you might say.

Back to Spring! Spring is probably the most popular dependency injection framework in Java; it's got a fairly simple declarative syntax, and it's got a *massive* ecosystem.

There are a few ways to integrate Hibernate into Spring, and we won't be able to cover them all; we'll cover one of the simpler ones, first, that provides direct Hibernate access (and thus looks very similar to code we've seen throughout the book.)

What we'll do first is define an umbrella project that has five modules in it (much as this book so far has a top-level project with modules for every chapter). Then, we'll define a `ch12common` project and use that to hold some resources we'll reuse for the rest of *this* chapter, and finally we'll dive into the Spring integration.

First is the `chapter12` project, which mostly organizes the other modules.

Listing 12-1. `chapter12/pom.xml`

```
<?xml version="1.0" encoding="UTF-8"?>
<project xmlns:xsi="http://www.w3.org/2001/XMLSchema-instance"
         xmlns="http://maven.apache.org/POM/4.0.0"
         xsi:schemaLocation="http://maven.apache.org/POM/4.0.0
         http://maven.apache.org/xsd/maven-4.0.0.xsd">
    <parent>
        <groupId>com.autumncode.books.hibernate</groupId>
        <artifactId>hibernate-6-parent</artifactId>
        <version>5.0</version>
    </parent>
    <packaging>pom</packaging>

    <modelVersion>4.0.0</modelVersion>

    <artifactId>chapter12</artifactId>

    <modules>
        <module>ch12common</module>
        <module>activej</module>
        <module>spring</module>
        <module>springboot</module>
    </modules>
</project>
```

Now let's dive into the ch12common project, which will have an object model for a *very* simple "blog" project - consisting of one entity, a Post - along with an interface for working with Post objects (and an implementation for working with Hibernate, as well, although we won't use the implementation in every project in this chapter. For that matter, we won't be using this "common" project in every section either; we're going to pick and choose as needed).

Here's the ch12common project model.

Listing 12-2. chapter12/ch12common/pom.xml

```
<?xml version="1.0" encoding="UTF-8"?>
<project xmlns:xsi="http://www.w3.org/2001/XMLSchema-instance"
         xmlns="http://maven.apache.org/POM/4.0.0"
         xsi:schemaLocation="http://maven.apache.org/POM/4.0.0
         http://maven.apache.org/xsd/maven-4.0.0.xsd">

    <parent>
        <groupId>com.autumncode.books.hibernate</groupId>
        <artifactId>chapter12</artifactId>
        <version>5.0</version>
    </parent>

    <modelVersion>4.0.0</modelVersion>

    <artifactId>ch12common</artifactId>

    <properties>
        <maven.compiler.target>11</maven.compiler.target>
        <maven.compiler.source>11</maven.compiler.source>
    </properties>

    <dependencies>
        <dependency>
            <groupId>org.hibernate.orm</groupId>
            <artifactId>hibernate-core</artifactId>
            <version>6.0.0.Alpha8</version>
            <scope>provided</scope>
        </dependency>
```

```
        <dependency>
            <groupId>com.h2database</groupId>
            <artifactId>h2</artifactId>
            <version>1.4.200</version>
        </dependency>

        <dependency>
            <groupId>ch.qos.logback</groupId>
            <artifactId>logback-classic</artifactId>
            <version>1.2.3</version>
        </dependency>
    </dependencies>
    <build>
        <plugins>
            <plugin>
                <groupId>org.apache.maven.plugins</groupId>
                <artifactId>maven-compiler-plugin</artifactId>
                <version>3.8.1</version>
            </plugin>
        </plugins>
    </build>
</project>
```

There are a few things to note here. First, Hibernate is included as a `provided` dependency, which means that it's in the classpath for this compilation unit but is *not* a transitive dependency. This means that any project that uses `ch12common` needs to provide Hibernate for itself.

We are doing this because we need Hibernate in the classpath, but we don't want to tell the other projects which Hibernate version to *use*. There's a potential for incompatibility here, if the version of Hibernate the other projects use doesn't use the same class structure as Hibernate 6, although as of this writing we're safe.

The other dependencies included - H2 and Logback - are transitive dependencies, so they'll be included in the classpath for anything that uses `ch12common`.

Back to the project! We have a configuration file for Hibernate as well.

Listing 12-3. chapter12/ch12common/src/main/resources/hibernate.cfg.xml

```
<?xml version="1.0"?>
<!DOCTYPE hibernate-configuration PUBLIC
    "-//Hibernate/Hibernate Configuration DTD 3.0//EN"
    "http://www.hibernate.org/dtd/hibernate-configuration-3.0.dtd">
<hibernate-configuration>
  <session-factory>
    <!-- Database connection settings -->
    <property name="connection.driver_class">org.h2.Driver</property>
    <property name="connection.url">jdbc:h2:./activej</property>
    <property name="dialect">org.hibernate.dialect.H2Dialect</property>

    <!-- Echo all executed SQL to stdout -->
    <property name="show_sql">true</property>
    <property name="use_sql_comments">true</property>

    <!-- Drop and re-create the database schema on startup -->
    <property name="hbm2ddl.auto">create-drop</property>

    <mapping class="ch12.Post"/>
  </session-factory>
</hibernate-configuration>
```

Here's our Post entity. Being written for the sake of example, it's mostly autogenerated.[3]

Listing 12-4. chapter12/ch12common/src/main/java/ch12/Post.java

```
package ch12;

import javax.persistence.*;
import java.util.Date;

@Entity
public class Post {
  @Id
```

[3] If you're wondering, Post was autogenerated by IDEA. Other IDEs can do the same thing, and the code would look pretty similar; it's "good enough" for the purposes of this chapter.

```
@GeneratedValue(strategy = GenerationType.AUTO)
Long id;
@Column(nullable = false, unique = true)
String title;
@Column(nullable = false)
@Lob
String content;
@Temporal(TemporalType.TIMESTAMP)
Date createdAt;

public Long getId() {
  return id;
}

public void setId(Long id) {
  this.id = id;
}

public String getTitle() {
  return title;
}

public void setTitle(String title) {
  this.title = title;
}

public String getContent() {
  return content;
}

public void setContent(String content) {
  this.content = content;
}

public Date getCreatedAt() {
  return createdAt;
}
```

```
  public void setCreatedAt(Date createdAt) {
    this.createdAt = createdAt;
  }

  @Override
  public String toString() {
    return "Post{" +
      "id=" + id +
      ", title='" + title + '\'' +
      ", content='" + content + '\'' +
      ", createdAt=" + createdAt +
      '}';
  }
}
```

Note our use of Date for the createdAt field. Ordinarily, we'd be better off with an OffsetDateTime, but integrating with the new Date-Time API in recent Java is occasionally problematic with some older libraries; if we weren't using a common utility library for use in multiple projects, we'd have done this "correctly" instead of using Date here.[4]

Our next class is a PostManager, an interface that does nothing more than specify that an implementation can provide a list of posts and can save a post. In a "real application," we'd want to provide for pagination, access to an individual post, a way to *update* a post, possibly a way to *delete* a post - the typical CRUD-type operations - but we've seen examples of those throughout the rest of the book, and they're not necessary here.[5]

Listing 12-5. chapter12/ch12common/src/main/java/ch12/PostManager.java

```
package ch12;

import java.util.List;

public interface PostManager {
```

[4] Using Date instead of OffsetDateTime is definitely a shortcut, mostly to prevent having longer program listings and extra dependencies that don't really show us anything new.

[5] If you've not seen examples of these kinds of operations yet, check out the rest of this book! It's a great book, you'll love it. The writer's hilarious.

```
  List<Post> getPosts();

  Post savePost(String title, String content);
}
```

Our last class in ch12common is a HibernatePostManager. This class replicates some of the code we've seen from the util project's SessionUtil - in the returnFromSession() method - and implements the PostManager interface. It also does nothing to create the SessionFactory from which it gets the Session - we'll be doing that in each one of our integration modules, when this class is used.

Listing 12-6. chapter12/ch12common/src/main/java/ch12/HibernatePostManager.java

```
package ch12;

import org.hibernate.Session;
import org.hibernate.SessionFactory;
import org.hibernate.Transaction;
import org.hibernate.query.Query;

import java.util.Date;
import java.util.List;
import java.util.function.Function;

public class HibernatePostManager implements PostManager {
  private final SessionFactory sessionFactory;

  public HibernatePostManager(SessionFactory factory) {
    this.sessionFactory = factory;
  }

  @Override
  public List<Post> getPosts() {
    return returnFromSession(session -> {
      Query<Post> postQuery = session.createQuery(
        "from Post p order by p.createdAt desc",
        Post.class
      );
      postQuery.setMaxResults(20);
```

```
      return postQuery.list();
    });
  }

  @Override
  public Post savePost(String title, String content) {
    return returnFromSession(session -> {
      Post post = new Post();
      post.setTitle(title);
      post.setContent(content);
      post.setCreatedAt(new Date());
      session.save(post);
      return post;
    });
  }

  public <T> T returnFromSession(Function<Session, T> command) {
    try (Session session = sessionFactory.openSession()) {
      Transaction tx = null;
      try {
        tx = session.beginTransaction();

        return command.apply(session);
      } catch (Exception e) {
        throw new RuntimeException(e);
      } finally {
        if (tx != null) {
          if (tx.isActive() &&
            !tx.getRollbackOnly()) {
            tx.commit();
          } else {
            tx.rollback();
          }
        }
      }
    }
  }
}
```

Now we can start looking at the actual Spring integration.

Our Spring application is going to be overly simple: simply storing a `Post` and retrieving it. Our other applications will provide a web interface for this, but Spring itself is a little simple for this; writing our own web integration and deployment layer is quite a bit of code that doesn't really do more than take up space.

The *responsibility* of our Spring application is rather simple: It needs to create a `SessionFactory` to provide to our `HibernatePostManager`, as well as providing the `HibernatePostManager` itself. It also needs to create a mechanism by which we can coordinate transactions within Spring components.

First, let's take a look at the project module itself, then we'll look at the code.

Listing 12-7. `chapter12/spring/pom.xml`

```
<?xml version="1.0" encoding="UTF-8"?>
<project xmlns:xsi="http://www.w3.org/2001/XMLSchema-instance"
         xmlns="http://maven.apache.org/POM/4.0.0"
         xsi:schemaLocation="http://maven.apache.org/POM/4.0.0
         http://maven.apache.org/xsd/maven-4.0.0.xsd">

    <parent>
        <groupId>com.autumncode.books.hibernate</groupId>
        <artifactId>chapter12</artifactId>
        <version>5.0</version>
    </parent>

    <modelVersion>4.0.0</modelVersion>
    <groupId>com.autumncode.books.hibernate</groupId>
    <artifactId>spring</artifactId>
    <version>1.0.0</version>

    <properties>
        <maven.compiler.target>11</maven.compiler.target>
        <maven.compiler.source>11</maven.compiler.source>
    </properties>

    <dependencies>
        <dependency>
            <groupId>com.autumncode.books.hibernate</groupId>
```

```
            <artifactId>ch12common</artifactId>
            <version>5.0</version>
        </dependency>

        <dependency>
            <groupId>org.hibernate.orm</groupId>
            <artifactId>hibernate-core</artifactId>
            <version>6.0.0.Alpha8</version>
        </dependency>

        <dependency>
            <groupId>org.springframework</groupId>
            <artifactId>spring-orm</artifactId>
            <version>5.3.8</version>
        </dependency>

        <dependency>
            <groupId>org.springframework</groupId>
            <artifactId>spring-context</artifactId>
            <version>5.3.8</version>
        </dependency>

        <dependency>
            <groupId>org.hibernate.orm</groupId>
            <artifactId>hibernate-hikaricp</artifactId>
            <version>6.0.0.Alpha8</version>
        </dependency>

        <dependency>
            <groupId>com.h2database</groupId>
            <artifactId>h2</artifactId>
        </dependency>
    </dependencies>
    <build>
        <plugins>
            <plugin>
                <groupId>org.codehaus.mojo</groupId>
                <artifactId>exec-maven-plugin</artifactId>
```

```
                <version>3.0.0</version>
                <configuration>
                    <mainClass>ch12.Main</mainClass>
                </configuration>
            </plugin>
            <plugin>
                <groupId>org.apache.maven.plugins</groupId>
                <artifactId>maven-compiler-plugin</artifactId>
                <version>3.8.1</version>
            </plugin>
        </plugins>
    </build>
</project>
```

This project is fairly straightforward; it imports the `ch12common` module (which means it gets H2 and Logback) and then imports Hibernate itself and two Spring dependencies: `spring-orm` (which provides Spring's interface with Hibernate via some convenient wrapper classes) and `spring-context` which gives us the basic annotations we'll use for configuration.

Off to the code!

We'll have a whopping *one* class to do all of this. It will create an `ApplicationContext` class – which is our entry point into the Spring resources – and request a `PostManager` from that context and interact with that `PostManager`. It will also declare the resources it needs: a `LocalSessionFactoryBean` resource (which provides the `SessionFactory`), the `PlatformTransactionManager`, and the `PostManager` itself.

Listing 12-8. `chapter12/spring/src/main/java/ch12/Main.java`

```
package ch12;

import org.hibernate.SessionFactory;
import org.slf4j.Logger;
import org.slf4j.LoggerFactory;
import org.springframework.context.ApplicationContext;
import org.springframework.context.annotation.
        AnnotationConfigApplicationContext;
import org.springframework.context.annotation.Bean;
```

```
import org.springframework.context.annotation.Configuration;
import org.springframework.core.io.ClassPathResource;
import org.springframework.orm.hibernate5.HibernateTransactionManager;
import org.springframework.orm.hibernate5.LocalSessionFactoryBean;
import org.springframework.transaction.PlatformTransactionManager;
import org.springframework.transaction.annotation.EnableTransactionManagement;

@Configuration
@EnableTransactionManagement
public class Main {
  @Bean
  LocalSessionFactoryBean sessionFactory() {
    LocalSessionFactoryBean sessionFactory = new LocalSessionFactoryBean();
    sessionFactory.setConfigLocation(new ClassPathResource(
    "/hibernate.cfg.xml"));

    return sessionFactory;
  }

  @Bean
  public PlatformTransactionManager hibernateTransactionManager() {
    HibernateTransactionManager transactionManager
      = new HibernateTransactionManager();
    transactionManager.setSessionFactory(sessionFactory().getObject());
    return transactionManager;
  }

  @Bean
  PostManager postManager(SessionFactory factory) {
    return new HibernatePostManager(factory);
  }

  public static void main(String[] args) {
    Logger logger = LoggerFactory.getLogger(Main.class);
    ApplicationContext context =
      new AnnotationConfigApplicationContext(Main.class);
```

```
    PostManager postManager = context.getBean(PostManager.class);
    logger.info(postManager.toString());
    postManager.savePost("foo", "bar");
    logger.info(postManager.getPosts().toString());
  }
}
```

The power of Spring in all this can be seen in the declaration for the method that returns a `PostManager`. We annotate it with `@Bean` - suggesting that Spring should provide an instance of `PostManager` as a Spring-managed object - and we require a `SessionFactory` parameter.

Spring will look for another managed instance that returns something *compatible with* a `SessionFactory` and *inject* it when calling this method to get a `PostManager`. It's also a simple, standard method; there's nothing that prevents us from calling it manually, but getting it from Spring means we get something that's built in such a way that everything it needs has been provided for it.

We're using the Hibernate `Session` here, but you could just as easily use the JPA `EntityManager` approach. You'd use a `LocalContainerEntityManagerFactoryBean` - and what a name - as well as some other different methods, but while the class names and interfaces would change, the process would remain largely the same.

The `main()` method is fairly simple, although it looks confusing at first: it simply builds an `ApplicationContext` using a class that scans for resources declared with annotations. It then acquires an instance that fulfills the definition it needs ("give me an instance that is a `PostManager`") and uses that to save a `Post` and list the `Post` entities it can find.

You could also set up the Hibernate configuration more declaratively, of course; here, we're using the XML configuration we've seen used over and over, but there's nothing suggesting you can't provide the XML configuration name as a resource or even parameterize the actual configuration declaratively as well.

To run this is a *little* involved, because of how Maven loads resources. You'd first run `mvn install` to install the project and its dependencies into a local Maven repository, and then, thanks to the use of the `exec-maven-plugin`, run `mvn exec:java` to execute the `ch12.Main` class with the project dependencies. It's not especially exciting to watch; we'll get more useful diagnostics in later sections of this chapter.

Our next sections will set up integrations with an HTTP endpoint, so we can actually interact with the frameworks with a browser or a utility like `curl` or `Postman`.

Spring Data with Spring Boot

Our next integration is with Spring Boot (`https://spring.io/projects/spring-boot`), leveraging the Spring Data project (`https://spring.io/projects/spring-data`) and, more specifically, Spring Data JPA (`https://spring.io/projects/spring-data-jpa`).

Spring Data abstracts the actual data access into a set of interfaces referred to as **repositories**, in a largely database-neutral way. We're targeting JPA (and Hibernate) here, of course, but you could rather simply target MongoDB, JDBC, Redis, Neo4j, or... well... any other supported database, and the primary changes would be in the configuration of the data sources, although there *are* some differences in capabilities.

We're also going to leverage Spring Web, so we will provide a REST endpoint (much like what we saw in Chapter 11, except with much less code).

Our project model is first, of course. We're going to include the `ch12common` module, but the *only* thing we're leveraging from that module is the `Post` entity itself. The `spring-boot-starter-data-jpa` dependency will include Hibernate 5[6] for us, and Spring Boot will also populate a reference to an H2 database for us by default.

Listing 12-9. `chapter12/springboot/pom.xml`

```xml
<?xml version="1.0" encoding="UTF-8"?>
<project xmlns:xsi="http://www.w3.org/2001/XMLSchema-instance"
         xmlns="http://maven.apache.org/POM/4.0.0"
         xsi:schemaLocation="http://maven.apache.org/POM/4.0.0
         http://maven.apache.org/xsd/maven-4.0.0.xsd">
  <parent>
    <groupId>org.springframework.boot</groupId>
    <artifactId>spring-boot-starter-parent</artifactId>
    <version>2.5.2</version>
    <relativePath/> <!-- lookup parent from repository -->
  </parent>
  <modelVersion>4.0.0</modelVersion>
```

[6] Spring Data hasn't been updated for Hibernate 6 as this is written. When the update for Hibernate 6 is made, the code will look functionally the same as it does here, although there may be some minor changes.

```
  <groupId>com.autumncode.books.hibernate</groupId>
  <artifactId>springboot</artifactId>
  <version>1.0.0</version>

  <properties>
    <java.version>11</java.version>
  </properties>

  <dependencies>
    <dependency>
      <groupId>org.springframework.boot</groupId>
      <artifactId>spring-boot-starter-web</artifactId>
    </dependency>

    <dependency>
      <groupId>org.springframework.boot</groupId>
      <artifactId>spring-boot-starter-data-jpa</artifactId>
    </dependency>

    <dependency>
      <groupId>com.autumncode.books.hibernate</groupId>
      <artifactId>ch12common</artifactId>
      <version>5.0</version>
    </dependency>
  </dependencies>

  <build>
    <plugins>
      <plugin>
        <groupId>org.springframework.boot</groupId>
        <artifactId>spring-boot-maven-plugin</artifactId>
      </plugin>
    </plugins>
  </build>
</project>
```

Our next type is actually our Repository interface. There's a *lot* going on under the surface here, but the short form is that Spring will create a proxy that provides a number of standardized create, read, update, and delete methods for you, based on the definition of the class. For what we need, we have methods already defined in the JPARepository interface: findAll() and save(). All we need to do is create an interface that provides the types for JPARepository, for the entity type (Post) and the entity's primary key type (Long).

Listing 12-10. chapter12/springboot/src/main/java/ch12/PostRepository.java

```
package ch12;

import org.springframework.data.jpa.repository.JpaRepository;

public interface PostRepository
  extends JpaRepository<Post, Long> {
}
```

There is a *lot* we're not using in Spring Data. We can actually define queries in our interface, with the query being inferred from the method name, for example, but this is a subject that wants its own book, and, yes, Apress has multiple excellent resources that can show you much more about Spring Data than this simple example can.

Our next class is a PostController, which leverages Spring Web to provide endpoints over HTTP. It's annotated as a @RestController, and its constructor requires a PostRepository - so Spring will look for a PostRepository and construct it appropriately for us. (You can also abstract this even further: you could have a controller leverage a service, which itself leverages multiple repositories to interact with your data sources. This chapter is full of academic-only concepts, so we're not fleshing things out completely, in the interest of zeroing in on example configuration.)

We have two endpoints declared here: one is at /, which gets a list of the most recent posts, and one is at /add, which allows us to add a post. Both are leveraged via HTTP GET, which isn't very wise, but we're not trying to demonstrate the *ideal* usage of Spring Web; doing it properly introduces a lot of validation code at the controller level which gets in our way. You could support POST by changing the annotation to @RequestMapping, if you like (it would handle multiple HTTP verbs), or @PostMapping, but using POST would mean processing the content differently, and that's a better subject for a book targeted at Spring Web.

Listing 12-11. chapter12/springboot/src/main/java/ch12/PostController.java

```
package ch12;

import org.springframework.data.domain.Sort;
import org.springframework.web.bind.annotation.*;

import java.util.Date;
import java.util.List;

@RestController
public class PostController {
  private final PostRepository postRepository;

  PostController(PostRepository postRepository) {
    this.postRepository = postRepository;
  }

  @GetMapping(value = "/", produces = {"application/json"})
  public List<Post> index() {
    return postRepository.findAll(
      Sort.by(Sort.Direction.DESC,"createdAt")
    );
  }

  @GetMapping(value = "/add", produces = {"application/json"})
  public Post addPost(
    @RequestParam("title") String title,
    @RequestParam("content") String content) {
    Post post = new Post();
    post.setTitle(title);
    post.setContent(content);
    post.setCreatedAt(new Date());
    postRepository.save(post);
    return post;
  }
}
```

The last class we have is `PostApplication` – which ties everything together – but all it does is serve as an entry point. Spring Boot scans the classpath for resources it needs and starts processes based on what it finds, so when it finds the `PostRepository`, it knows to initialize the database and associated resources – including Hibernate, of course – and when it finds the `PostController`, it cranks up an embedded web server.

Listing 12-12. `chapter12/springboot/src/main/java/ch12/PostApplication.java`

```
package ch12;

import org.springframework.boot.SpringApplication;
import org.springframework.boot.autoconfigure.SpringBootApplication;

@SpringBootApplication
public class PostApplication {
  public static void main(String[] args) {
    SpringApplication.run(PostApplication.class, args);
  }
}
```

We can test this with `curl`, after starting `ch12.PostApplication` (possibly with `mvn spring-boot:run`), using the following commands:

```
> curl -s -w "\n" http://localhost:8080/
[]
> curl -s -w "\n" "http://localhost:8080/add?title=foo&content=bar"
{"id":1,"title":"foo","content":"bar","createdAt":
"2021-07-24T17:02:58.042+00:00"}
> curl -s -w "\n" http://localhost:8080/
[{"id":1,"title":"foo","content":"bar","createdAt":
"2021-07-24T17:02:58.042+00:00"}]
```

We're using `-s` to turn off `curl` telling us about progress; otherwise, you get a rather instructive graph showing you how quickly the utility is able to retrieve less than 300 bytes of data, which isn't useful. We also use `-w "\n"` to append a newline after the content is displayed, because otherwise our next prompt is displayed immediately after the output of the request.

These are timestamped (guess when this was run!), but you should feel free to play with the endpoints as you like to see how the output differs.

Spring Boot is vastly configurable; here, we're relying on defaults for a lot of elements, which wouldn't be suitable for a "real application." As with Spring, Apress has multiple resources on leveraging the Spring Boot ecosystem; here, you see how trivial integration of Hibernate is.

Again, this is a Hibernate 5 integration and not a Hibernate 6 integration, as of this writing, but by the time you read this, they may have finalized migration to Hibernate 6.

ActiveJ

ActiveJ (`https://activej.io/`) is an alternative platform that focuses on high performance in delivering content. Unlike Spring Boot, it doesn't rely much on traditional Java architectural patterns for the enterprise space.[7] It tends to focus on microcontainers and asynchronous processes for excellent performance.

Asynchronous design, or "reactive programming," refers to designing processes that operate on streams of data rather than on the more traditional call-and-response models found in programming. Reactive programming tends to avoid code with side effects as much as possible, and it has its own mode of operation. We're not going to focus on a reactive model for Hibernate here, though; as with Spring, such a subject wants its own book.

Much like Spring, ActiveJ scans the classpath for injectable resources based on type, using the `@Provides` annotation, and it can inject references based on types as well.

For web resources, though, ActiveJ uses a `RoutingServlet` that maps resource by type and path into lambdas. The actual lambdas themselves aren't especially complicated, although their use inside the `RoutingServlet` can create some interesting data structures, as the lambdas receive only the `request` reference.

First, let's take a look at the project model, as usual.

[7] "It doesn't rely much on traditional Java architectural patterns" is a wordy way of saying it largely ignores Jakarta EE while reusing some of the same terms and concepts.

Listing 12-13. chapter12/activej/pom.xml

```
<?xml version="1.0" encoding="UTF-8"?>
<project xmlns:xsi="http://www.w3.org/2001/XMLSchema-instance"
         xmlns="http://maven.apache.org/POM/4.0.0"
         xsi:schemaLocation="http://maven.apache.org/POM/4.0.0
         http://maven.apache.org/xsd/maven-4.0.0.xsd">
    <parent>
        <groupId>com.autumncode.books.hibernate</groupId>
        <artifactId>chapter12</artifactId>
        <version>5.0</version>
    </parent>

    <modelVersion>4.0.0</modelVersion>

    <artifactId>activej</artifactId>

    <dependencies>
        <dependency>
            <groupId>io.activej</groupId>
            <artifactId>activej-launchers-http</artifactId>
            <version>4.3</version>
        </dependency>
        <dependency>
            <groupId>org.hibernate.orm</groupId>
            <artifactId>hibernate-core</artifactId>
            <version>${hibernate.core.version}</version>
        </dependency>
        <dependency>
            <groupId>com.fasterxml.jackson.core</groupId>
            <artifactId>jackson-databind</artifactId>
        </dependency>
        <dependency>
            <groupId>com.fasterxml.jackson.datatype</groupId>
            <artifactId>jackson-datatype-jsr310</artifactId>
        </dependency>
```

```
        <dependency>
            <groupId>com.h2database</groupId>
            <artifactId>h2</artifactId>
        </dependency>
        <dependency>
            <groupId>com.autumncode.books.hibernate</groupId>
            <artifactId>ch12common</artifactId>
            <version>5.0</version>
        </dependency>
    </dependencies>
</project>
```

As with our other examples in this chapter, we're including `ch12common`, which gives us the `Post`, `PostManager`, and `HibernatePostManager`, as well as a working Hibernate configuration. We're including Hibernate 6, as there's no innate Hibernate configuration (which is what we saw with Spring as well), along with the ActiveJ dependency itself.

We're also including Jackson (as we saw in Chapter 11) and the `jackson-datatype-jsr310` module, which allows us to serialize `Date` references as human-readable dates instead of numbers. (Our other modules do this for us without any intervention on our parts.)

Let's take a look at our resources, before we tie everything together.

The first resource we have is an `ObjectMapperFactory`. Jackson's `ObjectMapper` isn't threadsafe, and it's very light on resources; the preferred way to use it is to create a new one on use. With that said, we have specific requirements for ours: we want it to not serialize null references (if a data field is empty, we don't want to see it), *and* we want to serialize the dates as strings instead of numbers.

Listing 12-14. `chapter12/activej/src/main/java/ch12/ObjectMapperFactory.java`

```
package ch12;

import com.fasterxml.jackson.annotation.JsonInclude;
import com.fasterxml.jackson.databind.ObjectMapper;
import com.fasterxml.jackson.databind.SerializationFeature;
import com.fasterxml.jackson.datatype.jsr310.JavaTimeModule;
```

```
public class ObjectMapperFactory {
  public ObjectMapper buildMapper() {
    ObjectMapper mapper = new ObjectMapper()
      .setSerializationInclusion(
        JsonInclude.Include.NON_NULL
      )
      .disable(
        SerializationFeature.WRITE_DATES_AS_TIMESTAMPS
      );

    mapper.registerModule(new JavaTimeModule());
    return mapper;

  }
}
```

The next class has two methods that are rough analogs to servlets. Both methods accept an ActiveJ `HttpRequest` and return an `HttpResponse`, mapping the data into the appropriate form as necessary. On construction, it requires an `ObjectMapperFactory` from which it can build an `ObjectMapper` as well as a `PostManager`.

Listing 12-15. `chapter12/activej/src/main/java/ch12/Endpoints.java`

```
package ch12;

import com.fasterxml.jackson.core.JsonProcessingException;
import io.activej.http.HttpRequest;
import io.activej.http.HttpResponse;

import java.util.List;

public class Endpoints {
  PostManager postManager;
  ObjectMapperFactory mapperFactory;

  public Endpoints(
    PostManager postManager,
    ObjectMapperFactory mapperFactory
  ) {
```

```
    this.postManager = postManager;
    this.mapperFactory = mapperFactory;
  }

  HttpResponse getPosts(HttpRequest request) {
    try {
      List<Post> posts = postManager.getPosts();

      return HttpResponse
        .ok200()
        .withJson(mapperFactory
          .buildMapper()
          .writeValueAsString(posts)
        );
    } catch (JsonProcessingException e) {
      return HttpResponse
        .ofCode(500)
        .withPlainText(e.getMessage());
    }
  }

  HttpResponse addPost(HttpRequest request) {
    String title = request.getQueryParameter("title");
    String content = request.getQueryParameter("content");

    try {
      Post post = postManager.savePost(title, content);
      return io.activej.http.HttpResponse
        .ok200()
        .withJson(mapperFactory
          .buildMapper()
          .writeValueAsString(post)
        );
    } catch (JsonProcessingException e) {
      return io.activej.http.HttpResponse
        .ofCode(500)
```

```
        .withPlainText(e.getMessage());
    }
  }
}
```

Now let's tie everything together. Our PostApp does effectively the same thing we've seen in our Spring and Spring Boot examples; it declares a number of methods to return specific resources by type, annotated with @Provides, and starts an HTTP Server with whatever it finds. In our case, it's a RoutingServlet that dispatches URLs to various methods in our Endpoints class.

Listing 12-16. chapter12/activej/src/main/java/ch12/PostApp.java

```
package ch12;

import io.activej.http.AsyncServlet;
import io.activej.http.RoutingServlet;
import io.activej.inject.annotation.Provides;
import io.activej.launcher.Launcher;
import io.activej.launchers.http.HttpServerLauncher;
import org.hibernate.SessionFactory;
import org.hibernate.boot.MetadataSources;
import org.hibernate.boot.registry.StandardServiceRegistry;
import org.hibernate.boot.registry.StandardServiceRegistryBuilder;

import static io.activej.http.HttpMethod.GET;

public class PostApp
  extends HttpServerLauncher {
  @Provides
  ObjectMapperFactory mapper() {
    return new ObjectMapperFactory();
  }

  @Provides
  SessionFactory sessionFactory() {
    StandardServiceRegistry registry =
```

```
      new StandardServiceRegistryBuilder()
        .configure()
        .build();
    SessionFactory factory = new MetadataSources(registry)
      .buildMetadata()
      .buildSessionFactory();
    return factory;
  }

  @Provides
  PostManager getPostManager(SessionFactory factory) {
    return new HibernatePostManager(factory);
  }

  @Provides
  Endpoints endpoints(
    PostManager manager,
    ObjectMapperFactory mapperFactory
  ) {
    return new Endpoints(manager, mapperFactory);
  }

  @Provides
  AsyncServlet servlet(
    Endpoints endpoints
  ) {
    return RoutingServlet.create()
      .map(GET, "/", endpoints::getPosts)
      .map(GET, "/add", endpoints::addPost);
  }

  public static void main(String[] args) throws Exception {
    Launcher launcher = new PostApp();
    launcher.launch(args);
  }
}
```

As with the Spring Boot example, we can trivially test with `curl`. Note that the last command is fed into another command, `jsonpp`, which formats JSON for us:[8]

```
> curl -s -w "\n" http://localhost:8080/
[]
> curl -s -w "\n" "http://localhost:8080/add?title=foo&content=bar"
{"id":1,"title":"foo","content":"bar","createdAt":
"2021-07-24T17:09:36.125+00:00"}
> curl -s -w "\n" "http://localhost:8080/add?title=baz&content=bletch"
{"id":2,"title":"baz","content":"bletch","createdAt":
"2021-07-24T17:09:42.498+00:00"}
> curl -s -w "\n" http://localhost:8080/ | jsonpp
[
  {
    "id": 2,
    "title": "baz",
    "content": "bletch",
    "createdAt": "2021-07-24T17:09:42.498+00:00"
  },
  {
    "id": 1,
    "title": "foo",
    "content": "bar",
    "createdAt": "2021-07-24T17:09:36.125+00:00"
  }
]
```

ActiveJ is a relatively new entry in the framework wars, but it's been designed specifically for scalability and bears watching.

[8] For `jsonpp`, see `https://jmhodges.github.io/jsonpp/`; you can also substitute `json_pp`, depending on your desire and what you have installed.

Quarkus

Quarkus is a framework that targets developer ease of use, along with being readily and trivially deployable as a *native* image, which makes it very suitable for cloud environments. It relies on a set of extension points for optimizations and thus requires some effort to support newer technologies and releases like Hibernate 6. We're going to leverage the Quarkus ecosystem, but that means we're going to be targeting Hibernate 5 (just as we did with Spring Boot) until the ecosystem supports Hibernate 6; when *that* happens, Hibernate 6 integration is likely to be just as seamless as is presented here.

From a developer's standpoint, Quarkus is fantastically nice. There's a Maven command to create a Quarkus project, which gives you a rapid recompilation cycle for applications running under the JVM, as well as the option to build a native image using a Maven profile, if you've fulfilled the system requirements to do so.[9]

The basics of building a Quarkus application with access to Hibernate are fairly simple. However, we're going to approach this project differently, so we can leverage the tooling; we're going to create a project with no reliance on anything else in this book.

In the book's source code, this project is located under `chapter12/quarkus`; it is *not* a submodule of any other project in the book. It stands alone.

The first step we're going to take is to create a Quarkus project, with the following command:

```
mvn io.quarkus:quarkus-maven-plugin:2.0.2.Final:create \
    -DprojectGroupId=com.autumncode.books.hibernate \
    -DprojectArtifactId=quarkus \
    -DclassName="ch12.HelloWorld" \
    -Dpath="/hello"
```

This will create a `quarkus` directory, with a Maven wrapper and a `pom.xml`. The `pom.xml` is fairly long and will be fully standardized; we don't need to modify it in the slightest.

We can run this project already, by changing to the `quarkus` directory and running the following command:

```
mvn quarkus:dev
```

[9] To build a native image with Quarkus, you need to have the GraalVM installed as well as the native image tooling; see `https://quarkus.io/guides/building-native-image` for details and a tutorial.

This will compile the generated application and start a web server at port 8080 (the default): when we created the application, we told it to put an endpoint at `/hello`, and our application can do the following right out of the gate:

```
> curl -s -w "\n" http://localhost:8080/hello
Hello RESTEasy
```

It's time for us to integrate Hibernate.

To do this, we want to add two *extensions*, modules developed to help Quarkus generate an efficient integration into Hibernate. This is largely to enable Quarkus to optimize execution in not only the JVM but native environments; we aren't going to leverage native execution here, but the possibility is provided for.

The first extension is for Hibernate itself, and we want to add another extension for the H2 database. We can do that with the Quarkus tooling:

```
mvn quarkus:add-extension -Dextensions="quarkus-jdbc-h2,quarkus-hibernate-orm"
```

If you'd like, you can see all of the extensions available to you with `mvn quarkus:list-extensions`.

We can reuse the `Post.java` from the `ch12common` class; it's rather literally the same source as we've seen.

Listing 12-17. `chapter12/quarkus/src/main/java/ch12/Post.java`

```
package ch12;

import javax.persistence.*;
import java.util.Date;

@Entity
public class Post {
  @Id
  @GeneratedValue(strategy = GenerationType.AUTO)
  Long id;
  @Column(nullable = false, unique = true)
  String title;
  @Column(nullable = false)
  @Lob
  String content;
```

```
@Temporal(TemporalType.TIMESTAMP)
Date createdAt;

public Long getId() {
  return id;
}

public void setId(Long id) {
  this.id = id;
}

public String getTitle() {
  return title;
}

public void setTitle(String title) {
  this.title = title;
}

public String getContent() {
  return content;
}

public void setContent(String content) {
  this.content = content;
}

public Date getCreatedAt() {
  return createdAt;
}

public void setCreatedAt(Date createdAt) {
  this.createdAt = createdAt;
}

@Override
public String toString() {
  return "Post{" +
    "id=" + id +
    ", title='" + title + '\'' +
```

```
      ", content='" + content + '\'' +
      ", createdAt=" + createdAt +
      '}';
  }
}
```

We could reuse the PostManager and HibernatePostManager as well, or close to it, but we don't actually need to, and we can actually have simpler code without them. This is mostly because Quarkus will manage our transactions for us, and we want to add an annotation to inform Quarkus what resources we need, anyway.

Listing 12-18. chapter12/quarkus/src/main/java/ch12/PostManager.java

```
package ch12;

import java.util.List;

public interface PostManager {
  Post savePost(Post post);

  List<Post> getPosts();
}
```

The HibernatePostManager is annotated as a managed bean for Quarkus, with @ApplicationScoped, and receives a Hibernate Session via the @Inject annotation; we mark each method as @Transactional, and thus we have a natural (and enforced) transaction boundary. (This is why we reimplemented the class; with Quarkus' transaction management, we don't need a lot of the boilerplate code to handle transactions.) Apart from that, the actual acting code is very similar to the code we've seen elsewhere in the chapter.

Listing 12-19. chapter12/quarkus/src/main/java/ch12/HibernatePostManager.java

```
package ch12;

import org.hibernate.Session;

import javax.enterprise.context.ApplicationScoped;
import javax.inject.Inject;
import javax.persistence.TypedQuery;
```

```
import javax.transaction.Transactional;
import java.util.Date;
import java.util.List;

@ApplicationScoped
public class HibernatePostManager implements PostManager {
  @Inject
  Session session;

  @Transactional
  @Override
  public Post savePost(Post post) {
    post.setCreatedAt(new Date());
    session.save(post);
    return post;
  }

  @Override
  @Transactional
  public List<Post> getPosts() {
    TypedQuery<Post> postQuery = session
      .createQuery(
        "select p from Post p order by p.createdAt desc",
        Post.class
      );
    postQuery.setMaxResults(20);
    return postQuery.getResultList();
  }
}
```

There's only one piece left to configure for the persistence aspect of the application: we want to tell Quarkus about our database. We can do that with `application.properties`, in `src/main/resources`. We have quite a bit of control here, should we want it (see `https://quarkus.io/guides/hibernate-orm#hibernate-configuration-properties` for a full list of properties), but for the most part, we only want to tell Quarkus how to connect to the database and how to manage the schema. Here, we're mirroring the choices we've made for the rest of the book, where the application clears the database and resets the schema on every run.

Listing 12-20. `chapter12/quarkus/src/main/resources/application.properties`

```
# datasource configuration
quarkus.datasource.db-kind = h2
quarkus.datasource.username = sa
quarkus.datasource.password =
quarkus.datasource.jdbc.url = jdbc:h2:file:./quarkus

# drop and create the database at startup (use `update` to only update the
schema)
quarkus.hibernate-orm.database.generation=drop-and-create
```

All this is well and good – and works – but we've done nothing to provide access to anything that *uses* the `HibernatePostManager`. To do this, we need to add one more extension (to manage conversion to JSON) and an actual endpoint for HTTP.

We first need to add the `resteasy-jackson` extension:

```
mvn quarkus:add-extension -Dextensions="resteasy-jackson"
```

And now we can write a very simple `PostEndpoint`.

Listing 12-21. `chapter12/quarkus/src/main/java/ch12/PostEndpoint.java`

```
package ch12;

import javax.inject.Inject;
import javax.transaction.Transactional;
import javax.ws.rs.*;
import javax.ws.rs.core.MediaType;
import java.util.List;

@Path("/posts")
@Produces(MediaType.APPLICATION_JSON)
public class PostEndpoint {
  @Inject
  PostManager postManager;
```

```
  @GET
  @Transactional
  public List<Post> getPosts() {
    return postManager.getPosts();
  }

  @POST
  @Transactional
  public Post addPost(Post post) {
    return postManager.savePost(post);
  }
}
```

With this, we now have a working `/posts` endpoint with which we can interact via `curl`, once you've started the app with `mvn quarkus:dev`:

```
> curl -s -w "\n" http://localhost:8080/posts
[]
> curl -s -w "\n" \
-H "Content-Type: application/json" \
-X POST \
-d'{"title":"baz","content":"bletch"}' \
http://localhost:8080/posts
{"id":1,"title":"foo","content":"bar","createdAt":"2021-07-
24T23:10:45.794+00:00"}
>  curl -s -w "\n" http://localhost:8080/posts
[{"id":1,"title":"foo","content":"bar","createdAt":"2021-07-
24T23:10:45.794+00:00"}]
```

If you modify any of the classes to add debugging output or additional functionality (for error checking, for example), Quarkus will recompile on the fly for you and redeploy, which makes developing with it *quite* nice.[10]

[10] To be fair, Spring Boot offers a hot reload capability as well, but it's not quite as integrated as the Quarkus hot reload facility is.

Summary

What we've seen in this chapter is a very, very cursory overview of integrating Hibernate with a few different technologies: Spring, Spring Data JPA (built on Spring), ActiveJ, and Quarkus. In the case of Spring Boot and Quarkus, the tooling for Hibernate is very strongly integrated into the frameworks, so they might still be on Hibernate 5 as you read this; check the documentation (and the Web) for Hibernate 6 integration status.

In our next chapter, we'll go back to standard Hibernate and take a look at how we can *version* our data.

CHAPTER 13

Hibernate Envers

Hibernate Envers (www.google.com/url?q=https://hibernate.org/orm/envers/&sa=D&source=editors&ust=1628275087296000&usg=AOvVaw1fIkFMUR6OnHQP5ynNfRX_) is a project that provides access to what entities look like over time – that is, versioning entity states. This means that if you've marked an entity as being tracked by Envers, or "audited" – via the rather cleverly named `@Audited` annotation – that Hibernate will track changes made to that entity, and you can access the entity as it's existed through time.

What Does a "Version" Mean?

Before we jump too far into the rabbit hole, we should discuss what a version, or "revision," means.

A revision number, in Envers, is actually a type of count of database mutations[1] tracked for the **entire database**, not a counter for updates for a given entity. Thus, when we refer to a revision, we're actually referring to a reference to a snapshot of the database as it was at a specific point in time, for entities marked as being managed by Envers.

Revisions, then, aren't necessarily linear. You don't have an individual version attached to each entity – a `Post` might be attached revisions 1284, 1826, 19893, in order, rather than a more semantic versioning system of "version 1, 2, and 3." If we have an entity representing a `Purchase Order` with a primary key of `1207`, for example, it might get updated in three transactions: insertion is one transaction, with a state of `TO_BE_PROCESSED`. Then we might update it again, to say `PROCESSING`, and then again with `SHIPPED` – but there's no guaranteed relationship of the number of updates to the actual revision number. We'll even see that in our example code, actually.

[1] Database mutations include events where entities are inserted into a database table, or updated, or deleted.

J. B. Ottinger et al., *Beginning Hibernate 6*, https://doi.org/10.1007/978-1-4842-7337-1_13

Creating a Simple Project

Envers really is pretty simple, in concept: when changes are written to an entity within a transaction, it's "versioned" – assigned a revision – and updates are stored separately from the entity itself.[2] Thus, throughout the entire book, we could use our entities just as we've shown, with no awareness of Envers at all, but *if* the entities were marked as being audited, we'd be able to track every change applied to the entities.

Let's see how this is done. First, of course, we need our project model.

Listing 13-1. `chapter13/pom.xml`

```
<?xml version="1.0" encoding="UTF-8"?>
<project xmlns:xsi="http://www.w3.org/2001/XMLSchema-instance"
         xmlns="http://maven.apache.org/POM/4.0.0"
         xsi:schemaLocation="http://maven.apache.org/POM/4.0.0
         http://maven.apache.org/xsd/maven-4.0.0.xsd">
    <parent>
        <groupId>com.autumncode.books.hibernate</groupId>
        <artifactId>hibernate-6-parent</artifactId>
        <version>5.0</version>
    </parent>

    <modelVersion>4.0.0</modelVersion>

    <artifactId>chapter13</artifactId>

    <dependencies>
        <dependency>
            <groupId>com.autumncode.books.hibernate</groupId>
            <artifactId>util</artifactId>
            <version>${project.parent.version}</version>
        </dependency>
        <dependency>
            <groupId>org.projectlombok</groupId>
            <artifactId>lombok</artifactId>
```

[2] An Envers revision, then, refers to the updates that are applied to audited entities in a given transaction.

```
        </dependency>
        <dependency>
            <groupId>org.hibernate</groupId>
            <artifactId>hibernate-envers</artifactId>
        </dependency>
    </dependencies>
</project>
```

There's nothing particularly special in the pom.xml – we are including the hibernate-envers artifact, which provides the @Audited annotation, but that's really our main difference between this and our other chapter projects.

Our hibernate.cfg.xml is also very normal looking; we make a reference to chapter13.model.User (which we'll see very soon), but that's just a regular reference to an entity; there's nothing special about our Hibernate configuration, either.

Listing 13-2. chapter13/src/main/resources/hibernate.cfg.xml

```
<?xml version="1.0"?>
<!DOCTYPE hibernate-configuration PUBLIC
    "-//Hibernate/Hibernate Configuration DTD 3.0//EN"
    "http://www.hibernate.org/dtd/hibernate-configuration-3.0.dtd">
<hibernate-configuration>
  <session-factory>
    <!--  Database connection settings  -->
    <property name="connection.driver_class">org.h2.Driver</property>
    <property name="connection.url">jdbc:h2:file:./db13</property>
    <property name="connection.username">sa</property>
    <property name="connection.password"/>
    <property name="dialect">org.hibernate.dialect.H2Dialect</property>

    <!--  Echo all executed SQL to stdout  -->
    <property name="show_sql">true</property>
    <property name="use_sql_comments">true</property>

    <!--  Drop and re-create the database schema on startup  -->
    <property name="hbm2ddl.auto">create-drop</property>
```

```
    <mapping class="chapter13.model.User"/>
  </session-factory>
</hibernate-configuration>
```

Just for completeness' sake, we also have a `logback.xml` (stored in `src/main/resources` alongside the `hibernate.cfg.xml`), copied from our other chapters; it's got the same contents as every other `logback.xml`, so we'll save a tree[3] and not echo it *yet again*.

That leaves our entity itself. We're going to model a user, who has a set of groups; the model itself will be very simple, an entity with a few attributes and an element collection for the groups.

Listing 13-3. `chapter13/src/main/java/chapter13/model/User.java`

```
package chapter13.model;

import lombok.Data;
import lombok.NoArgsConstructor;
import org.hibernate.envers.Audited;

import javax.persistence.*;
import java.util.Arrays;
import java.util.HashSet;
import java.util.Set;

@Entity
@Data
@NoArgsConstructor
@Audited
public class User {
  @Id
  @GeneratedValue(strategy = GenerationType.AUTO)
  Integer id;

  @Column(unique = true)
  String name;

  boolean active;
```

[3] Or we'll save the *electronic version* of a tree, if you're reading this in an eBook and not on paper.

```
  @ElementCollection
  Set<String> groups;

  String description;

  public User(String name, boolean active) {
    this.name = name;
    this.active = active;
  }

  public void addGroups(String... groupSet) {
    if (getGroups() == null) {
      setGroups(new HashSet<>());
    }
    getGroups().addAll(Arrays.asList(groupSet));
  }
}
```

To enable auditing, all we need to do is add the @Audited annotation at the class level. What this annotation means is that when updates (including creates and deletes) are applied to the entity, its state should be saved as part of a specific revision when the transaction is committed; thus, we can change name and description in a single transaction and get one revision, or we can update name in one transaction, commit it, then update description in another transaction, and end up with two new revisions, one for each update.

We can update sets just as easily as we can update simple attributes, as shown with groups; changes to the set will be part of the revision.

As we've done in other chapters, we'll create some examples, starting with a BaseTest abstract class.

This class has a setup() method that basically creates a number of revisions[4] to a User entity, storing the primary key of the entity in a local array so it can be referred to in a lambda. It also has two utility methods to find a revision for a User at a specific point in its history; we'll explore how those work when we hit our second test, in the ValidateRevisionData class.

Be prepared: this has a lot of repetitive operations in a sequence!

[4] Our setup() also calls SessionUtil.getInstance().forceReload(), which causes a reinitialization of the entire database to a known state; if we don't do this, our tests will interfere with each other.

Listing 13-4. chapter13/src/test/java/chapter13/BaseTest.java

```
package chapter13;

import chapter13.model.User;
import com.autumncode.hibernate.util.SessionUtil;
import org.hibernate.Session;
import org.hibernate.envers.AuditReader;
import org.hibernate.query.Query;
import org.testng.annotations.BeforeClass;

import javax.persistence.EntityManagerFactory;

import static org.testng.Assert.*;
import static org.testng.Assert.assertEquals;

abstract class BaseTest {
  int[] userId = {0, 1};

  User createUser(Session session, String username) {
    User user = new User(username, true);
    user.setDescription("description");
    user.addGroups("group1");
    session.save(user);
    return user;
  }

  @BeforeClass
  public void setup() {
    SessionUtil.forceReload();

    SessionUtil.doWithSession(session -> {
      Query<User> deleteQuery = session.
        createQuery("delete from User u");
      deleteQuery.executeUpdate();
    });
```

```
SessionUtil.doWithSession((session) -> {
  User user = createUser(session, "user1");
  userId[0] = user.getId();
});

SessionUtil.doWithSession(session -> {
  User user = createUser(session, "user2");
  userId[1] = user.getId();
});

SessionUtil.doWithSession((session) -> {
  User user = session.byId(User.class).load(userId[0]);
  assertTrue(user.isActive());
  assertEquals(user.getDescription(),
    "description");
});

SessionUtil.doWithSession((session) -> {
  User user = session.byId(User.class).load(userId[0]);
  user.addGroups("group2");
  user.setDescription("1description");
});

SessionUtil.doWithSession((session) -> {
  User user = session.byId(User.class).load(userId[1]);
  user.addGroups("group2");
  user.setDescription("2description");
});

SessionUtil.doWithSession((session) -> {
  User user = session.byId(User.class).load(userId[0]);
  user.setActive(false);
});

SessionUtil.doWithSession((session) -> {
  User user = session.byId(User.class).load(userId[0]);
  assertFalse(user.isActive());
```

```
      assertEquals(user.getDescription(), "1description");
    });
  }

  User findUserAtRevision(
    AuditReader reader,
    Number revision) {
    return findUserAtRevision(
      reader,
      userId[0],
      revision
    );
  }

  User findUserAtRevision(
    AuditReader reader,
    int pk,
    Number revision) {
    reader.find(User.class, pk, revision);
    return reader.find(
      User.class,
      "chapter13.model.User",
      pk,
      revision
    );
  }
}
```

This is a lengthy class, but it's really (*really*) simple: the length is tied to its need to use separate transactions for a lot of updates in sequence. It only creates multiple users, and updates them, in multiple transactions; it also saves off the generated primary keys for later use.

Table 13-1. *User States in* `BaseTest`

id	name	description	groups	active	revision
1	user1	description	group1	true	1
2	user2	description	group1	true	2
1	user1	1description	group1,group2	true	3
2	user2	2description	group1,group2	true	4
1	user1	1description	group1,group2	false	5

Note the revisions, which are *not* counters of revisions *to the entities*. If they were, the revision of the third row would be 2, but it's not; this actually enables us to get a snapshot of the entire database by date, if we want, which is **incredibly** powerful. The *cost* of that power is that revisions aren't as simple to explain as they might otherwise be; we're no longer counting updates by entity, but by database transaction instead.

The main interface we use to interact with for revisions is the `AuditReader`, which we get from an `AuditReaderFactory`. Our basic pattern for usage is to get the available revisions via `AuditReader.getRevisions()` and then use `AuditReader.find()` or the `AuditReader.getQuery()` to load a specific revision.

`AuditReader` has a way to get a revision as it is applied at a certain point in time (and, likewise, a way to get the date for a specific revision). These mechanisms are likely to be more useful than `getRevisions()`, but would require constructing a fairly slow test harness. There's also an `AuditQuery` interface, which we'll see in action soon.

Let's take a look at a simple validation that revisions are being stored as we expect. We're going to create a `ValidateRevisions` test, extended from our `BaseTest` so it has access to a `User` with stored revisions.

You get an `AuditReader` from an `AuditReaderFactory`, passing in a `Session` for database access, like this:

```
AuditReader reader = AuditReaderFactory.get(session);
```

Thus, we need to make sure we're doing everything within the context of a `Session`. The first test just verifies that we have revisions for a `User` - the identifier of which is in `userId[0]`, stored in an array so we can use it in a lambda. We *get* the revisions through using `AuditReader.getRevisions()`, passing in the entity type (`User.class`) and a primary key for that type.

For the data from our `BaseTest`, getting the revisions for the `User` with id `1` should give us a list of `1,3,5`. If we don't have three revisions – which is set up by the `BaseTest.setup()` method – then something's gone wrong, but we can't necessarily test for *specific revision numbers* because revision numbers refer to when a snapshot was taken, not updates to an entity.[5] This has been repeated a few times, but the revision number is a lot like a counter of transactions, not updates to a specific entity.

Listing 13-5. `chapter13/src/test/java/chapter13/ValidateRevisionCountTest.java`

```
package chapter13;

import chapter13.model.User;
import com.autumncode.hibernate.util.SessionUtil;
import org.hibernate.envers.AuditReader;
import org.hibernate.envers.AuditReaderFactory;
import org.testng.annotations.Test;

import java.util.List;

import static org.testng.Assert.*;

public class ValidateRevisionCountTest extends BaseTest {
  @Test
  public void validateRevisionCount() {
    SessionUtil.doWithSession((session) -> {
      AuditReader reader = AuditReaderFactory.get(session);

      List<Number> revisions =
        reader.getRevisions(User.class, userId[0]);

      assertEquals(revisions.size(), 3);
    });
  }
}
```

[5] If you were to add *another* user to the BaseTest, for example, the revision numbers would change... but the number of revisions passed back for a specific entity would be the same, unless you added an update for that entity as well.

It's time for us to validate what those revisions contain. Let's create another test, the `ValidateRevisionData` test.

Listing 13-6. `chapter13/src/test/java/chapter13/ValidateRevisionDataTest.java`

```
package chapter13;

import chapter13.model.User;
import com.autumncode.hibernate.util.SessionUtil;
import org.hibernate.envers.AuditReader;
import org.hibernate.envers.AuditReaderFactory;
import org.testng.annotations.Test;

import java.util.List;
import java.util.Set;
import java.util.stream.Collectors;

import static org.testng.Assert.assertEquals;
import static org.testng.Assert.assertFalse;

public class ValidateRevisionDataTest extends BaseTest {
  @Test
  public void testUserData() {
    SessionUtil.doWithSession((session) -> {
      AuditReader reader = AuditReaderFactory.get(session);
      List<Integer> revisions =
        reader.getRevisions(User.class, userId[0])
          .stream()
          .map(Number::intValue)
          .collect(Collectors.toList());

      List<User> userRevs =
        revisions
          .stream()
          .map(rev -> findUserAtRevision(reader, rev))
          .collect(Collectors.toList());
```

```
      // first revision
      assertEquals(
        userRevs.get(0).getDescription(),
        "description"
      );
      assertEquals(
        userRevs.get(0).getGroups(),
        Set.of("group1")
      );

      // second revision
      assertEquals(
        userRevs.get(1).getDescription(),
        "1description");
      assertEquals(
        userRevs.get(1).getGroups(),
        Set.of("group1", "group2")
      );

      // third, and last, revision
      assertFalse(
        userRevs.get(2).isActive()
      );

      assertEquals(
        session.load(User.class, userId[0]),
        userRevs.get(2)
      );

      System.out.println(reader.getRevisionDate(2));
      System.out.println(reader.getRevisionDate(1));
    });
  }
}
```

This class does quite a bit more, but it's still pretty simple. The first thing it does is get the revisions, just as `ValidateRevisionCount` did, but then it does a map of those revisions into a list of `User` objects – which will correspond to the `User` entity's full history. The rest of the class is simply verifying that each revision has the changes we expect.

The first set of assertions (using `userRevs.get(0)`) validates the initial state of the `User`, which was with a simple description ("first description") and one group ("group1").

The second set of assertions checks the update of the groups and description, from the first update after the `User` was created.

The third set of assertions validates that the `active` flag has changed properly – and then we compare the third revision to the *current* state of the `User`, as shown by `Session.load()`, to demonstrate that the `AuditReader` is actually returning a valid entity representation as it is over time.

The way the `findUserAtRevision()` method works is by leveraging the `AuditReader.find()` method. There are lots of variations on this method; here are a few:

```
<T> T find(Class<T> cls, Object primaryKey, Number revision)
<T> T find(Class<T> cls, Object primaryKey, Date date)
<T> T find(Class<T> cls, String entityName, Object key, Number revision)
<T> T find(Class<T> cls, String entityName, Object primaryKey,
  Number revision, boolean includeDeletions)
```

We're leveraging the third of these, mostly because it gives us a chance to look at the `entityName` reference, which is a *little* misleading. In JPQL, the "entity name" of our `User` class is `"User"`, as in `from User u` – but here, it's actually the fully qualified entity name, so we need to pass `chapter13.model.User` instead, as that's what Envers is using to look up the audited entity.

The types are fairly clear, once we understand that minor hurdle: the concrete `Class` of the reference, the fully qualified entity name, the primary key of the entity (via `userId[0]`, in this case), and the revision number being passed in.

We can leverage the snapshot nature of revisions to grab data, too. Let's take a look at another test, `ValidateRevisionSnapshot`.

Listing 13-7. chapter13/src/test/java/chapter13/ValidateRevisionSnapshotTest.java

```
package chapter13;

import chapter13.model.User;
import com.autumncode.hibernate.util.SessionUtil;
import org.hibernate.envers.AuditReader;
import org.hibernate.envers.AuditReaderFactory;
import org.testng.annotations.Test;

import java.util.List;
import java.util.Set;
import java.util.stream.Collectors;

import static org.testng.Assert.*;

public class ValidateRevisionSnapshotTest extends BaseTest {
  @Test
  public void testUserData() {
    SessionUtil.doWithSession((session) -> {
      AuditReader reader = AuditReaderFactory.get(session);

      List<Integer> revisions =
        reader.getRevisions(User.class, userId[0])
          .stream()
          .map(Number::intValue)
          .collect(Collectors.toList());

      int indexOfLastRevision = revisions.size() - 1;
      int lastRevision = revisions.get(indexOfLastRevision);
      User lastUser = findUserAtRevision(reader, lastRevision);
      User prevUser = findUserAtRevision(reader, lastRevision - 1);

      assertTrue(lastRevision - 1 > revisions.get(indexOfLastRevision - 1));
      assertNotEquals(lastUser.isActive(), prevUser.isActive());
    });
  }
}
```

This class looks a lot more complicated than it actually is.

First, it gets the list of revisions - just like our `ValidateRevisionData` does.

Then it gets the "last revision" by calculating the position of the revisions in our list; we **should** have revisions 1, 3, and 5. (We'll test this, in fact, because otherwise we're not demonstrating anything at all.)

It then calls our `findUserAtRevision()` method, using revision 5 - the current revision - and revision 4, which is the previous *snapshot* of the database. The `User` at revision 4 should be the same as the `User` for revision 3 - after all, revision 4 updated our *other* user, not this one - and we can test that by looking at the `isActive()` status. If our assertion about the revisions is correct, revision 4 for the `User` should be set to active, and revision 5 should not.[6]

Our `BaseTest` runs rather quickly, or else we could use some informational methods in `AuditReader` to capture revision numbers for a given date (or when a given revision was written):

```
AuditReader reader=AuditReaderFactory.get(session);

Date revisionDate=reader.getRevisionDate(4);
// or
Date date=somePointInThePast();
Integer revisionNumber=reader
  .getRevisionNumberForDate(date)
  .intValue();
```

There are, of course, different *kinds* of revisions. Here, we've updated the `User` three times. However, we can also *delete* the user; what happens then? It's time to find out.

We're going to create a test that *deletes* the user so carefully created in our `BaseTest`, which will create a *sixth* revision in the context of that test. We'll actually have multiple tests in this class: one validates the creation of the fourth revision, and the others examine what happens when you query for the revision with `AuditReader.find()`.

[6] All of this explanation is assuming the revisions are progressing as in Table 13-1; there's no guarantee of this whatsoever, which is why we can't just refer to revision numbers as absolute concrete references. Our `BaseTest` forces a new database every test, so it *should* be consistent here, but there's no absolute guarantee.

Listing 13-8. chapter13/src/test/java/chapter13/HandleDeletedRevisionsTest.java

```
package chapter13;

import chapter13.model.User;
import com.autumncode.hibernate.util.SessionUtil;
import org.hibernate.envers.AuditReader;
import org.hibernate.envers.AuditReaderFactory;
import org.testng.annotations.BeforeClass;
import org.testng.annotations.Test;

import java.util.List;

import static org.testng.Assert.*;

public class HandleDeletedRevisionsTest extends BaseTest {
  @BeforeClass
  void deleteUser() {
    SessionUtil.doWithSession(session -> {
      User user = session.load(User.class, userId[0]);
      session.delete(user);
    });
  }

  @Test
  public void countRevisions() {
    SessionUtil.doWithSession(session -> {
      AuditReader reader = AuditReaderFactory.get(session);

      List<Number> revisions =
        reader.getRevisions(User.class, userId[0]);

      assertEquals(revisions.size(), 4);
    });
  }
```

```
  @Test
  public void findRevisionNoDeleted() {
    User user = runQueryForVersion(false);
    assertNull(user);
  }

  @Test
  public void findRevisionDeleted() {
    User user = runQueryForVersion(true);
    assertNotNull(user);
    assertNull(user.getName());
    assertNull(user.getDescription());
  }

  private User runQueryForVersion(
    boolean includeDeleted
  ) {
    return SessionUtil.returnFromSession(session -> {
      AuditReader reader = AuditReaderFactory.get(session);

      User user = reader.find(
        User.class,
        "chapter13.model.User",
        userId[0],
        6,
        includeDeleted
      );
      return user;
    });
  }
}
```

The `findRevisionNoDeleted()` test passes `false` for the `includeDeletions` parameter; in this case, what happens is that the `find()` returns `null`, because there's ... not actually a User, at a revision that's been deleted.

However, there might be cases where you want to trap data about the actual deleted entry (i.e., you are capturing the *event* of being deleted). For this case, you can pass `true` for `includeDeletions`, and you'll get back an actual entity, a `User`, in this case. However, the `User` is largely populated; you'll get `null` or default values for the simple attributes.[7]

Looking for Revisions with Specific Data

The `AuditReader` interface provides `find()`, as we've shown, but it also provides the ability to create a fairly fluent `AuditQuery`, which - apart from being largely typeless, requiring us to cast results - is rather useful.[8]

In our `User` transition, the `User` starts off as being marked `active`, with the last update marking the user as being inactive. We can actually find the last revision where the `User` was active by adding properties to an `AuditQuery`, as shown in the `FindLastActiveUserRevisionTest` class.

Listing 13-9. `chapter13/src/test/java/chapter13/FindLastActiveUserRevisionTest.java`

```
package chapter13;

import chapter13.model.User;
import com.autumncode.hibernate.util.SessionUtil;
import org.hibernate.Session;
import org.hibernate.envers.AuditReader;
import org.hibernate.envers.AuditReaderFactory;
import org.hibernate.envers.query.AuditEntity;
import org.hibernate.envers.query.AuditQuery;
import org.testng.annotations.Test;

import static org.testng.Assert.assertEquals;
```

[7] Oddly enough, the deleted `User` reference still has its `groups` collection populated. Envers can be… weird sometimes.

[8] See, Mr. Editor? I *do* know how to use irony! I'm rather fey about it.

```
public class FindLastActiveUserRevisionTest extends BaseTest {
  @Test
  public void findLastActiveUserRevision() {
    SessionUtil.doWithSession((session) -> {
      User user = getUserWhenActive(session);
      System.out.println(user);
      assertEquals(user.getDescription(), "1description");
    });
  }

  protected User getUserWhenActive(Session session) {
    AuditReader reader = AuditReaderFactory.get(session);
    AuditQuery query = reader.createQuery()
      .forRevisionsOfEntity(User.class, true, false)
      .addOrder(AuditEntity.revisionNumber().desc())
      .setMaxResults(1)
      .add(AuditEntity.id().eq(userId[0]))
      .add(AuditEntity.property("active").eq(true));

    User user = (User) query.getSingleResult();
    return user;
  }
}
```

Here, we have a `getUserWhenActive()` method that builds a query to find the most recent `User` set to `active`.

We tell the query *first* what type of entity we're looking for, with `forRevisionsOfEntity(User.class, true, false)`. The first boolean here is for "selected entities," which means we'll get actual `User` entities back and not information about the revisions themselves; the second boolean is for the selection of *deleted* entities, which we're not interested in.[9]

Next, we add an order to the results; we want the results in descending order of revision number (i.e., latest first).

[9] We're not interested in deleted entities because, first, they're *deleted*, we don't want them; second, we're actually looking for the last revision of the User such that they're marked as being *active*. A deleted `User` is by definition inactive (the `active` flag is set to false).

We are only interested in a single result, so we use `setMaxResults(1)`.

Then we add an `id` to the query, with a simple `add(AuditEntity.id().eq())` call – we're basically telling the query to add a predicate to the search. We add another predicate, on `AuditEntity.property("active")`, such that we're looking for an entity with a specific primary key that has a specific property value.

After that, it's simplicity itself; we run the query and expect a result; we check to make sure the `description` matches the revision we expect from our test data, et voilà!

An Example Reverting Data

Envers does not provide a mechanism by which we can easily *rewind* data to a previous known state; we can't tell Envers that we want revision 2 to be the "active" revision. We can, however, *access* revision 2 and set the current state of the entity to match the prior state.

Let's revisit `FindLastActiveUserRevisionTest` and extend it to revert a `User` marked inactive (and with a new description) to a prior state.

Listing 13-10. `chapter13/src/test/java/chapter13/RevertDataTest.java`

```
package chapter13;

import chapter13.model.User;
import com.autumncode.hibernate.util.SessionUtil;
import org.testng.annotations.Test;

import static org.testng.Assert.assertEquals;
import static org.testng.Assert.assertFalse;
import static org.testng.Assert.assertTrue;

public class RevertDataTest extends
  FindLastActiveUserRevisionTest {

  @Test
  public void revertUserData() {
    SessionUtil.doWithSession((session) -> {
      User auditUser = getUserWhenActive(session);

      assertEquals(auditUser.getDescription(), "1description");
```

```
      // now we copy the audit data into the "current user."
      User user = session.load(User.class, userId[0]);

      assertFalse(user.isActive());
      user.setActive(auditUser.isActive());
      user.setDescription(auditUser.getDescription());
      user.setGroups(auditUser.getGroups());
    });

    // let's make sure the "current user" looks like what we expect
    SessionUtil.doWithSession((session) -> {
      User user = session.load(User.class, userId[0]);
      assertTrue(user.isActive());
      assertEquals(user.getDescription(), "1description");
    });
  }
}
```

It's actually quite straightforward: we are reusing `getActiveUser()` from the `FindLastActiveUserTest` class, first; that's our source data for the update.

Then we load the `User` entity as it is from the database (the "current revision"). We know from our test data that the `active` flag should be `false`, but we check it here anyway.[10]

After that, well, we have a `User` reference that's being managed, since we just loaded it; we copy the data from the revision we loaded from `getActiveUser()` into the managed `User` reference. When the `Session` ends and the transaction is committed, the `Session` will create a *new* revision (with the data we just set) and write it into the database. The last part of our test reloads the user and validates the updates we just wrote.

[10] You should always trust your authors - why would we lie to you? - but one of the hallmarks of being trustworthy is never asking your readers to trust you. I'd rather show you instead.

Summary

Envers is an incredibly simple revision management library for Hibernate entities. It's unlikely that it will fit every requirement, but it *does* have very flexible query capabilities and can serve *most* auditing needs with the addition of a single, simple annotation to an entity class.

Hibernate is one of the most popular mechanisms in Java for providing persistence to relational systems. We've shown the features that will serve most applications, including basic persistence operations (creation, reads, updates, deletes), associations between object types, and providing and using audit data.

We've also seen a number of "better practices"[11] in use - with an emphasis on testing and build tools (through TestNG and Maven, respectively), and we've also seen how to use modern Java features to streamline some of our code (in particular with the use of lambdas to hide the transaction management in our later chapters).

We hope you've learned some fun and interesting and, above all, relevant information as you've read; and we also hope you've enjoyed reading the book.

[11] I wanted to say "best practices" but that sounded fairly egotistical.

Index

A

B

C

J. B. Ottinger et al., *Beginning Hibernate 6*, https://doi.org/10.1007/978-1-4842-7337-1

D

E

F

G

I

J, K

L

M

N

O

P

T

Printed in the United States
by Baker & Taylor Publisher Services